Transnational Business Governance Interactions

Transnational Business Governance Interactions

Advancing Marginalized Actors and Enhancing Regulatory Quality

Edited by

Stepan Wood

Canada Research Chair in Law, Society and Sustainability, Allard School of Law, University of British Columbia, Canada

Rebecca Schmidt

Assistant Professor of Law, Dublin City University, Ireland

Errol Meidinger

SUNY Distinguished Professor and Margaret W. Wong Professor of Law, Buffalo School of Law, The State University of New York, USA

Burkard Eberlein

Professor of Public Policy and Strategic Management, Schulich School of Business, York University, Canada

Kenneth W. Abbott

Jack E. Brown Professor of Law emeritus, Arizona State University, USA

Edward Elgar
PUBLISHING

Cheltenham, UK • Northampton, MA, USA

Published by
Edward Elgar Publishing Limited
The Lypiatts
15 Lansdown Road
Cheltenham
Glos GL50 2JA
UK

Edward Elgar Publishing, Inc.
William Pratt House
9 Dewey Court
Northampton
Massachusetts 01060
USA

A catalogue record for this book
is available from the British Library

Library of Congress Control Number: 2019951164

This book is available electronically in the Elgaronline
Social and Political Science subject collection
DOI 10.4337/9781788114738

MIX
Paper from
responsible sources
FSC® C013604

ISBN 978 1 78811 472 1 (cased)
ISBN 978 1 78811 473 8 (eBook)

Typeset by Westchester Publishing Services
Printed and bound by CPI Group (UK) Ltd, Croydon, CR0 4YY

Contents

Figures

Tables

Contributors

Kenneth W. Abbott is Jack E. Brown Professor of Law emeritus at the Sandra Day O'Connor College of Law, Arizona State University, Phoenix, USA.

Graeme Auld is Associate Professor and Director of the School of Public Policy and Administration, Faculty of Public Affairs, Carleton University, Ottawa, Canada.

Matthew Bach is Project Officer, Governance and Social Innovation at the European Secretariat of ICLEI – Local Governments for Sustainability, Freiburg, Germany.

Sophia Carodenuto is Assistant Professor at the Department of Geography, University of Victoria, Victoria, Canada.

Benjamin Cashore is Professor of Environmental Governance and Political Science, Director of the Governance, Environment and Markets Initiative and Director of the Program on Forest Policy and Governance at the School of Forestry and Environmental Studies, Yale University, New Haven, USA.

Donal Casey is Lecturer in Law and Deputy Director of Learning and Teaching at Kent Law School, University of Kent, Canterbury, United Kingdom.

Christopher (Chao-Hung) Chen is Associate Professor of Law at the School of Law, Singapore Management University, Singapore.

Burkard Eberlein is Professor of Strategic Management/Public Policy at the Schulich School of Business, York University, Toronto, Canada.

Paul Foley is Associate Professor of Environmental Policy at the School of Science and the Environment, Grenfell Campus, Memorial University of Newfoundland, Corner Brook, Canada.

Simin Gao is Associate Professor at the School of Law, Tsinghua University, Beijing, China.

Tetty Havinga is Associate Professor, Sociology of Law, at the Faculty of Law, Radboud University, Nijmegen, Netherlands.

Lasse Folke Henriksen is Associate Professor at the Department of Organization, Copenhagen Business School, Copenhagen, Denmark.

Errol Meidinger is SUNY Distinguished Professor, Margaret W. Wong Professor and Director of the Baldy Center for Law and Social Policy at the University at Buffalo School of Law, State University of New York, Buffalo, USA.

Natalie Oman is Assistant Professor of Legal Studies, Faculty of Social Science and Humanities, University of Ontario Institute of Technology, Oshawa, Canada.

Phillip Paiement is Assistant Professor of Jurisprudence, Tilburg Law School, Tilburg University, Tilburg, Netherlands.

Stefan Renckens is Assistant Professor in the Department of Political Science, University of Toronto, Toronto, Canada.

Rebecca Schmidt is Assistant Professor of Law at the School of Law and Government, Dublin City University, Dublin, Ireland.

Leonard Seabrooke is Professor at the Department of Organization, Copenhagen Business School, Copenhagen, Denmark.

Paul Verbruggen is Associate Professor of Private Law, Tilburg Law School, Tilburg University, Tilburg, Netherlands.

Oliver Westerwinter is Assistant Professor of Political Science at the Department of Political Science, University of St. Gallen, St. Gallen, Switzerland.

Jane K. Winn is Professor of Law at the School of Law, University of Washington, Seattle, USA.

Stepan Wood is Professor, Canada Research Chair in Law, Society & Sustainability, and Director of the Centre for Law and the Environment at the Peter A. Allard School of Law, University of British Columbia, Vancouver, Canada.

Acknowledgements

It is impossible to give proper recognition to everyone who contributed to the realization of this book. Most of the chapters made their first appearance at a workshop on "Theorizing Transnational Business Governance Interactions: Design, Structures, Mechanisms and Impacts" at York University in May 2016. The workshop and larger project were funded by a Partnership Development Grant (#890-2010-0126) from the Social Sciences and Humanities Research Council of Canada. The workshop benefitted immensely from the support of the Osgoode Hall Law School, the Schulich School of Business, and their respective Deans, Lorne Sossin and Dezsö Horváth. Jody-Ann Rowe-Butler of Osgoode and Susan Kimberley of Schulich provided expert logistical support.

Two of the authors also participated in an earlier graduate student research retreat generously hosted and funded by the Baldy Center for Law and Social Policy at the State University of New York at Buffalo.

York University, Arizona State University, the State University of New York at Buffalo, the University of British Columbia, the London School of Economics and Political Science, the Hertie School of Governance, the Robert Schuman Centre for Advanced Studies at the European University Institute, the Hague Institute for the Internationalization of Law's Transnational Private Regulation Project, the Hennick Centre for Business and Law (York University), the Schulich-ICAO Alliance for Accounting Research and Professional Competencies, the York Institute for Research and Innovation in Sustainability, the Canada Research Chairs program and York University's York Research Chairs program provided financial or in-kind support at various stages of the Transnational Business Governance Interactions project.

The editors wish to express their gratitude to the participants in the 2016 York workshop and numerous other scholarly meetings where the research and ideas presented in this book were tested, including workshops at the European University Institute, the Hertie School of Governance, the London School of Economics and Political Science, and meetings of the International Studies Association, the Law and Society Association and the ECPR Standing Group on Regulatory Governance. Among the many participants who helped sharpen their thinking, the editors are particularly grateful to Tim Bartley, Tanja Börzel, Karin

Buhmann, Tim Büthe, Fabrizio Cafaggi, Klaus Dingwerth, Marie-Laure Djelic, Luc Fransen, Thomas Gehring, Jessica Green, Lars Gulbrandsen, Anke Hassel, Virginia Haufler, Nicole Helmerich, Markus Jachtenfuchs, Gregory Jackson, Benedict Kingsbury, David Levi-Faur, Timothy Lytton, Christine Parker, Oren Perez, Tony Porter, Kerstin Sahlin-Anderson, Harm Schepel, Colin Scott, Gregory Shaffer, Susan Silbey, Klaus-Dieter Wolf and Peer Zumbansen.

A special debt of gratitude is owed to Julia Black, who was a core collaborator in the project's early stages and whose intellectual imprint on this book is evident. The editors are also grateful to Sasha Courville, Kristin Komives, Lara Koritzke and Vidya Rangan of the ISEAL Alliance, who encouraged the project and provided valuable insight from the world of transnational business governance.

Several student research assistants at Osgoode Hall Law School and the University of British Columbia's Allard School of Law helped with the York workshop and the resulting book, including Sarah Attardo (Osgoode JD 2018), Grace Chung (Allard JD candidate 2020), Heather Fisher (Osgoode JD 2017), Julia Roe (Allard JD candidate 2021), Nicholas Rosati (Allard JD candidate 2020) and Lawrence Wong (Allard JD 2019).

More information about the Transnational Business Governance Interactions project is available at http://tgiforum.org.

1. Transnational business governance interactions, regulatory quality and marginalized actors: An introduction

Stepan Wood, Burkard Eberlein, Errol Meidinger, Rebecca Schmidt and Kenneth W. Abbott

1.1 INTRODUCTION

Powerful actors including major states and corporations frequently exploit gaps, overlaps and conflicts in global governance to shape rules and decisions in their favour or evade regulation. They steer interactions amongst governance actors and institutions, creating inter-regime conflicts, exploiting the fragmentation of international law, orchestrating intermediaries, shopping for favourable fora and creating new ones (Raustiala and Victor 2004; Alter and Meunier 2009; Gehring and Oberthür 2009; Abbott et al. 2015; Blome et al. 2016). As important as it is to understand these manipulations, this book investigates the obverse: the circumstances in which governance interactions can be harnessed to advance the interests of marginalized actors and improve the quality of transnational regulation.

This introductory chapter proceeds as follows. In Part 2 we justify our focus on transnational business governance interactions (TBGIs). In Part 3 we turn to our central question when and how TBGIs can be harnessed to advance marginalized interests and enhance regulatory quality. We ask this question at three levels: regulatory capacities, outputs and outcomes. The first dimension, regulatory capacities, is drawn from the literature on regulation and includes symbolic and material resources along with capacities to learn and adapt. The second and third dimensions, regulatory outputs and outcomes, are drawn from the literature on regime effectiveness and include regulatory standards, institutional design features, regulatory synergies and uptake. The book explores whether and in what circumstances TBGIs can be steered to enhance transnational regulatory capacities, outputs and outcomes in general, and for marginalized actors in particular. Part 4 presents the plan of the book and summarizes the chapters.

1.2 TRANSNATIONAL BUSINESS GOVERNANCE INTERACTIONS

We coined the term transnational business governance interactions (TBGIs) to describe the interactive dynamics of transnational regulation, and proposed a framework to analyse these dynamics (Eberlein et al. 2014; Wood et al. 2015). We can summarize the concept by way of an example. In the 1980s, civil society groups in developed countries pressured governments and industry to combat tropical deforestation. In the 1990s, frustrated by states' failure to conclude a global forest treaty or to control deforestation, a coalition of civil society and business actors created the non-state Forest Stewardship Council (FSC) to set international standards for sustainable forestry and certify companies' compliance with those standards. Big retailers signed on, often in response to NGO threats to their brands, and FSC-certified forests and products multiplied. Forest owners and industry groups soon created their own competing certification schemes (Cashore et al. 2004). There is some evidence that this competition raised forest management standards and improved the governance of certification schemes (Overdevest 2010). Yet there is also evidence that upward convergence is superficial, masking persistent differences in transparency, accountability, rigour and effectiveness (Fransen 2011). These schemes also interact with national and international law in complicated ways. It is unclear, for example, what impact recent legality verification laws will have on them (Bartley 2014).

Comparable developments are occurring in many other economic sectors and issue areas. Transnational non-state governance actors and institutions interact with each other and with state-based actors and institutions at multiple spatial and temporal scales, with poorly understood effects on regulatory capacity, social and environmental standards, and marginalized actors.

The TBGI concept provides a common starting point for investigating these phenomena. *Governance* denotes deliberate efforts to change target actors' behaviour in furtherance of collective goals via norms, monitoring and enforcement (Black 2002, p. 170; Wood et al. 2015, pp. 337–8). Governance so understood is synonymous with 'regulation' or 'regulatory governance'. It is not restricted to states, international organizations or their formal governmental apparatus, but includes non-state and hybrid institutions created by a variety of actors and employing diverse regulatory techniques (Hood et al. 2001, p. 25; Scott 2004, pp. 161–6).

We focus on the governance of *business*, whether conducted by private firms or state-owned enterprises. The globalization of business generates some of the most serious and widespread contemporary governance challenges. The TBGI research agenda is, however, ripe for extension to other governance domains, such as health, education, migration, crime and security.

Transnational governance is governance in which non-state actors or institutions assert or exercise authority in the performance of one or more components of regulatory governance across national borders. These components include agenda-setting, norm formation, implementation, monitoring, enforcement and evaluation (ANIMEE). Actors and institutions have authority when relevant audiences perceive them as appropriately engaged in a regulatory task and their decisions as worthy of respect. But transnational governance is as much about the assertion and contestation of authority as about its exercise; our definition therefore includes asserted—not just accepted—authority.

We follow a rich vein of scholarship on transnational relations (Keohane and Nye 1971; Risse-Kappen 1995; Keck and Sikkink 1998), transnational law (Jessup 1956; Likosky 2002; Calliess and Zumbansen 2010; Halliday and Shaffer 2015) and global legal pluralism (Tamanaha 2001; Twining 2009; Berman 2012). Yet these literatures tend to focus on the emergence, operation, legitimacy or effectiveness of individual programs or regimes rather than their interactions with one another (Cutler et al. 1999; Dingwerth 2007; Hale and Held 2011). To the extent they consider interactions, it is usually between non-state and state regulation (Scott et al. 2011).

We also draw on the literatures on regulatory interactions (Hahn and Noll 1983), regulatory competition (Esty and Geradin 2001), international law fragmentation (M. A. Young 2012; Andenas and Bjorge 2015), interactive federalism (Schapiro 2006), interactive governance (Kooiman 2003; Edelenbos and van Meerkerk 2016), multilevel governance (Hooghe and Marks 2001; Bache and Flinders 2004), institutional interplay (Oberthür and Gehring 2006; Oberthür and Stokke 2011) and regime complexity (Raustiala and Victor 2004). But the TBGI agenda is distinctive in examining interactions amongst non-state actors and institutions in addition to interactions between state and non-state regulation, or within state regulation.

Finally, *interactions* are the mutual actions and reactions of governance actors, norms, institutions and systems. They can be deliberate or unintended, symmetrical or asymmetrical, cooperative or conflictual, orderly or chaotic. They engage agency (interactions amongst the makers, targets, interpreters, enforcers and beneficiaries of transnational regulatory governance) and social structure (interactions amongst transnational rules, principles, standards, programs, regimes, discourses, networks, technologies, legal orders and social systems). Interaction is neither desirable nor undesirable *per se;* it is inherent in all governance (Kooiman 2003).

Governance interactions occur and can be studied at various scales. At a micro scale, individual actors or norms interact within a single governance organization, program or jurisdiction. At a meso scale, governance initiatives or jurisdictions interact within regimes or organizational fields, while regimes, fields and discourses shape actors and norms. At a macro scale, regimes or fields interact within complexes or systems, and complexes or systems interact with one another (see Table 1.2).

Like early research into interactions amongst intergovernmental institutions (O. R. Young 2002), research into transnational governance interactions has reached a point where the lack of common concepts and data hinders the emergence of shared knowledge. We developed the TBGI analytical framework in response to this problem (Eberlein et al. 2014). The framework provides common definitions of central concepts and enables researchers to identify knowledge gaps, prioritize research and compare results. The framework disaggregates regulatory governance into the six components mentioned above: agenda-setting, norm formation, implementation, monitoring and information-gathering, enforcement, and evaluation and review. Interactions can occur within or between any of these components. The framework also poses six questions that researchers can ask about interactions in relation to each component: who or what interacts; what drives interaction; what are the mechanisms and pathways of interaction; what is the character of interaction; what are its effects; and how does interaction change over time? The framework thus produces a six-by-six matrix, which we apply to the chapters of this book in Table 1.1 (Eberlein et al. 2014; Wood et al. 2015).

The framework recognizes that interaction can involve heterogeneous entities (such as individuals, organizations, norms, discourses or systems) and often crosses organizational and spatial scales. The same actors can regulate while being regulated (Braithwaite and Drahos 2000, p. 10). The framework also acknowledges that actors and social structures co-evolve, interaction is both a cause and an effect, and it has diverse forms, pathways and causal mechanisms (Wood et al. 2015). In short, the TBGI framework is not monolithic or totalizing but promotes mutual intelligibility while accommodating heterogeneity and complexity.

A common analytical framework is only a starting point. Researchers must also theorize the interactive dynamics of transnational business governance. That is where this book comes in. It provides an integrative account of TBGIs that gains strength from a range of disciplines, theories and methods. The book draws on scholarly literatures in law, business, political science, sociology, environmental studies and other fields. Several of the contributors work across disciplines. Three (Bach, Carodenuto and Wood) have also been transnational business governance practitioners.

1.3 ENHANCING REGULATORY QUALITY AND ADVANCING MARGINALIZED ACTORS

The goal of this book is to generate insights into whether and how TBGIs, in all their variety, can be harnessed to enhance the quality of transnational regulation and advance the interests of marginalized actors. The chapters explore questions such as: which interactive strategies hold promise and who can use them (Verbruggen and Havinga, Chapter 2; Paiement, Chapter 11; Wood, Chapter 16)? Should the focus be on entrepreneurial individuals who spread regulatory models and norms (Meidinger, Chapter 3; Oman, Chapter 15); social networks (Auld and Renckens, Chapter 6; Henriksen and Seabrooke, Chapter 8); or isomorphic pressures (Gao and Chen, Chapter 13)? Why do TBGIs emerge, multiply and persist in some cases, while they stagnate, dwindle or fail to emerge in others (Westerwinter, Chapter 7; Winn, Chapter 5)? How do discursive and economic structures enable or constrain interactions (Casey, Chapter 9; Foley, Chapter 14)? How do various mechanisms and pathways of interaction operate (Bach, Chapter 12; Carodenuto and Cashore, Chapter 10; Schmidt, Chapter 4)?

Both regulatory quality and marginalized actors are contested concepts. We aim to specify them in ways that can attract relatively broad agreement while leaving open points of deep disagreement. We start with regulatory quality. We suggest assessing the relations between TBGIs and regulatory quality in terms of regulatory outputs and outcomes. We argue that their relations should also be assessed in terms of regulatory capacities—a factor overlooked by the literature on regulatory quality. We then define marginalized actors and suggest assessing their relations with TBGIs in the same terms: regulatory capacities, outputs and outcomes. Finally, we consider linkages and tensions between improving regulatory quality and advancing marginalized actors.

1.3.1 Regulatory Quality

The lament that no two definitions of regulatory quality coincide rings as true today as it did two decades ago (Gunningham et al. 1998, p. 25). Certain elements are nonetheless common to most accounts.

Effectiveness at achieving policy goals is a widely accepted element of regulatory quality, but there is disagreement whether the goal should be social and environmental improvement (Gunningham et al. 1998, p. 26) or ease of doing business (World Bank 2016; European Commission 2017). If the former, the emphasis is on increasing regulatory scope and ambition; if the latter, on reducing regulatory burdens (Pelkmans et al. 2000; Brown and Scott 2011). This book is in the former camp.

Efficiency, in many accounts, is the decisive element. Regulatory quality is a matter of optimizing regulatory benefits and burdens. Efficiency demands that regulatory goals be set at levels that maximize net benefits to society and that regulatory instruments be selected to achieve those goals at minimum cost (OECD 1995, 2005). Efficiency also requires advance assessment of costs, benefits, risks and impacts, as well as regular review and revision (OECD 1995; Ogus 1995; European Commission 2002). Assessments should consider all possible regulatory goals, instruments and actors (European Commission 2001; Brown and Scott 2011), as well as distributive consequences (OECD 1995; Baldwin and Cave 1999). Distributive equity is an independent criterion in some accounts (Gunningham et al. 1998, p. 26), but we do not include it here as it is central to our second theme, advancing marginalized actors.

Third, most accounts of regulatory quality emphasize *responsiveness*. Responsive regulation employs a flexible, pluralistic and complementary mix of actors, strategies and tools. It is tailored to variation in problem characteristics, industry structures, regulatory institutions, and actors' incentives and motivations (Ayres and Braithwaite 1992; Osborne and Gaebler 1992; Baldwin and Black 2008). It is also comprehensive, matching the scope of the problem (World Bank 2016).

Transparency, accountability and participation round out most recipes for regulatory quality. *Transparency* holds that regulation and regulatory processes should be clear, coherent, consistent, comprehensible and accessible (OECD 1995; Labory and Malgarini 2000). In some formulations, regulation should also be simple and practical (European Commission 2001; OECD 2005). *Accountability* requires regulators to justify their actions to, and submit to the scrutiny of, the general public or narrower constituencies of interested and affected parties (Radaelli and De Francesco 2007, p. 33; Alemanno 2015). Accountability and transparency are often combined with proportionality, due process and respect for the rule of law (OECD 1995).

Finally, *participation* means that all interested parties should have the opportunity to participate in regulatory governance processes (Lobel 2004). Broad and effective participation enhances regulation's legitimacy; expands the knowledge, experience, expertise and perspectives brought to bear on problems; helps identify unintended consequences; acts as a quality control check; and fosters compliance (OECD 1995). That said, the form and degree of participation thought to be necessary vary greatly, from mere notice and comment to joint decision-making.

Effectiveness, efficiency, responsiveness, transparency, accountability and participation are all subjects of ongoing debate. The chapters address them in different ways and to differing degrees. They devote more attention to effectiveness, transparency, accountability and participation than to efficiency or responsiveness.

1.3.2 Regulatory Outputs, Outcomes and Impacts

In the 1960s David Easton highlighted the need to distinguish between outputs, outcomes and impacts when investigating the consequences of political systems (Easton 1965). Put briefly, political systems produce *outputs* (regulations and other policy instruments) which lead to *outcomes* (changes in the behaviour, values or perceptions of regulatory targets) which in turn have *impacts* on social, economic, environmental or other conditions. International relations scholars have applied this schema to the effectiveness of international regimes (Underdal and Young 2004). We suggest applying it to all the dimensions of regulatory quality.

Outputs are relatively easy to assess. Outcomes can be tricky, and impacts even more so due to the multiplicity of forces, complexity of causal relations, diversity of contexts, pervasiveness of uncertainty and difficulty of specifying ideal results and no-regulation counterfactuals (O. R. Young 2017, pp. 28, 47). In addition, successful outputs and outcomes are no guarantee of progress in solving the targeted problems (ibid.). Thus, while impacts are our ultimate interest, we focus on regulatory outputs and, to a lesser extent, outcomes.

The outputs we emphasize are institutional designs and regulatory standards. Institutional designs include the structure and composition of decision-making organs and the rules and procedures by which they operate. Institutional designs can be more or less efficient, effective, responsive, transparent, accountable or participatory. Analysing institutional designs as outputs might seem odd: they seem more like inputs, shaping the production of regulatory outputs. But institutional designs are also outputs insofar as actors interact with one another and with existing institutions to design or redesign regulatory institutions. We are interested in how TBGIs can be steered to improve the design of regulatory institutions.

Regulatory standards include the rules, norms, guidelines, decisions and programs that regulatory institutions promulgate with a view to influencing the conduct of regulated actors. These are typically articulated at the norm formation stage, but also affect other stages (for example, best practice guidance for rule implementation and auditor competence requirements). We focus on the ambition and scope of standards. Standards can be more or less effective, efficient, responsive or transparent and can foster or hinder accountability and participation. We want to know whether TBGIs can be harnessed to increase the ambition and scope of regulatory standards. We are likewise interested in harnessing TBGIs to induce upward regulatory races, as well as regulatory ratchets that prevent backsliding (Braithwaite and Drahos 2000, pp. 518–20). Our emphasis on the strength and breadth of regulatory standards, rather than their efficiency or optimality, reflects the fact that in most regulatory domains 'ordinary citizens want higher standards of regulatory protection than they get' (ibid., p. 609).

Turning to regulatory outcomes, for the reasons mentioned earlier we do not assess the degree to which TBGIs change the social or environmental performance of regulated actors. Rather, we address two lower-order outcomes: the uptake of standards by regulatory targets and synergies amongst regulatory regimes. Greater uptake contributes to participation and (all else equal) effectiveness, and can also be associated with other components of regulatory quality. Synergy can enhance responsiveness (contributing to a smart, sophisticated ensemble of regulatory instruments and actors), transparency (through consistency and coherence) and efficiency (through cost-effectiveness).

Some chapters discuss other regulatory outcomes—including changes in regulated actors' behaviour—and the social and environmental impacts that are the ultimate object of our inquiry. We consider this evidence in the Conclusion, but systematic attention to impacts remains beyond the scope of this book.

1.3.3 Regulatory Capacity

Regulatory quality can be examined at yet another level: regulatory capacity. This concept is absent from most accounts of regulatory quality, but has received substantial attention from other scholars of regulation and public policy. Like regulatory quality, regulatory capacity is the subject of diverse perspectives. We understand it as a multidimensional endowment of resources and capabilities that enable regulatory actors to pursue goals and that must be mobilized for regulatory systems to function. These resources and capabilities include material and symbolic resources, organizational capacity, networks, capacity for feedback and learning, and resilience to shocks.

Material resources include technology, equipment, supplies, physical facilities and finances. Symbolic resources include authority, legitimacy, information, knowledge, skill, expertise, motivation and commitment (Black 2003, pp. 73–6). Legitimacy is amongst the most valuable regulatory assets and determinants of regulatory quality (Baldwin and Cave 1999; Alemanno 2015). Organizational capacity has material and symbolic dimensions and includes leadership and management, governance and operational structures, problem-solving ability, physical and communication infrastructure, and inter-organizational linkages (Lusthaus et al. 2002; Black 2003, pp. 78–9).

Social networks also cut across the material-symbolic divide, enabling members to mobilize relational assets including visibility, reputation, expertise, reliability and trust, not to mention access to information, people, organizations and material resources (Gulati 2007; Smith and Fischlein 2010; Westerwinter, Chapter 7; Henriksen and Seabrooke, Chapter 8).

Entire agendas for governance reform, including adaptive management (Lee 1993) and experimentalist governance (Sabel and Zeitlin 2008), are built around capacity for feedback, learning and adaptation. Cycles of innovation, monitoring, evaluation, learning and revision are a common feature of many accounts of reflexive or responsive regulation (Lobel 2004, pp. 395–400). Ciara Brown and Colin Scott (2011, pp. 477–9) argue that learning capacity should be a criterion for regulatory quality.

Finally, resilience refers to an actor or institution's ability to adapt to, overcome and recover from exogenous shocks while maintaining essential functions and structures (Holling 1973; Underdal 2004, p. 30; Bourbeau 2018, p. 7). Like learning, it is a valuable regulatory capacity.

Different components of regulatory governance demand different capacities (Black 2003). Lack of capacity at any point along the governance chain can jeopardize the performance of a regulatory system (Wood et al. 2015, p. 357). Mobilizing the capacities of multiple actors and institutions is essential to regulatory governance. At a minimum, a regulator must have capacity to promulgate standards and a regulatory target must have capacity to implement them. Single actors seldom possess all the capacities necessary to achieve their regulatory goals or ensure the operation of a regulatory regime. An actor's ability to enrol the capacities of other actors, regimes or networks is thus crucial to the achievement of regulatory goals.

Our catalogue of regulatory capacities is partial and contestable. Other scholars propose different lists. Kenneth Abbott and Duncan Snidal (2009) identify four essential regulatory competencies: independence, representativeness, expertise and operational capacity. We include expertise and operational capacity, while capturing independence and representativeness in our discussion of regulatory quality. Julia Black's (2003, p. 73) six critical resources—information, expertise, financial and economic resources, authority and legitimacy, strategic position and organizational capacity—are also covered more or less by our account.

Regulatory capacity should be integrated into analyses of regulatory quality. Regulation cannot be effective, efficient, responsive, transparent, accountable or participatory if regulatory actors and institutions lack the capacity to make it so. This is most evident for effectiveness: organizations with greater material and symbolic resources tend to be more effective, while low-capacity organizations face greater challenges. But the point also applies to other dimensions of regulatory quality. Information, expertise, organizational capacity and networks help ensure regulatory efficiency. Responsiveness cannot be achieved without some resilience and learning capacity. Transparency, accountability and participation require material resources and organizational capacities.

The relation between capacity and quality is not unidirectional. Regulatory quality both depends upon and contributes to regulatory capacity. For example, a regulatory regime is more likely to attract wide participation if it already enjoys authority and legitimacy and is committed to transparency, accountability and participation. Wider participation in turn will further enhance the regime's authority, legitimacy and commitment. Likewise, more efficient regulation frees up resources to enhance the capacity of relevant actors and institutions, including targets. The literature on regulatory quality largely overlooks these connections to capacity (exceptions include Baldwin and Cave 1999; Brown and Scott 2011; Alemanno 2015). Yet regulatory quality and capacity are thoroughly intertwined. We therefore incorporate regulatory capacity into our investigation of regulatory quality, alongside outputs and outcomes.

1.3.4 Marginalized Actors

The second theme of the book is concerned with challenging disparities of power in transnational governance. *Marginalized actors* are actors who have little or no role in the creation and operation of regulatory governance institutions, or influence over regulatory outputs and outcomes. Unlike actors who periodically exchange positions and symbols of power through routine governance contests, marginalized actors are systematically disadvantaged. The purposes, structures and rules of governance disfavour their interests, shared understandings reinforce their disadvantage, and they appropriate few material and symbolic rewards (Fligstein and McAdam 2012, p. 13).

Marginalization is multidimensional and contextual. At the extreme, it includes those who are utterly excluded from the social contract (Santos 2002, p. 457), possibly including indigenous and stateless peoples, refugees, illegal immigrants, the disabled, migrant labourers, unskilled or unemployed workers, slum dwellers, landless peasants, subsistence producers and people living with addiction or mental illness. Marginalized actors can also occupy intermediate social positions, such as women, ethnic minorities, consumers, workers, LGBTQ+ people, and their advocates (Kiai 2014). Business actors can be marginalized if they occupy marginal positions in global supply chains, such as subsistence producers in developing countries. Civil society groups can be marginalized in some contexts, as where they interact with global corporations and powerful states, but not in others, as where elite Northern NGOs purport to represent constituents to whom they are not accountable. Actors identified as marginalized in this book include suppliers in developing countries, small-scale producers, peripheral East Asian state and market actors, public interest NGOs, industry-affected communities, workers and indigenous peoples. Ultimately, however, marginalized actors should define and speak for themselves (Cornwall 2004; Agyeman et al. 2009).

We do not define marginalized actors in terms of whether their cause is just. Such characterizations are inherently contestable, even if consensus might be possible in some cases. Moreover, actors with legitimate claims may have interests or values that clash; any choice between them is based on contestable normative commitments. Finally, there is no external touchstone for the public interest; social life always involves 'a combination of pecuniary interest-pursuit and citizenship', and actors' 'definitions of their self-interest are generally congealed with a vision of the appropriate social order' (Meidinger 1992, unpaginated; see also 1987, pp. 365–6). Everyone enters regulatory governance interactions 'from the perspective of one's own preferences that are always already partial and contested or contestable but striving for universal recognition' (Koskenniemi 2012, p. 320), and actors generally advance their preferences and interests via public-regarding discourse (Ayres and Braithwaite 1992, p. 59).

Advancing marginalized actors can take weak and strong forms. In its weak form, it means harnessing TBGIs to better address marginalized actors' needs, mitigate adverse impacts on them, give them greater voice, and help them 'play' existing systems in their favour. These goals might be accomplished by, for example, increasing institutions' transparency, expanding participation and enhancing access to information (Gunningham et al. 1998, pp. 101–4). It might also include providing marginalized actors with resources to organize and participate effectively in regulatory governance (Ayres and Braithwaite 1992, pp. 18, 59). Such actions enable marginalized actors to get the most out of existing regulatory spaces, while expanding those spaces incrementally.

Such incremental advancement is the focus of this book. But the line between 'playing' the system and challenging it is blurry. Marginalized actors are always looking for cracks in the system, and routine contestation may shift imperceptibly to system rupture (Fligstein and McAdam 2012, pp. 97, 111). So we are also interested in the strong form of advancement: enhancing marginalized actors' chances to challenge and remake regulatory worlds. This entails developing skills and resources that enable marginalized actors to recognize when the limits of routine contention are reached; to fashion new conceptions that undermine existing regulatory settlements and attract wide support; to invent and deploy innovative regulatory forms; and to transform regulatory governance institutions or create new ones (ibid.).

Like regulatory quality, advancement of marginalized actors can be assessed at the level of regulatory capacities, outputs and outcomes. Thus we ask: Do TBGIs enhance marginalized actors' capacities to 'play the regulatory game' or to change the game? Do they enhance their material and symbolic resources? Do they improve their positions in regulatory networks, enhance their capacity for learning or increase their resilience? Do they lead regulatory institutions towards more participation, transparency and accountability? Do they produce regulatory standards that advance marginalized actors' interests and goals? And do they lead to regulatory outcomes that benefit marginalized actors?

1.3.5 Linkages

Enhancing regulatory quality and advancing marginalized actors are often aligned. Transparency, accountability and participation help marginalized actors, stave off capture by powerful actors, generate more regulatory options, provide information, strengthen standards and enhance effectiveness. Broader participation can enhance institutional legitimacy, an important regulatory capacity. And the more capacities marginalized actors can mobilize via networks, enrolment and other means, the better they can advance their interests. Most of the components of regulatory quality discussed in Part 3.1 are at least potentially consistent with advancing marginalized actors in the weak sense.

But regulatory quality and advancing marginalized actors are not always aligned. Enhanced regulatory capacity does not translate automatically into more ambitious standards, improved performance or greater protections. Efficiency and effectiveness can hamper marginalized actors' interests; broader participation can make regulatory processes more cumbersome and expensive. On the other hand, expanding marginalized voices often necessitates a more nuanced understanding of regulatory quality. Low-income communities in developing countries, for example, are likely to insist on adequate schooling and alternative economic opportunities as part of a regulatory strategy to eliminate child labour. Small-scale producers might accept tougher environmental or social standards only if accompanied by technical and financial support or enhanced market access.

1.4 PLAN OF THE BOOK

1.4.1 Overview

The book's two main parts correspond to its two themes. Part I primarily emphasizes harnessing TBGIs to improve regulatory quality, while Part II highlights issues of power and marginalization. Part III contains a concluding chapter that draws out key theoretical and practical lessons. The chapters cover a variety of sectors and issue areas. Eleven address specific economic sectors: agriculture and food (Verbruggen and Havinga, Chapter 2; Casey, Chapter 9), energy (Paiement, Chapter 11; Bach, Chapter 12), finance (Winn, Chapter 5; Gao and Chen, Chapter 13), fisheries (Auld and Renckens, Chapter 6; Foley, Chapter 14), forestry (Carodenuto and Cashore, Chapter 10; Oman, Chapter 15) and sport (Schmidt, Chapter 4). The others examine multiple sectors (Westerwinter, Chapter 7; Henriksen and Seabrooke, Chapter 8) or cross-sectoral initiatives (Meidinger, Chapter 3; Wood, Chapter 16). Issue areas examined include climate change (Paiement, Bach), corporate social responsibility (Wood), tropical deforestation (Carodenuto and Cashore), derivatives trading (Gao and Chen), food safety (Verbruggen and Havinga; Casey), financial technology (Winn), indigenous rights (Oman), sustainable events (Schmidt) and supply chain management (Meidinger).

The chapters cover the entire six-by-six TBGI analytical matrix (Eberlein et al. 2014, p. 8). Table 1.1 summarizes this coverage. Like most

Table 1.1 Coverage of the TBGI analytical matrix in this book

	Component of regulatory governance						
Dimension of interaction	**Agenda/goal setting**	**Norm formation**	**Implementation**	**Monitoring, information-gathering**	**Enforcement**	**Evaluation, Review**	**All/Un-differentiated**
Who or what interacts	Bach; Foley; Meidinger; Wood	Casey; Foley; Gao & Chen; Meidinger; Oman; Schmidt; Verbruggen & Havinga; Winn; Wood	Carodenuto & Cashore; Casey; Meidinger; Oman; Winn	Auld & Renckens; Casey; Meidinger; Paiement; Verbruggen & Havinga	Auld & Renckens; Casey; Meidinger; Paiement; Verbruggen & Havinga	Meidinger; Oman; Schmidt; Wood	Henriksen & Seabrooke; Westerwinter
Drivers and shapers	Bach; Foley; Wood	Casey; Foley; Gao & Chen; Meidinger; Schmidt; Verbruggen & Havinga; Winn	Casey; Meidinger; Winn	Casey; Meidinger; Verbruggen & Havinga	Casey; Verbruggen & Havinga	Schmidt; Wood	Henriksen & Seabrooke; Westerwinter
Mechanisms and pathways	Bach; Foley; Meidinger; Wood	Casey; Foley; Gao & Chen; Meidinger; Oman; Verbruggen & Havinga; Wood	Carodenuto & Cashore; Casey; Meidinger; Oman	Auld & Renckens; Casey; Meidinger; Paiement; Verbruggen & Havinga	Auld & Renckens; Casey; Meidinger; Paiement; Verbruggen & Havinga	Oman; Wood	Henriksen & Seabrooke; Westerwinter
Character of interaction	Bach; Foley; Meidinger; Wood	Foley; Gao & Chen; Meidinger; Oman; Schmidt; Verbruggen & Havinga; Wood	Meidinger; Oman	Auld & Renckens; Meidinger; Verbruggen & Havinga	Auld & Renckens; Meidinger; Verbruggen & Havinga	Meidinger; Oman; Schmidt; Wood	Henriksen & Seabrooke

Effects of interaction	Bach; Foley Meidinger; Wood	Casey; Foley; Gao & Chen; Meidinger; Oman; Schmidt; Verbruggen & Havinga; Winn; Wood	Carodenuto & Cashore; Casey; Meidinger; Oman; Winn	Auld & Renckens; Casey; Meidinger; Paiement; Verbruggen & Havinga	Auld & Renckens; Casey; Meidinger; Paiement; Verbruggen & Havinga	Meidinger; Oman; Schmidt; Wood	Henriksen & Seabrooke
Change over time	Meidinger; Wood	Casey; Gao & Chen; Oman; Schmidt; Verbruggen & Havinga; Winn; Wood	Carodenuto & Cashore; Casey; Meidinger; Oman; Winn	Auld & Renckens; Casey; Meidinger; Paiement; Verbruggen & Havinga	Auld & Renckens; Casey; Paiement; Verbruggen & Havinga	Oman; Schmidt; Wood	Henriksen & Seabrooke; Westerwinter

Note: Shading indicates the number of chapters addressing each cell of the TBGI matrix:

1–3 chapters 4–5 chapters ≥6 chapters

transnational governance research, they devote the greatest attention to norm formation, but agenda-setting, implementation, monitoring and enforcement also receive substantial treatment. The chapters analyse interactions involving numerous scales and units, ranging from individuals to entire social systems (Table 1.2).

1.4.2 Part I: Improving the Quality of Transnational Regulation

Part I opens on a cautiously optimistic note. Paul Verbruggen and Tetty Havinga (Chapter 2) explore interactions amongst the Global Food Safety Initiative (GFSI), transnational non-state food safety schemes and state actors in three countries. They argue that distributions of regulatory resources drive interactions, as actors seek to enrol one another's resources. Meta-regulator GFSI benchmarked non-state standards, which states recognized for enforcement purposes. These interactions raised standards, enhanced legitimacy for GFSI and benchmarked schemes, and improved state capacity. Yet mutual enrolment risks compromising enforcement agencies' independence.

Errol Meidinger (Chapter 3) explores interactions in sustainable supply chain management (SSCM). The main pathway of interaction is the supply chain; the main agent of interaction is the lead firm. Sustainability officers seek to enrol top management, cultivate direct supplier relationships and foster collaboration across supply chain tiers. The discourse is upbeat about these interactions, yet there is little evidence that they enhance regulatory capacities or improve standards.

Rebecca Schmidt (Chapter 4) examines sustainability standards for Olympic Games. She describes a process of cyclical regulation in which the International Olympic Committee (IOC) adopted rules for host city bids; prospective host cities proposed innovative environmental and social standards; the IOC incorporated these into its regulations; and subsequent aspiring host cities proposed further regulatory innovations. This cycle institutionalized local innovations as global standards and provided entry points for weaker actors.

Jane Winn (Chapter 5) presents a cautionary tale of failure to leverage TBGIs. EU regulators delegated the creation of the Single Euro Payments Area (SEPA) to banks, expecting them to fund the process. Banks resisted, and regulators ultimately reacted with a heavy hand, mandating use of SEPA for all payments. Winn argues that these interactions failed due to cognitive limitations. Regulators failed to recognize the public goods characteristics of proprietary payment systems, while banks systematically underestimated the magnitude of the costs and challenges posed by SEPA.

Table 1.2 Units and scales of analysis in this book

Chapter	Micro Actors or norms interact within a single organization, initiative or jurisdiction	Meso Initiatives or jurisdictions interact within regimes or fields; regimes, fields and discourses shape actors and norms	Macro Regimes or fields interact within complexes or systems; complexes or systems interact with one another
2. Verbruggen & Havinga		Global GFSI and national and transnational non-state food safety schemes interact with state actors and international organizations in a global food safety regime	
3. Meidinger	Sustainability, procurement and C-suite managers interact within lead firms; lead firms, suppliers, auditors, consultancies, NGOs, governments and others interact within and between tiers of global supply chains		
4. Schmidt	Local Olympic organizing bodies interact with state, market and civil society actors within and beyond host cities; cities interact with one another and the global IOC		
5. Winn		National, EU and global banking regulators interact with European banks and industry associations to create Single Euro Payments Area	
6. Auld & Renckens	Individual assessors, transnational auditing firms and local audited fisheries interact within global MSC		

(Continued)

Table 1.2 (Continued)

Chapter	**Micro** Actors or norms interact within a single organization, initiative or jurisdiction	**Meso** Initiatives or jurisdictions interact within regimes or fields; regimes, fields and discourses shape actors and norms	**Macro** Regimes or fields interact within complexes or systems; complexes or systems interact with one another
7. Westerwinter		Transnational governance initiatives interact within global networks	
8. Henriksen & Seabrooke	Issue professionals and transnational business governance organizations interact within two-level professional and organizational network		
9. Casey	GLOBALGAP interacts with national and global state, market and civil society actors within and outside GLOBALGAP		
10. Carodenuto & Cashore	National and subnational state, market and civil society actors in Cameroon interact with global REDD+ and FLEGT/VPA, which interact with each other in global tropical forest management regime		
11. Paiement		EU organs interact with extra-EU transnational sustainable biofuel schemes within a transnational assemblage	
12. Bach	Global OGCI interacts with member firms within OGCI, and with states, intergovernmental organizations, firms, industry associations, civil society actors and transnational governance schemes within a global climate governance regime; principles interact in a global climate governance discourse		
13. Gao & Chen		Global OTC and national futures trading schemes interact with each other and with national and international state actors within a global derivatives governance regime; dominant West interacts with marginal East	

14. Foley	Producers, states and other actors interact within fisheries eco-certification schemes; MSC interacts with territorial eco-certification schemes and transnational ethical eco-certification schemes; eco-certification schemes interact with state and non-state actors and institutions; neoliberal, embedded liberal and alter-globalization models of development interact with one another; all these interactions occur within three interacting spheres of action (social forces of production, state-civil society complexes, and world orders), each shaped by three interacting categories of power (material capabilities, ideas and institutions)
15. Oman	FSC members and organs interact within and between FSC International and FSC Canada; FSC, intergovernmental organizations and the transnational indigenous peoples' movement interact with one another and with international and Canadian law
16. Wood	Global ISO and ILO and national and global labour unions interact within and outside ISO, in a global social responsibility standardization field

Graeme Auld and Stefan Renckens (Chapter 6) apply social network analysis to Marine Stewardship Council (MSC) audits, analysing interactions amongst 15 audit firms over 16 years. They find that firms compete on audit scores and duration, with equivocal implications for regulatory quality. Auld and Renckens also examine the mobility of individual assessors, which can diffuse knowledge and good practice, but can lead audit firms to free-ride on others' training expenditure and limit audit firms' independence.

Oliver Westerwinter (Chapter 7) uses social network analysis to explain increasing overlaps amongst transnational multi-stakeholder governance initiatives. He shows that overlaps amongst initiatives are highly uneven over time and across issue areas, driven by shared issue areas, large size, clustering and popularity. These findings suggest, amongst other things, that marginalized actors should concentrate advocacy efforts on large, focal schemes.

Lasse Folke Henriksen and Leonard Seabrooke (Chapter 8) argue that two-level networks of issue professionals and organizations impede better regulation and advancement of marginalized interests. Issue professionals network to gain control over important issues. This analysis helps explain how regulatory capacities are developed and distributed, and why efforts to harness TBGIs often falter.

1.4.3 Part II: Advancing the Interests of Marginalized Actors

Donal Casey (Chapter 9) begins Part II by documenting the negative impact of early institutionalization on transparency, accountability and empowerment in the field of food safety. He traces the growth of the GLOBALGAP farm assurance system from an informal retailers' initiative to a powerful global regulatory organization. Early interactions amongst retailers, producers and suppliers enabled big business to entrench a dominant position. Governments, NGOs and marginalized smallholders pressed GLOBALGAP to adopt more inclusive governance processes and standards, but early institutionalization limited the potential of these interactions.

Sophia Carodenuto and Ben Cashore (Chapter 10) examine TBGIs in the implementation of international policies for timber legality (FLEGT/VPA) and avoidance of deforestation (REDD+) in Cameroon. These programs frustrated their own stated aim to empower local forestry operators and improve forest practices. International actors chose a complex, formal, technical approach that conflicted with their avowed choice of a logic of empowerment, thus excluding most Cameroonian forest operators and exacerbating governmental corruption and incapacity.

Phillip Paiement (Chapter 11) presents another story of harnessing TBGIs to support empowerment in theory, but creating disempowerment in practice. The EU, seeking to promote biofuels while ensuring their sustainability, delegated monitoring and enforcement to voluntary schemes. It recognized 19 such schemes, but failed to assess their transparency. This triggered a proliferation of schemes, but a downward trend in participation, transparency and accountability, empowering agribusiness interests at the expense of marginalized communities.

Matthew Bach (Chapter 12) suggests that TBGIs steered by major oil companies might contribute to tackling climate change. He examines agenda-setting interactions amongst the Oil & Gas Climate Initiative (OGCI), firms, industry associations and international organizations. He speculates that by endorsing a two-degree limit and promoting best practice, OGCI could trigger an upward regulatory ratchet, enrol powerful industry and interstate actors, and shift dialogue to a more proactive forum.

Simin Gao and Christopher Chen's (Chapter 13) analysis of TBGIs around financial derivatives trading focuses on responses by East Asian regulators and market operators to governance models exported from Western economies. The futures and over-the-counter (OTC) markets evolved separately, but each converged around a Western model through mimetic and normative isomorphism. After the global financial crisis, both regimes were disrupted by coercive isomorphism, consolidating Western dominance but generating some resistance by marginal Asian actors.

Paul Foley (Chapter 14) argues that the MSC's strained relationship with producers spurred the emergence of rival eco-certification schemes. Applying Robert Cox's (1987) critical international political economy, he argues that their counter-hegemonic potential is limited by a market-driven approach, large producers' entrenched advantage and international trade rules. New collaborations might overcome these constraints by shifting the MSC towards an embedded liberal model in which the state moderates market forces, or by building a more radical bottom-up coalition amongst fishery workers and transnational economic actors.

Natalie Oman (Chapter 15) is more sanguine about harnessing TBGIs. She documents an iterative process of interaction amongst the FSC, international law and national law around the norm of indigenous peoples' free, prior and informed consent (FPIC). Indigenous advocates leveraged the FSC's inclusive governance structure, interactions between its international and Canadian organs, and international human rights law to strengthen FPIC standards in the FSC. This opened an avenue towards a *de facto* consent power over forestry projects in Canada, and a stronger FPIC rule in customary international law.

Finally, Stepan Wood (Chapter 16) shows that despite being marginalized in the International Organization for Standardization (ISO), organized labour achieved remarkably favourable results in ISO 26000. He explains these interactions in terms of regulatory legitimation and enrolment. Organized labour overcame more powerful adversaries by leveraging the uneasy relationship between ISO, with a legitimacy 'deficit', and the International Labour Organization, which could enhance ISO's legitimacy. He proposes a triadic strategy through which marginalized actors can exploit such legitimacy differentials.

Overall, the chapters paint a decidedly mixed picture of the ability of TBGIs to improve regulatory quality and advance marginalized interests. Only five chapters find positive effects on one or both of those goals. In three chapters, TBGIs advanced both regulatory quality and marginalized actors' interests: Schmidt (Chapter 4), Oman (Chapter 15) and Wood (Chapter 16). Two chapters identify improvements in regulatory quality alone: Verbruggen & Havinga (Chapter 2) and Bach (Chapter 12); Westerwinter (Chapter 7) also suggests how TBGIs might improve regulatory quality. The remaining chapters find (or predict) mixed, unclear or negative effects. We explore these findings in more detail in the Conclusion.

REFERENCES

Abbott, Kenneth W., Philipp Genschel, Duncan Snidal and Bernhard Zangl (eds) (2015), *International Organizations as Orchestrators*, Cambridge, UK: Cambridge University Press.

Abbott, Kenneth W. and Duncan Snidal (2009), 'The governance triangle: regulatory standards institutions and the shadow of the state', in Walter Mattli and Ngaire Woods (eds), *The Politics of Global Regulation*, Princeton, NJ: Princeton University Press, pp. 44–88.

Agyeman, Julian, Peter Cole, Randolph Haluza-DeLay and Pat O'Riley (eds) (2009), *Speaking for Ourselves: Environmental Justice in Canada*, Vancouver: UBC Press.

Alemanno, Alberto (2015), 'How much better is better regulation: assessing the impact of the better regulation package on the European Union: a research agenda', *European Journal of Risk Regulation*, **6**, 344–56.

Alter, Karen J. and Sophie Meunier (2009), 'The politics of international regime complexity', *Perspectives on Politics*, **7** (1), 13–24.

Andenas, Mads and Eirik Bjorge (eds) (2015), *A Farewell to Fragmentation: Reassertion and Convergence in International Law*, Cambridge, UK: Cambridge University Press.

Ayres, Ian and John Braithwaite (1992), *Responsive Regulation: Transcending the Deregulation Debate*, Oxford and New York: Oxford University Press.

Bache, Ian and Matthew V. Flinders (eds) (2004), *Multi-Level Governance*, Oxford: Oxford University Press.
Baldwin, Robert and Julia Black (2008), 'Really responsive regulation', *Modern Law Review*, **71**, 59–94.
Baldwin, Robert and Martin Cave (1999), *Understanding Regulation: Theory, Strategy, and Practice*, Oxford and New York: Oxford University Press.
Bartley, Tim (2014), 'Transnational governance and the re-centered state: sustainability or legality?' *Regulation and Governance*, **8** (1), 93–109.
Berman, Paul Schiff (2012), *Global Legal Pluralism: A Jurisprudence of Law Beyond Borders*, New York: Cambridge University Press.
Black, Julia (2002), 'Regulatory conversations', *Journal of Law and Society*, **29** (1), 163–96.
Black, Julia (2003), 'Enrolling actors in regulatory systems: examples from UK financial services regulation', *Public Law*, 63–91.
Blome, Kerstin, Andreas Fischer-Lescano, Hannah Franzki, Nora Markard and Stefan Oeter (eds) (2016), *Contested Regime Collisions: Norm Fragmentation in World Society*, Cambridge, UK: Cambridge University Press.
Bourbeau, Philippe (2018), *On Resilience: Genealogy, Logics, and World Politics*, New York: Cambridge University Press.
Braithwaite, John and Peter Drahos (2000), *Global Business Regulation*, Cambridge, UK: Cambridge University Press.
Brown, Ciara and Colin Scott (2011), 'Regulation, public law, and better regulation', *European Public Law*, **17** (3), 467–84.
Calliess, Gralf-Peter and Peer Zumbansen (2010), *Rough Consensus and Running Code: A Theory of Transnational Private Law*, Oxford and Portland, OR: Hart.
Cashore, Benjamin, Graeme Auld and Deanna Newsom (2004), *Governing through Markets: Forest Certification and the Emergence of Non-State Authority*, New Haven, CT: Yale University Press.
Cornwall, Andrea (2004), 'Spaces for transformation? Reflections on issues of power and difference in participation in development', in Samuel Hickey and Giles Mohan (eds), *Participation: From Tyranny to Transformation?*, London: Zed Books, pp. 75–91.
Cox, Robert W. (1987), *Production, Power, and World Order: Social Forces in the Making of History*, New York: Columbia University Press.
Cutler, A. Claire, Virginia Haufler and Tony Porter (1999), *Private Authority and International Affairs*, Albany: State University of New York Press.
Dingwerth, Klaus (2007), *The New Transnationalism: Transnational Governance and Democratic Legitimacy*, Basingstoke, UK and New York: Palgrave Macmillan.
Easton, David (1965), *A Systems Analysis of Political Life*, New York: Wiley.
Eberlein, Burkard, Kenneth W. Abbott, Julia Black, Errol Meidinger and Stepan Wood (2014), 'Transnational business governance interactions: conceptualization and framework for analysis', *Regulation and Governance*, **8** (1), 1–21.
Edelenbos, Jurian and Ingmar van Meerkerk (2016), 'Introduction: three reflecting perspectives on interactive governance', in Jurian Edelenbos and Ingmar van Meerkerk (eds), *Critical Reflections on Interactive Governance: Self-Organization and Participation in Public Governance*, Cheltenham, UK and Northampton, MA, USA: Edward Elgar, pp. 1–28.
Esty, Daniel C. and Damien Geradin (eds) (2001), *Regulatory Competition and Economic Integration*, Oxford: Oxford University Press.
European Commission (2001), *Mandelkern Group on Better Regulation Final Report*, 13 November, Brussels: European Commission.

European Commission (2002), 'Action plan "simplifying and improving the regulatory environment"' (Communication) COM (2002) 278 final.
European Commission (2017), 'Better regulation guidelines', 7 July (Commission Staff Working Document) SWD (2017) 350.
Fligstein, Neil and Doug McAdam (2012), *A Theory of Fields*, Oxford and New York: Oxford University Press.
Fransen, Luc (2011), 'Why do private governance organizations not converge? A political–institutional analysis of transnational labor standards regulation', *Governance*, **24** (2), 359–87.
Gehring, Thomas and Sebastian Oberthür (2009), 'The causal mechanisms of interaction between international institutions', *European Journal of International Relations*, **15** (1), 125–56.
Gulati, Ranjay (2007), *Managing Network Resources: Alliances, Affiliations and Other Relational Assets*, Oxford: Oxford University Press.
Gunningham, Neil, Peter N. Grabosky and Darren Sinclair. (1998), *Smart Regulation: Designing Environmental Policy*, Oxford: Clarendon Press.
Hahn, Robert W. and Roger G. Noll (1983), 'Barriers to implementing tradable air pollution permits: problems of regulatory interactions', *Yale Journal on Regulation*, **1**, 63–92.
Hale, Thomas and David Held, (2011), *Handbook of Transnational Governance: Institutions and Innovations*, Cambridge, UK and Malden, MA: Polity.
Halliday, Terence C. and Gregory Shaffer (2015), 'Transnational legal orders', in Terence C Halliday and Gregory Shaffer (eds), *Transnational Legal Orders*, New York: Cambridge University Press, pp. 1–72.
Holling, C.S. (1973), 'Resilience and stability of ecological systems', *Annual Review of Ecology and Systematics*, **4**, 14.
Hood, Christopher, Henry Rothstein and Robert Baldwin (2001), *The Government of Risk: Understanding Risk Regulation Regimes*, Oxford: Oxford University Press.
Hooghe, Liesbet and Gary Marks (eds) (2001), *Multi-Level Governance and European Integration*, Lanham, MD: Rowman & Littlefield.
Jessup, Philip C. (1956), *Transnational Law. Storrs Lectures on Jurisprudence*, New Haven, CT: Yale University Press.
Keck, Margaret E. and Kathryn Sikkink (1998), *Activists Beyond Borders: Advocacy Networks in International Politics*, Ithaca, NY: Cornell University Press.
Keohane, Robert O. and Joseph S. Nye (1971), *Transnational Relations and World Politics*, Cambridge, MA: Harvard University Press.
Kiai, Maina (2014), *Report of the Special Rapporteur on the Rights to Freedom of Peaceful Assembly and of Association, Maina Kiai, to the Human Rights Council*, April, A/HRC/26/29.
Kooiman, Jan (2003), *Governing as Governance*, London: Sage.
Koskenniemi, Martti (2012), 'Hegemonic regimes', in Margaret A. Young (ed.), *Regime Interaction in International Law: Facing Fragmentation*, Cambridge, UK: Cambridge University Press, pp. 305–24.
Labory, Sandrine and Marco Malgarini (2000), 'Regulation in Europe: justified burden or costly failure?' in Giampaolo Galli and Jacques Pelkmans (eds) *Regulatory Reform and Competitiveness in Europe, Volume I: Horizontal Issues*, Cheltenham, UK and Northampton, MA, USA: Edward Elgar, pp. 81–126.
Lee, Kai N. (1993), *Compass and Gyroscope: Integrating Science and Politics for the Environment*, Washington, DC: Island Press.

Likosky, Michael (ed.) (2002), *Transnational Legal Processes: Globalisation and Power Disparities*, London: Butterworths.
Lobel, Orly (2004), 'The renew deal: the fall of regulation and the rise of governance in contemporary legal thought', *Minnesota Law Review*, **89**, 342–470.
Lusthaus, Charles, Marie-Hélène Adrien, Gary Anderson, Fred Carden and George Plinio Montalván (2002), *Organizational Assessment: A Framework for Improving Performance,* Washington, DC and Ottawa: Inter-American Development Bank and International Development Research Centre.
Meidinger, Errol (1987), 'Regulatory culture: a theoretical outline', *Law & Policy*, **9** (4), 355–86.
Meidinger, Errol (1992), 'Administrative regulation and democracy', Baldy Center for Law and Social Policy Working Paper, State University of New York at Buffalo, accessed 12 April 2019 at http://web2.law.buffalo.edu/faculty/meidinger/scholarship/regdem.html.
Oberthür, Sebastian and Thomas Gehring (eds) (2006), *Institutional Interaction in Global Environmental Governance: Synergy and Conflict among International and EU Rules*, Cambridge, MA: MIT Press.
Oberthür, Sebastian and Olav Schram Stokke (eds) (2011), *Managing Institutional Complexity: Regime Interplay and Global Environmental Change*, Cambridge, MA: MIT Press.
OECD (1995), *Recommendation of the Council of the OECD on Improving the Quality of Government Regulation (Adopted on 9 March 1995) Including the OECD Reference Checklist for Regulatory Decision-Making and Background Note*, OCDE/GD(95)95.
OECD (2005), *OECD Guiding Principles for Regulatory Quality and Performance*, Paris: OECD.
Ogus, Anthony (1995), 'Quality control for European regulation', *Maastricht Journal of European and Comparative Law*, **2**, 325–38.
Osborne, David and Ted Gaebler (1992), *Reinventing Government: How the Entrepreneurial Spirit Is Transforming the Public Sector*, Reading, MA: Addison-Wesley.
Overdevest, Christine (2010), 'Comparing forest certification schemes: the case of ratcheting standards in the forest sector', *Socio-Economic Review*, **8**, 47–76.
Pelkmans, Jacques, Sandrine Labory and Giandomenico Majone (2000), 'Better EU regulatory quality: assessing current initiatives and new proposals', in Giampaolo Galli and Jacques Pelkmans (eds), *Regulatory Reform and Competitiveness in Europe, Volume I: Horizontal Issues*, Cheltenham, UK and Northampton, MA, USA: Edward Elgar, pp. 461–526.
Radaelli, Claudio M. and Fabrizio De Francesco (2007), *Regulatory Quality in Europe: Concepts, Measures and Policy Processes*, Manchester: Manchester University Press.
Raustiala, Kal and David G. Victor (2004), 'The regime complex for plant genetic resources', *International Organization*, **58** (2), 277–309.
Risse-Kappen, Thomas (ed.) (1995), *Bringing Transnational Relations Back In: Non-State Actors, Domestic Structures and International Institutions*, Cambridge, UK: Cambridge University Press.
Sabel, Charles F. and Jonathan Zeitlin (2008), 'Learning from difference: the new architecture of experimentalist governance in the EU', *European Law Journal*, **14** (3), 271–327.
Santos, Boaventura de Sousa (2002), *Toward a New Legal Common Sense: Law, Globalization and Emancipation*, 2nd edn, London: Butterworths.

Schapiro, Robert A. (2006), 'From dualist federalism to interactive federalism', *Emory Law Journal*, **56** (1), 1–18.
Scott, Colin (2004), 'Regulation in the age of governance: the rise of the post-regulatory state', in Jacint Jordana and David Levi-Faur (eds), *The Politics of Regulation: Institutions and Regulatory Reforms for the Age of Governance*, Cheltenham, UK and Northampton, MA, USA: Edward Elgar, pp. 145–74.
Scott, Colin, Fabrizio Cafaggi and Linda Senden (2011), 'The conceptual and constitutional challenge of transnational private regulation', *Journal of Law and Society*, **38** (1), 1–19.
Smith, Timothy M. and Miriam Fischlein (2010), 'Rival private governance networks: competing to define the rules of sustainability performance', *Global Environmental Change*, **20**, 511–22.
Tamanaha, Brian Z. (2001), *A General Jurisprudence of Law and Society*, Oxford: Oxford University Press.
Twining, William (2009), *General Jurisprudence: Understanding Law from a Global Perspective*, Cambridge, UK: Cambridge University Press.
Underdal, Arild (2004), 'Methodological challenges in the study of regime effectiveness', in Arild Underdal and Oran R. Young (eds), *Regime Consequences: Methodological Challenges and Research Strategies*, Dordrecht, Netherlands: Kluwer Academic Publishers, pp. 27–48.
Underdal, Arild and Oran R. Young (eds) (2004), *Regime Consequences: Methodological Challenges and Research Strategies*, Dordrecht, Netherlands: Kluwer Academic Publishers.
Wood, Stepan, Kenneth W. Abbott, Julia Black, Burkard Eberlein and Errol Meidinger (2015), 'The interactive dynamics of transnational business governance: a challenge for transnational legal theory', *Transnational Legal Theory*, **6** (2), 333–69.
World Bank (2016), *Doing Business 2016: Measuring Regulatory Quality and Efficiency*, Washington, DC: World Bank Group.
Young, Margaret A. (ed.) (2012), *Regime Interaction in International Law: Facing Fragmentation*, Cambridge, UK: Cambridge University Press.
Young, Oran R. (2002), *The Institutional Dimensions of Environmental Change: Fit, Interplay, and Scale*, Cambridge, MA: MIT Press.
Young, Oran R. (2017), *Governing Complex Systems: Social Capital for the Anthropocene*, Cambridge, MA: MIT Press.

PART I

Improving the quality of transnational regulation

2. Transnational business governance interactions in food safety regulation: Exploring the promises and risks of enrolment

Paul Verbruggen and Tetty Havinga

2.1 INTRODUCTION

Food safety regulation has changed profoundly since the 1990s (Verbruggen and Havinga 2017). The globalization of food supply chains, the growing concentration of market power among food retailers and systemic risks of food safety outbreaks have challenged the capacities of national governments to regulate food safety (Marsden et al. 2010). Taken together, these developments have also been important elements triggering the rise of non-state food safety standards (Henson and Humphrey 2009, pp. 9–11). Such standards now govern a substantial portion of the global trade in food.

The rise of non-state food safety standards has had a significant impact on actors in global food supply chains. Dominant firms in these chains (typically multinational retailers and manufacturers) require producers and suppliers to meet these standards, effectively shifting compliance costs to actors up the chain. Actors supplying different retailers or markets are often confronted with multiple, partly overlapping standards, each with its own audit and certification protocols. The resulting compliance costs are said to impede market access for small and medium-sized enterprises (SMEs), especially those in developing countries (Martens and Swinnen 2012). This, in turn, has created concerns over the legitimacy of such standards in terms of democratic participation, transparency and accountability (Fuchs et al. 2011; Casey, Chapter 9).

A group of globally leading retailers established the Global Food Safety Initiative (GFSI) in 2000 in response to these and other concerns (Havinga and Verbruggen 2017). Rather than developing one single global food safety standard, GFSI benchmarks rival standards following a set of baseline requirements with a view to coordinate, converge and ratchet up existing standards and enhance compliance with food safety laws. GFSI's mission is to 'provide continuous improvement in food safety management systems to ensure confidence in the delivery of safe food to consumers worldwide' (GFSI 2019b).

GFSI actively engages with domestic state actors. Modern food law assigns key monitoring and enforcement competences to national and local authorities on the premise that they are best placed to address local problems and needs (MacMaoláin 2015, pp. 54–7). GFSI seeks to gain these authorities' recognition of its activities and benchmarked standards. Concurrently, these domestic state actors have reached out to involve GFSI-benchmarked standards in monitoring and enforcement policies.

In this chapter we discuss the unfolding interaction between GFSI and domestic state actors in the regulation of food safety. We offer an empirical account of how and to what extent national food safety agencies in Canada, China and the Netherlands have engaged with GFSI and its benchmarked schemes. We analyse these transnational business governance interactions (TBGIs) using the framework proposed by Eberlein et al. (2014) and Wood et al. (2015).

As our analysis will show, the interaction between GFSI and these different actors has developed for different reasons and in different ways, with different results. To critically discuss these findings, and to deepen the TBGI analytical framework, we draw on the concept of enrolment as developed by Black (2003). Regulatory enrolment is a strategy for linking actors possessing different regulatory capacities to enhance the capacity of both. It provides 'a normative framework for considering ways in which the capacity of the system as a whole might be enhanced effectively and legitimately by the careful deployment within it of the regulatory capacity of different actors' (ibid., p. 91). It adds to the TBGI framework a critical perspective on why and how certain actors link with each other, and with what results.

We start our analysis by discussing the emergence of GFSI as an institutionalized form of TBGIs among non-state food standards.

2.2 INSTITUTIONALIZING TBGIs: THE EMERGENCE OF GFSI

In 2000, 13 major retailers established GFSI with the purpose of coordinating the transnational food safety standards they had developed in the 1990s. As noted, GFSI sets meta-standards for food safety schemes. It assesses whether existing or new food safety schemes meet common benchmarks laid down in the GFSI Guidance Document (GFSI 2017b). Accordingly, GFSI is a transnational meta-regulator in the field of private food safety governance (Verbruggen and Havinga 2016).

As of 2017, 13 food safety schemes from nine scheme owners had been benchmarked against the GFSI Guidance Document and thus recognized by GFSI.[1] These included all major schemes around the world. What is more, most leading Western corporate food retailers and manufacturers require certification against GFSI-recognized schemes (Fulponi 2006; Havinga 2015, p. 67). Given this strong market uptake, the impact of GFSI on food safety practices on the ground is significant. According to its own statistics, GFSI meta-standards are applied in 77 000 factories and 150 000 farms in over 160 countries (GFSI 2017d). This implies that GFSI is a key institution in global food safety governance.

While GFSI was born out of a need to coordinate rival food safety schemes, it has also had an impact in terms of converging and ratcheting up the standards that make up these schemes. GFSI's benchmarking standards are widely regarded as the leading industry standard for transnational food safety schemes. Auditing and certification are one domain in which GFSI has been influential in shaping the design of these schemes (Fagotto 2017). GFSI helped to establish third-party certification as the leading approach to verifying conformity with the applicable standards (GFSI 2011). With its 2017 Guidance Document, GFSI aimed to ratchet up industry standards for auditor competence, unannounced audits and fraud prevention (Havinga and Verbruggen 2017, p. 191).

In the years following its creation, GFSI recognized the importance of engaging with the public sector (Havinga and Verbruggen 2017). It organized various meetings and events targeted at aligning its activities with national and international governmental organizations (IGOs). It established the Global Regulatory Affairs Working Group in 2009 to 'actively engage governments in recognizing and accepting GFSI-benchmarked schemes', further align industry and public sector efforts and integrate GFSI with the rules of the Codex Alimentarius Commission (Codex) and the Sanitary and Phytosanitary (SPS) Agreement of the World Trade Organization (WTO) (GFSI 2012, p. 3). The Group seeks to forge alliances with state actors by securing governmental recognition of third-party certification to GFSI-benchmarked schemes when determining compliance and enforcement actions, obtaining governmental feedback on GFSI programs, cooperating with governments and IGOs to gain alignment in regulatory capacity-building, and cooperating with Codex and national authorities to harmonize global food safety standards (International Forum on Food Safety and Health 2013).

While these objectives have not been fully achieved, GFSI participates in discussions on global food governance within Codex and the World Organisation for Animal Health (Havinga and Verbruggen 2017, pp. 196–7). It also takes part in regular meetings with officials from national and regional food agencies and has concluded memoranda of understanding with several governmental organizations. Our analysis will now focus on these interactions.

2.3 TBGIs BETWEEN GFSI AND DOMESTIC STATE ACTORS

GFSI's Global Regulatory Affairs Working Group considered the recognition and adoption of GFSI-benchmarked standards by domestic state actors as one of its core deliverables. In many jurisdictions food businesses are legally required (EU, Canada, US) or encouraged (China) to have food safety management systems (FSMSs). Since these systems were first introduced by individual corporations and expanded by non-state food safety schemes and GFSI (Havinga 2006), national laws built on these industry initiatives. GFSI saw the inclusion of FSMS requirements in public legal frameworks as an opportunity for engagement with governments.

In choosing with whom to engage, the Working Group first identified twenty countries of interest. One selection criterion was the willingness of national governments to engage with GFSI. High-priority countries included Canada, Chile, China, Japan, Mexico, South Africa, the Netherlands, UK and US. Alignment with the EU as a whole was also considered a priority.[2] In 2009, GFSI representatives met with EU officials as a 'first step in permitting a review of the relationship of food safety schemes to current legislation' (GFSI 2009). The activities of the Working Group included meetings at the national offices in these countries, invitations of senior officers of national food agencies to GFSI conferences and meetings with the GFSI Board, and the sharing of written information about GFSI. The Working Group chair described this effort as:

> (. . .) a long process of informing the government and officials, getting them to understand more about these standards and GFSI and the fact that it is a global standard and the process that GFSI uses to benchmark the various schemes. (Havinga and Verbruggen 2017, p. 199)

In the following we analyse the interactions between GFSI and national governments and food safety agencies by asking why, how and with what results these interactions have taken place. We focus on the cases of the Netherlands, Canada and China.[3] We include the Netherlands and

Canada because they are considered frontrunners in seeking collaboration with (trans)national food safety schemes and GFSI. In both countries concrete progress has been made towards integration of GFSI-benchmarked schemes in public monitoring and enforcement policies. Moreover, officials of both countries have taken the lead in organizing international meetings between representatives of governmental food authorities to discuss options for public-private cooperation. While the Netherlands has integrated a number of leading foreign schemes in its enforcement policies, Canada's progress is limited to a national scheme recognized by GFSI. We also include China in our analysis since the public-private partnerships that GFSI has established with Chinese state agencies are of a different nature and serve a different purpose when compared to GFSI's engagements with other domestic state actors, namely to resolve structural problems with the benchmarking of Chinese food safety standards.

2.3.1 The Netherlands

Historically, relations between government and industry in the Netherlands are of a corporatist character. The Dutch government has a long tradition of engaging with non-state actors in food policy-making. Industry and trade associations established various self-regulatory initiatives that were linked in some way to public policy or legislative frameworks (van Waarden 1985). As a result, food safety governance in the Netherlands has traditionally involved various forms of industry participation (Havinga and van Waarden 2013).

The national food safety authority, the NVWA (*Nederlandse Voedsel- en Warenautoriteit*), has continued this tradition. NVWA interprets current food safety laws[4] to enable it to build on private sector initiatives to bolster its risk-based enforcement policies (Verbruggen 2014, pp. 238–44). In this context, along with recurring institutional reforms and budget cuts that challenged its regulatory capacities, the NVWA accepted 14 national non-state quality assurance schemes to inform its enforcement policy. In addition, it concluded memoranda of understanding with seven food companies specifying the terms of collaboration and adapted inspections (Verbruggen and Havinga 2015).

A new phase in NVWA's engagement with the private sector is its integration of transnational food safety schemes in its enforcement policies. NVWA employs two strategies to influence these schemes and manage how they can be incorporated in its policy in a sound way. First, it challenges GFSI and its benchmarked schemes to strengthen these schemes' performance. Second, it uses an evaluative framework to assess the design of the schemes and their performance. With regard to the first strategy,

NVWA officials have met formally and informally with representatives of GFSI, transnational schemes, retailers and brand manufacturers to discuss the conditions under which NVWA accepts certification under these schemes as a factor to influence inspection frequency and enforcement action. Moreover, NVWA officials have spoken at the food safety conferences of GFSI and others, stressing the need to improve the performance of GFSI-benchmarked schemes. The main issues of concern for NVWA are the reliability of third-party certification, auditor competence and integrity, unannounced inspections, accreditation, food safety culture at certified businesses and fraud.

The NVWA's second strategy is the substantive assessment of non-state schemes (Havinga 2018, pp. 81–4). Such schemes are only accepted and integrated in NVWA's enforcement policy if they meet key design and performance criteria. After the horsemeat fraud scandal, the Dutch government established a task force of representatives from government, NVWA, and the meat, dairy and animal feed industries to discuss measures to restore consumer confidence in food. One result of this process was a policy document stating criteria for acceptance of non-state quality control systems that aim to safeguard food safety and integrity (NVWA 2014).[5] Transparency and the exchange of information are key elements of these criteria. Twenty-two schemes applied for acceptance (NVWA 2017b, p. 5). By mid 2019, the GFSI-recognized schemes of the British Retail Consortium (BRC), the International Featured Standards (IFS) and Food Safety System Certification (FSSC) had been accepted (NVWA 2019).

By recognizing these schemes, NVWA acknowledges that they support public enforcement action. NVWA takes into account whether or not a business is certified against an accepted non-state assurance scheme, for example in decisions about inspection frequency and scope, and sanctions. As a next step in the development of its relations with non-state schemes, NVWA aims 'to establish a long term [. . .] cooperation with scheme owners in order to strengthen the supply chain, exchange information where necessary and support official controls' (FSSC 22000 2017, quoting an NVWA official).

Given these developments and the attitude of NVWA in engaging with industry initiatives, GFSI saw the Netherlands as a key country where it could successfully align with a domestic state actor. As the chair of GFSI's Regulatory Affairs Working Group commented on NVWA's acceptance of the FSSC 22000 scheme: 'The NVWA is blazing the path for other governmental regulatory authorities to recognize the merits of GFSI-benchmarked schemes, the private assurance system and the benefit of utilizing accredited certifications in helping with the deployment of national inspectional resources, which ultimately leads to a strengthening of the food safety system' (FSSC 22000 2017).

2.3.2 Canada

Canada has a multi-layered governmental system dividing responsibilities for regulations and inspections between the federal, provincial and municipal governments (Hobbs et al. 2002, p. 78). The uptake of non-state food safety schemes in governmental policies was until recently mainly limited to export firms. In particular meat exports to the US had to comply with strict US regulations. In comparison to the UK and the Netherlands, the vertical integration of supply chains in Canada is less developed and as a result the role of retailers in driving food safety initiatives is not prominent (Nguyen et al. 2004).

However, several food safety incidents demonstrated that the food regulatory framework must be strengthened and keep pace with prevention-focused international food safety standards. In this context, the Canadian Food Inspection Agency (CFIA) sought to modernize its enforcement policy. In considering how to do this, CFIA consulted with many stakeholders, including GFSI. The agency 'recognizes that private certification schemes may play an important role in helping industry achieve food safety regulatory objectives, provided they can be assessed as being effective, credible and aligned with public policy objectives' (CFIA 2017b). CFIA's Private Certification Policy notes that certification under a private scheme that meets public law requirements should positively impact the risk-based strategy it uses to prioritize food businesses for inspection. To build this policy, CFIA first assessed whether and to what extent the GFSI Guidance Document and the accredited certification process complied with federal legislative requirements. Now that the Private Certification Policy is in place, many food businesses are expected to seek certification from a GFSI-benchmarked scheme in order to comply with the new *Safe Food for Canadians Act* (GFSI 2015b).[6]

Furthermore, Canada has set up a Food Safety Recognition Program 'which provides government recognition of on-farm and post-farm food safety systems developed and implemented by national industry organizations' (CFIA 2018). The program is led by CFIA with the participation of provincial and territorial governments. It aims to enhance food safety, maintain the confidence of Canadian consumers and facilitate market access. In 2013 Canadian chicken farmers were the first to achieve recognition under this program, the dairy farmers followed in 2016, and CanadaGAP in 2017. CanadaGAP is a non-state certification scheme for the fruit and vegetable industry that has been benchmarked by GFSI since 2010. Its CFIA recognition process began in 2004 and involved a technical review of the standard and the management system, third-party audits to assess implementation and performance, and an evaluation of third-party audits by Canadian government officials (CFIA 2017a). The CFIA takes into account companies' certification under several programs, including GFSI-recognized schemes, when determining the level of risk (Havinga 2018, pp. 70–72).

Importantly, Canada has also initiated, with the Netherlands, a series of informal meetings between government officials about public cooperation with non-state quality assurance schemes. These meetings include talks with representatives of the GFSI Board. In February 2017, some 100 representatives of 20 national governments and five IGOs met in Houston 'to share information on their approaches to private certification in order to foster a common understanding of benefits and challenges associated with leveraging private certification' in a regulatory context.[7]

In 2013, GFSI established a US-Canada Local Group to drive greater regulatory acceptance of GFSI-benchmarked schemes. GFSI advertises the recent CFIA policy framework on private certification schemes, its recognition of CanadaGAP, and its leading role in global meetings to further the collaboration between companies and governments to harmonize and strengthen food safety systems around the world (GFSI 2016, 2017c).

2.3.3 China

The People's Republic of China has been plagued with major food safety scandals and policymakers in China are increasingly concerned with food safety (Burns et al. 2015; Jensen and Zhou 2015, p. 168; An 2017). The food regulatory system is fragmented, and local government is not always willing to enforce the laws due to lack of resources, local protectionism and corruption (Thompson and Hu 2007). Food supply chains show little vertical coordination (let alone integration) and food is produced by a large number of low-educated, small-scale farmers. Moreover, civil society organizations representing the interests of consumers or manufacturers are missing. Industry associations are directly controlled by the government and are not key players in developing and disseminating food safety standards (An 2017).

Before 2009, food safety regulations were more lenient and less sophisticated than transnational food safety standards. The Chinese state has been focused on the production of high quantities of food and on economic growth, not on safe food (Gale and Buzby 2009, p. 3). After major food safety incidents, high refusal rates in exports and a growing lack of consumer confidence in domestically produced food, the central government established new food safety laws in 2009 and 2015. Along with this legislative overhaul came new systems for effective food controls (Roberts and Lin 2016). Since then, food businesses are required to have food safety experts and procedures. Compliance with Good Manufacturing Practices (GMP) and Hazard Analysis and Critical Control Points (HACCP) principles is encouraged. Since December 2016, businesses having a GMP or HACCP certificate may be considered to pose less risk to food safety and may benefit from less frequent official inspections.[8]

Despite this regulatory modernization, implementation and compliance remain problematic. Inspection and enforcement are complicated by governmental fragmentation, a lack of trained inspectors and insufficient resources (Kottenstede 2017, pp. 227–9). Chinese standards and certificates are not considered reliable at the international level (Gale and Buzby 2009, p. 26). This is a key explanation of why recognition of Chinese food safety standards by GFSI or another international forum that would lend these standards more credibility and authority is very important for China and its (agri)food sector.

Since its establishment in 2000, GFSI has developed a close relationship with China and various of its state actors.[9] China is important for GFSI and its corporate stakeholders: it is a significant market for the production of food and food ingredients, and many food manufacturers in Europe and North America source raw materials from China. GFSI initiates and participates in major food safety events in China. It has created a Chinese website and a local group called the China Food Safety Initiative. Transnational food safety schemes are in a difficult position to gain access to the Chinese market, as non-state standards need a government licence to operate legally. Only BRC has such a license. Chinese businesses that require a certificate against another transnational scheme to supply to foreign (Western) retailers now contract a foreign certification body accredited under a GFSI-recognized scheme, and auditors are flown into China to perform the audits (Kottenstede 2017, pp. 230–1). The Chinese government prefers certification against Chinese voluntary public standards (ChinaGAP, China HACCP). As a result of these legal, political and practical hurdles, the market uptake of transnational food safety schemes in China is still limited (An 2017).

GFSI has signed several memoranda of understanding with Chinese accreditation agencies and entered public-private partnerships to enhance food safety in China.[10] Moreover, the China HACCP scheme applied for GFSI recognition. Since this scheme is effectively government-owned, it did not (and could not) meet all requirements specified in the GFSI Guidance Document. For now, China HACCP has been considered 'technically equivalent' to the GFSI requirements. This status applies only to the technical food safety requirements (Part III of the GFSI Guidance Document) and does not include the scheme's governance and operational management components (Part II).[11] Experts remain sceptical about benchmarking Chinese standards against international standards (Kottenstede 2017, p. 229; interview with a member of the GFSI Regulatory Affairs Working Group).

GFSI's efforts to recognize China HACCP have led to an interesting development in its benchmarking activities. In 2015, GFSI introduced a new Government Standard Equivalence Process in its Guidance Document. This process is a tool to assess the technical requirements of state-owned certification standards against the GFSI Guidance Document. The governance or operational management of public certification schemes is not assessed. GFSI presents the process as:

> a positive initiative for building public-private partnerships providing a mechanism for governments to become familiar with the fundamental requirements and principles of the GFSI Guidance Document.
>
> It is also hoped that government certification systems will come forward to GFSI to undertake the standard equivalence process enhancing the relationships [between] government and the private sector, in the hope that there is a positive move toward global harmonisation and continuous improvement for food safety systems. (GFSI 2015c, unpaginated)

While this new strategy appears to be inspired by GFSI's experience in benchmarking Chinese schemes, it is clearly an attempt to institutionalize the assessment of public food safety certification standards and engage with government organizations at a substantive level. GFSI no longer only seeks to obtain public recognition of its benchmarking of non-state schemes, but also invites domestic public actors to submit their standards for benchmarking. A Canadian and a US voluntary government-owned standard responded to this call and have received the status of GFSI technical equivalence (GFSI 2019c).

2.4 UNDERSTANDING TBGIs: ENROLMENT IN FOOD SAFETY REGULATION

GFSI and domestic state actors in the Netherlands, Canada and China have engaged in both formal and informal relations to discuss and implement the integration of transnational food safety schemes in public enforcement policies. To understand better why, how and with what effect these TBGIs emerged, we draw on the concept of regulatory enrolment as developed by Julia Black (2003).[12] At its core, regulatory enrolment is a strategy for linking actors possessing different regulatory capacities to enhance the capacity of both (ibid., p. 84). For Black, regulatory capacity refers to 'the actual or potential possession of resources plus the existence of actual and potential conditions that make it likely that those resources will be deployed both now and in the future in such a way as to further the identified goals of those seeking to regulate' (ibid., p. 72). Key resources that shape the regulatory capacity of actors within a regulatory regime are information, expertise, financial and economic resources, authority and legitimacy, strategic position, and organizational capacity (ibid., pp. 73ff). These resources are not evenly distributed among actors, nor is actors' possession of them static or direct. These characteristics of regulatory capacity – dispersal, change and indirect disposal – invite thinking about ways in which actors possessing different kinds and degrees of regulatory capacity can be linked to one another to enhance the capacity of both actors and the effectiveness of the regime as a whole.

Evidently, regulatory enrolment does not guarantee regulatory outcomes. The actor who is enrolling another does not get full control over the activities of the actor being enrolled. The advantages of the strategy are to be found in the increased capacity of individual actors or the regime as a whole to achieve regulatory goals. For example, by being able to work with more detailed information about regulatory noncompliance provided by auditing firms, state actors may more accurately determine what type of enforcement action is required and refine their approach to secure compliance (Braithwaite 2008, p. 96). Furthermore, the ability to use or rely on additional resources may also enhance the transnational reach of public regulatory activities, which are typically confined to territorial borders (Drahos 2004, pp. 418–19). According to Black, a focus on regulatory capacities and their enrolment allows for 'considering ways in which the capacity of the system as a whole might be enhanced effectively and legitimately by the careful deployment within it of the regulatory capacities of different actors' (Black 2003, p. 91).[13]

Enrolment therefore provides a critical lens through which to analyse the drivers, modes and results of the interactions between GFSI, transnational schemes and domestic state actors. As we will show, these TBGIs are driven by changes in the configuration of the regulatory resources of the actors involved. Accordingly, enrolment adds to the TBGI framework a focus on regulatory resources as an explanatory variable for interaction and its results.

We will now discuss why, how and with what effect GFSI, transnational schemes and domestic state actors enrol each other in their regulatory activities. As the analysis will reveal, enrolment is not unilateral but mutual: each actor seeks to enrol the capacities of the others to further its own regulatory goals. We distinguish accordingly between four lines of enrolment.

2.4.1 Domestic State Actors Enrolling Transnational Schemes

Why do state authorities enrol transnational food safety schemes? The answer is very different for the Netherlands and Canada on the one hand, and China on the other. Dutch and Canadian authorities involve GFSI-benchmarked schemes in their activities principally because these schemes enhance their regulatory resources in several important ways. For one, transnational schemes possess significant audit and enforcement capacity. Audits under these schemes are carried out on (at least) an annual basis and address the full range of food safety requirements that need to be met under binding food safety laws. Consequently, certification bodies possess a wealth of compliance information about the audited firms that is likely to be more up-to-date than the information public agencies possess, given the typically much lower frequency of government inspections. These resources are much needed additions to public food safety agencies' operational resources, which have come under great pressure in the last decade due to budget cuts and increased consumer sensitivity and demand (Garcia Martinez et al. 2013). Most agencies do not have the means to perform frequent inspections of all food business operating sites.

The enrolment of transnational schemes in the enforcement policies of public agencies may thus compensate for the gaps in food safety enforcement. It also allows state agencies to deploy their resources more efficiently, to prioritize and focus on controlling high-risk products and underperformers. Firms that participate in a non-state scheme are audited regularly and the costs for these audits are not public expenditures. Moreover, certification against a recognized food safety scheme helps a firm to comply with legal obligations. This is particularly helpful for small firms that lack the expertise to apply the general food safety requirements, such as the HACCP principles (Fairman and Yapp 2005). Food safety consultants and auditors are contracted by firms to explain food safety laws and to help implement required FSMS. They possess an important strategic position in the regulatory regime in delivering food safety. The findings of a survey of officers of national food authorities also point to these benefits: food safety certification programs offer a welcome addition to authorities' inspection capacity, allowing public inspectorates to focus on high-risk sectors or firms. Respondents also expect the certification programs to improve food safety and assist food businesses in complying with food law (Havinga 2018, p. 13).

Another key reason for domestic state authorities to enrol transnational schemes concerns the latter's strategic positioning in global supply chains (Verbruggen 2016, pp. 473–4). The global scale of supply chains poses major challenges for state regulatory capacity. Global supply chains frequently involve stages of production in different jurisdictions. Furthermore, the sheer volume of trade in food products makes assessing compliance with food safety regulation more difficult.[14] The loss of strategic positioning by national food safety agencies in a global context, a lack of authority and legitimacy to regulate food production in other countries, and the costs of regulating once food products are imported to the home jurisdiction, invite these agencies to think about ways in which they could strengthen their regulatory capacity by enrolling the resources of others. Some enlist transnational certification schemes to fill the gap. By doing so, agencies like CFIA and NVWA seek to enrol resources of wealth, strategic position and organizational capacity in ever more globalizing supply chains.

In contrast to state actors in the Netherlands and Canada, the Chinese government does not seem to enrol transnational schemes. Rather, it seeks to limit the impact of transnational standards and certification systems in China, and favours national systems (Kottenstede 2017). As noted, foreign schemes are not allowed to operate in China unless they have a licence from the Chinese government. Only BRC applied for and obtained such a license.

Transnational schemes could enhance the Chinese government's inspection capacity the same as they do for Western governments. However, the Chinese government seems reluctant to enrol these resources as it gives preference to national public standards and inspection by government officials. The recent government policy declaring that food businesses in China having a GMP or HACCP certificate can benefit from a lower inspection frequency may enhance the appeal of voluntary schemes to food businesses. It is unclear, however, whether this policy also applies to BRC certificates or certificates from transnational food safety schemes based on GMP or HACCP principles.

2.4.2 Transnational Schemes Enrolling Domestic State Actors

Since our analysis did not specifically address the regulatory activities of individual transnational schemes but focused on GFSI instead, we have no systematic overview of their considerations and drivers in engaging with domestic state actors. However, we do know from our interviews that major transnational schemes (BRC, IFS, GlobalGAP, FSSC 22000, RiskPlaza) have applied under the acceptance scheme operated by NVWA.

They met with NVWA representatives and decided to amend their standards to meet NVWA's criteria. A key motive for the schemes to submit to these criteria appears to be that acceptance by NVWA adds to their legitimacy and credibility, and as such strengthens their market position. That market position may be bolstered in two ways. First, food businesses might be more inclined to obtain non-state certification because certification contributes to compliance with public laws and may even result in fewer or modified official controls. Second, accepted non-state schemes become more attractive than schemes that have no public recognition, so their market share will increase. Increased uptake in the market may result in economic gains for the scheme owners and their constituency. For retailers, manufacturers and traders that require their suppliers to be certified against such a scheme, a wider uptake results in a wider choice of suppliers (Verbruggen and Havinga 2015, p. 521).

2.4.3 GFSI Enrolling Domestic State Actors

GFSI's interest in enrolling domestic state actors lies in its aim to gain recognition for its activities from governments and to strengthen the market position of its constituencies and benchmarked schemes. To achieve these aims, GFSI has sought to raise awareness of its activities and achievements among government officials. It also amended its Benchmarking Guidelines in response to governments' concerns about auditor competence, audit integrity, and equivalence with official inspections. Its activities have begun to bear fruit in that the Dutch and Canadian food safety agencies have recognized a number of GFSI-benchmarked schemes for the purposes of their official inspection regimes. In addition, voluntary government-owned standards in Canada and the US have been considered technically equivalent to GFSI's benchmarking standards.

The main resource GFSI and its benchmarked schemes get from such interaction, especially in countries with a highly valued public food safety system, such as the Netherlands and Canada, is legitimacy and authority. Enrolment of credible public authorities compensates for non-state schemes' contested legitimacy in the public domain. Both governments and consumers remain hesitant to rely on such systems to ensure the safety of food. Recognition by a public authority assigns more authority and credibility to non-state systems.

The engagement of state actors with GFSI may also have contributed to the authority and credibility of GFSI and its benchmarked schemes at the substantive level. GFSI responded to concerns of governmental actors about the reliability of third-party certification by developing new guidelines on issues such as auditor competence, unannounced visits and food fraud. These guidelines must be met by transnational schemes that apply for recognition at GFSI. The interplay between GFSI and national and international governmental officials so far seems to have contributed to the ratcheting up of dominant transnational food safety schemes.

It should be noted, however, that the relationship between GFSI and China is of a completely different nature. Enrolment of the Chinese government by GFSI is not aimed at increasing its legitimacy and that of transnational schemes. GFSI first and foremost enrols Chinese government institutions to facilitate its constituents' access to the Chinese economy. The Chinese government remains the key gatekeeper to the Chinese market, which is important for global food companies that occupy key positions in GFSI.

2.4.4 Domestic State Actors Enrolling GFSI

National food authorities in the Netherlands and Canada engage with GFSI to tap into its organizational capacity and strategic positioning vis-à-vis transnational schemes. They see GFSI as providing leverage to pressure transnational schemes to change the design of third-party certification and improve their performance. A national food authority such as NVWA is in a rather weak position vis-à-vis major global players such as GFSI and BRC. The Netherlands is not a major power, and Dutch certified firms represent only a small portion of the global market for transnational food safety schemes. This weakness seems to be outweighed by GFSI's desire to enrol national governments and to highlight successful examples of this collaboration.

The enrolment of other domestic state actors can be a strategy to compensate for the unbalanced relation between domestic agencies and global non-state actors. NVWA is innovative in this regard. It has initiated meetings of national food authorities in Europe to discuss the value of non-state certification schemes for official food safety controls. Dutch and Canadian government officials also initiated meetings of national governmental officials in the slipstream of the annual GFSI global conferences in Berlin (2016) and Houston (2017). This enrolment of other national governments can strengthen the position of individual agencies vis-à-vis transnational actors.

GFSI plays a fundamentally different role in China than in the other countries addressed here. For the Chinese government the enrolment of GFSI has two distinct advantages. First, it assists the Chinese food industry to comply with more sophisticated food safety requirements. The Chinese government lacks expertise and knowledge regarding food safety assurance. Improving the level of food safety is important for both the Chinese market (as food scandals often have implications for political actors) and for the Chinese export industry (as important export markets require a minimum safety level). Cooperation with GFSI may add to the legitimacy of the Chinese regulatory system, both domestically and internationally. However, so far ChinaGAP has not been recognized by GFSI, China HACCP is assessed only in the technical equivalence program, and observers remain sceptical about the credibility of these schemes' certificates.

The interplay between GFSI and the Chinese government enrols different resources than does the interaction between GFSI and the Netherlands and Canada. This could be attributed to China's state-dominated, authoritarian economic and political system. Public authorities remain at the centre of the Chinese regulatory landscape. The Chinese party-state supports new actors only insofar as they remain controllable (van Rooij et al. 2016; Kottenstede 2017). Next to the dominant position of the state, the underdeveloped private sector and public distrust of private commercial entities to safeguard public interests such as food safety have also impeded industry from engaging in regulatory processes in China. Alternatively, the difference could be attributed to the different phases of state engagement with non-state standards organizations. Initially, governments in the Netherlands and Canada also wanted to stay in complete control, but this urge decreased over time as trust in these private sector bodies grew and public officials came to realise the potential advantages of alignment with them.

2.5 PROMISES AND RISKS OF ENROLMENT

Regulatory enrolment is a useful analytical tool to assess why and how regulatory actors seek to interlink with others. It offers insight into the opportunities to strengthen the regulatory capacity of individual actors and the regime as a whole by joining, borrowing or exchanging resources between various actors in the regime. We saw that both domestic state and transnational non-state actors (i.e. GFSI) try to enrol each other in their regulatory activities. Indeed, the process of enrolment in the domain of food safety regulation is characterized by reciprocity, that is, each side enrols the capacity of the other. The principal driver for this process is the actors' lack of vital resources to deliver their regulatory goals, inducing them to team up with other actors that may offer what they need. This idea that joining and borrowing between actors in the face of apparent regulatory incapacities is a driver of TBGI should be considered a key addition of the concept of regulatory enrolment to the TBGI analytical framework.

It would be easy to interpret the strategy of enrolment as a win-win proposition for the enrollers and the enrolled. In particular, in the field of food safety regulation national governments will use the information, wealth and strategic positioning of transnational schemes and, in return, these systems will gain legitimacy, public recognition and a stronger market position. However, the concept of enrolment does not draw sufficient attention to challenges and risks that might be concerned with public-private regulatory collaboration. In this section we will discuss potential risks related to conflicts of interest, non-state schemes' underperformance and state authorities' independence.

First, enrolment triggers a risk of conflicts between public and private interests. Although both government and industry have a clear common interest in the assurance of food safety, private interests do not completely overlap with public interests. For private parties (e.g. individual companies, certification bodies, GFSI) economic interests are important and quite often dominant. Where food safety interests conflict with economic interests, food safety may be disregarded. Companies might be induced to buy cheap products that violate food safety rules, and to omit costly or inconvenient audit procedures. For some companies and in some industries, short-term economic gain dominates and possible loss of reputation matters little. Certification bodies are primarily focused on their customers, who pay for certification and auditing services. This poses a major conflict of interest as these bodies are also expected to advance and assure a public good, namely food safety (Lytton and McAllister 2014). Accordingly, they are in constant limbo between not being too strict with (potential) customers and being strict enough to remain credible. Significant risks also emerge in operationalizing the cooperation between public and private entities. Confidentiality of compliance data, modes of exchange and verification of information about food safety incidents and risks, definition of responsibilities and competences within a cooperative initiative, and demands for public accountability in case of food safety incidents are important issues that may undermine the effectiveness of the whole enterprise (Verbruggen and Havinga 2015, pp. 521–3).

Second, underperformance of non-state food safety schemes may challenge public-private collaboration. Non-state schemes may not be capable or willing to conduct and maintain adequate food safety controls. The actual performance of such schemes has been criticized as too lenient and unreliable. Commentators have noted that these schemes lack enough qualified auditors and largely rely on announced inspection visits and administrative controls to verify compliance (Fagotto 2017). The conflicts of interest inherent in the design of non-state certification question the willingness of certified bodies to enforce food safety rules strictly. In addition, non-state schemes presuppose that audited food businesses are motivated to ensure food safety, but some food businesses may not place top priority on food safety and may be inclined to neglect food safety precautions and cover up non-compliance.

Third, incorporation of non-state food safety schemes in public food inspection policy may challenge state food authorities' independence as law enforcement agencies. By relying on non-state schemes to ensure food safety, public authorities might lose touch with the industry and fail to see what is happening on the ground. This will also eventually undermine the legitimacy and credibility of public food authorities. Regulatory capture is also a risk that emerges when government works closely with industry, as we saw in our discussion of Canada and the Netherlands.

Being aware of these potential risks, domestic state actors discuss with GFSI and non-state scheme owners what they see as these schemes' main weaknesses. They ask schemes to impose stricter standards concerning unannounced audits, auditor competence, integrity and independence, exchange of information on non-compliance, food fraud and authenticity controls, assurance in supply chains, and accreditation of certification bodies. They not only discuss these issues with representatives of GFSI and non-state food safety schemes, the Dutch and Canadian authorities also check how reliable the non-state systems are. Moreover, they have formulated conditions that must be satisfied before non-state certification is taken into account in governmental inspection policy.

Over time, non-state food safety schemes have become more elaborate. Discussions with state officials about their concerns over the design and performance of non-state schemes have contributed to this development. However, it is partly an autonomous development of non-state food safety schemes and the system of third-party certification and accreditation. The mutual enrolment as discussed here seems to have resulted in a ratcheting up of non-state schemes. From the perspective of improving food safety this can be considered a positive trend. However, the standards' stricter requirements and increased scope will also make it more costly and difficult for newcomers to join, that is, food businesses that are not certified against a GFSI-benchmarked scheme, and new schemes. Small food businesses and suppliers in developing countries are particular victims of this development. It becomes more and more difficult for them to comply with the increasing demands these schemes impose. Collaboration with non-state schemes also implies a shift of costs from the public expenditure towards private industry. Some private actors can bear these costs (and are happy to bear them because of the autonomy it entails); others cannot.

2.6 CONCLUSION: ENROLMENT AND THE TBGI FRAMEWORK

In this chapter we have argued that the concept of regulatory enrolment is a useful tool to analyse complex interactions between different state and non-state actors in a transnational regulatory regime. The concept focuses on regulatory resources, their fluid and dynamic character, and the ways in which actors draw upon others' resources to bolster or maintain their legitimacy and effectiveness. As such, enrolment helps explain why regulatory actors try to connect and collaborate with other actors. In this respect the concept is a valuable addition to the TBGI analytical framework.

Regulatory enrolment as observed in the field of global food safety regulation is a reciprocal process that strengthens the capacity of actors in the regime and the capacity of the regime as a whole. However, the concept of enrolment does not focus much attention on the possible drawbacks of the interaction between state and non-state actors. In the domain of food safety, and perhaps in others too, the state actors that enrol transnational non-state actors should be aware not only of the opportunities, but also of the risks this strategy entails. These risks should signal to state actors that they must carefully formulate the conditions for collaboration with non-state actors and clearly define their respective responsibilities for the attainment of regulatory goals.

NOTES

1. As of 2019, the number of recognized schemes had dropped to 11. GFSI 2019.
2. Other focus countries were Australia, Belgium, Brazil, Colombia, France, India, Korea, New Zealand, Peru, Thailand, and Turkey (GFSI 2014).
3. This analysis summarizes and updates our findings as presented in Havinga and Verbruggen 2017, pp. 201–10. Our analysis is built on interviews with two respondents at GFSI and two Dutch officials. We complemented these findings with a comprehensive survey conducted among officers of national food authorities on their collaboration with private food safety standards (Havinga 2018), and with documentary evidence publicly available on the Internet. Where such evidence was available, we refer to these public sources.
4. See in particular Regulation (EC) 882/2004 on official controls performed to ensure the verification of compliance with feed and food law, animal health and animal welfare rules [2004] OJ L165/1. See also Regulation (EC) 178/2002 laying down the general principles and requirements of food law, establishing the European Food Safety Authority and laying down procedures in matters of food safety [2002] OJ L31/1.
5. These criteria were modestly revised in September 2017 (NVWA 2017a).
6. *Safe Food for Canadians Act*, S.C. 2012, c. 24. Draft regulations were published in 2017 and finalized in 2018. *Safe Food for Canadians Regulations*, SOR/2018-108.
7. The quotation is from the agenda of a 2017 government-to-government meeting in Houston, Texas (on file with the authors). For a GFSI perspective on this meeting, see GFSI 2017a and Whitworth 2017a, b.
8. Yongkang An, personal communication.

9. For more details on the relationship between GFSI and China, see Kottenstede 2017 and Havinga and Verbruggen 2017.
10. Partnerships include those with the Certification and Accreditation Administration of China and the China Nutrition and Health Food Association (GFSI 2015a, d).
11. This seems to be contrary to the version of the GFSI Guidance Document in force at the time (Version 6), which provided that to be eligible for recognition by GFSI, a scheme must meet the requirements specified in Part II Section 2.
12. This analysis builds on Verbruggen 2016.
13. The idea behind regulatory enrolment has been discussed by many others. See Verbruggen 2016 for a discussion with relevant references.
14. The US Food & Drug Administration seeks to enrol non-state certification schemes to address this challenge. Since the adoption of the *Food Safety Modernization Act* (FSMA) in 2011, the Administration requires certification schemes to ensure that particular imported foods comply with US legal requirements (US Food & Drug Administration 2018).

REFERENCES

An, Yongkang (2017), *The Partial Food Safety Regulatory Regime in China: A Comparison with the United Kingdom and Germany*, unpublished PhD thesis, University College Dublin.

Black, Julia (2003), 'Enrolling actors in regulatory systems: examples from UK financial services regulation', *Public Law,* 63–91.

Braithwaite, John (2008), *Regulatory Capitalism: How It Works, Ideas for Making It Work Better*, Cheltenham, UK and Northampton, MA, USA: Edward Elgar.

Burns, John P., Jing Li and Xiaoqi Wang (2015), 'The political economy of Chinese food safety regulation: distributing adulterated milk powder in Mainland China and Taiwan', in Tetty Havinga, Frans van Waarden and Donal Casey (eds), *The Changing Landscape of Food Governance*, Cheltenham, UK and Northampton, MA, USA: Edward Elgar, pp. 96–113.

CFIA (Canadian Food Inspection Agency) (2017a), 'CanadaGAP successfully completes the Canadian Food Inspection Agency (CFIA) food safety recognition program', *CFIA Chronicle*, Fall, accessed 25 March 2019 at http://www.inspection.gc.ca/about-the-cfia/the-cfia-chronicle-edition-3/canadagap-successfully-completes-the-canadian-food/eng/1509030448145/1509030448497.

CFIA (2017b), *Private Certification Policy (Food Safety)*, accessed 25 March 2019 at http://www.inspection.gc.ca/about-the-cfia/accountability/consultations/regulatory-risk-based-oversight/private-certification-policy/eng/1452808755126/1452808821799?chap=0.

CFIA (2018), *Food Safety Recognition Program*, accessed 25 March 2019 at http://www.inspection.gc.ca/food/safe-food-production-systems/food-safety-enhancement-program/recognition-program/eng/1299860970026/1299861042890.

Drahos, P. (2004), 'Intellectual property and pharmaceutical markets: a nodal governance approach', *Temple Law Review,* **77** (2), 401–24.

Eberlein, Burkard, Kenneth W. Abott, Julia Black, Errol Meidinger and Stepan Wood (2014), 'Transnational business governance interactions: conceptualization and framework for analysis', *Regulation & Governance*, **8** (1), 1–22.

Fagotto, Elena (2017), 'Resolving gaps in third-party certification for food safety hybridization', in Paul Verbruggen and Tetty Havinga (eds), *Hybridization of Food Governance: Trends, Types and Results*, Cheltenham, UK and Northampton, MA, USA: Edward Elgar, pp. 54–77.

Fairman, Robyn and Charlotte Yapp (2005), 'Enforced self-regulation, prescription, and conceptions of compliance within small businesses: the impact of enforcement', *Law & Policy,* **27** (4), pp. 491–519.

FSSC 22000 (2017), *FSSC 22000 Accepted by NVWA*, accessed 25 March 2019 at http://www.fssc22000.com/documents/news-items/fssc-22000-accepted-by-nvwa.xml?lang=en.

Fuchs, Doris, Agni Kalfagianni and Tetty Havinga (2011), 'Actors in private food governance: the legitimacy of retail standards and multistakeholder initiatives with civil society participation', *Agriculture and Human Values,* **28** (2), 353–67.

Fulponi, Linda (2006), 'Private voluntary standards in the food system: the perspective of major food retailers in OECD countries', *Food Policy,* **31**, 1–13.

Gale, Fred and Jean B. Buzby (2009), 'Imports from China and food safety issues', *Economic Information Bulletin* No. 52, Washington, DC: US Department of Agriculture, Economic Research Service.

Garcia Martinez, Marian, Paul Verbruggen and Andrew Fearne (2013), 'Risk-based approaches to food safety regulation: what role for co-regulation?' *Journal of Risk Research,* **16** (9), pp. 1101–21.

GFSI (2009), *GFSI Newsletter*, Summer.

GFSI (2011), *Enhancing Food Safety through Third Party Certification*, Issy-les-Moulineaux, France: GFSI, accessed 25 March 2019 at https://www.mygfsi.com/gfsifiles/GFSI_White_Paper_-_Enhancing_Food_Safety_Through_Third_Party_Certification.pdf.

GFSI (2012), *GFSI Newsletter,* November.

GFSI (2014), *Global Regulatory Affairs TWG Progress: Sept 2014*, accessed 25 March 2019 at https://www.mygfsi.com/news-resources/latest-news/281-global-regulatory-affairs-twg-progress.html.

GFSI (2015a), *GFSI Embarks on Public-Private Partnership with China's CNCA to Accelerate Food Safety Development*, accessed 25 March 2019 at https://www.mygfsi.com/news-resources/latest-news/432-gfsi-embarks-on-public-private-partnership-with-china-s-cnca-to-accelerate-food-safety-development.html.

GFSI (2015b), *GFSI Focus Days Come to Canada: Key Time in Food Safety Regulatory Landscape*, accessed 25 March 2019 at https://www.mygfsi.com/news-resources/latest-news/425-gfsi-focus-days-come-to-canada-key-time-in-food-safety-regulatory-landscape.html.

GFSI (2015c), *Government Standard Equivalence Process: GFSI Guidance Document Version 6.4 Part III*, accessed 25 March 2019 at https://www.mygfsi.com/news-resources/latest-news/413-government-standard-equivalence-process-gfsi-guidance-document-version-6-4-part-iii.html.

GFSI (2015d), *Leveraging the Global Food Safety Initiative to Meet China Food Safety Challenges*, accessed 25 March 2019 at https://www.mygfsi.com/news-resources/news/press-releases/435-leveraging-the-global-food-safety-initiative-to-meet-china-food-safety-challenges.html.

GFSI (2016), *GFSI Applauds New Canadian Policy on Private Certification of Food Facilities*, accessed 25 March 2019 at https://www.mygfsi.com/news-resources/latest-news/454-gfsi-applauds-new-canadian-policy-on-private-certification-of-food-facilities.html.

GFSI (2017a), *30 Institutions Come Together with GFSI in a 'G30' of Food Safety*, accessed 25 March 2019 at https://www.mygfsi.com/news-resources/news/press-releases/652-30-institutions-come-together-with-gfsi-in-a-g30-of-food-safety.html.

GFSI (2017b), *GFSI Benchmarking Requirements, GFSI Guidance Document, Version 7*, Issy-les-Moulineaux, France: GFSI (on file with the authors).

GFSI (2017c), *GFSI-Recognised Certification Programme Achieves Full Government Recognition*, accessed 25 March 2019 at https://www.mygfsi.com/news-resources/news/press-releases/665-gfsi-recognised-certification-programme-achieves-full-government-recognition.html.

GFSI (2017d), *Key Figures*, accessed 25 March 2019 at https://www.mygfsi.com/files/Information_Kit/GFSI_Benefits_Infographic_2017.pdf.

GFSI (2019a), *Recognised Certification Programmes*, accessed 24 March 2019 at https://www.mygfsi.com/certification/recognised-certification-programmes.html.

GFSI (2019b), *What Is GFSI*, accessed 25 March 2019 at https://www.mygfsi.com/about-us/about-gfsi/what-is-gfsi.html.

GFSI (2019c), *GFSI Technical Equivalence for Government Certification Programmes*, accessed 21 August 2019 at https://www.mygfsi.com/certification/technical-equivalence.html

Havinga, Tetty (2006), 'Private regulation of food safety by supermarkets', *Law & Policy*, **28** (4), 515–33.

Havinga, Tetty (2015), 'Retail driven food safety regulation', in Abdelhakim Hammoudi, Christina Grazia, Yves Surry and Jean-Baptiste Traversac (eds), *Food Safety, Market Organization, Trade and Development*, Cham: Springer, pp. 59–76.

Havinga, Tetty (2018), 'The integration of private certification in governmental food controls: A survey on public-private collaboration in food safety governance', *Nijmegen Sociology of Law Working Papers Series No. 2018/01*, Nijmegen: Radboud University, accessed 21 August 2019 at http://hdl.handle.net/2066/198979.

Havinga, Tetty and Paul Verbruggen (2017), 'The global food safety initiative and state actors: paving the way for hybrid food safety governance', in Paul Verbruggen and Tetty Havinga (eds), *Hybridization of Food Governance: Trends, Types and Results*, Cheltenham, UK and Northampton, MA, USA: Edward Elgar, pp. 183–214.

Havinga, Tetty and Frans van Waarden (2013), *Veilig voedsel: Toezicht toevertrouwen?* Den Haag: Wetenschappelijke Raad voor het Regeringsbeleid Webpublicatie nr 70, accessed 12 May 2017 at https://www.wrr.nl/publicaties/publicaties/2013/03/14/veilig-voedsel-toezicht-toevertrouwen-sectorschets-toezicht-in-de-voedselsector---70.

Henson, Spencer and John Humphrey (2009), *The Impacts of Private Food Safety Standards on the Food Chain and on Public Standard-Setting Processes*, Paper Prepared for FAO/WHO, accessed 1 June 2016 at http://www.fao.org/docrep/012/i1132e/i1132e00.pdf.

Hobbs, Jill. E., Andrew Fearne and John Spriggs (2002), 'Incentive structures for food safety and quality assurance: an international comparison', *Food Control,* **13** (2), 77–81.

International Forum on Food Safety and Health (2013), 'Dr. Joseph Scimeca will join 2013 International Forum on Food Safety', accessed 25 March 2019 at http://www.ifofs.org/whatsnew/2013-04-04/58.html.

Jensen, Helen H. and Jiehong Zhou (2015), 'Food safety regulation and private standards in China', in Abdelhakim Hammoudi, Christina Grazia, Yves Surry and Jean-Baptiste Traversac (eds), *Food Safety, Market Organization, Trade and Development*, Cham: Springer, pp. 167–82.

Kottenstede, Kai (2017), 'Transnational private food standards in the People's Republic: hybridization with Chinese characteristics', in Paul Verbruggen and Tetty Havinga (eds), *Hybridization of Food Governance: Trends, Types and Results*, Cheltenham, UK and Northampton, MA, USA: Edward Elgar, pp. 215–39.

Lytton, Timothy D. and Lesley K. McAllister (2014), 'Oversight in private food safety auditing: addressing auditor conflict of interest', *Wisconsin Law Review* **22** (4), 289–335.

MacMaoláin, Caoimhín (2015), *Food Law: European, Domestic and International Frameworks*, Oxford: Hart Publishing.

Marsden, Terry, Robert Lee, Andrew Flynn and Samarthia Thankappan (2010), *The New Regulation and Governance of Food. Beyond the Food Crisis?* New York and London: Routledge.

Martens, Miet and Johan Swinnen (2012), 'Private standards, global food supply chains and the implications for developing countries', in Axel Marx and others (eds), *Private Standards and Global Governance: Economic, Legal and Political Perspectives,* Cheltenham, UK and Northampton, MA, USA: Edward Elgar, pp. 153–71.

Nguyen, Thanh, Anne Wilcock and May Aung (2004), 'Food safety and quality systems in Canada: an exploratory study', *International Journal of Quality & Reliability Management,* **21** (6), 655–71.

NVWA (2014), *Requirements for the Acceptance of Quality Systems by the Netherlands Food and Consumer Product Safety Authority*, accessed 12 May 2017 at http://ketenborging.nl/wp-content/uploads/Criteria-voor-acceptatie-Engels.pdf.

NVWA (2017a), *Criteria for Supervision Support Through Private Quality Systems*, accessed 25 March 2019 at http://ketenborging.nl/wp-content/uploads/EN-version-Criteria-for-supervision-support-through-private-quality-systems-25-9-17.pdf.

NVWA (2017b), *Zesde voortgangsrapportage Plan van aanpak NVWA*, accessed 25 March 2019 at https://www.rijksoverheid.nl/documenten/brieven/2017/05/16/zesde-voortgangsrapportage-plan-van-aanpak-nvwa.

NVWA (2019), *Kwaliteitsschema's en status*, accessed 25 March 2019 at http://ketenborging.nl/kwaliteitsschemas-en-status.

Roberts, Michael T. and Ching-Fu Lin (2016), 'China food law update: the 2015 food safety law and social governance on food safety', *Journal of Food law and Policy*, **12** (2), 238–63.

Rooij, Benjamin van, Rachel E. Stern and Kathinka Fürst (2016), 'The authoritarian logic of regulatory pluralism: understanding China's new environmental actors', *Regulation & Governance,* **10** (1), 3–13.

Thompson D and Hu Y (2007), 'Food safety in China', *Global Health Governance* 1/2, accessed 2 April 2014 at http://ghgj.org/Thompson_Food%20Safety%20in%20China.pdf.

US Food & Drug Administration (2018), *FSMA Final Rule on Accredited Third-Party Certification*, accessed 25 March 2019 at http://www.fda.gov/Food/GuidanceRegulation/FSMA/ucm361903.htm.

Verbruggen, Paul (2014), *Enforcing Transnational Private Regulation: A Comparative Analysis of Advertising and Food Safety*, Cheltenham, UK and Northampton, MA, USA: Edward Elgar.

Verbruggen, Paul and Tetty Havinga (2015), 'Food safety meta-controls in the Netherlands', *European Journal of Risk Regulation,* **6** (4), 512–24.
Verbruggen, Paul (2016), 'Understanding the "new governance" of food safety: regulatory enrolment as a response to change in public and private power', *Cambridge Journal of International and Comparative Law,* **5** (3), 445–76.
Verbruggen, Paul and Tetty Havinga (2016), 'The rise of transnational private meta-regulators', *Tilburg Law Review,* **21** (2), 116–43.
Verbruggen, Paul and Tetty Havinga (eds) (2017), *Hybridization of Food Governance: Trends, Types and Results,* Cheltenham, UK and Northampton, MA, USA: Edward Elgar.
Waarden, Frans van (1985), 'Varieties of collective self-regulation of business: the example of the Dutch dairy industry', in Wolfgang Streeck and Philip Schmitter (eds), *Private Interest Government: Beyond Market and State,* Beverly Hills: Sage, pp. 197–220.
Whitworth, Joseph J. (2017a), 'Dispatches from GFSI 2017 in Houston: GFSI on SENASICA, benchmarking requirements and Africa', *FoodNavigator.com,* 4 May, accessed 29 August 2019 at https://www.foodnavigator.com/Article/2017/05/04/More-alignment-on-private-and-public-food-safety-approaches.
Whitworth, Joseph J. (2017b), 'Dispatches from GFSI 2017 in Houston: regulators can use certification as element of risk assessment – GFSI', *FoodNavigator.com*, 8 May, accessed 29 August 2019 at https://www.foodnavigator.com/Article/2017/05/09/GFSI-on-auditor-competence-and-third-party-certification.
Wood Stepan, Kenneth W. Abbott, Julia Black, Burkard Eberlein and Errol Meidinger (2015), 'The interactive dynamics of transnational business governance: a challenge for transnational legal theory', *Transnational Legal Theory*, **6** (2), 333–69.

3. Governance interactions in sustainable supply chain management

Errol Meidinger

3.1 INTRODUCTION

Supply chains are a growing focus of transnational governance initiatives seeking to advance 'sustainability' goals such as environmental protection, community development, human rights and labour conditions.[1] 'Sustainable supply chain management' (SSCM) has become a category of practice and can be seen as an emerging movement that includes corporate managers, consultants, labour and environmental activists, and academics, among others. Their goal is to enlist the supply chain management capacities of businesses to pursue public purposes. This means systematically changing supply chain management.

This chapter analyses the relationships and strategies promoted by SSCM professionals in terms of the Transnational Business Governance Interactions (TBGI) framework (Eberlein et al. 2014). Part 2 lays the groundwork by discussing, respectively, data and research method, the TBGI framework, the key axioms of supply chain management as a discipline, the growth of 'sustainable' supply chain management, and the role of corporate management systems in the SSCM movement. Part 3, the heart of the chapter, summarizes and analyses public presentations and comments by SSCM professionals in terms of the TBGI framework. It seeks to characterize the types of interactions common in supply chains, as described by those professionals who see and work with them. It also summarizes what they see as the primary challenges and potential solutions for achieving sustainable supply chains. Part 4 considers the implications of those diagnoses and prescriptions for the goals of improving governance, ratcheting up environmental and social standards, and advancing marginalized interests.

3.2 SETTING THE SCENE: METHODS AND CONCEPTS

3.2.1 Data and Methods

The data used for this chapter are drawn from public presentations, comments, and discussions of approximately sixty SSCM professionals at two 'sustainable supply chain summits' organized by The Ethical Corporation in London in 2014 and 2015. Presenters included corporate procurement officials directly involved in supply chain management, a variety of supply chain consultants, facilitators, contractors, and NGO staffers active in SSCM initiatives. Each conference had approximately 150 attendees from approximately 100 different organizations. There was some overlap of attendees and organizations at the two conferences, but a rough count indicates approximately 85 percent of the attendees were unique at one or the other conference. I was one of only two professors at the first conference and the only one at the second.

The conferences were framed as business propositions where valuable information could be gathered and disseminated, benefiting all participants. They were relatively expensive to attend, with substantial fees for corporate attendees and nontrivial ones for NGOs and academics. The conferences provided valuable research settings by bringing together a much larger number and variety of practitioners than could possibly have been interviewed individually. The conference context also provided a significant research advantage in constraining speakers to make statements plausible and intelligible to their peers, a condition often not met in individual interviews (Becker 1970).

3.2.2 The Transnational Business Governance Interactions Framework

The TBGI framework posits that a key to understanding transnational governance is to describe and analyse patterns of interaction among the many diverse actors that constitute transnational governance (Eberlein et al. 2014). This is a necessary step to visualizing broad patterns in the rapidly emerging and changing transnational governance structures. To help sort out this 'blooming, buzzing confusion' (James 1890, p. 488), the framework seeks to organize interactions in terms of six generic kinds of tasks usually involved in regulatory governance: (1) framing the governance agenda and setting goals for it ('agenda setting'); (2) formulating norms and rules to be followed by those engaged in the activity of concern ('norm formation'); (3) implementing applicable goals, standards, and rules by those engaged in the activity ('implementation'); (4) gathering information on the state of the problem and monitoring the behaviour at issue ('monitoring'); (5) responding to non-compliance via sanctions and other forms of enforcement activities ('enforcement'); and (6) evaluating governance operations and providing feedback for possible improvement ('evaluation' – thus the combined acronym ANIMEE). The framework assumes interplay and overlap among these tasks, and, importantly, does not assume that they occur in a set sequence (Wood et al. 2015). Supply chain management is usually thought of in terms of implementation and monitoring; but as discussed below, it can also involve significant elements of the other four types of governance tasks.

Interactions in the TBGI schema can occur among quite different types of actors, ranging from individuals to organizations, to governance schemes, to institutions, to larger economic or discursive structures. While the concrete nature of interactions can thus be almost infinitely variable, the TBGI framework offers four general categories for patterns of interaction: competition, coordination, co-optation (hierarchy), and chaos. In SSCM discourse the actors of interest are mostly organizations, although primary producers in some supply chains can be individuals. The presumptive patterns of interaction in supply chains are hierarchy and coordination, but some emerging forms tend to be complex mixtures of the two, with some competition thrown in as well.

3.2.3 Supply Chain Management

Modern supply chain management built upon the relatively prosaic field of logistics, which sought to integrate all of an individual firm's production activities to achieve maximum productive efficiency (Kent and Flint 1997). By the mid-1980s, economic globalization and accelerated outsourcing had spawned the field of supply chain management to manage production chains involving multiple firms, and essentially to manage the supply chain as a single entity (Christopher 2011), still with the goal of maximizing efficiency. Three concepts from the supply chain literature are important here: (1) the idea of the value chain; (2) modelling the chain as network; and (3) supply chain coordination by a lead firm.

3.2.3.1 Value chain models

When a supply chain is rendered as a list of necessary tasks in producing a product, each of which should contribute efficiently to the overall value of the product, it follows fairly easily to think of each task in terms of its 'value added'. Each task is expected to justify itself by producing net value to the enterprise (Porter 1985). Any activity for which a producing firm does not enjoy comparative advantage is a candidate for outsourcing to a firm that can provide a cost or value advantage, and outsourcing is thus a possibility for every activity in the process.

Perhaps ironically, value chain analysis also provides a basis for normative critique. Once a quantified value is allocated to each task in the production process, it is possible to critically analyse the allocation of rewards. This has given rise to a branch of value chain analysis concerned with 'upgrading' – that is, directing a larger share of the value produced to under-rewarded supply chain participants, often primary producers in developing countries. Upgrading can be economic (more resources), social (better treatment of workers and communities) (Gereffi 2011), or environmental (Marchi et al. 2013).

3.2.3.2 Network models

While outsourcing has often been portrayed as a movement from hierarchy (integration in a single firm) to markets (coordination through arms-length inter-firm transactions), a great many inter-firm supply chain relationships do not fit the arms-length model, but instead involve various kinds of ongoing relationships. Figure 3.1's schematic model of a poultry supply chain shows transactional relationships running from farmers through a processor, distributors, and retailers (van der Vorst et al. 2007). The question for supply chain management is how those transactions are coordinated. While they could be simple market transactions based entirely on price and quantity, the importance of food quality and safety for all members of the chain suggests that the parties along the chain will want to be confident that standards are maintained, and that they will prefer to work with partners they consider reliable.

Gary Gereffi and colleagues (for example, Gereffi and Lee 2012) have developed three ideal types of supply network relationships:

- *Modular governance* for cases in which suppliers make products to a customer's specifications that are complex but relatively easy to codify. This type of coordination often relies heavily on standards.
- *Relational governance* for cases when buyers and suppliers rely on complex information that is not easily conveyed or readily understood. These situations call for frequent interactions and knowledge sharing based on mutual trust and social ties between the parties.
- *Captive governance* for cases involving a group of small suppliers who are dependent on one or a few buyers for resources and market access. Suppliers tend to operate under conditions determined by, and often specific to, individual buyers.

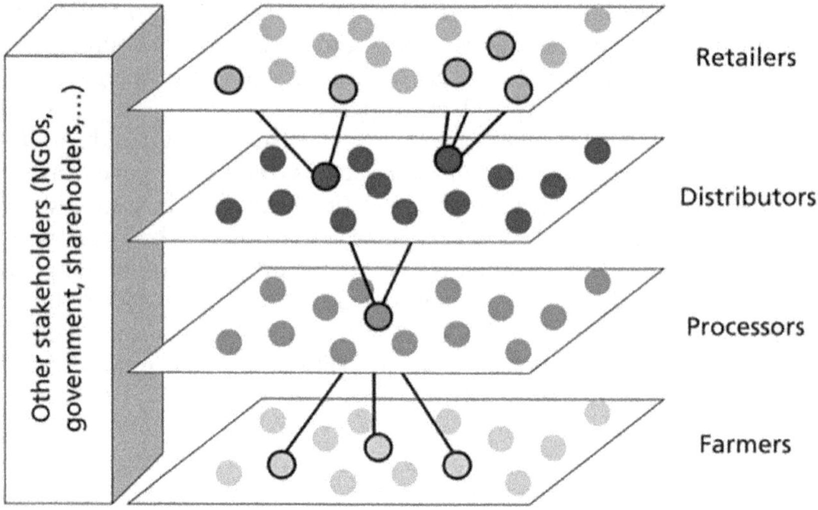

Source: van der Vorst et al. 2007, p. 15. Reproduced with permission.

Figure 3.1 Schematic diagram of a supply chain from the perspective of a processor within the total food supply chain network

These ideal types identify key aspects of the prescriptions of SSCM practitioners discussed in the next section. In addition, Figure 3.1 suggests several other important features of modern supply chains. First, supply chain relationships are not limited to actors in adjacent tiers: they can include horizontal relationships within a tier (although competition law may constrain them to certain forms). A supply chain manager for the British food retailer Tesco described the outsourced corporation as 'a long stringy chain for each thing it produces – more like a net . . . . When Tesco gets a kicking for horsemeat, all of the supermarkets get it', thus indicating a shared interest in food quality that could foster concerted action with other retailers.[2]

Second, supply chain relationships often jump tiers. (Before proceeding, it is helpful to note that numbered tiers are widely used as shorthand in the supply chain world. For example, from the perspective of retailers in Figure 3.1, farmers would be tier three suppliers.) Third, groups of actors spanning the various tiers can create networked alliances wherein they cooperate and trade regularly among themselves, while competing with other networked alliances. Fourth, at the same time, a member of a supply chain may also be involved in other supply chains. Thus, some actors may be parts of multiple supply chain networks and subject to multiple, potentially conflicting pressures from different customers.

Finally, as indicated by the rectangular column on the left side of Figure 3.1, the extended supply network can involve actors who are not engaged directly in making or handling the product. These can include government regulators, civil society organizations, shareholders, researchers, interested members of the public, and others. Indeed, actors can potentially inject themselves into supply chain networks if they can affect the value of any of the activities carried out by participants. Researchers, for example, might increase or decrease the value of a given activity by developing a new technology or procedure. NGOs might affect it by influencing consumer or public opinion regarding its desirable or undesirable effects.

3.2.3.3 Lead firm coordination

Where a supply network is extensive and complex, a distinctive coordination role will often be needed. Conventionally, the most economically powerful actor in the supply network – frequently a major retailer like Walmart, Tesco, or Home Depot, or a valuable brand merchandiser like Nike or Liz Claiborne – plays this role. This 'lead firm' exercises power over suppliers by setting terms of participation in the chain, often through private standards (Gereffi and Lee 2012). Such standards can expand to cover public welfare criteria such as workplace conditions and environmental practices, not just characteristics of the product per se, and perhaps create incentives for relational governance in terms of Gereffi and Lee's (2012) typology.

3.2.4 Sustainable Supply Chain Management

Adding public welfare goals to the traditional economic ones of price and functionality greatly increases the challenges of supply chain management. The goals cited by the SSCM presenters covered an almost dizzying array, ranging from broadly environmental ones (air quality, energy conservation, ecosystem service protection, land protection, toxins reduction, water conservation, waste minimization, and water quality) to broadly social ones (anti-corruption, anti-trafficking, community development, female empowerment, human rights, improved consumer values, labour rights, legality, poverty reduction, security, worker empowerment, and worker health and safety). Of course, many of these goals overlap, and SSCM is often used to encompass all of them. Nonetheless, their range is great, and the strategies for achieving them may be correspondingly diverse. Moreover, they may be somewhat at odds, involving normative choices for SSCM actors, as discussed in Parts 3.1 and 3.2 below.

The core strategy of SSCM advocates calls for powerful businesses to incorporate environmental and social goals into their supply chain management procedures. While they could in principle do so on their own initiative and in their own way, firms' policies are often shaped by broader, industry-wide standards programs such as the Forest Stewardship Council and Fairtrade International (Meidinger 2008), or even all-inclusive programs such as the UN Global Compact (UNGC) and the UN Guiding Principles on Business and Human Rights (UNGPs) (Leipziger 2017). Despite the formally voluntary nature of these programs, firms sometimes view them as de facto mandatory, since NGOs, civil society organizations, shareholder movements, and others pressure them to commit or risk significant brand damage.

De jure mandatory requirements are also emerging. Prominent examples include the US Dodd-Frank Act of 2010 (requiring publicly traded companies to issue reports on the possible use of conflict minerals in their supply chains);[3] the UK Modern Slavery Act of 2015 (requiring covered firms to prepare annual statements describing their policies, due diligence provisions, supply chain risks, measures, and effectiveness in countering human trafficking); the French Duty of Vigilance Law of 2017 (requiring firms to implement due diligence plans to protect against human rights and environmental risks in activities they control and in sub-contractors and suppliers on whom they have significant influence);[4] and the EU Directive on Disclosure of Non-Financial and Diversity Information (directing Member States to require large firms to report their CSR policies, due diligence implementation procedures, methods for managing principle risks, and results).[5]

3.2.4.1 Corporate management systems

These voluntary and mandatory initiatives rely centrally on corporate management systems. The idea is that the corporation creates a structured operating system that: (1) assesses the real or potential impacts of its activities on the concerns at issue; (2) develops a plan for managing those impacts; (3) monitors actual effects; and (4) assesses its degree of success and makes adjustments to improve its performance. Specific officials are designated to carry out the various tasks, and the organization achieves continuous improvement through an iterated evaluation and adjustment process.

An ideal typical example of the corporate management system approach to sustainability governance is the due diligence mandate laid out in the 2011 UN Guiding Principles on Business and Human Rights

(UNGPs) (United Nations 2011). They require the corporation to: (a) take adequate measures to 'avoid causing or contributing to adverse human rights impacts through [its] own activities'; and (b) 'seek to prevent or mitigate adverse human rights impacts directly linked to [its] operations, products or services by [its] business relationships, even if [it has] not contributed to those impacts' (ibid., p. 14, emphasis added). Activities are defined to include both acts and omissions, thus extending responsibility to possible failure to exercise leverage over supply chain partners to prevent negative effects (Wood 2012).

The corporation is to have an official, publicized, human rights policy promulgated by senior management and communicated to all linked parties, including business partners as well as states, shareholders, and potentially affected persons. It is to operationalize the policy though a human rights due diligence process that includes 'assessing actual and potential human rights impacts, integrating and acting upon the findings, tracking responses, and communicating how impacts are addressed' (United Nations 2011, p. 17): in other words, a human rights management system. The UNGPs envision that:

- Human rights due diligence will be incorporated into broader corporate risk management processes.
- The process will include risks not only to the corporation, but also to affected rights holders.
- Corporations with particularly large or complex supply chains may need to focus their attention on higher risk portions, rather than analysing their entire chains (ibid., p. 21).
- Appropriate actions regarding behaviour by other actors in their supply chains will vary with the 'extent of [the corporation's] leverage' (ibid.) and the nature of the problem.
- Risk assessments will include 'meaningful consultation with potentially affected groups' (ibid., p. 19).

3.3 GOVERNANCE INTERACTIONS IN SUSTAINABLE SUPPLY CHAIN MANAGEMENT

This Part analyses public presentations by, and follow-up conversations with, approximately 60 SSCM professionals. About three-quarters of them worked in supply chain management for lead firms; the remainder held a variety of advocacy or consulting roles. The analysis is organized in terms of the ANIMEE categories discussed above. While this organization is somewhat artificial in that few activities fall cleanly into one category or another, it is nevertheless helpful in focusing separately the different kinds of interactions involved in SSCM.

3.3.1 Agenda Setting

The agenda for SSCM seems to come from nearly everywhere. Major sources include labour and human rights movements dating from the 1940s; the modern corporate responsibility movement dating from the 1950s; the sustainable development movement dating from the 1970s; and the rapid proliferation of social and environmental certification programs that began in the late 1980s and early 1990s. As noted above, the SSCM agenda now contains many goals ranging across community, environment, health and safety, human rights, governance, and labour.

While businesses engaging in SSCM might therefore seem to be passive receivers of a broad and largely preformed agenda, they in fact play important formative roles by deciding which goals to pursue and to what extent. Two striking themes came up regarding lead firms' agendas for SSCM. First was the concept of a dynamic agenda. In one presenter's framing, this involves a progression in focus from compliance, to environmental stewardship, to value chain engagement, to sustainable innovation. The image of the buyer-supplier relationship thus changes from one of control and predictability to one of interaction and innovation. Second, an apparently growing number of SSCM managers espouse the goal of shaping not only supplier but also consumer behaviour. Some telephone companies, for example, promote eco-ratings for their handsets with the express goal of influencing retail customers to prefer ecologically superior phones, despite the seemingly low initial demand. This is a potentially significant effort to foster, rather than simply respond to, sustainability values.

External activists also significantly shape SSCM agendas. Former managers for US-based computer companies described how demonstrations by activists outside a Hewlett-Packard manufacturing facility in Oregon suddenly put the rare metal tantalum on their agenda when it would not otherwise have been. Their companies used relatively little of the metal, and their supplies came from several parts of the world, not just the Democratic Republic of Congo, where revenues from its sale were believed to be fuelling armed conflict. However, the demonstrations put it on their agenda in a powerful way, ultimately leading computer companies to establish a new conflict-free smelter audit program, to which many leading actors in the computer industry now subscribe. There are also many less dramatic examples of activists shaping the SSCM agenda, such as the Ethical Trading Initiative (ETI) described in the next sub-section.

3.3.2 Norm Formation

Norm formation merges and mingles with agenda setting. Indeed, agenda setting sometimes proceeds by actors promulgating and asserting standards to be followed in a particular governance arena, as was the case with forest certification (Meidinger 2006). Such initiatives typically draw on a broad existing body of received standards, goals, and maxims generated in variety of arenas, including intergovernmental forums. In the SSCM arena, many standards take the form of supplier codes of conduct or supplier responsibility standards. There could conceivably be as many different standards as purchasing firms, since the firms write the contracts specifying supplier performance. In practice, codes of conduct have long tended to be similar within industry groups (Jenkins 2001). Industry-developed codes of conduct have sometimes provoked counter-codes developed by NGOs or multi-stakeholder groups. The ETI, for example, was founded by a group of UK companies, NGOs, and trade unions to establish what they saw as a more credible standard for protecting worker rights worldwide than could be produced by corporations themselves (ETI 2019a). The ETI base code consists of nine standards that all member companies (currently over 80) must adopt (ETI 2019b). The ETI actively promotes the standard and participates in dialogues regarding implementation.

Although it is impossible to tally all sustainable supply chain codes, the International Trade Centre (ITC) currently lists 238 standards, codes, and protocols in its Standards Map, which is intended to help companies find standards that might apply to them (ITC 2019). This number grew by more than 20 in 2017. SSCM experts appear to agree strongly that there are too many standards in use and that some sort of harmonization or unification is necessary. One speaker stressed the need for a 'super-aligner' to harmonize all of the standards. The main reasons for this view, discussed further below, are practical. If codes are highly variable, they can be unnecessarily costly for suppliers to comply with, since multiple codes often apply to any given operation. They will probably also be more difficult for consumers to understand or trust.

New standards are being developed continually, in some cases to harmonize requirements within industries and in others simply to create relevant or workable standards for an otherwise uncovered type of supply chain. An example of the first is a collaborative standard-setting process by the chemical industry, Together for Sustainability (TfS), founded in 2011 by the chief procurement officers of six multinational chemical companies. Its purpose is to develop and implement 'a global program to assess, audit, and improve sustainability practices within the supply chains of the chemical industry' (TfS 2019). Development of the standard involved little direct participation by non-industry actors. Instead, it is based on the UNGC, which did involve significant participation by non-industry actors and Responsible Care, the chemical industry's pre-existing code of conduct, in which non-industry participation was limited and came relatively late (TfS 2019). The TfS process seems to have relied heavily on strong relationships with the Ethical Corporation, which gave it a prize, and with Ecovadis, which describes itself as a 'collaborative platform providing Sustainability Ratings for global sustainable procurements' (Ecovadis 2019). Thus, the interaction pattern here appears to be between a powerful, industry-specific group (TfS), a general supply chain sustainability rater (Ecovadis), and a sustainability-related business intelligence company (Ethical Corporation). Each is primarily business oriented, and yet they seem confident of their ability to promulgate, evaluate, publicize, and legitimate SSCM standards.

An example of a standard developed for an apparently previously uncovered supply chain is the Better Coal Code, developed by a group of major coal buyers 'to promote the continuous improvement of sustainability performance in their coal supply chain', specifically mining operations (Better Coal 2019). It was prepared by European coal buyers and facilitated by Business for Social Responsibility (BSR). BSR is a non-profit organization that seeks to 'catalyze change within business by integrating sustainability into strategy and operations, and to promote collaboration among companies and their stakeholders for systemic progress toward a just and sustainable world' (BSR 2019). Like TfS, the Better Coal Code is also built from existing standards, including International Finance Corporation investment standards, International Labour Organization standards, and the UNGPs.

Interestingly, the producers of the Better Coal Code are openly aware of potential antitrust law concerns posed by their collaboration in setting purchasing standards, and posted an antitrust policy directly on their website. The policy prohibits communications or agreements regarding banned subjects, including prices, pricing policies, terms of sale, customer lists, production costs, marketing plans, and the like (Better Coal 2011). Antitrust concerns regarding standard setting as well as other forms of industry collaboration are widespread. Collaboration is nonetheless occurring in many areas of SSCM, although one presenter reported that antitrust concerns undermined some important initiatives, including an effort to set toy company supply chain standards.

In sum, the primary norm formation interactions represented at the conferences seemed to be business-to-business interactions. They drew on existing examples and past experiences, and were doubtless heavily influenced by the possibility of NGO attacks, but seemed to have taken a significant amount of the rule-making process into business forums.

3.3.3 Implementation

The supply chains discussed at the conferences were highly variable. While some involved just a few suppliers of unique products to a single brand with a few retail outlets, others involved millions of suppliers going through dozens or hundreds of processors to dozens of different branded retailers. Interactions also necessarily reflected the different capacities of firms involved. Some supplier firms are large, complex, sophisticated corporations (for example in chemical supply chains), while others are small enterprises or individuals (for example in food supply chains). Although the nature of interactions with them therefore also varies greatly, and although the field is still very much in formation, there appeared to be several relatively typical types of interactions organized around lead firms.

3.3.3.1 Enrolling procurers and top officials

A frequently mentioned type of interaction takes place inside the lead firm, between sustainability and procurement officers. Procurement officers are generally under structural pressure to minimize expenses, with immediate costs usually counting for more than longer-term, somewhat uncertain risks. Sustainability officers are often in the position of advocating criteria that can raise short-term procurement costs. Hence, procurement officers often resist sustainability criteria. Numerous speakers mentioned the central importance of top-level executive commitment to SSCM. Without it, sustainability will inevitably give ground to ever-present cost pressures. Sustainability advocates must thus gain strong commitments from executives and seek ways to institutionalize them. This requires ongoing cultivation of executives, recruitment of new ones, and regular participation in high-level meetings to advocate sustainability in specific decisions. One common strategy for institutionalizing sustainable purchasing is through promulgation of formal, publicly announced company policies of the kind described above (purchasing policies and supplier codes of conduct). Another is to embed sustainability criteria in purchasing routines. A computer company executive, for example, described creating and implementing a new purchasing scorecard that includes numerous sustainability factors. According to this presenter, social and environmental scores can significantly raise or lower the scores of potential suppliers, thus advantaging sustainably run suppliers.

3.3.3.2 Enrolling suppliers

The conventional approach to ensuring supplier compliance with standards has been auditing, wherein buyers use auditors to ensure that suppliers meet sustainability standards. While auditing is very widely practiced, it has a number of limitations as discussed below in Part 3.4.1. Therefore, buyers have adopted a number of other interactive strategies to increase the likelihood of sustainability practices by suppliers.

Some companies have moved to shorten their supply chains and create direct relationships with suppliers, emphasizing relational governance. A presenter from one major food retailer, for example, said that the company buys as much as possible directly from farmers, believing that direct buying gives it more influence with suppliers and consequently increases compliance. It also posits that standards are more likely to be adopted when the company presents them directly to suppliers, rather than commissioning brokers, auditors, or certifiers to do so. The same retailer decided to use its own team to audit supplier practices, believing this strategy will be more successful because the team can decide what is really important, and can also demand that the supplier share information that it might refuse to share with a broker or auditor. The proposition that a lead firm might have greater success in selling standards was supported by another presenter who explained that, when his company started buying bananas directly from producers, 'guys on plantations said "you've got to be joking", "unions are ridiculous", etcetera. Eventually they got beyond that'.

Many companies use external auditors but also seek to maintain direct relationships between sustainability staff and individuals within the supplying companies. The rationale is similar: to create internal advocates in the supplier firm for adherence to sustainability practices. A related argument is the idea of embedding sustainability, of institutionalizing it in the operating procedures of the company. Finally, one major commodity buyer claimed to specialize in maintaining direct relationships with farmers through a sustained presence 'at the farm gate'. Olam International supplies branded giants like Nestlé and Unilever with commodities from four million different famers.

A third common prescription is to reward suppliers for achieving sustainability. Implicit in the relational governance strategy just discussed is the possibility of continuing trade with a committed customer, and this by itself can be a valuable protection against the vicissitudes of the open market, as one speaker explained. Still, many suppliers participate in more than one supply chain or require significant financial or organizational investment to achieve sustainability standards. A number of companies give public awards to successful suppliers. One classifies them in levels – bronze, silver, gold – that provide incentives for progress and recognize their achievements in making improvements. Nonetheless, many participants argued that the additional costs of achieving sustainability require additional revenue, a 'green premium'. Others countered that there is no need for a green premium, either because sustainable suppliers will thrive directly as a result of their improved operations (the so-called 'business case for sustainability') or, somewhat tautologically, that there is no reason to pay a green premium to people who are simply doing what they are supposed to do anyway. There were few agreed solutions for this problem.

3.3.3.3 Capacity building

An important feature of the widespread commitment to relational governance is its stress on capacity building. Given its potential to contribute to product quality and economic sustainability, capacity building receives a great deal of discussion and promotion, particularly with regard to marginal suppliers and small and medium enterprises. A common prescription, mentioned by many presenters, is that suppliers should be encouraged not simply to meet current standards, but to pursue continuous improvement. This, it is claimed, will instil innovation capacity and the ability to adapt to changing conditions. The underlying arguments have two interesting variants. One focuses on enhanced competitiveness and the ability to thrive in a difficult market. The other focuses on more humane work conditions. It argues that the relatively low level of sustainable production in many developing countries is tied to mistreatment of workers. The solution to achieving better results is to 'figure out how to turn disengaged, dissatisfied workers into engaged ones', as one speaker put it. The key to doing this, in turn, is to pay a living wage and allow freedom of association and collective bargaining, which are well correlated with a living wage. Some speakers argued that it is necessary to get suppliers to see the benefits of increased capacity so they 'will own it themselves' (in one presenter's words), which can also be seen as an apparently benign governmentality strategy – getting the governed to think the idea is their own and govern themselves accordingly without having true agency (Foucault 1991).

While the above are general prescriptions, one case description indicates the potential reach of the capacity building model. In describing the building of the Grancolombia Gold operation, presenters told a story of acquiring a legal gold concession in Colombia and dealing with major problems posed by 10000 illegal artisanal miners and 195 illegal mines. These included mercury pollution, child labour, prostitution, poverty, illegal gold sales, tax avoidance, and others. Grancolombia reacted not by evicting the miners, nor by making them employees, but by bringing them into their supply chain. They allowed artisanal miners into the first few levels of their industrial mine and helped them legalize their claims to land outside the concession. They paid the artisanal miners the London spot price for their gold, instead of the much lower black market prices they had been receiving. In return they insisted on the elimination of child labour, payment of taxes, social security contributions, and apparently entry into the formal legal system generally. Thus, the capacity building model included facilitating movement into an institutional framework in which SSCM could plausibly function. The story is not a simple or unalterably happy one, however. For example, the presenters noted active ongoing strikes they said were provoked by narcotraffickers who were losing out as a result of the legalizing economy. Moreover, the evidence is thin enough to counsel scepticism. Nonetheless, the example suggests the possible reach of capacity building beyond the boundaries of the firm to include public institutions more generally.

3.3.3.4 Collaboration

Perhaps the most common refrain among presenters was the importance of increased collaboration. Collaboration can occur at any level in supply chains, or among levels, and in relation to any of the ANIMEE components. Within tiers, collaboration can occur in standard setting, auditing (discussed in Part 3.4.1 below), data sharing, and so on. Such intra-tier collaboration raises the kinds of antitrust questions noted in the norm formation section (Part 3.2). Presenters disagreed about the degree to which antitrust law is a problem, but many had clearly thought and worried about it. One who was quite comfortable with antitrust law claimed that it leaves a 'tremendous amount of latitude to collaborate without getting too close', and that, while it can be constraining, the constraints are worth it: 'It costs some money for lawyers, but it's a fair price to pay for not having cartels.'

In the implementation process, collaboration occurs most often in the form of information sharing within tiers, usually about suppliers, as further discussed in Section 3.4.1 below. Between tiers, it can take the form of capacity building discussed above or simple joint problem solving regarding how to make a product better or in a better way. As one presenter remarked: 'It's simply about putting our challenges on the table and working them out together.' Another pointed out that often even big buyers cannot sway suppliers based on power alone, since the suppliers usually have other buyers. Hence, again, collaboration is necessary to achieve joint gains.

Cross-sector collaboration was occasionally mentioned, but described as extremely difficult. It was seen as desirable in two regards.

First, it can provide helpful examples of practices in other sectors. Second, it may help build enough of a power bloc to counter corruption in developing countries. Overall, however, there does not appear to be much direct cross-sector collaboration in SSCM. It mainly takes the indirect form of shared learning through websites, practice guides (Leipziger 2017), and episodic events such as the conferences discussed here.

3.3.3.5 Managing across non-contiguous tiers

Much of the analysis thus far has focused on direct buyer-supplier relationships. Yet there are key challenges involved in multi-tier supply chain management. The example of the computer companies forced to deal with tantalum, discussed above, involved suppliers several tiers upstream from the companies. The computer companies ended up organizing a meeting of the entire supply chain and eventually establishing a conflict-free smelter certification program that involves a 'bag and tag' program using radio-frequency identification devices to follow the minerals from mine to smelter. They thereby averted a potential boycott that would have been unnecessarily detrimental to non-conflict producers.

One of the computer company CSR managers opined that if they had done a human rights risk assessment beforehand, they 'would not have thought of this', since it was such a small part of such a large and complex supply chain. Given the complexity of many supply chains and the effective impossibility of examining them exhaustively, the common prescription was to 'cut through the complexity and figure out where the hotspots are', as one presenter put it. The CSR team can then focus on correcting problems in those processes before turning to others. Another presenter stressed that this is more difficult than it may seem, because investigation of risks often 'does not get rewarded'. She argued that corporate culture change is necessary to reward such activity. Another noted that the job is never ending, because suppliers regularly change, posing endless new challenges for finding and addressing hotspots – and presumably also for relational governance.

In sum, most success to date has occurred with first tier suppliers. Presenters agreed that knowledge of tiers three to five is usually quite murky. Investigation can lead, in one speaker's words, into 'people's back yards in developing countries'. One solution would be to rely on actors in tiers adjacent to the tiers at issue, since they can usually garner the necessary knowledge most easily. However, this requires a degree of enrolment into the mission, resource commitment, and supply chain integration that is often absent. The more suppliers, the more buyers, and the more rapid change in the industry, the more complex is the problem. Hence, supply chain managers are thrown back on frequent audits of what can be a quickly changing cast of suppliers.

3.3.4 Monitoring

Supply chain monitoring can helpfully be divided into micro and macro forms. The micro one – auditing – is widespread, although not necessarily frequent, in supply chain management. The macro one – systemic tracking of environmental and social effects of production practices – is rare, and is typically carried out by other actors, such as governments, academic researchers, or large NGOs.

3.3.4.1 Auditing

Auditing is the practice of checking whether an actor is meeting applicable requirements or commitments. Typically, it involves taking a list of requirements and checking them against the subject firm's behaviour or performance. Audits can be more or less intensive, but they have a tendency to take a standardized, bureaucratic form, perhaps in part to project an image of objectivity.

Presenters voiced several vigorous critiques of auditing. The first was that audits use up excessive resources. They involve a considerable amount of work for the auditor and can require even more work for the supplier, which may be subject to multiple audits from different buyers. A presenter estimated that an average Chinese factory producing for eight brands may have 20 audits per year. The factory will necessarily devote considerable resources to dealing with audits, and may come to see them as a nuisance to be skirted around – an imposition by 'them' on 'us'. Audits may be duplicative, in which case they may come to seem even more senseless, or they may be different in many small ways, in which case they impose additional costs of demonstrating compliance without necessarily producing useful information or improved operations. One response to this critique is that audits and reporting should be more standardized, and presenters reported that a fair bit of standardization seems to be occurring. A stronger response is that audits should be shared by multiple customers: 'An audit for one is an audit for all.' The TfS chemical supply chain audit system does this. Fifteen companies carry out and share 200 audits per year, thus covering the supply network and significantly reducing costs. According to the presenter, the joint audit process required considerable discussion and work with lawyers, but is working well.

A second critique is that audits do not always produce useful information. This may be because the goals at issue are difficult to measure. For example, compliance with the legal minimum wage may not provide a living wage. Or it may be because the audit, while covering all of the formal criteria, fails to deal adequately with intangible issues, such as worker morale, that require assessment. The auditor may not be empowered to exercise the kind of judgment that is required. Additionally, professional auditors are often very hesitant to give advice on how better to comply with standards, although they may order corrective actions. Like many government inspectors, auditors often see the provision of such advice as creating a conflict of interest.

A third critique is that audits often simply do not work. One presenter said that at one time his company thought, based on audits, that the vast majority of Chinese factories were compliant with fire safety laws. On closer inspection, however, they found that less than half were. One factory, according to the presenter, had five people on staff just to deal with auditors. His proposal, and evidently the strategy of his group, is to have people ('passionate people') actually work in the factories and live in the dorms. The same speaker argued that audit resources are better invested in coaching and mentoring, since the weakest producers need the most help. Speakers gave several other examples of audited workplaces that turned out to involve significant violations, including in developed countries. There was tacit acceptance that in many cases it may not be feasible for auditors to ferret out violations, since the audited companies control the situation and may be able to hide problems. Where the problems involve treatment of workers, as did most of the shared examples of undetected violations, a common suggestion is to focus on finding ways of empowering the workers. These methods might involve giving them language skills sufficient to defend themselves, helping them unionize, or setting up a call-in line where workers can report problems anonymously while not at work. Independent parties can then take those concerns to the companies. This last arrangement has reportedly been successful in both China and India, according to some presenters.

3.3.4.2 Transparency

Increased transparency has been touted for decades as a way of almost automatically enhancing social and environmental performance, because both the actor and others can see the level of performance and take action as a result. Rapid improvements in information management systems make this strategy particularly appealing in supply chain management. Retailers have long been able to use SKU (Stock Keeping Unit) codes to track merchandise back to specific suppliers, and potentially to discipline them for shoddy production. Now, QR (Quick Response) codes and other technologies make it possible for many actors along supply chains to see desired information. Edible QR codes, for example, are starting to become common on products like sushi, creating the possibility of supply chain governance interactions with interested consumers.

Such strategies are not always possible, particularly for components that will be transformed in the manufacturing process, as in the tantalum case. Still, transparency can also be achieved simply by making privately held information public. For example, the metal smelter could list its ore suppliers and the fabricator could list its smelter sources, as Intel partly did by naming its top 100 suppliers in its most recent CSR report (Intel Corporation 2018). However, this is rarely done. More commonly, corporations resist sharing supplier information for competitive reasons. A number of speakers were prepared to share certain information, for example the results of supplier audits, within industry groups, but few indicated willingness to share with the public as a whole. Indeed, some speakers and participants at the conference expressed great hesitancy about making public announcements of SSCM activities. When I inquired why, I was told by one presenter that it often seems unwise to 'stick your head above the parapet'. No matter how careful a company may be in sourcing products, an enterprising reporter or NGO may still be able to run an exposé demonstrating failed claims and portraying the company as deceitful.

3.3.5 Enforcement

As suggested above, non-compliance with sustainability standards can be high, including in audited firms. Presentations by sustainability professionals rarely referred to enforcement as conventionally understood (the application of rules backed by sanctions). Instead, they tended to emphasize relational governance strategies such as increasing engagement, mentoring, capacity building, and the like. Auditors commonly list corrective actions, which can be checked in the future. If non-compliance continues and is serious, buyers have the option of dropping non-compliant suppliers, provided they are replaceable. Often, however, buyers' enforcement powers are constrained by their limited market power and difficulty in arranging alternative suppliers. Moreover, dropping a supplier may do nothing to improve performance, since the supplier may simply leave the network and sell to less discriminating buyers. Thus, buyers are often inclined either to let violations pass, or to find cooperative ways of addressing them.

Other possible enforcers include governments, civil society organizations, worker organizations, and consumers. Host governments have formal jurisdiction over suppliers, and many violations of supplier codes are also violations of state laws. However, host-state agencies and legal systems often are very unreliable enforcers. As one speaker emphasized, developing countries usually want to increase their comparative advantage so as to be successful exporters, and one easy way to do this is to reduce formal and informal worker and environmental protections. A number of speakers expressed a desire for better host-state regulation, because it can reduce total enforcement costs (individual companies do not have to do it themselves), establish uniform standards, and generally create a more predictable business environment. However, there seems to be little sign of this happening. The appeal of lax standards to minimize costs and increase comparative advantage is strong in many places, as are the attractions of bribes for special treatment. Some recent trade agreements such as the Trans-Pacific Partnership (TPP) Agreement create a duty to enforce, but many years and much agitation will probably be required for such provisions to have significant effect (Meidinger 2019).

In some cases, the promise of activating civil society organizations or workers' organizations may be greater than the hope of increased state enforcement. However, many developing country governments strictly control protest actions, allowing them only when they suit government interests, which will often not be the case when supplier profits are threatened.

Consumer whistle blowers, finally, may be effective in some cases. However, often their only method is a consumer boycott, a very blunt instrument. It is often difficult to boycott only the products of 'bad' suppliers, and even if it is possible, the boycott may leave workers worse off (perhaps unemployed) than they would have been in their substandard work situations.

In sum, the enforcement system for SSCM is a spotty composite of relatively weak elements. This may mean that the capacity of SSCM to actually achieve any significant goals is severely limited. Differently viewed, it will have to rely on the aggregated, individually calibrated actions of many different enforcers, who often must rely on very limited information. Accordingly, enforcement as traditionally understood seems unlikely to play an important role in SSCM for some time to come.

3.3.6 Evaluation and Review

There is no overarching mechanism for evaluating or reviewing SSCM, although there is a rapidly growing flow of information. More and more corporations are issuing reports on their sustainability activities, including supply chain management, sometimes under Global Reporting Initiative (GRI) guidelines and sometimes on their own. But the amount of useful information they contain tends to be quite limited. They generally provide very little detail on their supply chains' structure or participants, typically for competitiveness reasons. Although some mention improvements in the performance of their supply chains, they very rarely detail the nature of the improvements, and almost never describe the severity of remaining problems. Thus, corporate responsibility reports rarely contain meaningful measures of effectiveness. This could change somewhat if GRI or OECD requirements (GRI 2013; OECD 2018) become more demanding, or perhaps even if the state of the art improves greatly. To date there is not much reason for optimism on either count.

Meanwhile, much of the broad evaluation and review activity that exists takes place in forums like the conferences discussed in this chapter. Those assessments are generally anecdotal and unsystematic. Outside the conferences, there is a growing body of academic research on SSCM. However, that research was not mentioned by the SSCM professionals, and the conferences were nearly devoid of academics. It thus appears that catalysing an effective evaluation and review function will require systematically connecting researchers to professional supply chain managers. While such connections may be developing in the business and human rights arena, it will take some time for meaningful networks of research and dialogue to generate information and analysis capable of supporting broad conclusions about the performance of SSCM.

3.4 CONCLUSION

This section offers some preliminary reflections about the role of SSCM in improving governance capacity, ratcheting up standards, and advancing marginalized interests.

3.4.1 Improving Governance Capacity?

Does the growth of SSCM enhance governance capacity? At a basic level, the answer would seem to be 'yes'. Clearly, it should be helpful for sustainability governance to conscript the previously unutilized supply chain management capacities of powerful businesses, and for them to institutionalize sustainability practices. It is much harder to say, though, just how helpful. At present, we have little information on what proportion of transnational supply chains are covered, or are likely to be within a reasonable time, or how effective SSCM strategies actually are. This is especially so because of the extreme shortage of information on actual enforcement actions by lead firms.

It is thus natural to be sceptical. And yet, a number of factors may bolster and accelerate the growth of SSCM. Important sources of capital, most recently the US $6 trillion investment fund BlackRock, are increasingly pressuring businesses in which they invest to demonstrate social responsibility or risk losing capital (Sorkin 2018). Regional trade agreements like the TPP Agreement also mandate state encouragement of corporate responsibility programs (Meidinger 2019). Risks of domestic legal liability for the actions of supply chain partners are also growing (Kinley and Navidi 2013–14).

Yet still, there remain grounds for serious scepticism. Capital only flows and businesses only succeed when there are profits, and profit requires cost control. Moreover, many of the lead firms pushing SSCM have near-monopsony power and relatively limited political accountability. The degree to which their behaviour can be reliably shaped by the power of norms over that of profits must remain subject to serious question. And finally, many of the goals of institutionalizing SSCM can also be seen as a kind of governmentality strategy (Foucault 1991). It thus becomes more questionable whether this is a true improvement in governance capacity.

3.4.2 Ratcheting Up Standards?

SSCM contains a significant commitment to continual improvement (ratcheting), and many of the presenters discussed ways of promoting and rewarding it. However, that improvement is centred on business goals, mainly productivity and adaptability. It is also constrained by the profit requirements noted above. Together, these requirements may place invisible upper limits on social and environmental standards.

Regardless of how far ratcheting might go in terms of protecting workers, communities, and the environment, it is important to stress that the SSCM concept of ratcheting seems to envision a change in the very nature of standards – away from specific outputs and toward greater organizational capacity for adaptation and innovation. Thus, it may be focused more on the characteristics of the organization than on the nature of its activities.

It remains possible, of course, that environmental and social standards will become more stringent as supply chain participants become more nimble and innovative, but the narratives examined in this chapter provide a limited basis at best for such a conclusion. Moreover, the dispersal of standard setting to so many diverse actors will make it difficult to discern how much ratcheting up actually occurs. Standards may be strict in some areas and weak in others, absent the 'super-aligner' called for by some of the presenters.

3.4.3 Advancing Marginalized Interests?

The primary form of empowerment in SSCM is through rules. Rules are used to define protections for workers, communities, and the environment. Thus, much of what might be thought of as empowerment is top-down and takes the form of protection by more powerful actors. It occurs mainly through codes that already specify the legitimate expectations of the protected interests. The labouring oar has been largely in the hands of lead firms. Several SSCM practitioners did describe programs in which firms empower workers by giving them a voice through hotlines, language training, unions, and other arrangements. Overall, however, worker and community empowerment still seem to be a relatively small part of the SSCM repertoire. The majority of presentations focused on effectuating more control by lead firms to get suppliers to follow practices protecting people and nature in a predictable manner. As long as that focus holds, empowerment of marginalized interests in SSCM seems likely to remain limited.

NOTES

1. Helpful comments by Matthew Bach, Guyora Binder, Todd Brown, Abigail Cooke, Matt Dimick, James Gardner, Jennifer Hunt, Meredith Lewis, Tara Melish, Jessica Owley, Christine Parker, John Henry Schlegel, Margaret Shannon, Mateo Taussig-Rubbo, David Westbrook, and my co-editors are gratefully acknowledged, as is research funding provided by the Baldy Center for Law & Social Policy, The State University of New York at Buffalo.
2. Throughout this chapter, where I quote SSCM professionals without citation to a published source, the source is public presentations by them at the SSCM conferences I attended for the purposes of this research, or follow-up conversations I had with them. The conferences are described in Part 2.1.
3. Dodd-Frank Wall Street Reform and Consumer Protection Act, Pub. L. No. 111-203, § 929-Z, 124 Stat. 1376, 1871 (2010) (codified at 15 U.S.C. § 78p).
4. *Loi* n° 2017-399 du 27 mars 2017 relative au devoir de vigilance des sociétés mères et des entreprises donneuses d'ordre, JO 28 mars 2017, texte n° 1.
5. Directive 2014/95/EU of the European Parliament and of the Council of 22 October 2014 amending Directive 2013/34/EU as regards disclosure of non-financial and diversity information by certain large undertakings and groups [2014] OJ L330/1.

REFERENCES

Becker, Howard S. (1970), *Sociological Work: Method and Substance*, New Brunswick, NJ: Transaction Publishers.

Better Coal (2011), *Anti-Trust Compliance Policy Statement – Principles*, Gillingham, UK: Better Coal, accessed 6 April 2019 at https://bettercoal.org/wp-content/uploads/2018/04/Bettercoal-Anti-trust-Policy-1.pdf.

Better Coal (2019), *Who We Are*, accessed 6 April 2019 at https://bettercoal.org/who-we-are.

BSR (Business for Social Responsibility) (2019), *About Us*, accessed 6 April 2019 at http://www.bsr.org/en/about.

Christopher, Martin (2011), *Logistics & Supply Chain Management,* 4th edn, New York: Prentice-Hall.

Eberlein, Burkard, Kenneth W. Abbott, Julia Black, Errol Meidinger and Stepan Wood (2014), 'Transnational business governance interactions: conceptualization and framework for analysis', *Regulation and Governance,* **8** (1), 1–21.

Ecovadis (2019), *About Ecovadis*, accessed 6 April 2019 at https://www.ecovadis.com/about-us.

ETI (Ethical Trading Initiative) (2019a), *ETI's Origins*, accessed 6 April 2019 at http://www.ethicaltrade.org/about-eti/why-we-exist/etis-origins.

ETI (Ethical Trading Initiative) (2019b), *ETI Base Code*, accessed 6 April 2019 at http://www.ethicaltrade.org/eti-base-code.

Foucault, Michel (1991), 'Governmentality', in G. Burchell, C. Gordon and P. Miller (eds), *The Foucault Effect: Studies in Governmentality*, London: Harvester Wheatsheaf, pp. 87–104.

Gereffi, Gary (2011), 'Global value chains and international competition', *Antitrust Bulletin,* **56** (1), 37–64.

Gereffi, Gary and Joonkoo Lee (2012), 'Why the world suddenly cares about supply chains', *Journal of Supply Chain Management*, **48** (3), 24–32.

GRI (Global Reporting Initiative) (2013), *G4 Sustainability Reporting Guidelines, Part 1: Reporting Principles and Standard Disclosures*, Amsterdam: GRI, accessed 6 April 2019 at https://www.globalreporting.org/resourcelibrary/GRIG4-Part1-Reporting-Principles-and-Standard-Disclosures.pdf.

ITC (International Trade Centre) (2019), *Standards Map: Your Roadmap to Sustainable Trade*, accessed 6 April 2019 at http://www.standardsmap.org/identify.

Intel Corporation (2018), *Corporate Responsibility at Intel: 2017–2018 Report*, Santa Clara, CA: Intel Corporation, accessed 6 April 2019 at http://csrreportbuilder.intel.com/PDFfiles/CSR-2017_Full-Report.pdf.

James, William (1890), *The Principles of Psychology*, **1**, New York: Henry Holt & Co.

Jenkins, Rhys (2001), 'Corporate codes of conduct: self-regulation in a global economy', UNRISD Technology, Business and Society Programme Paper No. 2, UN Research Institute for Social Development (April), accessed 6 April 2019 at http://www.unrisd.org/80256B3C005BCCF9/search/E3B3E78BAB9A886F80256B5E00344278.

Kent, John L. Jr. and Daniel J. Flint (1997), 'Perspectives on the evolution of logistics thought', *Journal of Business Logistics,* **18** (2), 15–29.

Kinley, David and Jahan Navidi (2013–14), 'The long arm of human rights risk: supply chain management and legal responsibility', *Business and Human Rights Review* (*Allen & Overy LLP*), **3**, 10–13.

Leipziger, Deborah (2017), *The Corporate Responsibility Code Book,* 3rd edn, London: Routledge.

Marchi, V. D., E.D. Maria and S. Micelli (2013), 'Environmental strategies, upgrading and competitive advantage in global value chains', *Business Strategy and the Environment*, **22**, 62–72.

Meidinger, Errol (2006), 'The administrative law of global private-public regulation', *European Journal of International Law,* **17**, 47–87.

Meidinger, Errol (2008), 'Multi-interest self-governance through global product certification programs', in Olaf Dilling, Martin Herberg and Gerd Winter (eds), *Responsible Business? Self-Governance in Transnational Economic Transactions*, Oxford: Hart, pp. 259–91.

Meidinger, Errol (2019), 'The TPP and environmental regulation', in Benedict Kingsbury, David M. Malone, Richard B. Stewart and Atsushi Sunami (eds), *Megaregulation Contested: Global Economic Ordering after TPP,* New York and Oxford: Oxford University Press, pp. 175–95.

Porter, Michael T. (1985), *Competitive Advantage: Creating and Sustaining Superior Performance*, New York: Free Press.

OECD (2018), *OECD Due Diligence Guidance for Responsible Business Conduct*, Paris: OECD, accessed 6 April 2019 at http://mneguidelines.oecd.org/OECD-Due-Diligence-Guidance-for-Responsible-Business-Conduct.pdf.

Sorkin, Andrew Ross (2018), 'BlackRock's message: contribute to society, or risk losing our support', *New York Times Dealbook* (15 January), accessed 6 April 2019 at https://www.nytimes.com/2018/01/15/business/dealbook/blackrock-laurence-fink-letter.html.

TfS (Together for Sustainability) (2019), *What Is Together for Sustainability?,* accessed 6 April 2019 at https://tfs-initiative.com/about-us-2.

United Nations (2011), *Guiding Principles on Business and Human Rights: Implementing the United Nations 'Protect, Respect and Remedy' Framework*, Geneva: Office of the UN High Commissioner for Human Rights, accessed 6 April 2019 at https://www.ohchr.org/Documents/Publications/GuidingPrinciplesBusinessHR_EN.pdf.

van der Vorst, Jack G.A.J., Carlos A. da Silva and Jacques H. Trienekens (2007), 'Agro-industrial supply chain management: concepts and applications', Agricultural Management, Marketing and Finance Occasional Paper No. 17, United Nations Food and Agriculture Organization, accessed 6 April 2019 at http://www.fao.org/3/a-a1369e.pdf.

Wood, Stepan (2012), 'The case for leverage-based corporate human rights responsibility', *Business Ethics Quarterly*, **22**, 63–98.

Wood, Stepan, Kenneth W. Abbott, Julia Black, Burkard Eberlein and Errol Meidinger (2015), 'The interactive dynamics of transnational business governance: a challenge for transnational legal theory', *Transnational Legal Theory*, **6** (2), 333–69.

4. Local practices, transnational solutions? The role of host cities in the cyclical process of environmental regulation of sports mega-events

Rebecca Schmidt

4.1 INTRODUCTION

Transnational regulation is a 'dynamic, co-regulatory and co-evolutionary process' that involves a variety of actors and institutions (Wood et al. 2015, p. 340). The transnational business governance interactions (TBGI) project acknowledges this and, rather than relying on one narrative of how transnational governance and governance interactions come about, it provides a framework setting out features that any theory of transnational business governance interactions should take into account (ibid.). The role of transnational actors, whether international organizations, civil society or business entities, in developing and putting forward transnational regulation has been analysed in many different contexts (e.g. Slaughter 2004; Büthe and Mattli 2011; Abbott et al. 2015). Less pronounced in these and many other studies is the role local government entities play in transnational multi-stakeholder regulation. This chapter argues that such entities can innovate transnational regulatory processes and can also provide an entrance point for other actors, such as local communities, non-governmental organizations (NGOs) and other actors promoting the provision of public goods, to develop and influence transnational regulation.

To this end, the chapter presents a case study of the environmental protection and sustainability framework implemented within the context of the Olympic Games. Since the 1990s, the Olympic movement has implemented increasingly extensive environmental regulations. From the start, the local, host city level has played a crucial role in the development and expansion of this regulatory regime. Two host cities, Lillehammer and London, stand out for their innovative approaches to environmental and sustainability regulation in the preparation and execution of their respective Games. By providing the role model of the first green Games, Lillehammer set a standard that was translated into the initial environmental framework at the level of the International Olympic Committee (IOC). Later innovations, such as London's sustainability management system, were also integrated into the movement's regulatory structure and became binding for subsequent Games. The chapter terms the dynamic at work in this case study 'cyclical regulation'. In this context, as in many other transnational regulatory settings (Braithwaite and Drahos 2000, p. 10), local governments function as both rule takers and rule innovators; they are both regulators and regulated.

Although the chapter examines a single case study, it has broader relevance for several reasons. In recent years, local government entities have become increasingly important actors in a transnational regulatory context. Often the local level is more open for regulatory innovations, providing a sphere where innovations can be tested before they are promoted on a larger scale.[1] It is also a place where local and transnational business and civil society actors find an entrance point to promote their respective regulatory agendas, leading to complex regulatory interactions and structures.[2] This open and experimental character is revealed particularly in recent trends to apply and integrate new technologies as governance tools. Summarized under the 'smart city' concept, a range of new technologies are applied to respond to regulatory and infrastructural challenges in city governance (ISO 2014). Such developments lead to enhanced local level engagement in transnational regulatory processes, which warrants further research.

The chapter adopts the following structure: the theoretical framework and empirical approach are presented in Part 2, Part 3 contains the case study and this is followed by a discussion of the findings in Part 4, before a short conclusion.

4.2 THEORETICAL FRAMEWORK AND EMPIRICAL APPROACH

Global regulation occurs in highly interrelated ways, through fluid interactions of multiplicities of actors, institutions, and sources over time and across scales. Literature addressing the complexity of business governance interactions is vast (e.g. Büthe 2010; Grabosky 2013; Eberlein et al. 2014; Wood 2015). Kenneth Abbott and Duncan Snidal propose the governance triangle to examine the interactions between different types of actors (states, NGOs and firms) (Abbott and Snidal 2009). Scholars of new regulation and governance portray the multifaceted interactions of public and private organizations, instruments, and norms (Braithwaite and Drahos 2000; Black 2001; Eberlein et al. 2014). Focusing on the role of local level actors as transnational regulatory innovators and on the process through which these innovations are taken up by transnational regulators and disseminated into different contexts, this chapter links to the TBGI framework in two ways. First, it depicts contexts within which local-transnational interactions take place. For the area of sport regulation, it unearths the key mechanisms and pathways of such interactions. Secondly, regarding the normative ambition of this volume for better regulation and the advancement of marginalized actors, the chapter points to different entrance points within a cyclical regulatory process that weaker actors and advocates for higher standards can deploy in pursuing their goals.

Beyond its linkage with the TBGI framework, further preliminary remarks are necessary. The first concerns the term 'regulatory innovation', which is used throughout this chapter. Based on Black, Lodge, and Thatcher's definition, it should be understood as normatively neutral, referring to 'changes in the performance of regulatory functions, institutional structures and organizational processes which have an impact on the regulatory regime' (Black et al. 2005). If in the present examples local actors function as regulatory innovators, they initiate such changes transnationally through experimentation and the dissemination of local experiences and practices.

This leads to the second set of remarks, regarding the overlaps and similarities of this chapter with other strands of literature. One notable related body of scholarship discusses experimentalist governance (Dorf and Sabel 1998; Sabel and Zeitlin 2008; Sabel and Zeitlin 2012). Experimentalist governance describes processes, particularly found within EU governance, whereby a superordinate regulator sets framework goals together with lower level entities (e.g. member states). Those goals are then implemented by the lower level authorities, who have considerable freedom regarding the ways in which implementation occurs. In a third step, implementation strategies are reported to the higher level, and their performance is measured and evaluated comparatively. Based on this evaluation, framework goals and metrics are regularly revised (Sabel and Zeitlin 2012 p. 3; Sabel and Zeitlin 2008, p. 271; see also Dorf and Sabel 1998). Comparable processes can be found in the case at hand, where each new Olympics provides an experimental playing field for the host city to implement and further the environmental regulatory framework of the Olympic Movement. Successful regulatory innovations are taken up by the IOC and integrated into its general framework. Future host cities must implement those, and, by implementing them, they test their viability in different settings and over time.

Literature on regulatory intermediaries also provides a comparative approach to understand the general complexity of environments, where 'regulation often operates indirectly via chains of intermediation' (Abbott et al. 2017b, p. 5) and takes place across different scales (ibid., p. 5). Concretely, regulatory intermediaries come into play where a direct relationship between regulator and target (R and T) is either inefficient or impossible. In such contexts intermediaries step in or are engaged to provide assistance and resources to accomplish the regulatory goal, constituting a regulator-intermediary-target (RIT) triad (Abbott et al. 2017a, 3). Intermediation can be done through the provision of expertise to facilitate 'implementation, monitoring behaviour of regulatory targets and building assurance and trust' (ibid. pp. 3–4). Often intermediaries are orchestrated by the regulator, who uses 'soft techniques' to 'engage them and their capacities into the regulatory process' (Abbott et al. 2017a; Abbott et al. 2015). In the case at hand, there is a direct relationship between the IOC and host cities. However, especially regarding environmental protection and sustainability we also find the inclusion of third parties into the regulatory processes. Thus, NGOs, civil society representatives and international organizations are active in further developing the environmental framework and in monitoring compliance by host cities with existing standards.

The concept of cyclical regulation that I develop in this chapter diverges from these approaches. The nuances will be developed in more detail throughout the chapter. Preliminarily, one can distinguish three main differences. First, unlike experimentalist governance, cyclical regulation does not take place within a more or less clearly determined and legally enforceable hierarchy (e.g. the EU). In the Olympic example, host cities volunteer or, more precisely, compete to host the Games, and regulatory innovation is one aspect of this competition. The transnational regulator sometimes adopts their ideas and procedures and implements rules accordingly. In other cases, the context is even more anarchic. Innovations are adopted without any formal process, only because the proffering entity is regarded as conveying sufficient expertise and experience. Thus, there is at least initially no formalized relationship that determines responsibilities for innovation.

Secondly, there is no clear allocation of roles between regulators, intermediaries and targets as in the RIT framework: local level actors are not really intermediaries, as they have minimal ties with and no authority over future host cities. One can say that the transnational regulator exercises some orchestration activity, since it encourages local regulatory innovation through its competitive selection process. Yet local entities act either independently or within an authority relationship with the transnational regulator in which they are rule takers as well as rule innovators. To change the behaviour of future host cities, the IOC must implement the innovation in its regulatory framework and in future host city contracts. Here, one can find overlap with the experimentalist framework, in that the boundaries between rule makers and rule takers are blurred (Dorf and Sabel 1998, p. 354).

Finally, the cyclical regulatory innovation process I describe is usually not linked to one particular regulatory regime. Because innovations are taken up at different regulatory levels and by different regulatory systems (municipality, transnational sports regulator, the events management sector, etc.), they involve and spread across a large variety of regimes, which often have no direct relationship to the original sector (sports in the case at hand).

Beyond these differences, this chapter, while situated in these strands of literature, particularly emphasizes the importance of local level entities (especially cities) for the global economy and as a consequence for business regulation. This role has been pointed out for some time (Hall 1966; Friedmann and Wolff 1982; Sassen 2001; Herrschel and Newman 2017). From the 1960s onwards and since the end of the Cold War, cities have become central 'control sites in the international economic order' (Sassen 2001, p. 5). This development not only impacts the dynamics within the city (e.g. increased socio-economic inequality), it also alters the relationship between the city and the state in which it is located (ibid., p. 8). Globalization and communication technologies have increased interconnectedness between cities. Municipalities are no longer responsible only to their residents and to higher-level national or subnational governments. They have complex relationships with each other and with transnationally operating actors, relationships that are characterized by cooperation, competition and other forms of interactions, such as intermediary functions. Local actors can therefore become creators and facilitators of global norms (Herrschel and Newman 2017).

In the context of sport, the importance of the local level is not surprising, as it is the point where the transnational regime interacts with a variety of different entities. The Games are the single most important deliverable of the Olympic movement, and outside actors have the greatest opportunities to influence the Olympic regime in the preparation and execution phase of the Games. For a few decades, local and transnational NGOs and activist groups have either treated the Games as a platform to spread their message, or have used the local level to impact regulation in the sports regime as a whole (Dansero 2012; Hayes and Karamichas 2012; Whitson 2012; Renou 2012).

4.3 HOST CITIES AND SUSTAINABILITY REGULATION IN THE SPORT CONTEXT

4.3.1 The Selection of Host Cities

Events such as the Olympic Games have been labelled mega-events. The term is used to describe 'large-scale cultural (including commercial and sporting) events, which have a dramatic character, mass popular appeal and international significance' (Roche 2000, p. 1). This significance includes the broad reach these events have globally and the impact they have at the local level (Roche 2000; Horne and Manzenreiter 2006; Hayes and Karamichas 2012). The Olympics are broadcast to more than 200 national territories and reach up to 4.8 billion people. The London Olympics broadcast rights alone created a revenue of US $3.9 billion (IOC 2012). These mega-events have a significant social, economic and political dimension beyond the Olympic Movement and the sporting community. Mega-events are also considered to 'increasingly provide a platform for economic growth oriented approaches to environmental protection and amelioration'. In this scenario, the IOC and other sport organizations function 'as regulatory authority for the development and dissemination of environmental best practice and sustainable technologies, facilitating the creation and growth of new markets' (Hayes and Karamichas 2012, pp. 10–11).

The IOC's strong position vis-à-vis potential host cities at the selection phase is important for its role as a regulatory authority. Its power is reduced later in the process, but it can still exert control through the Coordination Commission, which is closely involved in the preparation from the IOC side. Finally, the IOC can withdraw the Games from a host city, although this measure of last resort has never been applied (IOC 2019: Rule 37 and associated bylaw). To understand how standards developed by one host city are implemented in the preparations for subsequent Games, one must look at the way host cities are selected. By selecting new host cities based on experiences from previous preparation and execution phases, lessons learned at one host city serve as a basis for the next one. Crucial in this context is the bidding phase, where the IOC scrutinizes the candidature files and suggests improvements necessary to be considered in the selection process (ibid., Rule 33 and associated bylaw).

The selection process is not static, rather it changes and expands with almost every Games. Through a recent reform put in place by the IOC's Agenda 2020, the general structure of the selection process has changed in an even more substantial way (IOC 2014b). Under the old regime, in effect before 2015, potential host cities underwent two selection stages: a candidature acceptance and a candidature phase (IOC 2016c). In the first phase, potential host cities were required to answer a questionnaire provided by the IOC (2016b). The information gathered was then assessed with that collected in other categories, and a decision to proceed to the next phase was made on this basis. Cities that made it to the candidature phase were then required to submit a detailed candidature file. This file included a section on environment and metrology. Here the candidate provided information on its environmental approach, for example geographical features, environmental plans, venue construction and development projects (IOC, 2010). At both stages environmental concerns were part of the criteria by which a host city was chosen. The last selection process that formally still applied this old system took place in 2014–15 for the host city of the 2022 Olympics. However, both candidates (Beijing and Almaty) had already adjusted their bids to be in line with the new approach (Host City 2015).

The new approach was introduced through the Olympic Agenda 2020 reform process, implemented in 2015, which introduced several changes in the bidding process. The first part of the bidding is now called invitation phase. The idea behind the invitation phase is to provide support to future host cities in putting together their candidature file, by sharing best practice and encouraging 'legacy and sustainability [. . .] to ensure the Games act as a catalyst for positive development of tangible and intangible legacies for the city and the region' (IOC 2016d). During the candidature phase, aspiring host cities make an official bid. The candidature phase has three stages, which are again characterized by dialogue between the cities and the IOC. In each stage the cities submit parts of their candidature files. In support, the IOC provides feedback, hosts workshops and at one point has the candidature cities participate in an Olympic Games observer programme, through which they receive behind-the-scenes insight into the details of how to deliver the Games (ibid.). After the final part of the candidature file is submitted, the IOC Evaluation Commission visits each city and provides a report distributed to all IOC members. During the IOC Session (the annual meeting of the IOC's plenary organ), the new host city is selected and the host city contract is signed (ibid.).

Once a host city is chosen, all commitments made in the candidature files become binding and must be implemented by the local organizing committee. They form part of the host city contract, which includes references to the host city contract principles, operational requirements, the Games Delivery Plan and the Olympic Charter (IOC 2018 p. 13). To fulfil these commitments, local organizing committees must cooperate with governmental authorities and other stakeholders to implement appropriate policies across the city and country. Experts from the IOC and other organizations (such as the United Nations Environment Programme (UNEP) or Worldwide Fund for Nature [WWF]) may assist the local committee in the development and implementation of environmental policies (Sustainability and Legacy Commission 2017). Finally, together with external actors such as UNEP, NGOs or the media, the IOC Coordination Commission monitors the process to ensure 'maximum fulfilment of commitments and maximum use of the opportunity to improve environmental conditions and practices' (ibid.; Schmidt 2018, p. 166).

The following sections outline how IOC environmental regulation was implemented and expanded in a cyclical fashion by three innovative host cities.

4.3.2 The City as Regulatory Target and Innovator – Three Case Studies

4.3.2.1 Lillehammer – early environmental standards in the sport context

The first step towards a green Olympics was taken in the early 1990s. Increased environmental awareness in Western societies put the Games' environmental impact in the spotlight. The Winter Olympics in Albertville, France in 1992 were viewed by many as an 'environmental disaster' and caused widespread and well-covered protests by environmentalist groups (Cantelon and Letters 2000, p. 299). The IOC's lack of an environmental policy was criticized in particular (ibid.). The Lillehammer Games in 1994 provided a response to these complaints and affected the entire Olympic Movement. Unlike previous Olympic Games, Lillehammer had an environmental policy in place to help execute the Games in a green and sustainable manner (Myrholt 1996; IOC 2014a). The reason for this was, on the one hand, the long tradition and experience of environmental protection in Norway, and, on the other, the IOC's inexperience in this field, leaving room for local innovation. Long before the Games took place, Norwegians had developed a 'strong culture and affiliation to nature', and at the time of the Games there was a 'powerful environmental lobby' and grassroots movement active in the country, which had strong public support (Myrholt 1996).

This background was reflected in the organization and preparation of the Lillehammer Games. The preparation and execution of the Games involved a partnership of three actor groups: the private sector, local authorities and 'volunteer environmental organizations' (ibid., p. 2). The initial environmental policy was based on a proposal drafted jointly by the Lillehammer Olympic Organizing Committee and Friends of the Earth Norway. This 'precipitated a process, starting from grassroots, which set managers, politicians and environmental volunteers on a steep learning curve and turned the Games into a project-based "environmental showcase"' (ibid., p. 3). This success story was eagerly taken up by the IOC. In the aftermath, the Olympic Charter was amended to make environmental protection the third pillar of Olympism, along with sport and culture. The IOC furthermore set up the Sports and Environment Commission, now called the Sustainability and Legacy Commission, and drafted the Agenda 21 – Sport for Sustainable Development (IOC 2014a). More recently this Agenda has been complemented by Agenda 2020, a list of 40 recommendations for the Movement's future, in which sustainability, broadly conceived, plays a crucial role (IOC 2014b). Apart from using the Lillehammer Games as a role model, the IOC also started a partnership with UNEP for the development of various policies and programs within the Olympic movement. Nonetheless, the local experiences from the Lillehammer Games were essential in the development of the Movement's environmental policy. Since Lillehammer, environmental concerns and sustainability have increasingly become a significant issue in both the application and execution phase of the Games. The environment was a factor as early as the selection of the Sydney Games (Myrholt 1996).

4.3.2.2 London – sustainability and event management

The regulatory framework governing environmental factors of the Olympic Games developed gradually from one event to the next, yet it is important to mention the special role of London as a regulatory innovator. Sustainability management, as developed and implemented by its Organizing Committee, was not a requirement of the IOC at the time of the bid. In fact, the goal pursued by the London organizers was to hold the first sustainable Olympics, going beyond the concept of 'green Games' and involving also economic and social aspects (LOCOG 2012, p. 11). The framework for this approach was provided in the London 2012 Sustainability Plan, 'Towards a One Planet 2012', which was developed by two NGOs – BioRegional and WWF (LOCOG 2009). This framework understands sustainability in the context of mega-events as having global dimensions beyond the local context. One element of the London framework that had a broad reach beyond the Games was the management system approach. The organizing committee's decision to adopt this approach led to the creation of the British Standards Institution's BS 8901 standard and later the ISO 20121 standard. These standards set specifications for sustainable event management systems. The London Organizing Committee and the Olympic Delivery Authority were certified to ISO 20121. The local city administration and the organizing committee did not create ISO 20121, however. This was left to national and international standard setting processes. Thus, first the BSI developed BS 8901, through a drafting process conducted by consultants from Arup and the Events Industry Association (EIA) using input from the wider events industry sector (BSI 2007). In the aftermath, BSI together with the Brazilian national standards body, ABNT, submitted a joint proposal for the development of ISO 20121 to ISO and provided the secretariat of the working group developing the ISO standard (ISO 2012, p. 10).

In addition to securing an international standard against which their management system could be implemented and evaluated, the London organizers desired a framework for reporting publicly on the sustainability of the Games. To this end, they collaborated with the Global Reporting Initiative (GRI) and the IOC to develop an Event Organizers Sector Supplement of the GRI Sustainability Reporting Guidelines (ibid., p. 12).

The London Organizing Committee considered this comprehensive sustainability management approach necessary because it was under enormous public scrutiny. This approach also reflected the political and legal context in which preparation of the London Olympics took place. Around the time of the bid, the newly elected Labour government had started implementing its 'better regulation' agenda, which was intended to constitute a 'Third Way' between the deregulatory approach pursued since the late 1970s and a return to the interventionist welfare state (Baldwin et al. 2010, p. 7; Giddens 2000, p. 27). The Third Way emphasized market-based regulatory strategies (Yeung 2010, p. 66; Better Regulation Task Force 2003) that employ market mechanisms, such as competition, to pursue public policy goals. It also emphasized management-based regulation, a reflexive approach that aims at stimulating self-critical reflection by regulated entities in light of broad public criteria and goals. Thus, management-based regulation asks firms 'to produce plans that comply with general criteria designed to promote the targeted social goal' (Coglianese and Lazer 2003). Regulatory criteria 'specify elements that each plan should have, such as the identification of hazards, risk mitigation actions, [and] procedures for monitoring and correcting' (ibid., p. 694). In some cases, government regulations provide mechanisms to approve or ratify these plans (ibid., p. 694). Management systems standards, of which

ISO 20121 is an example, are often used by regulated firms to implement management-based regulation. Indeed, their use is often encouraged and sometimes even required by regulators.

Management-based regulation is particularly useful when regulated entities are heterogeneous and the regulator's capacity to monitor and assess output is limited (ibid., p. 705). Management-based regulation has the advantage of pushing more responsibility to the firm level, where the technical knowledge is usually located. Using private, third-party expert auditors and certifiers to verify compliance reduces the burden on governmental resources (ibid., p. 696).

The London organizers were familiar with this regulatory strategy and saw benefits for the complex regulatory context of a large-scale event such as the Olympics. In London, such an approach integrated well into existing administrative and private management structures and ultimately ensured that the organizers reached their sustainability targets (LOCOG 2012).

Both BS 8901 and ISO 20121 were drafted for all types of events, not just sports events. Furthermore, ISO 20121 is intended to be used by a whole range of actors in the event management sector, including 'event organizers, event owners, the workforce, supply chain (such as caterers, stand constructors, transport companies), participants and attendees' (ISO 2012, p. 4). The London Olympics in 2012 were both the impetus for ISO 20121 and the first time that the new standard was implemented. Since the 2012 Games ISO 20121 has been applied in a variety of contexts ranging from the 2013 Eurovision Song contest to the Danish Presidency of the European Council (ISO 2013). COP15, the Copenhagen UN Conference on Climate Change, was certified to BS 8901; Microsoft hosted the first event in the US to be BS 8901 certified in 2009 (ibid.; BSI 2009; Schmidt 2018, p. 185).

4.3.2.3 Rio, agenda 2020 and current sustainability requirements for host cities

Since London, sustainability management has become a requirement for the organization of any future Olympic Games. The current Host City Operational Requirements stipulate that a 'sustainability strategy, sustainability implementation plans, governance arrangements for sustainability matters, sustainability management systems, sustainability reports and a Games impact study must be implemented' (IOC 2018, pp. 165-167). Rio de Janeiro had the sustainable management approach already well embedded, announcing the development of the Rio 2016 Sustainability Management Plan in its candidature file (Rio 2009, p. 95). London designed its management system in line with both the

London Sustainable Development Framework, which provides a vision for sustainability in the city and objectives to guide decision-making (IOC 2016a), and international environmental management systems standards, namely the European Union's Eco-Management and Audit Scheme (EMAS) and ISO 14001 (LOCOG 2004, p. 76). Rio, for its part, referred to the Rio Environment Summit of 1992 as well as local environmental traditions. The Rio Candidature File referenced the ISO 14000 family of environmental management system standards, the ISO 26000 social responsibility guidance standard, the GRI, the One Planet Living Approach, the United Nations Human Development Index and the Sustainable Development Index for different purposes. For instance, the ISO 14000 standards were referenced as a way to ensure green procurement (Rio 2009, pp. 99 and 105). Not coincidentally, the initial proposal for creating the new ISO 20121 standard was jointly submitted by BSI and Brazil's national standards body, ABNT (ISO 2012, p. 10). Despite these stipulations, however, Rio fought an uphill battle to fulfil the sustainability obligations in its host city contract, and its sustainability legacy has been mixed.

4.3.2.4 The way forward

The examples above show continual development towards stronger sustainability standards. As mentioned, it was not only during the preparations of the Games in Lillehammer or London that changes and improvements to the regulatory framework were made. This also happened in other host cities. There are also examples of less successful Olympic Games, however. The 2014 Sochi Olympics were highly problematic regarding sustainability. In fact, many observers considered them an environmental failure. Important NGOs ceased collaboration with the Organizing Committee because they believed it was failing to fulfil the requirements set out in the host city contract (WWF Russia, no date).

Sustainability and sustainability management are nonetheless now well-established principles in the preparation and execution framework of Olympic Games. The Agenda 2020 stresses the importance of sustainability throughout its provisions (IOC 2014b). Recommendation 4 emphasizes the need to 'include sustainability in all aspects of the Olympic Games', commits the IOC to '[d]evelop a sustainability strategy to enable potential and actual Olympic Games organizers to integrate and implement sustainability measures that encompass economic, social and environmental spheres in all stages of their project' and calls on the IOC to '[a]ssist newly elected Organising Committees to establish the best possible governance for the integration of sustainability throughout the organisation' (IOC 2014b, p. 12).

The bidding process for the 2024 Olympic Games contained extensive sustainability requirements. The Operational Requirements, which complement the Host City Contract by providing detailed regulatory requirements on many aspects of the Games preparations, require a number of sustainability aspects to be integrated into the Games Delivery Plan. These include a general sustainability strategy, implementation plans, governance arrangements, a sustainability management system, sustainability reporting and an impact study (IOC 2018, pp. 165-167).

The London approach of introducing a sustainability management framework is thus now fully integrated within the Olympic Games planning and execution procedures. In the last bidding round, the two remaining candidate cities, Paris and Los Angeles, included detailed sections on sustainability. Both relied on ISO 20121 for their sustainability management system (Paris 2017, p. 88; Los Angeles 2017, p. 64). ISO 20121 has thus become the de facto standard governing sustainability management in the context of the Olympic Games.

4.4 INNOVATION, CYCLICAL REGULATION AND TRANSNATIONAL BUSINESS GOVERNANCE INTERACTIONS

4.4.1 Local Level Innovation in Cyclical Regulation – A Case of TBGIs?

This part argues that the Olympic case study shows that the local level can function as a place of innovation in complex regulatory processes. Here one can distinguish between the local level generally and global cities in particular.

The role of the local level generally in complex transnational governance processes has been examined most notably in literature on subsidiarity in the EU and in federal systems. The principle of subsidiarity serves various purposes, from avoiding centralization to accommodating different local and national value systems (Craig 2012, pp. 72–3). It also includes an understanding that the local (as well as national) level has unique abilities not enjoyed by higher-level entities: local authorities are much closer to their constituencies; they understand specific local conditions and preferences, and thus they can govern in a more fitting and accepted manner. By being closest to residents, they provide a contact point for citizens' concerns and complaints. Often this takes place through traditional venues that constituencies are familiar with (e.g. town hall meetings) and that are supported by established administrative structures. For similar reasons, both federal and central governments employ the local level as implementers of their regulation. This is often done by granting some degree of discretion that can even amount to independent local rule making (e.g. municipal bylaws).

However, subsidiarity and well-established administrative structures do not entirely account for the innovative potential of local entities. Though there is acknowledgement that the local level is in many cases better equipped to interpret, implement, or even amend rules, innovative potential is not necessarily encouraged in traditional legislative frameworks. Thus, when looking at local innovation, one must go beyond those roles to consider the transformation that many major urban centres have undergone in recent decades – in short, the emergence of the phenomenon of global cities. Once this is considered, it comes as no surprise that local entities are playing a much more prominent role in transnational processes. Big cities often unite business capacity, expertise and cutting-edge technologies in a small space. Local level officials, more generally, have frequent interaction with local business, NGOs and citizens. Consequently, cities like London can access a large pool of expertise and resources – a pool that is at least not readily available to a more specialized transnational regulator such as the IOC.

Given the potential for regulatory innovation at the local level, what is its relationship to transnational regulation? How are regulatory innovations taken up at higher levels? In some contexts, the interplay between different regulatory levels is well developed and even legally framed (Sabel and Zeitlin 2012). However, often it is not. In the case at hand we observe a cyclical process that is semi-structured. The IOC is the initial regulator, a rule maker in terms of the RIT framework (Abbott et al. 2017a). Cities that want to stand a chance in the selection process need to comply with parameters provided by the IOC during the bidding process. However, because of the competitive nature of the selection process, cities engage in innovation to achieve an advantage over their competitors. As such, they expand their role, set new standards, and become a kind of 'secondary regulator' (Abbott et al. 2017a, p. 19). In contrast to the RIT framework from which this term is taken, host cities are intermediaries only insofar as they enforce rules on local suppliers. They are not intermediaries in relation to future host cities. At this transnational scale, the IOC incorporates successful innovations into its own regulatory framework and then makes them binding for future host cities. At this point former host cities are out of the picture or play a marginal role.

In summary, host cities are both rule takers and rule innovators. They are innovators in that they expand existing regulatory frameworks and they are rule takers when they comply with the requirements that the IOC has set out for the bidding process. The practical dispersion of regulatory competences forces both host cities and the IOC to cooperate with each other, yet not in an ongoing but in a temporal manner. This temporality of the relationship leads to a cyclical process with regard to the overall regulatory framework for environmental protection in the sports context. The innovations of one host city are implemented into the requirements set out for the next one and tailored to the specific context. The IOC monitors these efforts and adapts its overall framework periodically. However, because of the specific and unique character of each Olympics, there is a discrepancy between the goals of the IOC's long-term regulatory perspective and the goals of the organizing committees in executing successful Games (Chappelet and Kübler-Mabbott 2008, p. 93).

4.4.2 Higher Social and Environmental Standards and Transferability of Local Regulatory Innovations

We now turn to a short discussion on whether the cyclical phenomenon of local innovation and transnational dissemination leads to higher social and environmental standards within the sports sector and beyond. This is a complex question that requires research that is not possible within the limited space of this chapter. However, we can observe a number of trends revealed in the Olympics case that find application beyond the scope of the case study.

First, we shall look at the possibility of ratcheting up standards through local level innovation. Here we can see clearly that over time transnational standards became much more comprehensive as new methods and principles were added that often originated locally. As such we can say that in the Olympics case, local level innovation led to an upward trend in standards. This was partly due to the IOC's limited capacities regarding both environmental regulation and municipal governance. Especially initially, the IOC had little in-house environmental expertise. Established local practices and venues to gather input were welcomed as a way to expand the existing transnational framework. Since Lillehammer, the rules for environmentally friendly and sustainable Games have been constantly expanding. Current expectations for host cities are extensive and take up as much space in the candidature files as security or transport (e.g. Paris 2017). This trend is consistent with the experimentalist literature. Because of limited capacities at the central (supranational or federal) level, local actors are involved, and their expertise is used to continually improve regulation (Dorf and Sabel 1998; Sabel and Zeitlin 2008; Sabel and Zeitlin 2012).

Regarding the effective implementation of these improved standards in future Games, the picture is more mixed. Here, two specificities of the

Olympics play an important role. First, regional diversity – the Olympics take place around the world, not only in Western democracies with high environmental standards. Differences in local circumstances mean that a model that led to a large success in one context had only average results in others (such as Rio); and some host cities face a much steeper uphill battle in successfully implementing all promises made in the bid (Woody 2016). Moreover, there were clear outliers such as Sochi 2014, where many environmental promises made in the bidding process and enshrined in the host city contract were not kept (WWF Russia, no date). Second, once the Games are allocated, a sunk cost dynamic sets in. As time passes, it becomes almost impossible to reallocate the Games, taking away the strongest leverage tool from the IOC. Thus, in cases where the host cities are lagging behind in implementing their environmental obligations it is not always possible to correct these dynamics.

As a result, the case study points to the limitations of local level innovation. When implemented in different contexts, regulatory innovations must be adapted and altered to fit changed circumstances. Thus, for any innovation it is important to assess its transferability and to understand how far it can work in different circumstances.

4.4.3 The Role of Weaker Actors in Cyclical Regulation

The second central issue concerns the role of weaker actors in innovative local processes. Again, generalization is difficult given the focus on one specific case. Yet several lessons learned from the present example might be transferable to other contexts. First, as stated above, the special context of the Olympics provides weaker actors a platform and a point of entrance. These sports mega-events receive significant publicity and in return are under severe public scrutiny. NGOs and other civil society groups have for a long time used such events as venues to draw public attention to local or global (environmental) issues. Some of these issues were host country-related, rather than directly linked to the event itself (e.g. Free Tibet protests in the context of the 2008 Beijing Olympics). However, it was through the interplay of the local level with the global that the push for innovation could happen. For the London Olympics, for instance, meticulous planning was considered necessary to avoid negative press coverage that might delegitimize the event. This was to be achieved through strong procedures and comprehensive involvement by a variety of concerned actors, such as the BioRegional and the WWF regarding the sustainability strategy.

Secondly, established paths for certain groups representing weaker actors exist in some host cities, for example in Lillehammer and London.

Lillehammer had a strong local environmental grassroots movement, which the organizers involved in the planning and execution of the event. London, too, built its framework on a concept developed by a local NGO, BioRegional. BioRegional had already established a record of creating and promoting sustainable business and, in that context, it had also cooperated with local authorities for some time (Riddlestone 2014). It was therefore easy for BioRegional to get involved in the preparation of the 2012 Olympics and to develop the sustainability strategy. Both points show that the local level can function as an entrance point especially for smaller, more local advocacy groups representing weaker actors and concerns for public goods. Such involvement is even easier if there is increased scrutiny of local authorities; and it also is easier for actors with already established connections to local authorities.

A number of problems must not be overlooked. First, there is a limited pool of local actors that can gather the necessary expertise to be regulatory innovators in the context of mega-events. In the Olympics case, only host cities with established environmental regulation frameworks could trigger an expansion of the transnational framework. Other host cities struggled to comply with existing rules. Consequently, local level innovative activities are often limited to economically advanced communities in the West. These innovations are then transferred to other contexts, where they may not work in the same manner. The IOC tries to bridge this gap through its own initiatives, such as host city workshops, the Olympic Games Observer Programme and the Coordination Commission, and by bringing on board third parties such as UNEP or the WWF. As was pointed out above, the success of these measures is mixed (for the case of Sochi, see WWF Russia, no date). Local circumstances do not always allow for broad participation. In more authoritarian jurisdictions, exclusion rather than inclusion might be the chosen path. Finally, not all processes are necessarily inclusive and even those that are inclusive favour some actors over others. In the preparation of the sustainability management system for the London Games, at least on the level of policy creation, actors with closer ties to the business sector (BSI, but also BioRegional) were involved to a much higher degree.

4.5 CONCLUSION

This chapter pursued two goals. First, it identified the role local actors play in transnational regulatory interactions. In contrast to more structured interactions such as the ones described in the experimentalist governance literature, the role of local actors in the case at hand is much broader, more unpredictable, and often more innovative. This then led to a thorough examination of the type of regulatory interaction engaged. Focus was put on the cyclical ways in which innovation takes place. Here again, the current example provided a different story from those found in related literature, particularly on orchestration and regulatory intermediaries. In the RIT model, actors (rule makers, intermediaries and rule takers) have fairly well-defined roles. In the example at hand, however, the actors involved change their role frequently, leading to dynamic and to a degree anarchic processes that are less predictable from the outset.

Secondly, the chapter, in line with the general goal of this volume, examined whether the described interactions led to higher social and environmental standards and the advancement of weaker actors. Here it found that local innovation ratcheted up sustainability standards in the sports sector. However, given the less predictable frame in which the interactions took place, local level dynamics sometimes also had the opposite effects and not even existing standards were met. Finally, participation of weaker actors was ensured through specific local-transnational dynamics. Yet, the chapter also cautioned against generalizing these dynamics as the Olympics provide a very specific setting involving public attention that is unsurpassed outside the sporting context.

NOTES

1. One highly topical example is 'smart city regulation'. There are currently several initiatives within ISO to standardize this development. Though strongly industry driven, local practices serve as a starting point for those standards (ISO 2015).
2. The complexity is examined elsewhere, using a similar case study (Schmidt 2018). In this chapter the local level constitutes one component among many others, such as the state level, the transnational sport regulator and transnational business standard setting bodies.

REFERENCES

Abbott, K.W. and D. Snidal (2009), 'The governance triangle: regulatory standards institutions and the shadow of the state', in W. Mattli and N. Woods (eds), *The Politics of Global Regulation*, Princeton, NJ: Princeton University Press, pp. 1–44.

Abbott, K.W., P. Genschel, D. Snidal and B. Zangl (2015), 'Orchestration: Global governance through intermediaries', in K.W. Abbott, P. Genschel, D. Snidal and B. Zangl (eds), *International Organizations as Orchestrators*, Cambridge, UK: Cambridge University Press, pp. 3–36.

Abbott, K.W., D. Levi-Faur and D. Snidal (2017a), 'Introducing regulatory intermediaries', *Annals of the American Academy of Political and Social Science*, **670**, 6–13.

Abbott, K.W., D. Levi-Faur and D. Snidal, D. (2017b), 'Enriching the RIT framework', *Annals of the American Academy of Political and Social Science*, **670**, 280–88.
Baldwin, R., M. Cave and M. Lodge (2010), 'Introduction: regulation – the field and the developing agenda', R. Baldwin, M. Cave and M. Lodge (eds), *The Oxford Handbook of Regulation*, Oxford: Oxford University Press, pp. 3–16.
Better Regulation Task Force (2003), *Principles of Good Regulation*, accessed 21 August 2019 at http://webarchive.nationalarchives.gov.uk/20100407162704/http:/archive.cabinetoffice.gov.uk/brc/upload/assets/www.brc.gov.uk/principlesleaflet.pdf.
Black, J. (2001), 'Decentring regulation: understanding the role of regulation and self-regulation in a "post-regulatory" world', *Current Legal Problems*, **54**, 103–46.
Black, J., M. Lodge and M. Thatcher (2005), *Regulatory Innovation: A Comparative Analysis*, Cheltenham, UK and Northampton, MA, USA: Edward Elgar Publishing.
Braithwaite J. and P. Drahos (2000), *Global Business Regulation*, Cambridge, UK: Cambridge University Press.
BSI (2007), *Sustainable Events? BSI Invites Organisers, Venues and Suppliers to Trial New Standard*, Press Release, 3 May.
BSI (2009), *Microsoft Convergence® 2009 Achieves the First BS 8901*, accessed 28 August 2019 at https://www.bsigroup.com/en-GB/about-bsi/media-centre/press-releases/2009/1/Microsoft-Convergence-2009-achieves-the-first-BS-8901/.
Büthe, T. (2010), 'Private regulation in the global economy: a (p)review', *Business and Politics,* **12**, article 1.
Büthe T. and W. Mattli (2011), *The New Global Rulers – Privatization of Regulation in the World Economy*, Princeton, NJ: Princeton University Press.
Cantelon H. and M. Letters (2000), 'The making of the IOC environmental policy as the third dimension of the Olympic movement', *International Review for the Sociology of Sport,* **35**, 294–308.
Chappelet, J.-L. and B. Kübler-Mabbott (2008), *The International Olympic Committee and the Olympic System: The Governance of World Sport*, 1st edn, Abingdon: Routledge.
Coglianese, C. and D. Lazer (2003), 'Management-based regulation: prescribing private management to achieve public goals', *Law & Society Review,* **37**, 691–730.
Craig, P. (2012), 'Subsidiarity: a political and legal analysis', *Journal of Common Market Studies* **15**, 72–87.
Dansero, E., B. Del Corpo, A. Mela and I. Ropolo. (2012), 'Olympic games, conflicts and social movements: the case of Torino 2006', in G. Hayes and J. Karamichas (eds), *Olympic Games, Mega-Events and Civil Societies*, Basingstoke, Hampshire: Palgrave Macmillan, pp. 195–218.
Dorf, M.C. and C.F. Sabel (1998), 'A constitution of democratic experimentalism', *Columbia Law Review* **98**, 267–473.
Eberlein, B., K.W. Abbott, J. Black, E. Meidinger and S. Wood (2014), 'Transnational business governance interactions: conceptualization and framework for analysis', *Regulation & Governance* **8**, 1–22.
Friedmann, J. and G. Wolff (1982), 'World city formation: an agenda for research and action', *International Journal of Urban and Regional Research* **6**, 309.
Giddens, A. (2000), *The Third Way and Its Critics*, Cambridge, UK: Polity Press.
Grabosky, P. (2013), 'Beyond responsive regulation: the expanding role of non-state actors in the regulatory process', *Regulation & Governance* **7**, 114–23.
Hall, P.G. (1966), *The World Cities,* London: Weidenfeld and Nicolson.

Hayes, G. and J. Karamichas (2012), 'Introduction: Sport mega-events, sustainable development and civil societies', in G. Hayes and J. Karamichas (eds). *Olympic Games, Mega-Events and Civil Societies*, Basingstoke, Hampshire: Palgrave Macmillan, pp. 1–27.
Herrschel, T. and P. Newman (2017), *Cities as International Actors: Urban and Regional Governance Beyond the Nation State*, London: Palgrave Macmillan.
Horne J. and W. Manzenreiter (eds) (2006), *Sports Mega-Events: Social Scientific Analyses of a Global Phenomenon*, Malden/Oxford: Blackwell Publishing.
Host City (2015), *IOC: Agenda 2020 Reforms Apply to Almaty and Beijing*, accessed 21 August 2019 at http://www.hostcity.com/news/event-bidding/ioc-agenda-2020-reforms-apply-almaty-and-beijing.
IOC (International Olympic Committee) (2010), *2018 Candidature Procedure and Questionnaire, XXIII Olympic Winter Games*, accessed 21 August 2019 at https://stillmed.olympic.org/media/Document%20Library/OlympicOrg/Documents/Host-City-Elections/XXIII-OWG-2018/Candidature-Acceptance-Procedure-for-the-XXIII-Olympic-Winter-Games-2018.pdf.
IOC (2012), *IOC Marketing: Media Guide*, accessed 21 August 2019 at http://www.olympic.org/Documents/IOC_Marketing/London_2012/IOC_Marketing_Media_Guide_2012.pdf.
IOC (2014a), *Lillehammer 1994 Set the Stage for Sustainable Games Legacies*, accessed 21 August 2019 at http://www.olympic.org/news/lillehammer-1994-set-the-stage-for-sustainable-games-legacies/219117.
IOC (2014b), *Olympic Agenda 2020: 20+20 Recommendations*, Lausanne: IOC, accessed 21 August 2019 at http://www.olympic.org/documents/olympic_agenda_2020/olympic_agenda_2020-20-20_recommendations-eng.pdf.
IOC (2016a), *A Sustainable Development Framework for London*, accessed 21 August 2019 at https://www.london.gov.uk/moderngov/Data/Environment%20Committee/20040318/Agenda/4%20Framework%20PDF.pdf.
IOC (2016b), *Election of the 2018 Host City*, accessed 21 August 2019 at https://www.olympic.org/2018-host-city-election.
IOC (2016c), *Host City Election for the Olympic Winter Games 2022*, accessed 21 August 2019 at https://www.olympic.org/2022-host-city-election.
IOC (2016d), *Olympic Games Candidature Process*, accessed 21 August 2019 at https://www.olympic.org/all-about-the-candidature-process.
IOC (2018), *Host City Contract Operational Requirements—June 2018*, accessed 21 August 2019 at https://stillmed.olympic.org/media/Document%20Library/OlympicOrg/Games/Host-City-Contract/HCC-Operational-Requirements.pdf.
IOC (2019), *Olympic Charter*, accessed 28 August 2019 at https://www.olympic.org/documents/olympic-charter.
ISO (International Organization for Standardization) (2012), *Sustainable Events with ISO 20121*, accessed 21 August 2019 at http://www.iso.org/iso/sustainable_events_iso_2012.pdf.
ISO (2013), *Event Sustainability Management – ISO 20121 Passes 2012 Olympic Games Test*, accessed 21 August 2019 at http://www.iso.org/iso/home/news_index/news_archive/news.htm?Refid=Ref1690.
ISO (2014), *Smart Cities Preliminary Report 2014*, accessed 21 August 2019 at https://www.iso.org/files/live/sites/isoorg/files/developing_standards/docs/en/smart_cities_report-jtc1.pdf.

ISO (2015), *How to Measure the Performance of Smart Cities*, accessed 21 August 2019 at https://www.iso.org/news/2015/10/Ref2001.html.

Kitchin, R. (2014), 'The Real-Time City? Big Data and Smart Urbanism', *GeoJournal,* **79**, 1–14.

LOCOG (London Organising Committee of the Olympic Games and Paralympic Games) (2004), *Candidature File*, accessed 21 August 2019 at http://webarchive.nationalarchives.gov.uk/20070305103412/http:/www.london2012.com/news/publications/candidate-file.php.

LOCOG (2009), *London 2012 Sustainability Plan: Towards a One Planet 2012*, 2nd edn, London: LOCOG.

LOCOG (2012), *London 2012 Post-Games Sustainability Report – A Legacy of Change*, London: LOCOG.

Los Angeles (2017), *LA2024 Candidature File Part 3*. accessed 21 August 2019 at https://la24-prod.s3.amazonaws.com/assets/pdf/LA2024-canditature-part3_english.pdf.

Myrholt, O. (1996), 'Greening the Olympics', *Our Planet* 8.2.

Paris (2017), *Paris 2024 Candidature File Part 3*, accessed 21 August 2019 at https://library.olympic.org.

Renou, X. (2012), 'Resisting the torch', in G. Hayes and J. Karamichas (eds), *Olympic Games, Mega-Events and Civil Societies*. Basingstoke, Hampshire: Palgrave Macmillan, pp. 236–46.

Riddlestone, S. (2014), *Turning 20 – A Look Back at Growing Up*, accessed 21 August 2019 at http://www.bioregional.com/blood-sweat-and-twenty-years-later.

Rio (2009), Rio de Janeiro 2016, Candidature File (on file with the author).

Roche, M. (2000), *Mega-Events and Modernity: Olympics and Expos in the Growth of Global Culture*, London: Routledge.

Sabel, C.F. and J. Zeitlin (2008), 'Learning from the difference: the new architecture of experimentalist governance in the EU', *European Law Journal,* **14** (3), 271–327.

Sabel, C.F. and J. Zeitlin (2012), 'Learning from difference: the new architecture of experimentalist governance in the EU', in C.F. Sabel and J. Zeitlin, *Experimentalist Governance in the European Union: Towards a New Architecture*, Oxford: Oxford University Press, pp. 1–28.

Sassen, S. (2001), *The Global City: New York, Tokyo, London,* 2nd edn, Princeton, NJ: Princeton University Press.

Schmidt, R. (2018), *Regulatory Integration Across Borders: Public-Private Cooperation in Transnational Regulation*, Cambridge: Cambridge University Press.

Slaughter, A.-M. (2004), *A New World Order*, Princeton, NJ: Princeton University Press.

Sustainability and Legacy Commission (2017), *Sustainable Development Is at the Heart of the Olympic Games*, accessed 21 August 2019 at https://www.olympic.org/sustainability-and-legacy-commission.

Whitson, D. (2012), 'Vancouver 2010: the saga of Eagleridge Bluffs', in G. Hayes and J. Karamichas (eds), *Olympic Games, Mega-Events and Civil Societies,* Basingstoke, Hampshire: Palgrave Macmillan, pp. 219–35

Wood, S. (2015), 'Transnational governance interactions: a critical review of the legal literature', *Osgoode Hall Law School Legal Studies Research Paper Series*, No. 35/2015, accessed 8 October 2019 at http://ssrn.com/abstract=2644465

Wood, S., K.W. Abbott, J. Black, B. Eberlein and E. Meidinger (2015), 'The interactive dynamics of transnational business governance: a challenge for transnational legal theory', *Transnational Legal Theory,* **6**, 333–69.

Woody, C. (2016), '"I have never faced a crisis like this": Rio's problems are growing worse as the Olympics get closer', *Business Insider*, 16 June, accessed 21 August 2019 at http://uk.businessinsider.com/brazil-olympics-violence-economic-ticket-sales-problems-2016-6?r=US&IR=T.

WWF Russia (No date), *2014 Olympics in Sochi*, accessed 21 August 2019 at https://wwf.ru/en/about/positions/sochi2014.

Yeung, K. (2010), 'The regulatory state', in R. Baldwin, M. Cave and M. Lodge (eds), *The Oxford Handbook of Regulation,* Oxford: OUP, p. 64–84.

5. Transnational governance of innovation in payment services: A case study of the Single Euro Payments Area

Jane K. Winn

5.1 INTRODUCTION

Payment systems are an essential element of the infrastructure of modern markets. Until very recently, they have generally been operated almost exclusively by banks. Even though the tempo of payment system innovation is accelerating, most modern systems still depend almost entirely on the legacy computer systems known as 'core banking systems', which allow banks to comply with regulatory requirements for operational risk. Banks at the cutting edge of technological innovation a generation ago now find themselves encumbered with aging computer systems they cannot easily replace, even as they must confront increasing pressure to become more nimble from regulators and disruptive payment service innovators.

Many years before the current wave of disruptive innovation in payment services erupted around the world, European Union regulators launched a project that became known as the Single Euro Payments Area (SEPA), which required the integration of many complex, incompatible legacy national payment systems into a single transnational payment system. This chapter analyses the SEPA project as a case study of how the challenges facing banks, regulators and innovators hoping to transform cross-border payment systems may be amplified if regulators disregard the importance of transnational business governance interactions (TBGIs). When EU regulators mandated the removal of barriers to cross-border electronic fund transfers (EFTs) in euros in 1999, they anticipated that the SEPA project could be completed within a couple of years. When work began on SEPA, neither banks nor regulators could have imagined that it would actually require nearly two decades to accomplish the task.

Viewed from one angle, modern payment systems are made up of private property in the form of bank computer systems and the digital artefacts representing money that move through them. Viewed from another angle, however, payment systems constitute an essential element of the infrastructure of modern markets and thus also display some properties of public goods. While ownership rights over private property are exclusive and private goods are exhausted once consumed, pure public goods can simultaneously be enjoyed by all citizens equally and cannot be exhausted by use. Fireworks displays, ideas outside the scope of intellectual property rights and national defence are classic examples of public goods (Cowen undated). Payment systems have public goods characteristics because they increase the liquidity of markets by making it easier to share information about the value of goods and services being exchanged, that is, prices. Financial stability can also be thought of as a public good (Holthausen and Rochet 2005; Evans and Schmalensee 2008). To ensure the stability of financial markets and markets for other goods and services, regulators establish prudential standards to safeguard the safety and soundness of payment systems. As a quid pro quo for the privilege of engaging in the banking business, banks are required to bear the costs of prudential regulation.

Controversy surrounding the banks' collective management of conventional payment systems has grown as a result of rapid changes in payment technologies and conditions in markets for payment services. The idea of unbundling payment services from the banking business is gaining traction because it is now technologically feasible for non-bank financial service providers to compete directly with banks. In addition, public scepticism is growing about the value of regulatory regimes that suppress competition, such as the one that sheltered banks from competition from non-bank payment services for most of the twentieth century. Although the basic business of banking – taking deposits and making loans – might once have overshadowed payment services in its strategic significance for banks, that is no longer true. Payment services have become a major profit centre for many banks, and hence of great strategic interest to them (see for example, Long 2016). But at the same time that bank regulators have realized that '[r]etail payments are the backbone of the real economy' (European Central Bank 2013, n.p.), they have also become more open to the idea of allowing disruptive FinTech (financial technology) innovators to offer new payment services in competition with banks, thus undermining the profitability of banks' payment services.

This chapter examines one example of this growing political controversy, the demand by EU regulators that European banks overhaul their systems for processing cross-border fund transfers as part of the process of building the internal market. European regulators' initial goal in launching the SEPA project was clear and simple: they wanted the difference between domestic and cross-border euro transfers to be eliminated for citizens within the Eurozone. When this policy was established in the late 1990s, sending EFTs within each European country was already quick and easy, but sending cross-border EFTs between the countries that planned to join the Eurozone was notoriously slow and expensive. The SEPA project was designed to erase the differences between domestic and cross-border euro transfers from the customers' perspective.

While end-user performance criteria were easy to specify, the business process reengineering challenges of getting there turned out to be immense, and were systematically underestimated by both regulators and industry. To meet risk management standards set by regulators while providing competitive services, most banks rely on 'core banking systems'. A core banking system is the 'underlying system of record for credits and debits that maintains transactions, histories and balances' (Geurden et al. 2016). Most banks began to use mainframe computers to run their core banking systems in the 1970s and 1980s. In later decades, new technologies were grafted onto aging legacy core banking systems to extend their functionality, resulting in systems that were ever more complex to maintain.

Just as refurbishing an airport while it remains in use is vastly more difficult than building a new one from scratch, the process of gradually migrating away from an aging legacy computer system to a new one is complex, expensive, slow and risky. In 2014, the UK Co-operative Bank wrote off the £300 million it had invested in its attempt to migrate to a new computer system when it was forced to admit that the effort had failed and it went back to using its old legacy system (Peppard and Thorp 2014). Yet trying to keep the old legacy system running may not work much better: In 2013, when UK bank RBS experienced a catastrophic failure of its aging legacy banking system following a botched software upgrade, its customers were denied access to their accounts for days or weeks and the cost to RBS topped £1 billion (Wilson 2013). Bank examiners charged with oversight of banks' operational risk management tend to be even more risk-averse than bankers, further complicating the process of decommissioning legacy core banking systems and replacing them with new systems (Crosman 2015).

During the 1970s and 1980s, different countries in Europe established national EFT systems that were integrated into the mainframe core banking systems of each country's banks. Each national EFT system was compatible with all the core banking systems in that country, but none of the national EFT systems was interoperable with the others. Cross-border fund transfers were slow and expensive because they had to be processed by hand, and merely changing the currency to euros on both sides of the transaction could not solve that problem. Banks were thus required to retrofit their legacy core banking systems to create the equivalent of a new pan-European network based on SEPA technology and business process standards.

No cost-benefit study was undertaken before the SEPA project was launched, and it appears that both regulators and banks grossly underestimated its costs. The problem of unexpectedly difficult and expensive technological problems was compounded by EU regulators' rejection of the notion that a pan-European EFT network constituted a public good. This denial made it easy for them to reject any obligation to ensure that the banks could in some way defray the cost of creating this network. The cost of modifying their legacy systems and business practices to accommodate the SEPA system thus fell squarely on the banks.

In recent years, EU regulators have unleashed on European banks a torrent of law reforms to accelerate the pace of innovation in European payment services. These include the E-Money Directive II,[1] the Payment Account Directive,[2] the Payment Services Directive 2,[3] the Interchange Fee Regulation,[4] and the Fourth Anti-Money Laundering Directive,[5] as well as all the technical standards issued by the European Banking Authority (EBA) in connection with these directives and regulations (see generally Winn 2017). While the years of effort invested in SEPA may have contributed something to the growth of TBGIs in the domain of payment services in Europe, it seems more likely to have hardened regulators' resolve to resort to mandatory regulation whenever they believe they detect recalcitrance on the part of industry. Although it is not yet clear whether the recent spate of EU law reforms designed to promote innovation and competition in European payment systems will enjoy any more success than SEPA did, it has already become clear that TBGIs – regulatory governance interactions in which banks themselves exercise authority in the performance of one or more components of a regulatory governance process across national borders (Eberlein et al. 2014) – are unlikely to play a major role in EU policy in the field of payment law reform in the future.

This chapter proceeds as follows. Part 2 describes how the rapid pace of technological innovation in financial services has fuelled the rise of new types of transnational business governance schemes in payment systems around the world, as well as contributing to the transformation of some traditional self-regulatory schemes, such as clearinghouses. Part 3 reviews the history of the troubled relationship between EU regulators and banks throughout the SEPA migration process as a case study of the difficulty of sustaining productive TBGIs in the face of unexpected obstacles to technological change. Part 4 assesses the likely legacy of SEPA in the field of EU payment law reform, comparing progress in building a pan-European real-time payment system with the controversy surrounding implementation of the 'open banking' mandate in the Payment Services Directive 2. Part 5 concludes by suggesting that EU regulators' ambivalence toward TBGIs in the domain of payment services may shed light on the EU's failure to achieve its Lisbon Agenda goals of increasing the global competitiveness of European businesses.

5.2 TRANSNATIONAL BUSINESS GOVERNANCE INTERACTIONS AND PAYMENT SYSTEMS

This chapter considers the impact of law reform efforts intended to accelerate the transformation of financial services using the TBGI analytical framework (Eberlein et al. 2014). Transnational business governance in this context refers to 'systematic efforts to regulate business that involve a significant degree of non-state authority in the performance of regulatory functions across national borders', while 'interactions' refer to 'the myriad ways in which governance actors and institutions engage with and react to one another' (Eberlein et al. 2014, p. 2). The TGBI framework helps to capture the complex interplay among global regulatory governance institutions, national regulators, private law regimes and private self-regulatory schemes.

A payment is the transfer of an abstract claim to value denominated in money (Proctor 2009, p. 9). Payment systems are networks through which economic agents transfer value together with information about those value transfers. As networks, payment systems may be characterized by strong network effects or positive externalities, because the value of a payment system for each user increases as a function of the total number of users of that network (see generally Shapiro and Varian 1999). Most payment systems are heavily regulated by governments, usually through oversight by a country's central bank, because such systems are an essential part of the infrastructure of markets. As such, their efficiency and stability can affect the productivity of a national economy as a whole. The strong network effects mentioned above tend to encourage concentration of payment systems into a single network, which may raise competition law issues (Weinberg 1996, p. 1). The anti-competitive impact of network effects on payment systems can be exacerbated if they operate as 'two sided markets', in which a platform operator (such as a card network) brings two different groups (such as retail merchants and consumers) together by charging one a relatively high price for access while subsidizing participation by the other (Rochet and Tirole 2003).

Long before political controversy erupted over the appropriate relationship between banks' payment systems and those operated by non-bank FinTech innovators, TBGIs were common in global financial markets. Two important global governance institutions that influence national payment system regulations through 'soft law' guidance are the Committee for Market and Payment Infrastructures (CMPI), based in Basel, and the Financial Action Task Force (FATF), established to increase coordination among national regulators in the fight against money laundering. Payment system risks have always been a central focus of the Basel Committee on Banking Supervision (Basel Committee), founded in 1974 following an international banking crisis triggered by the failure of Bank Herstatt to settle its cross-border payment obligations (Bank for International Settlements 2018). The CMPI, the Basel Committee's sister body, is the most important transnational regulatory governance body focused on payment systems issues. Its roots date back to 1980 (Bank for International Settlements 2016). Operators of global payment networks such as the Society for Worldwide Interbank Financial Telecommunications (SWIFT) business-to-business EFT network, and payment card networks maintained by Visa, MasterCard and UnionPay, serve as important global self-regulatory schemes with regard to the transactions executed over their systems.

These emerging global payment regulatory schemes generally take effect by influencing national regulatory frameworks. The regulatory oversight of payment systems is normally one element of a larger process of assuring the safety and soundness of national banking systems. The intensity of the regulatory oversight imposed on payment systems may be one reason that global technology giants such as Google have not yet tried to launch a 'digitally native' bank to compete head on with traditional banks. Zac Townsend, founder of a successful FinTech start-up, explained the problem in these terms:

> The problems are primarily regulatory. It is very hard to buy a bank. It is very hard to capitalize it. Banks are very restricted in their operations. Regulators are very scared of innovation. They are very scared of a bank that does not make money in the way that other banks make money. The reason they're uncomfortable is the reason we all should be uncomfortable: banks aren't really meant to make money. They're meant to serve as a rock-solid repository for other people's money. . . . The question is, 'Could you actually operate a bank like a technology company?' The answer is probably no. And I'll give you the simplest reason, which is what every regulator has told me: they are uncomfortable with

> a bank that grows more than 20 percent year over year. The number one historical indicator of a bank that is about to go belly-up is one that has a lot of growth. But a good Silicon Valley start-up grows 20 percent month over month. (Ross 2016, p. 169)

While new payment services offered by innovative FinTech start-up companies garner a great deal of media attention, the day-to-day operations of the electronic payment systems that are part of the economic foundation of most modern economies still depend largely on banks' aging legacy core banking systems. Like a duck that appears to float serenely on the surface of the water while its feet paddle madly just below, the massive scale of the computing functions performed by core banking systems may appear effortless to a bank customer making an automated teller machine (ATM) withdrawal. But enormous computing resources may be required to achieve that appearance of effortlessness: while Google's vast data centres are capable of processing 60 000 searches per second, mainframe computers in banks can be capable of handling more than 1 million transactions per second (Smith 2014). Legacy bank computer systems tend to be rigid, complex and increasingly difficult to maintain or modify, while the information technology systems used by the banks' disruptive competitors tend to be flexible, modular and relatively easy to modify in response to changing requirements (Quintero et al. 2015).

While it may be obvious to everyone in the banking industry that legacy core banking systems will have to be overhauled before the revolutionary potential of disruptive FinTech innovation can be fully realized, there is no sign that either politicians or regulators, constrained by lingering popular hostility to banks left over from the Global Financial Crisis, have figured that out. Banking industry experts have come up with a variety of colourful metaphors to describe how difficult it is for a bank to replace its legacy core banking system with something fit for purpose for financial markets today:

- Trying to change engines on an airliner at 30 000 feet (Kelly 2014 7.10 p. 55);
- Trying to build a Tesla from a Model T foundation (Belmaker 2016);
- Trying to perform multiple heart transplants simultaneously on the same patient (Planet Compliance 2016); and
- Undergoing open heart surgery with your eyes open and no anaesthesia (Crosman 2013).

Although legacy bank computer systems may not be able to provide bank customers the same end-user experience that their disruptive competitors offer, they do provide a definitive system of record that maintains absolute data consistency throughout all of the bank's computer systems at all times. Consistent with CPMI standards on the management of risk in payment systems and Basel Committee operational risk standards, banking supervisors in advanced economies will not permit banks to use the kinds of flexible, loosely coupled information technology systems that their more nimble competitors use, if doing so would lead to any deterioration in the capacity, speed, accuracy, security or availability of their core system of record processes. With no safe, obvious transition path away from their aging legacy systems, and under constant pressure to reduce costs and solve urgent problems, bank managers may feel they have no choice but to keep piling more temporary fixes on top of systems already buckling under the strain (Louwe Kooijmans et al. 2012, p. 1; Matthan 2016).

In some respects, the problem of legacy system modernization resembles the Year 2000 (Y2K) software glitch that received considerable attention at the end of the twentieth century. Earlier generations of programmers truncated the year to two digits instead of four to save precious resources at a time when processing capacity was limited. So there was concern that when the year 2000 arrived, software programs containing two-digit years might crash if they interpreted the beginning of the new century as 1900 rather than 2000. The problem was the same across all computer systems, and while Y2K remediation might have been expensive, there was a clear consensus on what needed to be done: change the dates in the old programs to four digits. The problem of aging core banking systems is also related to the limitations of outdated information system design principles, but is immensely more complex and varied than Y2K problems, because each bank's core banking system was unique when it was built, and has only become more unique as it has been extended and updated over many years. Furthermore, no clear consensus has emerged among banks, technology vendors and regulators about the best design for the next generation of powerful bank computer systems. This compounds the challenges facing bank executives and directors trying to navigate a way out of this maze.

5.3 THE SINGLE EURO PAYMENTS AREA

As the project to create a single European currency was taking shape in the 1990s, EU regulators decided that individuals in the Eurozone should be able to transfer euros across borders within the Eurozone as quickly and easily as they transfer them within their own country. From a policy perspective, this goal was a 'natural consequence' of the broader policy goal of uniting the Single Market under a common currency (European Central Bank 2006, p. 4). The clarity of this general purpose was not matched with equal decisiveness in its execution, however. Because EU regulators did not view the new market infrastructure they required as a public good, they did not see any reason to allocate any public resources to pay for its construction. In an early work in the nascent field of law and economics, then law professor, later judge Richard Posner described the practice of 'taxation by regulation' as arising when governments choose not to pay directly for public services out of their own tax revenues, but to require a regulated industry to use profits earned from other activities to subsidize the provision of those public services (Posner 1971, p. 22). Because constructing the new pan-European payment system generated no new revenues for the banks to offset the cost to them of constructing it, EU regulators were in effect requiring European banks to use cross-subsidies to cover those costs.

Before the 1992 Treaty on the European Union (the Maastricht Treaty) authorized creation of a common currency as the next step toward European Monetary Union, ensuring the technical interoperability of national payment systems had not been a concern of European policymakers. Cross-border wholesale electronic payments were handled efficiently within the SWIFT network, and the volume of cross-border retail electronic payments was small (Committee of Governors of the Central Banks of the Member States of the European Economic Community 1992, p. 285). Starting as early as the 1960s in some countries and finishing as late as the 1980s in others, the banking industry of each EU member state, in collaboration with its national central bank, had set up a national automated clearing and settlement system for domestic payment transactions. By the time the goal of a single currency was established in 1992, each member state had its own automated clearing house (ACH) with its own national policies, procedures, technical specifications and governance mechanisms. None of the national systems had been designed to interoperate with any other national systems.

Creating a pan-European infrastructure for fund transfers in euros became a high priority for EU regulators over the course of the 1990s (European Monetary Institute 1996). While most domestic fund transfer systems in Europe were fully automated by the 1990s, cross-border transfers were still processed manually through a system of correspondent banks, resulting in high costs and slow processing times (European Central Bank 1999, p. 5). In studies conducted the early 1990s, the Commission discovered that the average cost of a cross-border transfer was the equivalent of € 24 for a transfer of € 100 at a time when the corresponding cost of most domestic fund transfers in Europe was measured in pennies. In 1999, the European Central Bank (ECB) found that fees had not come down much: they ranged from € 3.50 to € 26 for smaller amounts and from € 31 to € 400 for larger amounts. In addition, while the processing times for domestic payment transactions were 1–3 days, cross-border transactions averaged 4.8 days, with 15 percent taking more than a week. Furthermore, banks in some countries charged additional fees for balance of payments reporting, currency conversion, postage and other communication charges.

In 1999, European regulators informed European banks that they were expected to find a way to eliminate the difference in cost and processing times for domestic and cross-border euro transfers as quickly as possible – preferably in time for the launch of the new euro notes and coins on 1 January 2002 (European Central Bank 1999, p. 12). The banks were reluctant to undertake the difficult, expensive process of reengineering their domestic EFT networks to support a common European standard when only about one percent of all the EFTs they processed involved cross-border transactions. While EU regulators did not deny that current transaction volumes were low, they believed that once the vicious cycle of low transaction volumes and high fees suppressing consumer demand was broken, latent demand would surface (European Central Bank 1999, p. 12).

The ECB also decided not to assume direct responsibility for operating a new European-level ACH for small-value euro payments, but instead to assume the role of a 'catalyst for change' by engaging in a dialogue with banks about how best to achieve the goal of creating a new 'domestic' fund transfer system for the Eurozone (European Central Bank 1999, p. 15). By contrast, the ECB took the lead in developing TARGET (Trans-European Automated Real-time Gross Settlement Express Transfer System), a new pan-European large-value payment fund transfer system launched in 1999, because it was responsible for the safety and soundness of European banks, and large-value fund transfer systems pose systemic risks to the banking system that small-value fund transfer systems do not (European Central Bank 1999, p. 8). Furthermore, because the Euro Banking Association had already created the EURO1 network and many national ACHs had already set up bilateral relationships with other national ACHs, there was no evidence that a new small-value payment network operated by the ECB was needed. Although neither EURO1 nor the bilateral arrangements had yet achieved significant transaction volumes, this was attributed to the continued dependence on manual rather than automated processes (European Central Bank 1999, pp. 9–10).

In its new role as the catalyst for change in Eurozone payments, the ECB informed the banks in 1999 that it expected whatever kind of new cross-border service they devised to be capable of providing the equivalent of domestic 'straight-through processing' services by 2002 (European Central Bank 1999, p. 7). The ECB held up the highly centralized and automated Visa and MasterCard networks in Europe as examples of what should be possible for cross-border EFTs (European Central Bank 1999, pp. 8–9). The ECB noted that the European Committee for Banking Standards had already developed the International Bank Account Number (IBAN), International Payment Instruction (IPI) and Bank Identifier Code (BIC) standards (European Central Bank 1999, p. 10; Janczuk-Gorywoda 2015). There is no evidence that EU regulators were aware that making changes in the format of account numbers could be a complex and difficult undertaking for banks with aging legacy core banking systems. Before changing the format of the text of an EFT instruction to achieve interoperability across different software applications, a bank must analyse its existing system of internal controls to make sure that the bank's exposure to operational risks is not increased by any of the technical changes being made and it remains in compliance with all its regulatory obligations. In addition, dozens, hundreds or even thousands of separate software applications would have to be modified.

As the 2002 target date for the launch of euro notes and coins approached, EU regulators realized little progress was being made in establishing the pan-European EFT system they believed was necessary to the success of the euro. EU regulators then shifted to a new channel of communication to ensure that their message would be received and interpreted correctly by the banks. Late in 2001, the Commission issued a regulation setting the price of cross-border euro transfers equal to the price of domestic euro transfers,[6] which abruptly transformed cross-border euro transfer activities from a profitable line of business into one that haemorrhaged money. Representatives of the European banking industry met in May 2002 to come up with a strategy for mitigating the losses they were now suffering as a result of the EU's taxation-by-regulation strategy. After the meeting, they issued a strategy paper, Euroland: Our Single Euro Payments Area (European Payments Council 2002), describing the strategy they had devised. In June 2002, the bankers established the European Payments Council (EPC), composed of representatives of 65 banks representing all categories of European banks (such as commercial banks and saving banks), several banking industry trade associations and the Euro Banking Association. The EPC immediately began work developing standards, rulebooks and frameworks that would be the foundation of a pan-European interoperable fund transfer system.

In 2001, when the banks realized that the Commission was preparing to mandate lower prices for cross-border euro payments, they proposed a Multilateral Interchange Fee Convention permitting an interchange fee of € 3 to be charged to help defray the costs of building the SEPA system. Such an interchange fee would have created a financial incentive similar to those provided by the international Visa and MasterCard card networks to drive adoption of the new SEPA network. The Commission was already embroiled in a long-running battle with the card networks over the level of interchange fees they charged, however, and so was unwilling to agree to such an incentive system for SEPA.[7] After the Commission rejected the interchange fee proposal, the banks were left with no viable mechanism for recovering the costs of reengineering their national ACH systems to conform to SEPA standards. Yet EU regulators continued to expect prompt compliance notwithstanding the lack any viable cost recovery mechanism, repeatedly expressing their frustration with the slow pace of progress:

> Despite efforts on the part of the European public institutions, the banking sector has failed to address in a serious manner the issue of cross-border retail payments in euro and the situation remains highly unsatisfactory. (European Central Bank 2001, p. 6)

EU regulators felt entitled to exercise a veto over any part of the SEPA migration process that was not to their liking, and at the same time, without any sense of irony, they also insisted that it was really a market-driven process through which the banks should respond to market demand (see for example, European Central Bank 2010, p. 9):

> . . . the EPC has so far made very little visible progress in meeting the expectations of euro area citizens, who want all credit transfers in the euro area to be domestic, implying that national schemes, standards and business practices must be replaced by pan-European ones. (European Central Bank 2004, p. 12)

When European regulators denied the banks' request to create incentives for participating in the SEPA migration process with interchange fees, they overlooked the fact that, to the extent that payment systems provide equal access to liquidity and stability to all market participants, they operate as a form of public good. Producers of public goods have difficulty recouping their production costs because they cannot exclude anyone from enjoying their output; the result is often market failure in the form of underproduction of those public goods. Had EU regulators recognized that payment systems embody the characteristics of both public and private goods, they could have anticipated that not allowing interchange fees would undermine SEPA migration.

In 2002, the EPC issued the Convention on a Basic Standard for Euro Retail Cross-Border Credit Transfers in the Countries of the EU (the Credeuro Convention) and in 2003, the Interbank Charging Principles Convention (Wandhofer 2011). The implementation of these early efforts at creating the equivalent of a domestic euro scheme for the Single Market was based largely on the efforts of the major banks that had previously operated the correspondent banking system; in effect, it permitted other banks to outsource the processing of cross-border euro transactions to those banks rather than coming into compliance themselves. In 2006, the Commission made it clear that any solution not based on full participation of all participants in the system would not be acceptable:

> [SEPA] will be deemed a success when the full potential of economies of scale and scope and competition are realised with the euro-zone. This means savings for users and lower costs for providers. This vision does not allow for developments that will only take us half the way. A mini-SEPA that only delivers solutions for cross-border payments in Europe is not acceptable. (European Commission 2006, p. 4)

At a 2006 OECD Policy Roundtable focused on competition policy for payment card networks, Weibe Ruttenberg of the ECB affirmed the fundamentally political nature of the SEPA project when he said: 'For banks, SEPA is not an option. It will be implemented. Should banks fail to deliver, a structure will be put in place.'[8]

So the EPC went back to the drawing board to develop more comprehensive schemes. In 2008, the SEPA Credit Transfer scheme was officially launched, followed by the SEPA direct debit scheme in 2009 (see European Payments Council 2019a, b for current information). That same year, the EU repealed its 2001 Regulation on cross-border euro payments,[9] replacing it with a Regulation that expanded the scope of pricing parity between domestic and cross-border euro transfers to cover more types of payments and pushed for greater use of the new IBAN standard in cross-border euro payments.[10] To facilitate the implementation of the SEPA direct debit scheme, the new Regulation authorized banks to collect an interchange fee of € 0.088 from 2009 to 2012; a subsequent Regulation in 2012 authorized banks to collect an interchange fee in connection with direct debit transactions that were reversed.[11] What the banks had been hoping for would have generated significantly more fee income than these two limited exceptions to regulators' no interchange fee policy.

By 2010, however, it had become clear that simply removing barriers to migration to the new SEPA schemes would never be enough to bring SEPA migration to a conclusion, in the absence of significant incentives to participate. The banks lobbied EU regulators for help concluding the SEPA project (European Payments Council 2010). In 2012, the EU Parliament and Council complied by issuing the SEPA End Date Regulation, which made the use of the EPC schemes mandatory even for purely domestic euro transfers within a single Eurozone country. The regulation set 1 February 2014 as the end date for the use of non-SEPA compliant fund transfer schemes for euro countries and 31 October 2016 for non-euro countries.[12]

There is no evidence that, when EU regulators issued the original mandate to Eurozone banks to construct what later became known as SEPA, either the regulators or the banks conducted any form of cost-benefit analysis. In the 1990s, when EU regulators developed their basic vision of SEPA, they were under no legal obligation to develop realistic estimates of what it would cost the banks to build the pan-European EFT network they envisaged. While the notion of cost-benefit analysis for EU action was established in 1992 with the Maastricht Treaty,[13] it was not until 2002 that the EU required a regulatory impact assessment for all major projects and legislation.[14] With no formal framework for estimating costs and benefits, the magnitude of costs of getting every commercial bank, savings bank, cooperative bank, corporate biller and small and medium-sized enterprise that sent or received payments by electronic fund transfer all enrolled in a new pan-European system were not apparent to either EU regulators or European bankers. Had leaders of the EU banking industry realized in the 1990s what a burden SEPA migration would become, it is easy in retrospect to guess that they might have pushed back harder. Once EU regulators had control over the SEPA migration agenda, however, the banks were never able to retake the initiative.

5.4 MANDATING THE TRANSFORMATION OF PAYMENT SYSTEMS

The conventional wisdom about the delays associated with the SEPA migration process places the blame squarely at the banks' feet:

> The introduction of a new intra-bank payments system which is supposed to speed up financial transactions across the European Union has been delayed as a result of 'lazy banks...dragging their heels', a leading business group has claimed. (Pope 2014, unpaginated; see also Kleiss 2011)

A more careful examination suggests, however, that the relative paucity of TBGIs among regulators and industry during the SEPA migration process might have made it difficult for the industry to educate regulators about the challenges they faced, such as legacy system modernization. In a classic work on public administration published in 1936, John Gaus noted:

> Much of the effort of public administration today is rightly expended upon establishing procedures and agencies whereby the general policy enacted in the law and application with the active collaboration of groups of citizens most affected . . . [O]nly this process of conference, adjustment, statement and restatement of facts and opinions will bring any widespread conviction to a substantial group of citizens that the resulting policy is their policy and that the administrators of it are their officials. (Gaus 1936, quoted in Lynn 2001, p. 150).

While such collaborative dialogue may exist between regulators and the banking industry within each individual member state, the long, slow, difficult process of completing the SEPA project suggests how difficult it may be to reproduce that type of collaborative dialogue at the EU level.

Although bankers may generally be perceived as quite effective in lobbying to advance their interests in political and regulatory arenas, in the years following the Global Financial Crisis widespread popular hostility toward banks generally may have limited the effectiveness of such efforts (Nelson 2009; Leopold 2010; Masters 2010). Furthermore, the banks themselves appear to have miscalculated the importance and difficulty of what EU regulators were demanding in the late 1990s, perhaps because operational issues are routinely accorded less weight by managers in their strategic thinking than revenue generating activities. European banks appear not to have taken very seriously regulators' early entreaties to reduce the high costs of cross-border fund transfers within the Single Market, only snapping to attention when it became clear that the regulators had found a way to shift those costs away from bank customers and onto the banks with the 2001 cross-border euro payments Regulation.[15] The banks are hardly alone in making such miscalculations: ignoring complex, difficult business process reengineering problems or underestimating their cost are common management responses to the need for large, complex business process reengineering projects (Clemons et al. 1995).

The banks' miscalculations appear to have been exacerbated by unwarranted optimism among European regulators that the goals of the Lisbon Strategy would soon be realized. Launched in 2000, the Lisbon Strategy's aim was to make Europe 'the most competitive and dynamic knowledge-based economy in the world capable of sustainable economic growth with more and better jobs and greater social cohesion' (European Parliament 2000, para 5). By any objective measure, the Lisbon Strategy did not succeed, although the causes of its failure remain a subject of considerable debate (Wyplosz 2010). Unwarranted optimism about the feasibility of Lisbon Strategy goals in connection with the SEPA project manifested themselves in the form of pronouncements that a 'market-driven' policy could generate essential infrastructure for the Single Market without recourse to outsourcing, interchange fees or distorting cross-subsidies. If EU regulators had been more familiar with the scale and severity of the banks' legacy computer system problems and the concerns of bank examiners about the risks of trying to migrate from those legacy systems to newer systems, they might have been less impatient with the slow progress in completing the SEPA project. But as the president of Estonia, the most digital nation in Europe, noted: 'We don't have, in Europe at least, people at the policy-making level who understand what IT is about' (quoted in Ross 2016, p. 246).

Had the EPC had been permitted by regulators to play a larger role in the SEPA migration process, TBGIs might also have played a greater role in the SEPA migration process. The TBGI framework identifies six components of regulatory governance: agenda-setting, norm formation, implementation, monitoring, enforcement and evaluation/review (Eberlein et al. 2014, p. 6). EU regulators set the agenda for SEPA and in response industry established the EPC to coordinate their response and lower their cost of complying with the 2001 cross-border payments Regulation. In 2013, the ECB formally removed any vestigial agenda-setting authority the EPC might have accrued over the course of the SEPA migration process, and gave a newly created Euro Retail Payments Board (ERPB) under its direct control full responsibility for setting retail payments policy in Europe. If the EPC had been granted sufficient autonomy to oversee the SEPA migration process generally rather than merely being responsible for developing the schemes governing technical aspects of implementation, then outsourcing, interchange fees or both might have played a role. The EPC struggled to achieve implementation of the SEPA Credit and Debit schemes because – notwithstanding EU regulators' confidence that latent demand for cross-border fund transfers would emerge once a pan-European framework was in place – no compelling economic incentive for compliance ever emerged. The fact that full compliance with the SEPA could not be achieved without a legislative mandate supports the argument that the payment network created by SEPA should be seen as a public good paid for via 'taxation by regulation' imposed on the banking industry. Because SEPA schemes govern both technology and business processes, after the SEPA end date passed and older national EFT systems were decommissioned, any bank wishing to participate in SEPA had no choice but to comply. So although the EPC has no enforcement duties per se, it continuously monitors how SEPA schemes are being used and works with industry to keep them updated.

In 2014, the ERPB noted with concern the rise of 'instant payment' schemes in Eurozone domestic markets, and invited the EPC to develop a plan for an EU-level response (ERPB Secretariat 2015). Instant payment schemes are payment services that operate on a 24/7/365 basis providing real-time or near real-time settlement, unlike traditional EFT systems, which normally operate only Monday to Friday during banking hours and settle one or two days after a transaction originates. The ERPB approved the plan that the EPC presented in 2015 to launch the effort to develop an 'SCT Inst' (SEPA Credit Transfer-Instant) payment scheme in 2016. The new system went live in 2017, and a public consultation was planned for 2018 to provide the foundation for the first update of the SCT Inst scheme. While it is too soon to know whether the SCT Inst scheme will be a success, it is clear that the ERPB recognized the value the EPC could provide in terms of mobilizing bank support for a pan-European competitor to domestic euro instant payment schemes.

But the arrival of the 2018 deadline for banks' compliance with the 'open banking' mandate in the 2015 Payment Services Directive 2 found EU regulators reluctant to engage in a collaborative dialogue with the industry most affected by the law reform. The open banking mandate brings new third-party payment services under the oversight of national regulators and, in return, requires banks to accept instructions from their customers granting those third-party payment services direct access to their bank accounts. In order to safeguard the privacy and security of bank customers' information, banks and third-party payment services are required to use 'strong customer authentication'. Both the mandate to accommodate customer requests to allow third-party payment services to access their accounts and the mandate to use strong customer authentication place enormous regulatory compliance burdens on banks still struggling to modernize their legacy computer systems. Responsibility for developing regulatory technical standards that would make it possible both for the third-party payment services to have easy access to their users' bank accounts and for the banks to restrict access to their customers' accounts to remain in compliance with operational risk standards fell to the EBA.

These strong authentication standards became a political football as conflict escalated in 2017 among the banking industry, new payment services, the EBA and the Commission over how the open banking mandate would be implemented (Srivastava and Powell 2017). The EBA published a Discussion Paper in 2015 setting out its preliminary analysis of the issues. After the EBA analysed the many responses it received to its Discussion Paper, it published a Consultation Paper in 2016 containing a draft regulatory technical standard for comment. In consultation with the ECB, the EBA analysed the even larger number of responses it received to its Consultation Paper and in February 2017 issued its final proposal for a regulatory technical standard for strong customer authentication. The Commission found the EBA's final proposal too accommodating of the banks' concerns, however, and in May 2017, exercised its prerogative to change the EBA's final proposal. In June 2017, the EBA responded by objecting to the Commission's changes. In November 2017, the Commission responded to that criticism by modifying some of the changes it had earlier made in the EBA's text, but in December 2017, the EBA complained that it had not even been consulted before the latest round of changes were made. The Commission responded in February 2018 by assuring the EBA that the Commission had taken its concerns into account in the November revisions (Reid and Chertkow 2018). The final regulatory technical standard became effective in March 2018.[16]

Under the 2010 European Banking Authority Regulation, the EBA has the authority to develop regulatory technical standards as part of the process of implementing EU-level banking law reforms, when requested to do so by the Commission.[17] As part of its standard-setting mandate, the EBA works to facilitate a broad consensus amongst all interested stakeholder groups to support the regulatory technical standards it issues. While this is a very different process than the voluntary consensus process characteristic of standard setting in the United States (Office of Technology Assessment 1992; Winn 2009, pp. 185–219), the standard-setting processes managed by the EBA nevertheless appear to be open, transparent and as pragmatic as possible. The fact that the Commission felt so free to disregard the EBA's expert opinion reflecting the deliberative processes it facilitated as cavalierly as it disregarded the EPC's expert opinions reflecting the deliberative processes it had facilitated a decade earlier during the SEPA implementation process does not bode well for the future success of the EU's open banking mandate.

5.5 CONCLUSION

When EU regulators required European banks to reengineer their national payment systems in order to create a new pan-European electronic fund transfer system, they believed they were acting as the catalyst of a market-driven reform process. The challenges that surfaced during the SEPA migration process call to mind the challenges that surfaced in another epic construction project dogged by controversy and cost overruns: the Sydney Opera House. Started in 1957 with a budget of AUD $7 million and an estimated completion date of 1963, the Sydney Opera House was not finished until 1973 at a cost of $102 million, more than one thousand per cent over budget. Like the Danish architect Jørn Utzon, who blamed the Australian contractors for the cost overruns and delays, EU regulators attributed the slow pace of progress in achieving SEPA to industry recalcitrance. Such an explanation, however, overlooks the possibility that the project design itself was flawed.

After EU regulators required banks to set the price of cross-border at the same level as domestic euro transfers, the banks responded by creating the EPC to take the lead on developing technologies that could lower the banks' cost of compliance. The EPC's early promise as a self-regulatory organization intended to facilitate productive TBGIs that might have lowered the cost and reduced the time required to complete SEPA was never realized, however, because regulators incessantly overrode whatever industry consensus emerged within the EPC. EU regulators' interest in fostering TBGIs faded once it became clear that the EPC could not guarantee rapid implementation of SEPA and that that it was getting bogged down in controversy. Industry interest in using the EPC to foster TBGIs was undermined by the lack of any concrete, immediate economic payoff for participating in it. Neither regulators nor industry factored in the cost of legacy system modernization when SEPA was launched; as the enormous cost compliance with regulators' political vision of a single market later became clear to industry, impatient regulators were no longer in any mood to engage in evidence-based policy-making.

The problems that emerged during the SEPA migration process can help shed some light on the EU's failure to achieve its Lisbon Strategy goals of increasing the global competitiveness of European businesses. While EU regulators felt comfortable attributing to themselves the role of catalyst, they were clearly not comfortable allowing the EPC to play such a role. As the EPC's autonomy to engage in agenda-setting or norm formation outside the realm of technical standards was curtailed, the possibility that TBGIs might develop and smooth the path toward SEPA implementation faded. As regulators became increasingly frustrated by what appeared to them to be inexplicable delays, they resorted to ever more heavy-handed measures to compel industry's compliance with their wishes, which in turn made it ever less likely that they would develop a clear understanding of the root causes of the delays that could inform their policy choices going forward. While the collaborative dialogue between the EPC and ECB with regard to developing a pan-European instant payment scheme shows great promise as an arena within which

TBGIs might develop, implementation of the Payment Services Directive 2's open banking mandate appears likely to suffer from the same downward spiral of frustrated expectations on the part of regulators unwilling or unable to factor commercial realities into their policy calculus.

NOTES

1. Directive 2009/110/EC of the European Parliament and of the Council of 16 September 2009 on the taking up, pursuit and prudential supervision of the business of electronic money institutions amending Directives 2005/60/EC and 2006/48/EC and repealing Directive 2000/46/EC [2009] OJ L267/7 (E-Money Directive II).
2. Directive 2014/92/EU of the European Parliament and of the Council of 23 July 2014 on the comparability of fees related to payment accounts, payment account switching and access to payment accounts with basic features [2014] OJ L 257/214 (Payment Account Directive).
3. Directive (EU) 2015/2366 of the European Parliament and of the Council of 25 November 2015 on payment services in the internal market, amending Directives 2002/65/EC, 2009/110/EC and 2013/36/EU and Regulation (EU) No 1093/2010, and repealing Directive 2007/64/EC [2015] OJ L337/35 (Payment Services Directive 2).
4. Regulation (EU) 2015/751 of the European Parliament and of the Council of 29 April 2015 on interchange fees for card-based payment transactions [2015] OJ L123/1 (Interchange Fee Regulation).
5. Directive (EU) 2015/849 of the European Parliament and of the Council of 20 May 2015 on the prevention of the use of the financial system for the purposes of money laundering or terrorist financing, amending Regulation (EU) No 648/2012 of the European Parliament and of the Council, and repealing Directive 2005/60/EC of the European Parliament and of the Council and Commission Directive 2006/70/EC [2015] OJ L141/73 (Fourth Anti-Money Laundering Directive).
6. Regulation (EC) 2560/2001 of the European Parliament and of the Council of 19 December 2001 on cross-border payments in euro [2001] OJ L344/13 (Cross-Border Euro Payments Regulation 1), repealed by Regulation (EC) 924/2009 of the European Parliament and of the Council of 16 September 2009 on cross-border payments in the Community and repealing Regulation (EC) No 2560/2001 [2009] OJ L266/11 (Cross-Border Euro Payments Regulation 2).
7. Opinion of the Economic and Social Committee on the 'Proposal for a Regulation of the European Parliament and of the Council on Cross-border Payments in Euro' (2002/C 48/29) [2002] OJ C48/141, para 2.12.
8. Organisation for Economic Co-Operation and Development, Directorate For Financial and Enterprise Affairs, Competition Committee, *Competition and Efficient Use of Payment* Cards, 4 October 2007, DAF/COMP (2006) 32, p. 355.
9. Cross-Border Euro Payments Regulation 1.
10. Cross-Border Euro Payments Regulation 2.
11. Regulation (EU) 260/2012/EU of the European Parliament and of the Council of 14 March 2012 establishing technical and business requirements for credit transfers and direct debits in euro and amending Regulation (EC) No 924/2009 [2012] OJ L94/22.
12. Ibid., amended by Regulation (EU) 248/2014/EU of the European Parliament and of the Council of 26 February 2014 amending Regulation (EU) No 260/2012 as regards the migration to Union-wide credit transfers and direct debits [2014] OJ L84/1 (SEPA End Date Regulation).
13. Treaty on European Union, 7 February 1992 [1992] OJ C191/1, art 130R (now art 174(3)).
14. European Commission, 'Communication from the Commission on Impact Assessment' (Communication) COM (2002) 276 final.

15. Cross-Border Euro Payments Regulation 1.
16. Commission Delegated Regulation (EU) 2018/389 of 27 November 2017 supplementing Directive (EU) 2015/2366 of the European Parliament and of the Council with regard to regulatory technical standards for strong customer authentication and common and secure open standards of communication [2018] OJ L69/23.
17. Regulation (EU) 1093/2010 of the European Parliament and of the Council of 24 November 2010 establishing a European Supervisory Authority (European Banking Authority), amending Decision No 716/2009/EC and repealing Commission Decision 2009/78/EC [2010] OJ L331/12 (European Banking Authority Regulation), recitals 21–6 and arts 8(2) and 10–16.

REFERENCES

Bank for International Settlements (BIS) (2016), *About the CPMI*, accessed 8 April 2019 at https://www.bis.org/cpmi/info.htm?m=3%7C16%7C29.

Bank for International Settlements (BIS) (2018), *History of the Basel Committee*, accessed 8 April 2019 at http://www.bis.org/bcbs/history.htm.

Belmaker, Gidon (2016), 'Why banks refuse to upgrade core banking systems', *Tearsheet*, 24 August, accessed 8 April 2019 at http://www.tearsheet.co/uncategorized/why-banks-refuse-to-upgrade-core-banking-systems.

Clemons, Erik K., Matt E. Thatcher and Michael C. Row (1995), 'Identify sources of reengineering failures: a study of the behavioral factors contributing to reengineering risks', *Journal of Management Information Systems*, **12** (2), 9–36.

Committee of Governors of the Central Banks of the Member States of the European Economic Community (1992), *Payment Systems in EC Member States (Blue Book)*, 1st edn, Frankfurt: Committee of Governors of the Central Banks of the Member States of the European Economic Community, accessed 8 April 2019 at https://www.ecb.europa.eu/paym/intro/book/html/index.en.html.

Cowen, Tyler (undated), 'Public goods', *The Library of Economics and Liberty, Basic Concepts Collection*, accessed 8 April 2019 at http://www.econlib.org/library/Enc/PublicGoods.html.

Crosman, Penny (2013), 'Can big four core banking vendors' oligopoly be broken?', *American Banker*, 7 October, accessed 8 April 2019 at https://www.americanbanker.com/news/can-big-four-core-banking-vendors-oligopoly-be-broken.

Crosman, Penny (2015), 'Small banks take a test flight in the cloud', *American Banker*, 21 July, accessed 8 April 2019 at https://www.americanbanker.com/news/small-banks-take-a-test-flight-in-the-cloud.

Eberlein, Burkard, Kenneth W. Abbott, Julia Black, Errol Meidinger and Stepan Wood (2014), 'Transnational business governance interactions: conceptualization and framework for analysis', *Regulation & Governance*, **8** (1), 1–21.

ERPB Secretariat (2015), *Annual Report of the Euro Retail Payments Board 2014-2015*, Frankfurt: European Central Bank, accessed 8 April 2019 at https://www.ecb.europa.eu/paym/retpaym/euro/html/index.en.html.

European Central Bank (1999), *Improving Cross-Border Retail Payment Services: The Eurosystem's View*, Frankfurt: European Central Bank, accessed 8 April 2019 at https://www.ecb.europa.eu/pub/pdf/other/retailpsen.pdf.

European Central Bank (2001), *Towards an Integrated Infrastructure for Credit Transfers in Euro*, Frankfurt: European Central Bank, accessed 8 April 2019 at https://www.ecb.europa.eu/pub/pdf/other/credtransfeuroecofinen.pdf.

European Central Bank (2004), *Towards a Single Euro Payments Area: Third Progress Report*, Frankfurt: European Central Bank, accessed 8 April 2019 at https://www.ecb.europa.eu/pub/pdf/other/singleeuropaymentsarea200412en.pdf.

European Central Bank (2006), *Towards a Single Euro Payments Area: Objectives and Deadlines, Fourth Progress Report*, Frankfurt: European Central Bank, accessed 8 April 2019 at https://www.ecb.europa.eu/pub/pdf/other/singleeuropaymentsarea200602en.pdf.

European Central Bank (2010), *Single Euro Payments Area: Seventh Progress Report, Beyond Theory into Practice*, Frankfurt: European Central Bank, accessed 8 April 2019 at https://www.ecb.europa.eu/pub/pdf/other/singleeuropaymentsarea201010en.pdf.

European Central Bank (2013), New Euro Retail Payments Board will reinforce market governance (Press release), 19 December, accessed 8 April 2019 at https://www.ecb.europa.eu/press/pr/date/2013/html/pr131219.en.html.

European Commission (2006), *Consultative Paper on SEPA Incentives*, Brussels: European Commission.

European Monetary Institute (1996), *Payment Systems in the European Union (Blue Book)*, 2nd edn, Frankfurt: European Monetary Institute, accessed 8 April 2019 at https://www.ecb.europa.eu/paym/intro/book/html/index.en.html.

European Parliament (2000), *Lisbon European Council 23 And 24 March 2000: Presidency Conclusions*, accessed 8 April 2019 at http://www.europarl.europa.eu/summits/lis1_en.htm.

European Payments Council (2002), 'Euroland: our single Euro payment area!' White Paper (May), Brussels: European Payments Council, accessed 8 April 2019 at https://www.europeanpaymentscouncil.eu/document-library/other/euroland-our-single-payment-area.

European Payments Council (2010), *Formal Declaration on SEPA Migration End-Date(s)*, 14 June, Brussels; European Payments Council, accessed 8 April 2019 at https://www.europeanpaymentscouncil.eu/document-library/other/sepa-council-formal-declaration-sepa-end-dates.

European Payments Council (2019a), *SEPA Credit Transfer*, accessed 8 April 2019 at https://www.europeanpaymentscouncil.eu/what-we-do/sepa-credit-transfer.

European Payments Council (2019b), *SEPA Direct Debit*, accessed 8 April 2019 at https://www.europeanpaymentscouncil.eu/what-we-do/sepa-direct-debit.

Evans, David S. and Richard Schmalensee (2008), 'Markets with two-sided platforms', in ABA Section of Antitrust Law (ed.), *Issues in Competition Law and Policy*, **1**, Chicago: ABA Book Publishing, pp. 667–93.

Gaus, John M. (1936), 'A theory of organization in public administration', in John M. Gaus, Leonard D. White and Marshall E. Dimock (eds), *The Frontiers of Public Administration*, Chicago: University of Chicago Press, pp. 66–91.

Geurden, Wim, Matthias Loh, Jan Muralitharan and Bob Reveal (2016), *Surgically Replacing Core Banking Platforms: A Perspective on Alternative Approaches*, London: EY (Ernst & Young).

Holthausen, Cornelia and Jean-Charles Rochet (2005), 'Incorporating a "public good factor" into the pricing of large-value payment systems', European Central Bank Working Paper Series No. 507, accessed 8 April 2019 at https://www.ecb.europa.eu/pub/pdf/scpwps/ecbwp507.pdf.

Janczuk-Gorywoda, Agnieszka (2015), 'Evolution of EU retail payments law', *European Law Review*, **40** (6), 858–76.

Kelly, Christopher (2014), *Failings in Management and Governance: Report of the Independent Review into the Events Leading to the Co-operative Bank's Capital Shortfall*, 30 April, accessed 8 April 2019 at https://www.co-operative.coop/investors/kelly-review.

Kleiss, Marion (2011), 'SEPA: banks must act now or pay later', *The Global Treasurer*, 20 December, accessed 8 April 2019 at https://www.theglobaltreasurer.com/2011/12/20/sepa-banks-must-act-now-or-pay-later.

Leopold, Les (2010), 'Capitalism is dead, long live the billionaire bailout society', *Huffington Post*, 24 April, accessed 8 April 2019 at https://www.huffingtonpost.com/les-leopold/capitalism-is-dead-long-l_b_471180.html.

Long, Heather (2016), 'ATM and overdraft fees top $6 billion at the big 3 banks', *CNN Money*, 14 January, accessed 8 April 2019 at http://money.cnn.com/2016/01/14/investing/atm-overdraft-fees/index.html.

Louwe Kooijmans, Alex, Rishi Balaji, Yasodhar Patnaik and Saket Sinha (2012), 'A transformation approach to smarter core banking', *IBM Redbooks*, 23 September, accessed 8 April 2019 at http://www.redbooks.ibm.com/abstracts/redp4764.html.

Lynn, Laurence E. Jr. (2001), 'The myth of the bureaucratic paradigm: what traditional public administration really stood for', *Public Administration Review*, **61** (2), 144–60.

Masters, Brooke (2010), 'Tsunami of regulation batters banks', *Financial Times*, 21 May.

Matthan, Rahul (2016), 'RegTech will change the way we regulate', *Livemint*, 26 October, accessed 8 April 2019 at http://www.livemint.com/Opinion/8WcbKsj7my7ZrPiuN9mOkL/RegTech-will-change-the-way-we-regulate.html.

Nelson, Fraser (2009), 'Politics: Fraser Nelson Launches the spectator's inquiry into the causes of the recession, *The Spectator*, 11 February, accessed 8 April 2019 at https://www.spectator.co.uk/2009/02/politics-10.

Office of Technology Assessment (1992), *Global Standards: Building Blocks for the Future*, Washington, DC: US Government Printing Office.

Peppard, John and John Thorp (2014), 'The IT project that brought a bank to its knees', *Harvard Business Review*, 15 May, accessed 8 April 2019 at https://hbr.org/2014/05/the-it-project-that-brought-a-bank-to-its-knees.

Planet Compliance (2016), 'What the heck is RegTech?', *Planet Compliance*, 8 June, accessed 8 April 2019 at http://www.planetcompliance.com/2016/06/08/what-the-heck-is-regtech.

Pope, Conor (2014), '"Lazy banks" behind six month SEPA delay', *Irish Times*, 9 January, accessed 8 April 2019 at https://www.irishtimes.com/business/lazy-banks-behind-six-month-sepa-delay-1.1649640.

Posner, Richard (1971), 'Taxation by regulation', *Bell Journal of Economics*, **2** (1), 22–50.

Proctor, Charles (ed.) (2009), *Goode on Payment Obligations in Commercial and Financial Transactions*, 2nd edn, London: Sweet & Maxwell.

Quintero, Dino, William M. Genovese, KiWaon Kim, Ming Jun MJ Li, Fabio Martins, Ashish Nainwal, Dusan Smolej, Marcin Tabinowski and Ashu Tiwary (2015), *IBM Software Defined Environment*, Armonk, NY: IBM, accessed 24 April 2018, at http://www.redbooks.ibm.com/redbooks/pdfs/sg248238.pdf

Reid, Emily and Jonathan Chertkow (2018), 'PSD2: commission responds to EBA on RTS on strong customer authentication', *Lexology*, 23 February, accessed

8 April 2019 at https://www.lexology.com/library/detail.aspx?g=ca4c00fd-e258-4915-bd0f-3a861ef14b9e.
Rochet, Jean-Charles and Jean Tirole (2003), 'Platform competition in two-sided markets', *Journal of the European Economic Association*, **1** (4), 990–1029.
Ross, Alec (2016), *Industries of the Future*, New York: Simon & Schuster.
Shapiro, Carl, and Hal R. Varian (1999), *Information Rules: A Strategic Guide to the Network Economy*, Boston, MA: Harvard Business School Press.
Smith, Bryan (2014), 'How do banks maintain financial data? Mainframes', *Information Week Bank Systems & Technology*, 12 December, accessed 8 April 2019 at http://www.banktech.com/infrastructure/how-do-banks-maintain-financial-data-mainframes/a/d-id/1318116.html.
Srivastava, Arun and Richard Powell (2017), 'PSD2: strong customer authentication: a political football?', *Lexology*, 7 July, accessed 8 April 2019 at https://www.lexology.com/library/detail.aspx?g=3e1616a7-012b-4148-9e2a-36a0be0deae9.
Wandhofer, Ruth (2011), 'The king is dead, long live the king', *European Payments Council News & Insights*, 11 July, accessed 8 April 2019 at https://www.europeanpaymentscouncil.eu/news-insights/insight/king-dead-long-live-king.
Weinberg, John A. (1996), 'Network externalities and public goods in payment systems', paper presented at Conference on the Foundations of Policy Toward Electronic Money, Federal Reserve Bank of Minneapolis, 3 December, accessed 8 April 2019 at https://www.minneapolisfed.org/research/conferences/research-events---conferences-and-programs/conference-on-the-foundations-of-policy-toward-electronic-money.
Wilson, Harry (2013), 'RBS IT "glitch" leaves bank facing £1bn bill', *The Telegraph*, 3 December, accessed 8 April 2019 at https://www.telegraph.co.uk/finance/newsbysector/banksandfinance/10491846/RBS-IT-glitch-leaves-bank-facing-1bn-bill.html.
Winn, Jane K. (2009), 'Globalization and standards: the logic of two-level games', *I/S: Journal of Law and Policy for the Information Society*, **5** (2), 185–218.
Winn, Jane K. (2017), 'Regulatory developments in the E.U.: structures and frameworks', in Edward Morse (ed.), *Electronic Payments in the 21st Century*, Chicago: ABA Publishing, pp. 207–38.
Wyplosz, Charles (2010), 'The failure of the Lisbon strategy', *VOX*, 12 January, accessed 8 April 2019 at http://voxeu.org/article/failure-lisbon-strategy.

6. Micro-level interactions in the compliance processes of transnational private governance: The market for Marine Stewardship Council auditors and assessors

Graeme Auld and Stefan Renckens

6.1 INTRODUCTION

Transnational private certification regimes comprise a bundle of regulatory functions intended to promote responsible business practices. They are rule setters, generating standards that define appropriate environmental and social practices for a given sector or issue area. Companies that seek voluntarily to comply with these standards must pass an independent, third-party audit. This compliance-assessment function is usually conducted by separate organizations that we term *auditors*. *Accreditation agencies* check to ensure that these auditors can properly implement the assessment procedures of the rule-setting governor. The accredited auditors then perform the independent audits to verify the compliance of an applicant company, contracting individual *assessors* (usually in teams of three to five) who have specific expertise relevant to the applicant company and the regime's standards.

In this chapter, we explore these compliance functions from a micro-level perspective by examining interactions among actors within a single private regime (Eberlein et al. 2014). We focus on characterizing the pool of auditors and assessors, how this pool has evolved and the kinds of intra-pool interactions that exist. Our premise is that this pool and its intra-pool dynamics – what we conceptualize as markets for auditors and assessors – matter for the functioning and outcomes of the compliance process. A few studies have highlighted the potential importance of these compliance agents (McDermott 2012). We seek to build from and extend these initial studies and push for further research into these micro-level interactions within a transnational private governance regime.

To undertake this analysis, we examine the Marine Stewardship Council (MSC), a prominent transnational private certification program for sustainable wild-capture fisheries. Our analysis uses a dataset comprising all 312 fisheries that sought MSC certification from 1999 to November 2015; it includes details on the fishery audits (i.e. timing, scores, features of the fishery, stakeholder objections), the organization performing the audit and the composition of the audit team. Considering that auditors are profit-driven businesses, we highlight the impact on the auditor pool of changes in market demand for the MSC certificate by adding data collected on the market campaigns conducted by Greenpeace and other environmental groups that led to a series of commitments from seafood buyers. Our data come from MSC audit reports, the MSC website and Greenpeace websites and reports. As a whole, these data allow us to describe the evolving pool of auditors and assessors working with the MSC, characterize different forms of interactions, and propose potential consequences of these interactions for regulatory outcomes.

Our analysis shows that there has been increasing competition among MSC accredited auditors, in the sense that as demand for audits increased, the number of auditors entering the market also increased. However, a closer look at this relationship shows that the competition among auditors has largely constituted a duopoly and that consolidation in the auditor market influences competitive pressures. Furthermore, we find that there are considerable differences across the auditors in terms of assessment outcome variables (duration, scores, objections), especially between those accredited early (2001) and those accredited in a second period (2006–08). By exploring the sharing of assessors by the auditors, we find that over the 15 years of MSC assessments each auditor has on average employed six assessors whom other auditors have also employed. We also find important connections among the auditors over time: newly accredited auditors use assessors who gained experience working for early accredited auditors, pointing towards learning across auditors by means of mobile individual assessors. At the same time, we observe that some new auditors draw in new assessors who subsequently work for other existing auditors. As a result, following Power (1997, 2003) and Hatanaka and Busch (2008), we show that while auditors may be organizationally independent, they may not be operationally independent.

The MSC is not a unique case. Any transnational private governance regime that involves third-party certification will include assessors and auditor(s). We therefore see our analysis as elucidating an important, and so far little studied, facet of this form of governance.

We proceed in four steps. First, we review the features of private regimes and justify our focus on auditors and assessors as important compliance agents. Second, we introduce the empirical case and review the results of our descriptive analysis. Our conclusions provide directions for further research on compliance processes within private regimes.

6.2 TRANSNATIONAL PRIVATE REGIMES AND COMPLIANCE AGENTS

Transnational private governance regimes have emerged in recent decades to create a vibrant field of governance activities aimed at addressing myriad social and environmental problems. Diverse initiatives count as governance in this area of work. Only a subset of these initiatives focus on regulatory governance – the purposeful use of rules to steer behavioural outcomes – what Abbott and Snidal (2009) termed regulatory standard-setting initiatives (see also, Cashore 2002).

Private certification programs are a prominent type of regulatory governance. They have evolved to constitute complete regulatory regimes (Scott 2002) in that they involve processes for, at minimum, (re)negotiating, implementing and monitoring rules, and adjudicating disputes. Rule implementation and monitoring – what we examine in this chapter as encompassing the compliance process (Renckens and Auld 2016) – are typically handled by organizations at arm's length from the rule maker, whereby a regime engages intermediaries to bring rule targets' behaviour in line with the regime's rules (Abbott et al. 2017).[1] The compliance process has evolved to include three distinct agents (Auld 2014): the auditor (at arm's length to both the rule maker and the company to be certified) contracted to conduct the compliance check; the accreditation agency that checks whether the auditor is organizationally qualified to conduct the audits; and the expert assessors hired by the auditor to conduct individual audits. Rule targets that pass an initial audit are then subject to surveillance audits every year and must be re-assessed in a new full audit after, typically, five years.

The incentives for rule targets to comply with the private regime's rules are exogenous to the regime. Unlike government regulations that are mandatory and can include specific sanction mechanisms such as fines, license removals, or even criminal prosecutions, private regimes rely on the evaluative judgments of market players as a compliance driver (Cashore 2002). This has meant that an important source of compliance incentives has come from purchasing decisions by individual consumers and corporate sustainability commitments, which are often spurred by NGO campaigns.

Our premise is that the organizations and individuals involved in this compliance process are consequential for how certification operates and for its regulatory and political outcomes and impacts (Auld and Renckens 2017; Renckens and Auld 2016). Work on technical and product standards and financial accounting support this premise. Galland (2017), for instance, documents the political power of Bureau Veritas, a large auditor, by detailing how it used its European-wide operations to circumvent efforts by the French government to re-establish state oversight of tramway and cableway technical safety inspection. Work on regulatory inspections has also recently turned greater attention to the importance of characteristics of inspectors and inspection teams for inspection outcomes (e.g. Muehlenbachs et al. 2016; Short et al. 2016).

This new direction for studies of regulatory inspection is an extensive and longstanding research agenda for students of financial audits – an area of work beyond the scope of this chapter to fully review. In short, there are at least three relevant tracks to this work. First, studies have examined the changing nature of audit markets through descriptive studies of the degree of competition – measured by concentration ratios and the Herfindahl indices, for instance (e.g. Wolk et al. 2001) – and studies connecting measures of competition to outcomes, such as audit quality (Newton et al. 2013) and audit fees (Maher et al. 1992). Second, considering similar outcomes, studies examine the characteristics of the auditors, such as size and reputation (Francis 1984). Third, this area of research has also examined the role of individual assessors, connecting personal experience and characteristics to the same outcomes examined in the market-level studies (Cahan and Sun 2015).

In spite of this well-established literature, the majority of research on private regimes has not examined auditors and assessors as potentially important agents that affect the processes and outcomes of compliance, despite their widespread importance to this form of governance. The small set of studies that do focus on these agents speaks to their import. McDermott (2012) documents how stakeholders in British Columbia, Canada held divergent views on the trustworthiness of the six different auditors that were accredited to certify for the Forest Stewardship Council (FSC) in the province. A sense of shared values, more than perceived competence, stood out as key to trust, which highlights the significance of these compliance agents for the credibility of the certification program as a whole. Maletz and Tysiachniouk (2009), by contrast, emphasize the importance of expertise for compliance outcomes. Through case studies of two Russian companies audited against the FSC, the authors document how the 'knowledge, experience and personal disposition' of assessors affected how the FSC's generic standards were translated into specific requirements for the two forest companies. Relatedly, a study by Toffel et al. (2015) examining labour violations in factory audits across 47 countries from 2004 to 2009 finds that assessors who have taken more skills training are associated with audits noting more labour violations, whereas the years an assessor has worked for an audit organization had no statistically significant relationship with the number of violations reported in audits.

We contribute to this burgeoning research focus for private regimes by beginning with a descriptive effort to characterize the compliance agents (both auditors and assessors) and how they interact within the compliance process. We focus on the fisheries sector and one prominent private regime, the MSC.

6.3 THE MARINE STEWARDSHIP COUNCIL

The MSC was established in the mid-1990s as a partnership of the World Wide Fund for Nature (WWF) and Unilever. The program became independent of its founders in 1999 and has since been a lead standard-setting and certification program for responsible capture fisheries. The MSC fishery standard relevant for this chapter's time frame consisted of three principles and associated criteria and indicators, addressing the sustainability of the operator's targeted fish stock(s), broader environmental consequences of the fishery, and the fishery's management and operational systems (MSC 2010).[2]

The MSC requires compliance before a fishery can enjoy the benefits of participation. Companies that want to be certified by the program must complete an independent audit, performed by auditors that are accredited to certify against the MSC standard. The MSC initially did the accreditation in-house; it now has this work done by Assurance Services International (ASI, formerly Accreditation Services International).

To achieve certification and gain access to the MSC on-product label, a fishery must pass the audit with overall scores of at least 80 out of 100 for all three principles; these average scores are calculated using weights for the performance indicators associated with the principles. Stakeholders can also issue an objection to the audit decision, after which the current practice is for an adjudicator to review the concerns and decide whether certification can be granted.

6.4 THE MARKET FOR AUDITORS

The number of accredited MSC auditors has steadily increased. Table 6.1 shows that 15 different auditors have been accredited in four distinct waves: in 2001, five auditors were accredited (Moody / Intertek, SGS, SCS,

Table 6.1 Characteristics of the auditors accredited for MSC audits

Auditor	Date Accredited	Audits Count (%)	Team Size Mean (s.d.)	Accreditation wave
SGS	1 January 2001	8 (3%)	3.38 (0.18)	First
SCS	1 January 2001	32 (10%)	3.5 (0.15)	
Tavel	5 March 2001	7 (2%)	4.57 (0.37)	
Moody / Intertek[1]	1 May 2001	116 (37%)	3.72 (0.09)	
ME Certification[2]	1 September 2001	20 (6%)	3.2 (0.16)	
IMO[3]	21 November 2006	1 (<1%)	5	Second
OIA	6 December 2006	5 (2%)	4.8 (0.66)	
Food Certification/ Acoura Marine[4]	16 July 2007	47 (15%)	4.17 (0.12)	
Bureau Veritas	4 October 2007	12 (4%)	3.67 (0.19)	
MRAG	20 December 2007	22 (7%)	3.27 (0.12)	
DNV	11 August 2008	23 (7%)	3.48 (0.12)	
Global Trust / SAI	5 March 2010	14 (4%)	3.5 (0.14)	Third
SFS	7 December 2010	3 (1%)	5 (0.58)	
Marine Certification	3 May 2016	1 (<1%)	3	Fourth
TQCS	N/A	1 (<1%)	6	N/A

Notes:
1. Formerly Intertek Moody Marine, it now operates under Intertek Fisheries Certification. On 9 December 2015, Intertek voluntarily ended its accreditation for MSC fishery assessments, while it continues to perform Chain of Custody assessments.
2. Transferred from MacAlister Elliott and Partners.
3. Since 2 March 2015, IMO has withdrawn from fisheries certification, but still performs Chain of Custody assessments.
4. Formerly Food Certification International.

ME Certification, and Tavel); between 2006 and 2008, another six were accredited (Food Certification/Acoura Marine, DNV, MRAG, Bureau Veritas, OIA and IMO); two more were accredited in 2010 (Global Trust/ SAI and SFS); and the latest (Marine Certification) received accreditation in 2016.

When we pool all the audits conducted through November 2015, we see that more than half have been conducted by two auditors – Moody / Intertek (37 per cent) and Food Certification / Acoura Marine (15 per cent). Moody also bought Tavel in 2010 furthering its dominance (SeafoodSource 2010). It was then acquired by Intertek on 27 April 2011 (Intertek 2012). Finally, Table 6.1 provides figures for the average size of the audit teams for each of the auditors. Most congregate around 3.5

to 4.5 members per team; indeed, the average across the entire sample is 3.72 (s.d. 0.052).

The increasing pool of accredited auditors is partly explained by the changing market demand for MSC certificates. As we noted above, compliance incentives for private regimes are exogenous. Actors other than the private regime generate them. In the case of the MSC, rising demand can be traced to specific events at the end of 2005 and the beginning of 2006 (Figure 6.1). In October 2005, Greenpeace UK started a public campaign aimed at naming and shaming supermarkets for their insufficient attention to fisheries products' sustainability (Greenpeace 2005). It released the first of a series of annual reports evaluating the seafood purchasing practices of UK supermarkets, a market segment recognized to be highly competitive (Schurman and Munro 2010). The reports did not advocate

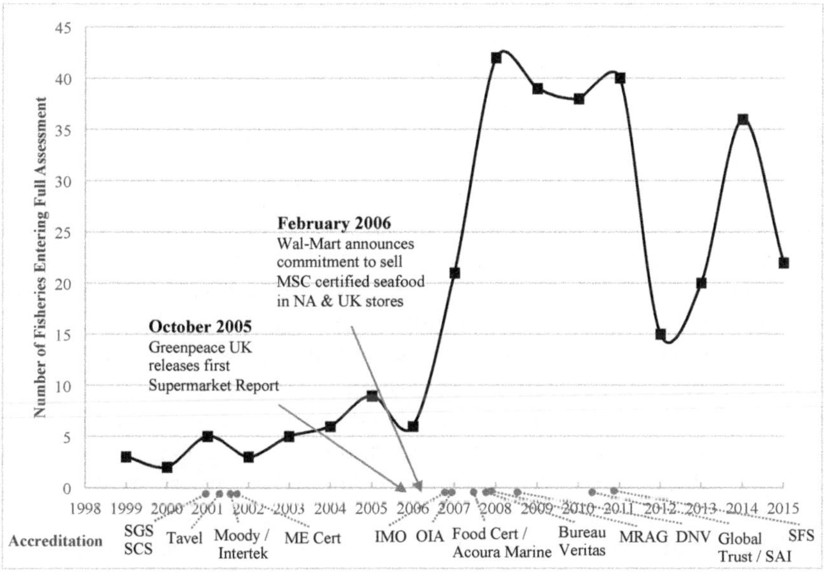

Note: While the first audit started in 1999, the first auditors were only accredited in 2001. This is likely because the initial accreditation processes were occurring concurrently with the first official fisheries audits.

Legend: NA=North America.

Figure 6.1 Fisheries under audit January 1999–November 2015, and auditor accreditation dates

MSC certification as such – indeed, Greenpeace has continuously voiced concerns over the MSC (e.g. Greenpeace 2009) – yet the campaign served to pressure supermarkets to respond. Commitments to purchase certified seafood offered targeted companies one way to claim they were doing something. The campaign could claim quick success when Wal-Mart and ASDA (the UK affiliate of Wal-Mart) announced in early 2006 that they would commit to purchase MSC certified fisheries products (Auld and Cashore 2013).

Only 33 fisheries started the certification process before 2006, an average of just under five fisheries per year. According to Martin et al. (2012), in this same period, only 58 fisheries had undergone confidential pre-audit assessments, which are used by fisheries to assess their potential performance before entering the formal audit process. From 2006 to 2015, the number of fisheries starting formal audits jumped. A total of 279 fisheries sought full audits over this time period, for an average of almost 28 fisheries per year, nearly as many per year as had sought full audits in the first six years of the MSC's existence. A total of 389 fisheries underwent confidential pre-audit assessments from 2006 to 2012 (Martin et al. 2012). These numbers underlie the pronounced increase in fisheries seeking certification captured in the rise in active audits documented in Figure 6.1.

This externally driven increase in demand for certification implies that a private regime does not necessarily need to lower its standards to increase corporate participation, as is hypothesized in the often mentioned trade-off between strictness and support (cf. Bernstein and Cashore 2007). Fisheries that initially did not see the (market) benefit of getting certified – even though they would have passed the audit – may now be incentivized to engage. Yet fisheries that expect to have a more difficult time passing an audit may also decide to get audited. This may more dramatically change the composition of the applicant pool, in terms of difficulty of assessment or likelihood of success, even though the mentioned pre-audit assessments may weed out the worst performers.

Notwithstanding the incentives for new fisheries to get audited, the entry of new auditors was ostensibly a response to this dramatic rise in the number of fisheries seeking certification. In 2011, there were times when 111 fisheries were being audited. We know from Table 6.1, however, that Moody / Intertek was successful in capturing a large proportion of this increasing demand. How did this happen? A more informative picture of the audit market emerges when we examine the activities of auditors for the time span of our data. A first important pattern is the ratio of active auditors to active audits. This ratio has fluctuated from a low of 0.6 to a high of 8.2. Over the span of our data, the average ratio is 5.7 (s.d. 1.81). This means that there have been times when very few fisheries were seeking audits compared to the pool of available auditors, and other times when the auditors have had many more fisheries to potentially audit.

But, as Table 6.1 suggests, the auditors have not been equally successful in securing contracts to audit particular fisheries. We can see a pattern of dominance emerge when we plot two trends for the top three auditors (Moody / Intertek, SCS and Food International / Acoura Marine): the number of active audits and the number of completed audits (Figure 6.2). These trends show that until the end of 2005, SCS and Moody kept pace with each other. They each had seven active audits at the time; Moody had completed seven and SCS had completed five, which together represented 75 per cent of all completed audits. After 2005, they diverge. Moody ramped up its auditing work, capturing a high of 75 per cent of active audits in September 2008 and reaching a high in absolute terms of 56 active audits in May 2010 (representing 60 per cent of all active audits). SCS, by contrast, stagnated. Over the same time period, it averaged only four active audits. Its share of the active audits averaged 9 per cent over this same time period.

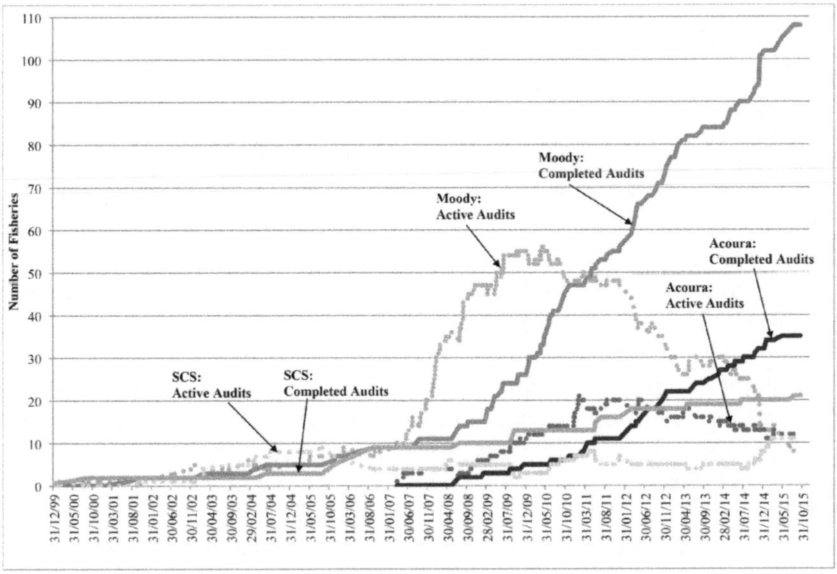

Figure 6.2 Active and completed audits for the top three MSC auditors

Figure 6.2 also details the later rise of Food Certification / Acoura Marine. This auditor began audits in April 2007 and reached a high point of 21 active audits by February 2011, which represented 20 per cent of all active audits at that time. This high also marked the changing fortunes of Moody / Intertek, which, by this time, only accounted for 47 per cent of the active audits. And, as the figure highlights, by 2015, all three auditors had converged towards a similar level of audit activity. The decline in Moody / Intertek's activities was likely an early signal of its December 2015 announcement that it would voluntarily end its accreditation for MSC fishery audits.

What underlies the dynamics of this audit market? While it is evident that rising demand helps us understand the entry of new auditors, it does not appear to help explain why some were able to capture more of the audit market. As work on financial audits indicates, auditor features may matter, such as their capacities and resources as well as the alignment of MSC audit work with their business strategies. For instance, a large auditor such as Moody / Intertek might find it easier to dedicate the resources needed to compete and win audit contracts. From the perspective of audited fisheries, the relative performance of auditors and their fees could also matter. As an initial attempt to understand this in the context of private governance, we examine performance differences across the auditors. We know from previous work that there were concerns about inconsistencies across auditors in the MSC's early years (Ward 2008). Perhaps auditors were more or less stringent in their interpretation of the MSC standard, meaning some auditors were able to capture a greater hold of the market given that fisheries likely preferred a relatively less stringent audit for the same certification program, all else being equal. There is some evidence in our data to suggest that this may be the case.[3] For fisheries that began audits before 2007, Moody / Intertek certified 17 fisheries, giving these fisheries an average score of 88.05 (95 per cent C.I. 87.10 – 88.99). SGS certified four fisheries, with an average score of 83.44 (95 per cent C.I. 80.61 – 86.27), while SCS certified 13 fisheries, with an average score of 86.27 (95 per cent C.I. 84.85 – 87.71). These numbers imply that Moody / Intertek's scoring was higher than its dominant competitors in the first years of the MSC's operations. Additionally, according to these numbers, SGS was the most stringent scorer. Yet, SGS also faced three objections to its four early audits. This may have meant that fisheries were less inclined to contract SGS for future audits, and it may have also given SGS less reason to see continued engagement with the MSC as a worthwhile business activity. Indeed, as Table 6.1 shows, SGS had only engaged in four additional audits by November 2015.

Turning to the second wave of accreditation, we can compare Moody / Intertek and SCS to their main competitor – Food Certification / Acoura Marine. From 2006 onward, the average audit scores awarded by these three competitors indicate that SCS became more variable in its audits, while its average score increased only slightly (average of 86.6; 95 per cent C.I. 83.70 – 89.54). Moody / Intertek's average score dropped to 86.7 (95 per cent C.I. 85.96 – 87.38) to become more aligned with the scoring practices of SCS. And, interestingly, Food Certification / Acoura Marine had even lower scores, averaging 84.9 (95 per cent C.I. 84.21 – 85.64) for the fisheries it audited. Thus it does not appear that Food Certification / Acoura Marine offered less stringent audits (measured by higher scores for fisheries) as a way to attract fishery clients away from Moody / Intertek.

However, a different picture emerges when we compare the duration of the certification processes in which the auditors were involved. This is a measure of how long a fishery takes to proceed from announcing that it is pursuing certification to when the audit is complete and a final decision has been released. Auditors lack complete control over the length of this time period, yet fisheries will experience a longer certification process as costly because it means they cannot claim to be certified or access any market benefits until the process is finished. When we compute averages for the auditors active for the time period 2006 to 2015 (the time period that follows the uptick in market demand for MSC), we see that Moody / Intertek was involved in considerably longer certification processes than its main competitors. Its certification processes took on average 864 days (95 per cent C.I. 758.73 – 969.50) or just under 2.5 years. Both SCS and Food Certification / Acoura Marine were much faster, with average durations, respectively, of 566 days (95 per cent C.I. 487.65 – 644.18) and 555 days (95 per cent C.I. 452.08 – 657.03). Given that these differences will matter for fisheries, the discrepancies between these three main competitors are quite striking.

While we observe such outcome differences (audit score and duration) among auditors, it is unclear both theoretically and empirically how the direction of these differences should be interpreted. A shorter certification process, for example, can be the result of a more experienced auditor or audit team, the availability of a larger pool of assessors or characteristics of the fishery (a smaller, better organized or less complex fishery). But a shorter certification process is not necessarily better than a longer one, since it can also indicate a less rigorous audit. Similarly, higher audit scores can result from less experienced auditors and assessors, a more lenient audit process or beneficial fishery characteristics. In a crowded auditor market with a few dominant players, then, there are multiple competing incentives. Auditors may want to retain clients for future re-assessments and build a reputation as a trusted and fair auditor. At the same time, they need to take into account the bottom line and their likelihood of survival when entering a new market. Examining strategic behaviour to reconcile these objectives is an important avenue for future empirical research.

6.5 THE MARKET FOR ASSESSORS

These differences among auditors are also interesting for a second facet of our analysis – that is, the human resource pool available to auditors. Recall that audits are conducted by audit teams with an average of three to four members. Thus, a different way of looking at competitive relationships among auditors is to move the analysis one level down to the individuals the auditors employ to perform the audits. This level of analysis elucidates the degree to which auditors that are organizationally independent are also operationally independent. It also points to another dimension of competition, one that focuses on securing competent experts to carry out audits.

Our dataset comprises 281 individuals who have been assessors for MSC accredited auditors. Many of these assessors worked for different auditors. For instance, one assessor could have been on an audit team for a fishery audited by Moody / Intertek in one year and on the audit team for a fishery audited by IMO at some later date. In our dataset, the average assessor has conducted just over four audits and has worked for 1.32 different auditors; two assessors in our dataset have worked for five different auditors and another five have worked for four different auditors. A total of 54 have worked for at least two different auditors. This implies that there are links among the different auditors that may be important to understand.

Despite this pattern of movement between auditors, our most prolific assessor has performed 52 out of a total of 55 audits for one auditor (Moody / Intertek), with an additional two for Food Certification / Acoura Marine and one for DNV. Our next two most prolific assessors have been employed by three and two auditors, respectively, with the second-ranked assessor performing 25 audits for Food Certification / Acoura Marine, nine for Moody / Intertek, and one for SGS, while the third-ranked assessor performed 16 audits for Moody / Intertek and 10 for DNV. Still, the movement of assessors among auditors does indicate a degree of interdependence that just examining the organizational level would miss.

Using social network analysis, we can examine the exchange of assessors among the different auditors. Since we know which auditor conducted each audit, we are able to examine the movement of assessors among the different auditors through their work as assessors for specific fisheries. To do this, we treat the audited fisheries as nodes and the assessors as edges. This means that two fisheries will be connected in our network if they share a common assessor. Using these ties, we can examine what happens to the network when a newly accredited auditor enters the auditor market. We can do this because we know the exact dates each audit began and when it was completed or when it ended because the fishery failed certification or withdrew from the audit.

Figure 6.3 illustrates the sharing of assessors that occurred as Food Certification / Acoura Marine and Tavel entered the auditor market. The network represents every fishery under audit as of 19 October 2007, a date chosen to highlight the entry of Food Certification to the auditor market. By this time, Food Certification, as it was known then, had begun four audits. The first occurred in April 2007, and three more followed before the end of 2007. One assessor who had previously worked for Moody joined all four of these audit teams. This one assessor, therefore, appears to be a key link between the two auditors; this individual had knowledge of two previous Moody audits. Such mobile assessors may be significant given Granovetter's (1973) argument about

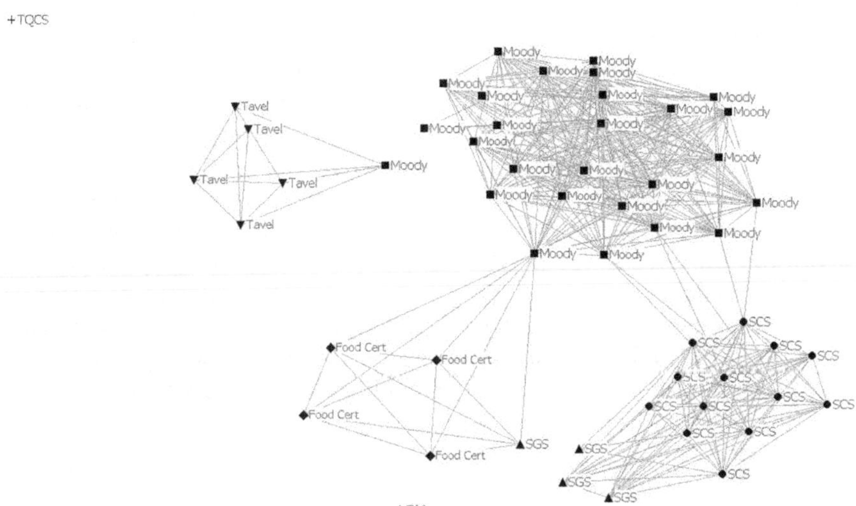

Note: Nodes represent fisheries certified by a given auditor; edges represent assessors that have worked on more than one audit.

Figure 6.3 Assessor movement across auditors with entry of Food Certification/Acoura Marine and Tavel to the MSC auditor market (audits from 1999 to 19 October 2007)

the strength of weak ties – a situation where limited rather than many ties connect communities, facilitating the spread of innovations. A mobile assessor may represent a weak tie between the two auditors, diffusing certain knowledge and practices to the new auditor. This is interesting particularly when we compare the experience of Food Certification with the pattern for Tavel. Tavel was linked to Moody via a fishery that had an audit team whose members had never previously worked with any of the other assessors employed by Moody to that date. This link may have been less effective in spreading lessons learned.

We can extend this approach to analysing the entry of other auditors to the market in the second wave of accreditation. MRAG's first audit began on 3 December 2007, and the team included assessors who had in total worked on six previous Moody audits and two SCS audits. DNV began its first audit on 18 August 2008, and none of the assessors who worked on this audit had worked on an MSC audit previously. This was also true for Bureau Veritas' first audit, which began on 10 February 2009. However, DNV's second and third audits drew heavily on assessors who had previously worked with Moody, one of whom had conducted 15 audits and the other had completed two. The final auditor active in this time period was ME Certification. Its first audit took place on 9 February 2009, and the team included one assessor who had been on four audits for Moody and another who had completed two audits for Tavel.

As well, we can see the counter trends: assessors who moved from Moody to MRAG also moved back to Moody; and assessors who began work with DNV subsequently worked on audits for Moody. Thus, the role of mobile assessors does not appear to advantage only the late movers. In some instances, the entry of new auditors may open up a new pool of assessors previously untapped by the first movers, thus expanding the available supply of assessors for all auditors. This will not necessarily increase the overall level of competition among assessors. Assessors may be chosen for their geographic or species-specific knowledge as well as their location, thereby increasing competition in sub-pools only.

6.6 CONCLUSION

The descriptive analysis in this chapter provides initial insights into some of the micro-level interactions among auditors and assessors in the compliance process of a prominent transnational private governance regime, the MSC. From a TBGI perspective, two main insights jump out. First, while the number of auditors increased over time, creating the potential for a more competitive market – initially at least partly due to increased market demand – in practice the auditor market can be described more accurately as a duopoly. Second, while auditors may be organizationally independent, their operational independence may be limited due to the sharing of assessors.

Several future directions emerge from our analysis, all of which would usefully extend beyond the initial descriptive analysis we have provided. First, research is needed on the impact of competition on regulatory outcomes. In particular, the hypothesis that increased competition leads to more lenient audits needs further examination (cf. Bennett et al. 2013). Competition might also help explain delays some auditors experience when they successfully gain clients for audits, but then must compete for a limited pool of qualified assessors. As we found, interestingly, Moody's time to audit increased during the period when it was engaged in the most active audits. Such delays may, subsequently, influence outcomes if the auditor decides to contract less experienced or new assessors.

Second, the sharing of assessors may pose strategic challenges for an individual auditor. Once trained, an assessor may move to another auditor meaning the first auditor pays some fixed cost of training that subsequent auditors can then benefit from. Assessor movements across auditors should, therefore, be further examined, including assessors' motives for their mobility and potential incentives auditors can offer to decrease such mobility.

Third, private regimes engage compliance agents with varied backgrounds. In most instances, the auditors working for a new private regime, such as the MSC, have prior experience conducting compliance assessments for technical and public regulatory standards. That is, the private regimes are much newer than the auditors that do the compliance-assessment work. When examining the impact of regulatory expertise and competition on regulatory outcomes and overall regime effectiveness, we should therefore be cognizant of not only the interactions among auditors and assessors within one regime, but also of the connections with other regimes, the acquired general auditing expertise in addition to content-specific expertise, and the reasons behind moving into and out of the market of auditors for a particular new private regime.

Finally, a comparative analysis of private regimes will highlight differences in both the auditor and the assessor markets. Some private regimes employ the MSC model of allowing competition among auditors. Other regimes, however, use one dedicated auditor (such as FLOCERT in the case of Fairtrade International) or some other model of compliance verification, which is closely linked to the historical development of a regime (Auld and Renckens 2017; Loconto 2017). Examining the impact of these different models on auditor and assessor interactions is an important avenue for future research.

NOTES

1. Some early certification programs did not use arm's length organizations for these functions. For instance, Fairtrade International only introduced an arm's length audit function in 2003 and the Forest Stewardship Council created an arm's length accreditation organization – Accreditation Services International, now Assurance Services International (ASI) – in 2005.
2. A new standard was released in April 2015, following a two-year review. The program has an additional set of rules – termed chain of custody rules – for tracking certified products through the seafood supply chain. These include provisions about guaranteeing the validity of the MSC supply, creating temporal and/or physical separation of MSC seafood from other supplies all along a supply chain, and label compliance requirements. Operators are also checked to ensure they have management systems in place to ensure conformance with chain of custody rules and that they are overseeing and ensuring compliance of subcontractors they work with.
3. These descriptive statistics do not, of course, account for self-selection processes, whereby fisheries with particular characteristics, which influence their audit scores, choose certain auditors over others.

REFERENCES

Abbott, K.W., D. Levi-Faur and D. Snidal (2017), 'Theorizing regulatory intermediaries: the RIT model', *The Annals of the American Academy of Political and Social Science,* **670** (1), 14–35.

Abbott, K.W. and D. Snidal (2009), 'Strengthening international regulation through transnational new governance: overcoming the orchestration deficit', *Vanderbilt Journal of Transnational Law,* **42** (2), 501–78.

Auld, G. (2014), *Constructing Private Governance: The Rise and Evolution of Forest, Coffee, and Fisheries Certification,* New Haven, CT: Yale University Press.

Auld, G. and B. Cashore (2013), 'Mixed signals: NGO campaigns and NSMD governance in an export-oriented country', *Canadian Public Policy-Analyse De Politiques,* **39** (S2), 143–56.

Auld, G. and S. Renckens (2017), 'Rule-making feedbacks through intermediation and evaluation in transnational private governance', *The Annals of the American Academy of Political and Social Science,* **670** (1), 93–111.

Bennett, V.M., L. Pierce, J.A. Snyder and M.W. Toffel (2013), 'Customer-driven misconduct: how competition corrupts business practices', *Management Science,* **59** (8), 1725–42.

Bernstein, S. and B. Cashore (2007), 'Can non-state global governance be legitimate? An analytical framework', *Regulation & Governance,* **1** (4), 347–71.

Cahan, S.F. and J. Sun (2015), 'The effect of audit experience on audit fees and audit quality', *Journal of Accounting, Auditing & Finance,* **30** (1), 78–100.

Cashore, B. (2002), 'Legitimacy and the privatization of environmental governance: how non-state market-driven (NSMD) governance systems gain rule-making authority', *Governance,* **15** (4), 503–29.

Eberlein, B., K.W. Abbott, J. Black, E. Meidinger and S. Wood (2014), 'Transnational business governance interactions: conceptualization and framework for analysis', *Regulation & Governance,* **8** (1), 1–21.

Francis, J.R. (1984), 'The effect of audit firm size on audit prices: a study of the Australian market', *Journal of Accounting and Economics,* **6** (2), 133–51.

Galland, J.-P. (2017), 'Big third-party certifiers and the construction of transnational regulation', *The Annals of the American Academy of Political and Social Science,* **670** (1), 263–79.
Granovetter, M.S. (1973), 'The strength of weak ties', *American Journal of Sociology,* **78** (6), 1360–80.
Greenpeace (2005), *A Recipe for Disaster: Supermarkets' Insatiable Appetite for Seafood,* London: Greenpeace.
Greenpeace. (2009), *Assessment of the Marine Stewardship Council (MSC) Fisheries Certification Programme*, accessed 28 March 2019 at http://www.greenpeace.org/usa/wp-content/uploads/legacy/Global/usa/report/2009/7/assessment-of-the-msc.pdf?2dea3c.
Hatanaka, M. and L. Busch (2008), 'Third-party certification in the global agrifood system: an objective or socially mediated governance mechanism?', *Sociologia Ruralis,* **48** (1), 73–91.
Intertek (2012), *Your Global Quality Partner. Annual Report 2011,* London: Intertek Group plc.
Loconto, A. (2017), 'Models of assurance: diversity and standardization of modes of intermediation', *The Annals of the American Academy of Political and Social Science,* **670** (1), 112–32.
Maher, M.W., P. Tiessen, R. Colson and A.J. Broman (1992), 'Competition and audit fees', *The Accounting Review,* **67** (1), 199–211.
Malets, O. and M. Tysiachniouk (2009), 'The effect of expertise on the quality of forest standards implementation: the case of FSC forest certification in Russia', *Forest Policy and Economics,* **11** (5), 422–8.
Martin, S.M., T.A. Cambridge, C. Grieve, F.M. Nimmo and D.J. Agnew (2012), 'An evaluation of environmental changes within fisheries involved in the Marine Stewardship Council certification scheme', *Reviews in Fisheries Science,* **20** (2), 61–9.
McDermott, C.L. (2012), 'Trust, legitimacy and power in forest certification: a case study of the FSC in British Columbia', *Geoforum,* **43** (3), 634–44.
MSC (Marine Stewardship Council) (2010), *MSC Fishery Standard: Principles and Criteria for Sustainable Fishing*. London: MSC.
Muehlenbachs, L., S. Staubli and M.A. Cohen (2016), 'The impact of team inspections on enforcement and deterrence', *Journal of the Association of Environmental and Resource Economists,* **3** (1), 159–204.
Newton, N.J., D. Wang and M.S. Wilkins (2013), 'Does a lack of choice lead to lower quality? Evidence from auditor competition and client restatements', *Auditing: A Journal of Practice & Theory,* **32** (3), 31–67.
Power, M. (1997), *The Audit Society. Rituals of Verification,* Oxford: Oxford University Press.
Power, M. (2003), 'Evaluating the audit explosion', *Law & Policy,* **25** (3), 185–203.
Renckens, S. and G. Auld (2016), 'Compliance processes in transnational private governance: explaining variation in fisheries sustainability certification', Paper presented at the Conference on Disclosing Sustainability: The Transformative Power of Transparency?, Wageningen University, Wageningen, 24–25 June.
Schurman, R. and W.A. Munro (2010), *Fighting for the Future of Food: Activists Versus Agribusiness in the Struggle over Biotechnology,* Minneapolis, MN: University of Minnesota Press.
Scott, C. (2002), 'Private regulation of the public sector: a neglected facet of contemporary governance', *Journal of Law and Society,* **29** (1), 56–76.

SeafoodSource (2010), *Moody Marine Acquires Rival Certifier*, accessed 28 March 2019 at https://www.seafoodsource.com/news/environment-sustainability/moody-marine-acquires-rival-certifier.
Short, J.L., M.W. Toffel and A.R. Hugill (2016), 'Monitoring global supply chains', *Strategic Management Journal,* **37** (9), 1878–97.
Toffel, M.W., J.L. Short and M. Ouellet (2015), 'Codes in context: how states, markets, and civil society shape adherence to global labor standards', *Regulation & Governance,* **9** (3), 205–23.
Ward, T.J. (2008), 'Barriers to biodiversity conservation in marine fishery certification', *Fish and Fisheries,* **9** (2), 169–77.
Wolk, C.M., S.E. Michelson and C.W. Wootton (2001), 'Auditor concentration and market shares in the US: 1988–1999 a descriptive note', *The British Accounting Review,* **33** (2), 157–74.

7. The evolution of transnational governance overlaps: A network approach[1]

Oliver Westerwinter

7.1 INTRODUCTION

Throughout the 20th century, states were at the centre of global governance. International regimes and international organizations were the dominant modes of cooperation (Krasner 1983; Keohane 1984; Abbott and Snidal 1998). Yet, beginning in the 1970s and accelerating in the 1980s and 1990s, global governance started to evolve in new directions. States have become only one set of actors among a larger and more heterogeneous group of participants in global governance that includes firms, business associations, and non-governmental organizations (NGOs) (Keohane and Nye 1971; Cutler et al. 1999; Hall and Biersteker 2002; Avant et al. 2010; Avant and Westerwinter 2016). With these new actors came new forms of governing in which varying mixes of state and non-state actors cooperate to govern global problems by engaging in information sharing, rule-making and standard-setting, implementation, monitoring, and enforcement (Abbott and Snidal 2009; Avant et al. 2010; Avant and Westerwinter 2016). These new forms of governance include transnational public-private governance initiatives (TGIs) (Abbott and Snidal 2009; Westerwinter 2019a). In TGIs, states and/or intergovernmental organizations (IGOs)[2] cooperate with business and civil society actors to govern transnational problems that no actor alone has the knowledge and resources to address effectively (Abbott and Snidal 2009, p. 45).[3] Examples include the World Commission on Dams in the environment domain (Dingwerth 2007), the Global Alliance for Vaccines and Immunization in the health sector (Liese and Beisheim 2011), and the International Code of Conduct for Private Security Service Providers' Association (ICoCA) in the security area (Avant 2016).

The number of TGIs in the international system has been growing rapidly since the 1990s in absolute terms and even more so relative to

IGOs. Using a new dataset that contains information on IGOs and TGIs (Westerwinter 2019a, 2019b), we observe that from 63 in 1990, within 24 years the number of TGIs increased by about 590 percent to a total of 435 in 2014. This evidence is consistent with other studies of transnational governance initiatives (Abbott and Snidal 2009; Abbott et al. 2016). According to Abbott and Snidal (2009), transnational governance networks are a recent phenomenon. While few such arrangements existed before 1994, since then their number has increased steadily (Abbott and Snidal 2009, pp. 53–5). Likewise, Abbott et al. (2016, p. 248) find that 'private transnational regulatory organizations' formed by different mixtures of business and civil society actors have proliferated in recent decades. Although the absolute number of IGOs was still higher at 316 in 1990, TGIs became the most frequent form of cooperation in the dataset as of 2009.

Recent work in political science and international law examines new forms of global governance (Pauwelyn et al. 2012; Burca et al. 2013; Eberlein et al. 2014; Green 2014; Avant and Westerwinter 2016). However, studies often focus on specific types of governance arrangements in isolation and comparative research is typically limited to a small number of cases. Further, the evolution of new forms of transnational governance and their relationships with each other across issue areas and over time has so far received little attention. Consequently, research on the factors that shape whether TGIs overlap with one another and how these overlaps change over time is still at its early stages. Yet, as long as we do not take into account the development of the scope and pattern of overlaps among new forms of transnational governance, our analyses of the dynamic patchwork of contemporary global governance remain partial and incomplete (Lake 2010).

In this chapter, I start to fill this research gap. Using information on 457 TGIs from the new Transnational Public-Private Governance Initiatives in World Politics (TGIWP) dataset (Westerwinter 2019a) and methods of network analysis, I investigate how the overlaps through shared state participants among TGIs evolved across issue areas and over time.[4] I explore whether transnational governance overlaps have been driven by competition or cooperation among TGIs and whether their evolution is shaped by large TGIs. I also examine the extent to which the evolution of transnational governance overlaps is based on dynamics endogenous to the network of TGIs, such as clustering and popularity. My results suggest that the evolution of TGI overlaps is overall driven more by cooperation than competition among governance initiatives as suggested by the fact that TGI overlaps are more common within than across issue areas. In addition, TGI size in terms of number of participants positively affects TGI overlap. In other words, governance initiatives with more participants tend to overlap more frequently with other initiatives than those with fewer participants. I also find evidence for clustering and popularity as driving forces of the evolution of TGI overlaps.

This chapter makes three distinct contributions to the growing literature on transnational governance interactions. First, I empirically map the evolution of overlaps among TGIs across issue areas and over time based on the most comprehensive dataset on TGIs to date. Second, I specify and test hypotheses about the drivers and constraints of overlaps among TGIs using statistical network analysis. Given that the literature on transnational governance interactions is largely dominated by single and small-*n* case studies (Cashore et al. 2004; Fransen 2011; Abbott 2012; Overdevest and Zeitlin 2014; Porter 2014), the results of my analysis provide a step towards a more systematic empirical analysis that moves beyond individual governance regimes and issue areas. Finally, from a methodological perspective the chapter demonstrates the usefulness of descriptive and inferential network methods for exploring new avenues in the study of transnational governance interactions.

The remainder of the chapter proceeds in four steps. First, I develop some initial hypotheses about the drivers and constraints of transnational governance overlaps. The second section presents the data and the operationalization of the variables that I use in my empirical analysis. It also discusses the methods of inferential network analysis applied in this chapter. In section three, I present the results of my empirical analysis. A final section concludes, discusses the limitations of my analysis, and identifies areas for future research.

7.2 OVERLAPS AMONG TRANSNATIONAL PUBLIC-PRIVATE GOVERNANCE INITIATIVES

TGIs operate in an institutional environment that is replete with other governance arrangements. International relations used to be called a space that was 'thin' in terms of institutions (Waltz 1979). This description is hardly accurate anymore. Contemporary global governance is characterized by an increasing level of institutionalized cooperation (Avant et al. 2010; Lake 2010; Abbott et al. 2016; Avant and Westerwinter 2016; Barnett et al. 2016). Whether it takes the form of IGOs (Pevehouse et al. 2004), international agreements (Koremenos 2016), informal intergovernmental organizations (Vabulas and Snidal 2013), or TGIs (Westerwinter 2019a), studies agree that over recent decades, and particularly since the end of the Cold War, cooperation among states, but also among state and non-state actors, has been on the rise in many issue areas of world politics. Accordingly, recent work proposes to explore what happens when the global institutional fabric 'thickens' (Abbott et al. 2016). When states, business actors, and civil society organizations decide to cooperate in governing a transnational problem, they can choose from a broad menu of institutional forms, each of which brings together public and private actors in different configurations and confers different weight and authority to each group in the governance process (Abbott and Snidal 2000, 2009). Which institutional option is selected is the result of a transnational bargaining game in which each group of actors deploys its power resources to shape institutional design decisions in its favour (Abbott and Snidal 2009; Westerwinter 2014).

The institutions that exist in an issue area prior to the creation of a new governance arrangement shape its creation and development (Eberlein et al. 2014; Wood et al. 2015; Abbott et al. 2016). They may serve as institutional focal points in the creation of new governance arrangements that are then promoted or blocked by the actors that dominate them. For example, in the context of the governance of forestry, the International Tropical Timber Organization served as a focal institution in the late 1980s, but powerful states prevented action on timber labelling, which facilitated the development of the Forest Stewardship Council as a non-state alternative (Cashore et al. 2004). Looking at relationships between IGOs and non-state actors in global governance, Abbott et al. (2015) identify four patterns: IGOs compete with, collaborate with, delegate to, and orchestrate non-state actors. The literature on regime complexes addresses some of the outcomes of institutional density, particularly the conditions under which forum-shopping occurs (Raustiala and Victor 2004; Busch 2007; Alter and Meunier 2009). Finally, Eberlein et al. (2014) and Wood et al. (2015) look at how different transnational business governance efforts interact, arguing that scholars need to disaggregate the governance process itself to identify patterns in the outcomes of institutional overlap and interaction.

The central questions raised by the existence of multiple institutions at the global level are concerned with the degree to which these institutions compete with, complement, or reinforce each other. For example, competing institutional arrangements may lead to a lowering of regulatory standards to attract new members (Vogel 2009). Two institutions may also operate within the same issue area but address different sub-issues or operate at regional versus global levels. This allows them to define a functional and institutional niche for themselves, which in turn facilitates the acquisition of resources, authority, and support in ways that are complementary rather than competitive. Institutional arrangements may also reinforce one another. For example, in the conflict minerals area, the Organisation for Economic Co-Operation and Development (OECD) Guidelines on Due Diligence and the Conflict Smelter Scheme both reference and incorporate a purely public standard set by the US Dodd-Frank financial legislation (Haufler 2016).

One way in which forces of cooperation and competition among TGIs could be detected in their evolution over time is by examining the overlaps among governance initiatives through shared members within issue areas. Here, the underlying idea is to examine whether two TGIs with the same issue focus are more or less likely to have members in common. An overlap in issue focus bears a potential for competition for resources, participants, and political influence because the overlapping institutions seek to address the same or a similar set of governance problems. At the same time, operating in the same issue area has the potential to facilitate the overlap of members and the combination of governance efforts across TGIs. Through shared participants, institutions can exchange knowledge and expertise regarding the set of governance problems they care about, coordinate the standards that they create, exchange lessons learned, and build synergies among their participants. I explore these possibilities by examining the following competing hypotheses:

Hypothesis 1: Two TGIs that operate in the same issue area are more likely to have common participants.

Hypothesis 2: Two TGIs that operate in the same issue area are less likely to have common participants.

In addition to cooperation and competition, it could also be that the size of governance initiatives affects the evolution of their overlaps. Larger TGIs, that is TGIs with more participants, can draw on a wider and deeper pool of material and non-material resources, such as funds, personnel, and technical expertise, which allow them to more effectively build and maintain relationships with other governance arrangements than smaller initiatives. The more participants a TGI has, the more prolific it can be in its interactions with other governance initiatives and the higher the likelihood that it shares members with other initiatives. At the same time, a large number of participants can serve as a signal for the legitimacy, or at least acceptance, of the goals and mission of a TGI by a broad range of stakeholders. This may particularly hold if a TGI is based on a broad participation of public actors, such as states and IGOs. Such participation, in turn, may increase the incentives for other TGIs to establish a relationship with these initiatives because they seek to benefit indirectly from their legitimacy by being recognized as associated with them. This leads to my third hypothesis:

Hypothesis 3: Large TGIs are more likely to have common participants with other TGIs.

Finally, in addition to factors exogenous to the network of TGIs, overlaps among TGIs may be driven by endogenous dynamics within the TGI network. First, the emergence of overlaps among TGIs could be driven by clustering among TGIs. This implies that the likelihood that two TGIs overlap with each other through shared participants is positively affected by these two TGIs overlapping with the same third TGI (the friend of my friend is my friend). Two TGIs that overlap with the same third TGI are able to obtain information about each other's missions, goals, and participants which, everything else being equal, puts them in a better position to establish a relationship with one another if they are interested in doing so. Second, it is plausible to expect that, once a TGI overlaps with other TGIs, other yet unconnected TGIs pay increased attention to this already well-connected governance initiative and seek to establish a relationship with this TGI themselves. One way of doing this is to include states and non-state actors as participants that are also members of well-connected TGIs. In doing so, the not well-connected TGI may gain access to the resources, recognition, and legitimacy of the already well-connected governance initiative. If this popularity dynamic is present in the TGI network, we would expect to observe a tendency towards TGIs having more than one overlap relationship with other TGIs in the network of TGIs. This leads to my two last hypotheses:

Hypothesis 4: Two TGIs that have common participants with the same third TGI are more likely to have common participants with each other.

Hypothesis 5: TGIs tend towards having common participants with more than one TGI.

7.3 DATA, MEASUREMENT, AND METHODS

To test my hypotheses, I use information from the new TGIWP dataset (Westerwinter 2019a). At the time of writing, this dataset contained information on 457 TGIs in a broad range of issue areas and covered the time period between 1885 and 2016. No undisputed definition of the universe of TGIs in world politics exists, and it is unclear how many initiatives this universe of cases contains. While there is consensus that the number of transnational public-private governance arrangements has risen dramatically over recent decades, numbers range across sources. Kaul (2006, p. 219), for example, shows that the number of transnational public-private partnerships has increased from 50 in the mid-1980s to at least 400 in the 2000s. Similarly, Abbott and Hale (2014) document the existence of 223 global solution networks of varying mixtures of states, businesses, NGOs, and other actors. Focusing on environmental governance, Andonova (2010, p. 25) reports the creation of over 400 so-called type II partnerships in the aftermath of the 2002 United Nations (UN) World Summit on Sustainable Development and the initiation of more than 150 collaborations between UN agencies, states, and non-state actors between 1998 and 2008 under the auspices of the UN Fund for International Partnerships. Finally, Widerberg and Stripple (2016) show that even within a single issue area, such as climate change, the number of existing governance arrangements reported varies considerably across databases. This ambiguity is at least partially due to the lack of a widely shared definition of transnational public-private governance arrangements (Börzel and Risse 2005; Abbott and Snidal 2009). Therefore, building on existing research, I develop my own definition of TGIs and use it to specify the criteria for selecting initiatives into the sample.

For purposes of this chapter, I define TGIs as institutions that: (1) involve at least one state and/or IGO, one business actor, and one civil society actor; (2) perform tasks that are related to governing transnational problems; and (3) are institutionalized to the extent that they provide a basis for regular interactions among their participants.[5] First, I focus on institutions that are of a multi-stakeholder nature and bring together actors from the public sector, the private for-profit sector, as well as the private non-profit sector. In other words, my definition of a TGI zooms in on the centre of the governance triangle proposed by Abbott and Snidal (2009). State actors are governments, government agencies, or representatives of government agencies. Institutions in which the only public participant is a local government actor, such as a municipality or a city, are not included in the sample. IGOs may participate in a TGI either through their main secretariat or their organizational branches. Business actors encompass firms, business associations, and business foundations. Civil society actors may be NGOs, NGO coalitions, or universities and research institutes.

Second, TGIs are built to fulfil a task or set of tasks that is related to providing governance beyond the level of individual states. Governance tasks that TGIs may be concerned with include the creation of rules and standards that govern the behaviour of states, corporations, and other actors; the implementation of rules and standards; the financing of projects; and the facilitation of information exchange and networking related to a transnational problem. Other governance tasks that may be part of the activities of TGIs are agenda-setting as well as the monitoring, enforcement, and adjudication of rules and standards (Abbott and Snidal 2009; Avant et al. 2010). In other words, TGIs are explicitly focused on contributing to governing transnational problems or the provision of global public or collective goods. As a consequence, the sample of TGIs used in this chapter does not include, for example, transnational criminal and terrorist networks.

Third, TGIs are institutionalized to the extent that they provide a basis for regular interactions among their participants (Börzel and Risse 2005; Schäferhoff et al. 2009). This criterion distinguishes TGIs with some form of organizational structure, such as a chair, regular administrative support, or regular meetings of participants, from instances of cooperation that are of an irregular, ad-hoc nature. For example, one-off meetings or projects of public and private actors are not captured by my definition of a TGI. Therefore, the sample does not include spontaneous project-based collaboration between states and/or IGOs, business, and NGOs that do not generate some form of organizational structure.

All institutions that meet these three requirements are part of the population of TGIs in world politics as understood here and are therefore included in the data collection. An example of a TGI that governs issues related to global health is the Global Fund to Fight AIDS, Tuberculosis and Malaria (GF) (Liese and Beisheim 2011). Based on the participation of states, the private sector, and NGOs, the GF garners, manages, and disburses resources to fight HIV/AIDS, tuberculosis, and malaria. Founded in 2002, the GF has a governing board and its work is supported by the Global Fund Secretariat, the Global Fund's Office of the Inspector General, as well as other institutional structures (Global Fund to Fight AIDS, Tuberculosis and Malaria 2019). In the security area, the International Code of Conduct for Private Security Service Providers' Association (ICoCA) was founded in 2013 (Avant 2016). Building on the International Code of Conduct for Private Security Service Providers process that started in 2009, the ICoCA brings together states, private security companies, and a range of civil society organizations that collaborate to create and monitor standards for private security service providers and how states make use of their services. The ICoCA meets on an annual basis in the form of its general assembly, has its own secretariat, and working bodies focused on different substantive aspects of the governance of private security providers (ICoCA 2019).

The data used in this chapter is a sample of the population of TGIs in world politics. The creation of the sample took place between 2015 and 2016. To identify TGIs, the definition of a TGI was applied to seven source databases that were identified as containing information about transnational governance arrangements. These databases include the Global Solution Network database (Global Solution Networks 2019), the UN Environment Programme's Climate Initiatives Platform (UN Environment Programme 2019), and the UN's Sustainable Development Goals Partnerships Platform (UN 2019). The team of researchers also searched all organizations that are recorded as 'networks' in the Yearbook of International Organizations (Union of International Associations 2019). Further, the research team applied the TGI criteria described above to the organizations documented in the databases of Andonova et al. (2016) as well as ongoing research projects at the University of Zürich and Duke University.[6] Finally, the research team searched websites of TGIs that were included in the sample for references and links to identify additional organizations that meet the TGI definition. Thus, in total, eight sources were used to identify cases for the dataset. Across these sources, 457 TGIs were identified for inclusion in the dataset. A list with the names of all TGIs in the sample is available from the author upon request.[7]

I use descriptive and inferential network analysis to investigate the evolution of the pattern of overlaps among TGIs over time. In terms of inferential network analysis, I use temporal exponential random graph models (TERGMs) to examine how TGI overlaps have developed over time and what factors have shaped this development (Hanneke et al. 2010; Cranmer and Desmarais 2011). TERGMs are an extension of the basic exponential random graph model (ERGM) for the analysis of longitudinal network data. The ERGM is a general model for statistical inference with network data (Robins et al. 2007; Lusher et al. 2013). ERGMs are probability models for networks on a given set of actors with the response variable being the probability of the observed collection of network ties. They allow modelling the network generating process that underlies an observed pattern of relationships as a function of both exogenous actor and dyad covariates, on one hand, and endogenous structural effects on the other (e.g. the friend of my friend is my friend).[8]

Importantly, the ERGM relaxes the assumption of conditional independence of observations that is critical for conventional statistical analysis (Cranmer and Desmarais 2011). In fact, one of the primary advantages of ERGMs, as opposed to the conventional regression framework, is that they allow for explicitly characterizing interdependencies among units. Thus, using ERGMs to analyse the evolution of TGI overlaps helps to avoid faulty inference on the independent variables of interest and allows for direct modelling of the complex relational interdependencies at work in the TGI network.

The dependent variable in my models is the pattern of overlaps among TGIs in a given year *t*. In the inferential network analysis, I focus on TGI overlaps in the period 1980–2014.[9] I measure TGI overlaps as the number of shared state participants between two TGIs, *i* and *j*. I dichotomize shared state participants, which results in a dependent variable that is coded 1 if two TGIs have at least one state member in common in year t, and 0 otherwise. Let Ω be an $n \times n$ matrix, where the element ω_{ij} represents the relation directed from TGI *i* to TGI *j*, $(i, j = 1,\ldots, n)$ and *n* is the number of TGIs in the network. TGI overlap ties are non-directional and, therefore, $\omega_{ij} = \omega_{ji}$. The elements of Ω can, thus, be formally defined as follows:

$$\omega_{ij} = \omega_{ji} = \begin{cases} 1 & \text{if TGI } i \text{ and TGI } j \text{ have at least one shared state participant in year } t \\ 0 & \text{otherwise.} \end{cases} \quad (7.1)$$

While using joint state participants as an approximation of TGI overlaps in the context of a large-*n* analysis is useful, it also has limitations. TGIs that share a large number of state participants are likely to face higher odds of interacting with each other, both at the institutional level as well as through their shared members. However, it is possible that two TGIs with a large number of shared state members do not interact. Likewise, TGIs with few or no shared state members may still interact in the context of governing the policy problems they are designed to address. Furthermore, the operationalization of TGI overlaps in the form of joint state members does not allow us to differentiate between different qualities of connections as well as between the implications of which states are joint members of two TGIs (e.g. two TGIs that have Germany and the United States as joint members versus two TGIs that are connected because they share Guinea-Bissau and Burundi as members).

Alternatively, one could examine shared participants other than states, such as business actors, NGOs, or IGOs. While this is in principle possible, it would be challenging to normalize these memberships by the number of total actors that existed in the international system in a given year (something that is feasible with shared state members). Working without such a normalization runs the risk that increases in shared members are just a reflection of increases in overall numbers of actors in the international system and not necessarily an indicator for increases in overlaps among governance initiatives. Thus, despite its limitations, operationalizing TGI overlaps as shared state members is a useful first step in broadening the existing research on transnational governance interactions towards incorporating more general large-*n* analyses. The results obtained from this analysis provide the basis for more detailed theoretical and empirical explorations in future research.

To test hypotheses 1 and 2, I examine whether TGIs that operate in the same issue area are more or less likely to share state members. For this purpose, I group TGIs into nine issue areas: security, trade and commerce, environment, development, human rights, health, finance, social affairs, and technical. For each issue area, I create a TGI-by-TGI matrix that indicates whether two TGIs are concerned with the same kind of policy issue. If hypothesis 1 is supported, I expect a positive coefficient for this variable in the TERGMs. If hypothesis 2 is supported, the coefficient on the *shared issue area* variable should be negative. I also include a variable that captures the lower of the number of issue areas in which two TGIs operate in order to control for issue area activity.

To examine hypothesis 3, I include a variable that measures, for each pair of TGIs, how large the smaller of the two TGIs is in terms of its total number of participants. For each TGI in the dataset, the total number of participants is the sum of its state, IGO, business, and civil society participants. If it is true that larger TGIs have a stronger tendency to overlap with other TGIs, then the coefficient of this variable should be positive. In addition, to examine whether particular groups of participants are consequential for the pattern of overlaps among TGIs, I differentiate overall participation into participation of states, IGOs, business actors, and civil society organizations. For each group, I create a variable that measures the lower of the two participant counts of a pair of TGIs. For example, the variable *number business low* captures the lower of the two business actor participant counts in a pair of TGIs.

To capture the tendency towards clustering within the TGI network described in hypothesis 4, I examine whether we can observe triadic closure within the TGI network. If clustering shapes the pattern of TGI overlaps, then if TGI *i* overlaps with TGI *k* and TGI *j* overlaps with *k,* then *i* and *j* are also likely to have an overlap tie. To capture this effect, I include a measure for the geometrically weighted edgewise shared partner distribution (GWESP) proposed by Snijders et al. (2006) in the TERGMs. GWESP is useful from a modelling perspective as it captures specific linear combinations of an entire distribution of shared partner statistics. Importantly, GWESP is 'shown to work well in practice in overcoming model degeneracy and producing models that fit a wide range of data well' (Goodreau et al. 2009, p. 111). The expectation of clustering in the form of triadic closure in the TGI network should result in a positive coefficient on the GWESP statistic.

To examine hypothesis 5, I include a statistic that measures node popularity in the TGI network. It describes the number of times that two TGIs, *i* and *j,* have an overlap tie with the same TGI, *k*. I include this structural dependency in the TGI variable in the TERGM specification as a 2-star statistic. A 2-star is defined as a node, *i,* and a set of two different nodes, *k,* such that *i* has direct ties with both nodes *k*. If hypothesis 5 is supported, I expect a positive coefficient for this variable in the TERGMs.

7.4 EMPIRICAL ANALYSIS

I start my empirical analysis by examining the distribution of TGIs across issue areas. While the recent growth of TGIs is striking, it is not universal. We observe more of a turn towards TGIs as institutional arrangements for governing transnational problems in some issue areas than in others. In 2014, about 64 percent of all initiatives in the dataset are concerned with social problems; 50 percent deal with environmental issues, including climate change and sustainable energy-related problems. Forty-one percent deal with development, and 25 percent address health problems. TGIs have also begun to enter the realms of high politics, with 25 percent of the TGIs in the data dealing with trade and commerce, 5 percent with finance, and 4 percent with security issues.[10] IGOs, by contrast, are most prominent in the areas of social affairs, development, trade and commerce, and technical issues. Since the dataset only contains a sample of all TGIs in world politics, these figures should be interpreted cautiously. Nevertheless, we can see that TGIs are not equally distributed among issue areas and that they are not limited to low politics issues. They are also important for governing economic and security problems.

If we move from this static snapshot to an examination of the evolution of TGIs in different issue areas, we observe variation in the growth trajectories of TGIs across issue areas. The beginning of the rise of TGIs as forms of global governance varies markedly across issue areas. The creation of TGIs in the environment, development, health, and social affairs domains can be traced back to the 1970s. It began to increase slowly in the 1970s and 1980s, and then exponentially in the 1990s. For TGIs operating in the technical and trade and commerce areas, we observe a similar growth pattern, although here growth started later and its intensity has so far remained below that of environment, development, health, and social affairs TGIs. In the areas of finance, security, and interestingly human rights, the speed and intensity of TGI growth has remained low until today. Thus, both in terms of TGI distribution and growth patterns we observe striking differences across issue areas.

But what if we move from the level of individual TGIs towards analysing their overlaps? Is the frequency of TGIs in different issue areas related to the amount of overlap that we observe between governance initiatives? To address this question, I examine the networks of TGIs and the patterns of ties within them over time. As a first step, I create networks that include as nodes all TGIs that were created up to a particular year. For example, the 1990 TGI network includes as nodes all TGIs that have been created before or in 1990 and were not terminated until 1990. To identify ties between TGIs, i.e. TGI overlaps, in a given year, I measure the shared state participants of two TGIs. Thus, ties between TGIs can be either absent or present. If they are present, ties can be constituted by a minimum of one shared state participant between two TGIs up to a maximum of as many shared state participants as the international system has states in a particular year.[11]

Figure 7.1 shows the evolution of the overlaps among TGIs based on shared state participants using network density. Network density is a descriptive measure of network analysis and captures the overall level of connectedness of nodes in the network as a ratio of present ties over all possible ties. Thus, in the TGI network, density captures the extent to which TGIs in a given year were connected through shared state participants. Larger values indicate high levels of TGI overlap, while low density suggests little overlap. As we can see from the left-hand panel of Figure 7.1, the overall amount of overlap among TGIs has varied between a maximum of 0.53 in 1980 and a minimum of 0.39 in 1997. Overall, we observe a downward trend in TGI overlap based on shared state participants between 1980 and 2014. After a sharp decline in the 1980s and 1990s, the level of overlap reached its minimum in 1997 and then increased again slightly in the early 2000s. In 2014, we have a TGI network density of 0.41, which indicates that 41 percent of all possible shared state participant ties between the TGIs in the data were realized.

If we move from the aggregate of the network of all TGIs to those that are focused on particular issue areas, the picture becomes more nuanced. First of all, as shown in the right-hand panel of Figure 7.1, we see that the overall density of TGI overlaps varies across issue areas and from the

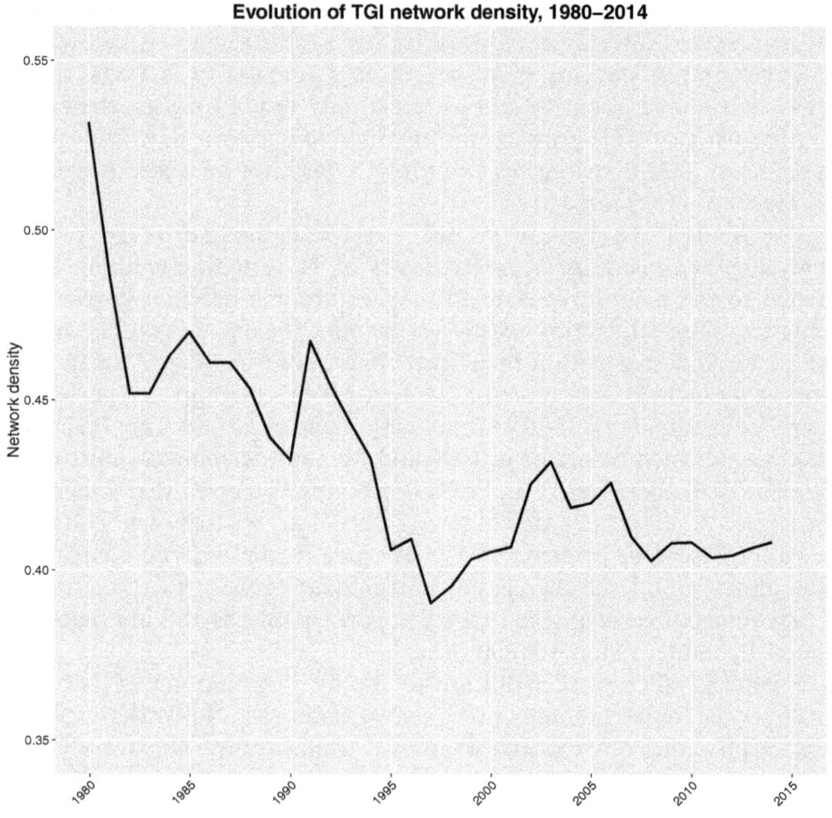

Figure 7.1 TGI overlaps, 1980–2014

aggregate network of all TGIs. TGIs that govern health issues overlap more often than TGIs in general and in other issue areas. The same holds for trade and commerce TGIs until the early 2000s. By contrast, finance and security TGIs show less overlaps than TGIs in general. We also see that the evolution of TGI overlaps differs across issue areas. In the health and trade and commerce areas, we have an overall downward trend in the level of TGI overlaps over time. In the finance and security areas, we observe an increase of overlaps. Environment TGIs are characterized by a relatively steady level of overlap density that ranges between 0.55 and 0.42 between 1980 and 2014. Thus, the frequency of TGIs in an issue area does not directly translate into high levels of overlap among initiatives. Issue areas with a large number of TGIs operating within them, such

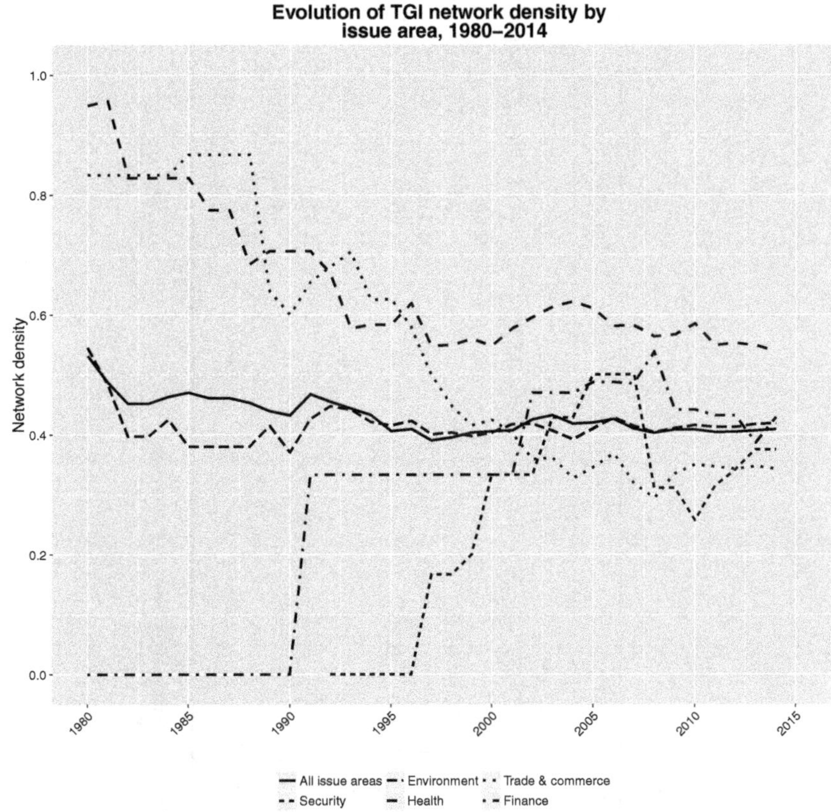

Figure 7.1 (*Continued*)

as the environment domain, do not necessarily reflect a high level of TGI overlaps relative to other issue areas. By contrast, issue areas with relatively few TGIs compared to others, such as health and trade and commerce, have relatively high levels of TGI overlaps.

How can we explain this pattern of evolution of overlaps among TGIs? What factors make two TGIs likely to overlap through shared state participants? To shed light on this question, I estimate TERGMs for the TGI-by-TGI network between 1980 and 2014. The models presented in Table 7.1 provide a first test of my five hypotheses.[12] In all four models, shared issue area is positively correlated with the likelihood of the presence of a shared state participants tie between two TGIs. Two TGIs that operate in the same issue area are more likely to overlap

Table 7.1 TERGMs TGI network evolution, 1980–2014

	Model 1	Model 2	Model 3	Model 4
Edges	–0.474*	–12.658*	–15.977*	–23.137*
	[–0.491; –0.458]	[–13.131; –12.209]	[–16.394; –15.595]	[–24.670; –22.564]
Shared issue area	0.113*	0.087*	0.062*	0.050*
	[0.104; 0.129]	[0.077; 0.102]	[0.051; 0.073]	[0.029; 0.074]
Number issue areas low		0.446*	0.502*	0.419*
		[0.431; 0.463]	[0.489; 0.517]	[0.361; 0.496]
Number participants low			0.562*	0.464*
			[0.543; 0.578]	[0.394; 0.517]
Clustering				4.938*
				[4.409; 6.097]
Popularity				0.008*
				[0.005; 0.011]

Note: * 0 outside the confidence interval. Confidence intervals based on 5000 bootstrap iterations.

through shared member states than two TGIs that focus on different issues. This effect is statistically significant in all models. In light of my hypotheses, it seems that cooperation among TGIs with the same issue focus is a stronger driver of TGI overlaps than competition among governance initiatives that operate in the same issue domain. Hypothesis 1 receives support, while there is no evidence in the data in support of hypothesis 2.

Furthermore, the total number of participants of a TGI (*number participants low*) is consistently positively and statistically significantly associated with TGI overlap. In other words, large TGIs seem likely to overlap with other initiatives. This lends support to hypothesis 3. Is this effect driven by a particular group of TGI participants or is it consistent independent of whether we examine state participants, business participants, civil society organizations, or IGOs? The models in Table 7.2 shed light on this question by differentiating between TGI size based on the four constitutive groups of TGI participants. As we can see in model 9, once we control for other types of participants, the number of civil society organizations in TGIs has a negative, and the number of states a positive and statistically significant effect on the likelihood of two TGIs overlapping via shared state participants. The number of business actors and IGOs has no effect that is distinguishable from 0. Thus, it seems that pairs of TGIs that involve larger numbers of civil society organizations are less likely to overlap, while TGIs with larger numbers of state participants are more likely to overlap. We also see that differentiating between different groups of TGI participants does not affect the results with respect to shared issue area as a driver of the evolution of TGI overlaps.

Finally, we also find evidence that dynamics endogenous to the TGI network are important drivers of the evolution of the pattern of relationships within it. Specifically, we find a substantively strong and statistically significant tendency towards clustering within the TGI network. Two TGIs that are connected via shared member states to the same third TGI also have an increased likelihood of overlapping with each other through shared state members. Importantly, clustering within the TGI network is the substantively strongest driver of TGI overlaps in all models. This suggests that compared to shared issue area and TGI size, clustering is a substantively more important driver of the evolution of TGI overlaps. Similarly, TGIs seem to overlap with more than one other TGI at a time. As the positive and statistically significant coefficient on the popularity variable suggests, there seems to be a tendency towards popularity in the network of TGI overlaps. Together, these findings lend support to hypotheses 4 and 5.

Table 7.2 TERGMs TGI network evolution number of participants differentiated, 1980–2014

	Model 5	Model 6	Model 7	Model 8	Model 9
Edges	–20.291*	–20.983*	–21.551*	–31.430*	–31.440*
	[–22.238; –19.661]	[–22.649; –20.396]	[–23.418; –20.945]	[–38.197; –30.215]	[–37.165; –30.244]
Shared issue area	0.047*	0.037*	0.066*	–0.007	–0.000
	[0.026; 0.074]	[0.016; 0.064]	[0.044; 0.093]	[–0.025; 0.009]	[–0.018; 0.016]
Number issue areas low	0.360*	0.380*	0.403*	0.719*	0.717*
	[0.310; 0.427]	[0.328; 0.453]	[0.348; 0.475]	[0.666; 0.776]	[0.665; 0.775]
Number business low	0.065*				0.070*
	[0.044; 0.092]				[0.050; –0.102]
Number civil society low		0.177*			–0.038*
		[0.153; 0.191]			[–0.077; –0.017]
Number FIGOs low			0.504*		0.099*
			[0.438; 0.554]		[0.085; 0.109]
Number states low				1.887*	1.872*
				[1.722; 2.017]	[1.707; 2.019]
Clustering	4.956*	4.926*	4.917*	4.983*	4.970*
	[4.394; 6.238]	[4.371; 6.062]	[4.380; 6.194]	[3.957; 9.236]	[3.959; 8.583]
Popularity	0.008*	0.008*	0.008*	0.005*	0.005*
	[0.006; 0.011]	[0.006; 0.011]	[0.005; 0.011]	[0.003; 0.008]	[0.003; 0.008]

Note: *0 outside the confidence interval. Confidence intervals based on 5000 bootstrap iterations.

7.5 CONCLUSION

In this chapter, I examine the evolution of the pattern of overlaps among TGIs. I also analyse the factors that facilitate and constrain TGI overlaps. Based on new data, I find that the rise of TGIs as a mode of global governance has played out differently across different issue areas. While, over the past 20 years we see a strong increase in TGIs in the environment, development, and social affairs domains, there is much less growth in the human rights, finance, and security areas. I also observe variation in the evolution of TGI overlaps both across issue areas and over time. TGIs operating in the health and trade and commerce domains tend to overlap to a greater extent with each other than TGIs that are active in other issue areas including environment, security, and finance. Thus, the mere frequency of TGIs in an issue area does not directly translate into an increase in the extent of TGI overlaps. This variation opens up room for the empirical analysis of the driving and constraining forces that shape overlaps among TGIs.

Using inferential network analysis, I start analysing the factors that are related to TGI overlaps. My results indicate that TGIs that operate in the same issue area are more likely to overlap. This suggests that cooperation among governance initiatives that operate in the same issue domain could be one of the driving forces underlying TGI overlaps. I also find that large TGIs have a stronger tendency to overlap with other initiatives. Larger TGIs can draw on the material and political resources of a larger number of participants, which makes interactions with other governance initiatives more feasible. Finally, I find that dynamics endogenous to the TGI network shape the evolution of TGI overlaps. Specifically, my analysis shows that TGI overlaps are driven by clustering as well as popularity within the TGI network. Thus, the extent to which TGIs overlap and variations in patterns of overlaps over time are driven by both the characteristics of governance initiatives and their participants as well as dynamics that play out within the network of TGIs.

The theoretical discussion and empirical analysis provided in this chapter offer insights into some of the questions that lie at the centre of this edited volume and point to avenues for future research on transnational governance interactions. I show that the editors' initial observation that transnational governance interactions emerge, multiply, and persist in some cases, while they dwindle, collapse, or fail to emerge in others, applies across issue areas and over time, although these dynamics play out differently in different issue areas and at different points in time. Furthermore, my analysis emphasizes that the set of drivers and constraints of transnational governance interactions consists of a broad range of factors at various levels of analysis and includes characteristics of governance initiatives and their participants, as well as endogenous dynamics within the population of governance initiatives.

Future studies can take these findings into several directions. First, while I treat the characteristics of governance initiatives and their participants as exogenous to the evolution of the overlaps among them, researchers could explore whether the characteristics of governance initiatives and their participants co-evolve with the network of relationships among initiatives. For example, does the size of a governance initiative affect its likelihood of overlapping with other initiatives or do governance initiatives attract more participants and therefore grow in size as a function of their increased connectedness in the network of governance initiatives? Second, it is unlikely that the network of overlaps among transnational governance initiatives evolves independent of the overlaps among other types of international institutions, such as IGOs. Future studies may investigate whether the ups and downs of transnational governance overlaps occur in response to overlaps among other forms of global governance.

NOTES

1. This research was funded by the Swiss Network for International Studies. I am grateful for the excellent research assistance of Christian Andres, Ruslan Aybazov, Tino Good, Stefano Jud, Rosie Keller, Laura Leibundgut, Giulia Parini, Dominik Schneeberger, Johannes Schultz, and Keto Schumacher in preparing this chapter. I also thank Ken Abbott, Burkard Eberlein, Stefan Renckens, Virginia Haufler and Stepan Wood for helpful suggestions. I especially thank Sharlene Westerwinter for sharing her thoughts and for always supporting me.
2. IGOs are traditional intergovernmental organizations, such as the United Nations, the World Bank, or the World Trade Organization. According to the Correlates of War project, an international institution is an intergovernmental organization if it has at least three member states, holds regular plenary meetings at least once every ten years, and possesses a permanent secretariat and corresponding headquarters (Wallace and Singer 1970; Shanks et al. 1996; Pevehouse et al. 2004). IGOs are distinct from informal intergovernmental organizations (IIGOs) in which states participate in regular meetings to make policies and coordinate behavior without a formal institutional support structure (Vabulas and Snidal 2013).
3. In policy-oriented studies, TGIs are often referred to as multi-stakeholder initiatives (Truex and Soreide 2010; Jerbi 2012; MSI Integrity 2017).
4. In this chapter, I use a preliminary version of the Transnational Public-Private Governance Initiatives in World Politics data. Westerwinter (2019a) introduces the full dataset.
5. Westerwinter (2019a) expands this definition and includes transnational membership and scope of activities as an additional characteristic of TGIs.

6. I thank Katja Michaelowa and her team at the University of Zürich as well as Ben Collins and Suzanne Katzenstein (Collins and Katzenstein 2016) and their team at Duke University for sharing their databases.
7. Westerwinter (2019a) presents an updated version of the TGI dataset used in this chapter that includes information on 636 TGIs that were created between 1885 and 2017.
8. Thus, the statistical approach pursued in this chapter goes beyond existing technical solutions to interdependence (e.g. Heagerty et al. 2002), which tend to obscure rather than reveal substantively interesting patterns of interdependence and can create their own problems (for a discussion, see Gartzke and Gleditsch 2008).
9. Few TGIs existed prior to the 1980s, which yields sparse TGI overlaps. This creates problems for estimating TERGMs. I therefore drop the years prior to 1980 from the analysis. I also drop the years 2015 and 2016 since there are only five TGIs in total in the dataset that were founded after 2014.
10. The issue areas in which TGIs operate are not coded as mutually exclusive, that is one TGI can be active in more than one issue area.
11. To identify the states that existed in the international system in a given year, I use the Correlates of War Project data on the composition of the international system (Correlates of War Project 2019).
12. Goodness of fit analyses indicate that none of the models presented in Tables 7.1 and 7.2 have degeneracy problems.

REFERENCES

Abbott, Kenneth W. (2012), 'The transnational regime complex for climate change', *Environment and Planning C*, **30** (4), 571–90.

Abbott, Kenneth W. and Duncan Snidal (1998), 'Why states act through formal international organizations', *Journal of Conflict Resolution*, **42** (1), 3–32.

Abbott, Kenneth W. and Duncan Snidal (2000), 'Hard and soft law in international governance', *International Organization*, **54** (3), 421–56.

Abbott, Kenneth W. and Duncan Snidal (2009), 'The governance triangle: regulatory standards institutions and the shadow of the state', in Walter Mattli and Ngaire Woods (eds), *The Politics of Global Regulation,* Princeton, NJ: Princeton University Press, pp. 44–88.

Abbott, Kenneth W., Philipp Genschel, Duncan Snidal and Bernhard Zangl (2015), 'Orchestration: global governance through intermediaries', in Kenneth W. Abbott, Philipp Genschel, Duncan Snidal and Bernhard Zangl (eds), *International Organizations as Orchestrators,* Cambridge: Cambridge University Press, pp. 3–36.

Abbott, Kenneth W., Jessica F. Green and Robert O. Keohane (2016), 'Organizational ecology and institutional change in global governance', *International Organization*, **70** (2), 247–77.

Abbott, Kenneth W. and Thomas Hale (2014), 'Orchestrating global solution networks: a guide for organizational entrepreneurs', manuscript, Arizona State University.

Alter, Karen J. and Sophie Meunier (2009), 'The politics of international regime complexity', *Perspectives on Politics*, **7** (1), 13–24.

Andonova, Liliana B. (2010), 'Public-private partnerships for the earth: politics and patterns of hybrid authority in the multilateral system', *Global Environmental Politics*, **10** (2), 25–53.

Andonova, Liliana B., Thomas N. Hale and Charles Roger (2016), 'National policy and transnational governance of climate change: substitutes or complements?' Forthcoming International Studies Quarterly.
Avant, Deborah (2016), 'Pragmatic networks and transnational governance of private military and security services', *International Studies Quarterly,* **60** (2), 330–42.
Avant, Deborah D., Martha Finnemore and Susan K. Sell (2010), 'Who governs the globe?', in Deborah D. Avant, Martha Finnemore and Susan K. Sell (eds), *Who Governs the Globe?,* Cambridge: Cambridge University Press, pp. 1–31.
Avant, Deborah and Oliver Westerwinter (2016), 'Introduction: networks and transnational security governance', in Deborah Avant and Oliver Westerwinter (eds), *The New Power Politics. Networks and Transnational Security Governance,* Oxford: Oxford University Press, pp. 1–18.
Barnett, Michael, Jon Pevehouse and Kal Raustiala (2016), 'The future of global governance', paper prepared for the workshop, 'The Future of Global Governance?', Social Trends Institute, Barcelona, Spain, 1–3 December.
Börzel, Tanja A. and Thomas Risse (2005), 'Public-private partnerships: effective and legitimate tools of transnational governance?', in Edgar Grande and Louis W. Pauly (eds), *Complex Sovereignty: Reconstituting Political Authority in the Twenty-first Century,* Toronto: University of Toronto Press, pp. 195–216.
Burca, Grainne de, Roebert O. Keohane and Charles Sabel (2013), 'New modes of pluralist global governance', *International Law and Politics*, **45** (3), 723–81.
Busch, Marc L. (2007), 'Overlapping institutions, forum shopping, and dispute settlement in international trade', *International Organization,* **61** (4), 735–61.
Cashore, Benjamin, Graeme Auld and Deanna Newsom (2004), *Governing Through Markets: Forest Certification and the Emergence of Non-State Authority*, New Haven, CT: Yale University Press.
Christiansen, Thomas and Christine Neuhold (2012), 'Introduction', in Thomas Christiansen and Christine Neuhold (eds), *International Handbook on Informal Governance* (eds), Cheltenham, UK: Edward Elgar, pp. 1–15.
Collins, Ben and Suzanne Katzenstein (2016), 'Mapping MSIs: normative implications and strategies going forward', working paper, MSI Integrity.
Correlates of War Project (2019), *State System Membership*, accessed 27 August 2019 at http://www.correlatesofwar.org/data-sets/state-system-membership.
Cranmer, Skyler J. and Bruce A. Desmarais (2011), 'Inferential network analysis with exponential random graph models', *Political Analysis,* **19** (1), 66–86.
Cutler, Claire A., Virginia Haufler and Tony Porter (eds) (1999), *Private Authority and International Affairs*, Albany, NY: State University of New York Press.
Dingwerth, Klaus (2007), *The New Transnational. Transnational Governance and Democratic Legitimacy*, Houndmills, Basingstoke, UK: Palgrave Macmillan.
Eberlein, Burkard, Kenneth W. Abbott, Julia Black, Errol Meidinger and Stepan Wood (2014), 'Transnational business governance interactions: conceptualization and framework for analysis', *Regulation and Governance*, **8** (1), 1–21.
Fransen, Luc (2011), 'Why do private governance organizations not converge? A political-institutional analysis of transnational labor standards regulation', *Governance*, **24** (2), 359–87.
Gartzke, Erik and Kristian Skrede Gleditsch (2008), 'The ties that bias. Specifying and operationalizing components of dyadic dependence in international conflict', unpublished manuscript, University of California, San Diego.

Global Fund to Fight AIDS, Tuberculosis and Malaria (2019), *Global Fund Overview*, accessed 27 August 2019 at https://www.theglobalfund.org/en/overview/.
Global Solution Networks (2019), *Global Solution Networks*, accessed 27 August 2019 at http://gsnetworks.org/.
Goodreau, Steven M., James A. Kitts and Martina Morris (2009), 'Birds of a feather, or friend of a friend? Using exponential random graph models to investigate adolescent social networks', *Demography*, **46** (1), 103–25.
Green, Jessica F. (2014). *Rethinking Private Authority. Agents and Entrepreneurs in Global Environmental Governance*, Princeton, NJ: Princeton University Press.
Hall, Rodney Bruce and Thomas J. Biersteker (eds) (2002), *The Emergence of Private Authority in Global Governance*, Cambridge, UK: Cambridge University Press.
Hanneke, Steve, Wenjie Fu and Eric D. Xing (2010), 'Discrete temporal models for social networks', *Electronic Journal of Statistics*, **4**, 585–605.
Haufler, Virginia (2016), 'Corporations, governance networks, and conflict in the developing world', in Deborah Avant and Oliver Westerwinter (eds), *The New Power Politics. Networks and Transnational Security Governance,* Oxford: Oxford University Press, pp. 224–44.
Heagerty, Patrick, Michael D. Ward and Kristian S. Gleditsch (2002), 'Windows of opportunity: window subseries empirical variance estimators in international relations', *Political Analysis*, **10** (3), 304–17.
ICoCA (International Code of Conduct for Private Security Service Providers' Association) (2019), *Respect for Human Rights: Promoting Responsible Private Security*, accessed 27 August 2019 at https://icoca.ch/en.
Jerbi, Scott (2012), 'Assessing the roles of multi-stakeholder initiatives in advancing the business and human rights agenda', *International Review of the Red Cross*, **94** (887), 1027–46.
Kaul, Inge (2006), 'Exploring the policy space between markets and states. Global public-private partnerships', in Inge Kaul and Pedro Conceicao (eds), *The New Public Finance: Responding to Global Challenges,* Oxford: Oxford University Press, pp. 219–68.
Keohane, Robert O. (1984), *After Hegemony. Cooperation and Discord in the World Political Economy*, Princeton, NJ: Princeton University Press.
Keohane, Robert O. and Joseph S. Nye (1971), 'Transnational relations and world politics: an introduction', *International Organization*, **25** (3), 329–49.
Koremenos, Barbara (2013), 'What's left out and why? Informal provisions in formal international law', *Review of International Organizations*, **8** (2), 137–62.
Koremenos, Barbara (2016), *The Continent of International Law: Explaining Agreement Design*, Cambridge, UK: Cambridge University Press.
Krasner, Stephen D. (ed.) (1983), *International Regimes*, Ithaca, NY: Cornell University Press.
Lake, David A (2010), 'Rightful rules: Authority, order, and the foundations of global governance', *International Studies Quarterly*, **54** (3), 587–613.
Liese, Andrea and Marianne Beisheim (2011), 'Transnational public-private partnerships and the provision of collective goods in developing countries', in Thomas Risse (ed.), *Governance Without a State? Policies and Politics in Areas of Limited Statehood,* New York: Columbia University Press, pp. 115–43.
Lusher, Dean, Johan Koskinen and Garry Robins (eds.) (2013), *Exponential Random Graph Models for Social Networks,* Cambridge, UK: Cambridge University Press.

MSI Integrity (2017), *The New Regulators? Assessing the Landscape of Multi-Stakeholder Initiatives. Findings from a Database of Transnational Standard-Setting Multi-Stakeholder Initiatives*. Technical report, MSI Integrity and the Duke Human Rights Center at the Kenan Institute for Ethics.

Overdevest, Christine and Jonathan Zeitlin (2014), 'Assembling an experimental regime: transnational governance interactions in the forest sector', *Regulation and Governance*, **8** (1), 22–48.

Pauwelyn, Joost, Rameses A. Wessel and Jan Wouters (2012), *Informal International Lawmaking*, Oxford: Oxford University Press.

Pevehouse, Jon, Timothy Nordstrom and Kevin Warnke (2004), 'The correlates of War 2 International Governmental Organizations Data Version 2.0', *Conflict Management and Peace Science*, **21** (2), 101–19.

Porter, Tony (2014), 'Technical systems and the architecture of transnational business governance interactions', *Regulation and Governance*, **8** (1), 110–25.

Raustiala, Kal and David G. Victor (2004), 'The regime complex for plant genetic resources', *International Organization*, **58** (2), 277–309.

Robins, Garry, Pip Pattison, Yuval Kalish and Dean Lusher (2007), 'An introduction to exponential random graph (p*) models for social networks', *Social Networks*, **29** (2), 173–91.

Shanks, Cheryl, Harold K. Jacobson and Jeffrey H. Kaplan (1996), 'Inertia and change in the constellation of international governmental organizations, 1981–1992', *International Organization*, **50** (4), 593–627.

Snijders, Tom A.B., Philippa Pattison, Garry Robins and Mark S. Handcock (2006), 'New specification for exponential random graph models', *Sociological Methodology*, **36** (1), 99–153.

Truex, Rory and Tina Soreide (2010), 'Why multi-stakeholder groups succeed and fail', Policy Research Working Paper 5495, World Bank.

UN (United Nations) (2019), *Sustainable Development Goals Partnerships Platform*, accessed 27 August 2019 at https://sustainabledevelopment.un.org/partnerships/.

UN Environment Programme (2019), *Climate Initiatives Platform*, accessed 27 August 2019 at http://climateinitiativesplatform.org/index.php/Welcome.

Union of International Associations (2019), *The Yearbook of International Organizations*, accessed 27 August 2019 at https://uia.org/yearbook.

Vabulas, Felicity and Duncan Snidal (2013), 'Organization without delegation: informal intergovernmental organizations (IIGOs) and the spectrum of intergovernmental arrangements', *Review of International Organizations*, **8** (2), 193–220.

Vogel, David (2009), 'The private regulation of global corporate conduct', in Walter Mattli and Ngaire Woods (eds), *The Politics of Global Regulation,* Princeton, NJ: Princeton University Press, pp. 151–88.

Wallace, Michael and J. David Singer (1970), 'Intergovernmental organization in the global system, 1815–1964: a quantitative description', *International Organization*, **24** (2), 239–87.

Waltz, Kenneth N. (1979), *Theory of International Politics*, New York: Random House.

Westerwinter, Oliver (2014), 'The politics of transnational institutions: power, bargaining, and institutional choice', PhD dissertation, European University Institute.

Westerwinter, Oliver (2019a), 'Transnational public-private governance initiatives in world politics: introducing a new dataset', forthcoming paper, *Review of International Organizations*.
Westerwinter, Oliver (2019b), 'Contextual design: existing international institutions and new transnational governance', manuscript, University of St. Gallen.
Widerberg, Oscar and Johannes Stripple (2016), 'The expanding field of cooperative initiatives for decarbonization: a review of five databases', *WIREs Climate Change*, **7** (4), 486–500.
Wood, Stepan, Kenneth W. Abbott, Julia Black, Burkard Eberlein and Errol Meidinger (2015), 'The interactive dynamics of transnational business governance: a challenge for transnational legal Theory', *Transnational Legal Theory*, **6** (2), 333–69.

8. Issue control in transnational business governance interactions

Lasse Folke Henriksen and Leonard Seabrooke

8.1 INTRODUCTION

In this chapter we focus on the role of professional networks in transnational business governance interactions (TBGIs). Professional networks, in many ways, provide the context of interaction for issue-specific work within and across transnational business governance (TBG). Those setting the rules and standards in TBG, promulgating them and making sure they are implemented and evaluated increasingly consider themselves 'professionals'. This entails that work practices pertaining to all stages of the governance process move from being considered non-professional to undergoing some degree of professionalization. A field that is professional entails participants directing attention at each other as professional peers. This can evoke a sense of community and belonging around collective professional identities and mutual recognition around shared competencies and methodology. Professionalization in issue-specific governance fields can also, however, follow messier trajectories where expertise based on institutional experience becomes the driver of peer recognition. Studying the character and structure of the professional networks involved in TBGIs is important to understand how these interactions play out and what their likely outcomes are.[1]

In this chapter we argue that people we call 'issue professionals' have risen as a prominent actor type within the institutionally hybrid fields of governance that we witness in TBG. These fields entail intense interactions between institutionally diverse actors, such as firms, NGO, states and international organizations, at one or several stages of the governance process. Issue professionals are actors who are seen as 'knowing well' within an issue-specific field of governance; recognition among their professional peers is often based on a combination of specialized technical expertise and institutional mobility (Seabrooke and Henriksen 2017).

The remainder of the chapter consists of four sections. Part 2 locates key hurdles to productive TBGIs that are identified by contributors to this volume. We suggest that there is some analytical purchase in addressing these hurdles via our professional-organizational nexus framework. Part 3 introduces this framework, based around the concept of issue professionals as an important ideal-type actor in TBG. Part 4 elaborates further on our framework, locating the professional-organizational nexus and examining issue control as an outcome of two-level network dynamics in TBGIs. Part 5 discusses how professional and organizational characteristics can be matched to identify where there are likely opportunities for issue professionals to make the most of their TBGIs.

8.2 TRANSNATIONAL BUSINESS GOVERNANCE INTERACTIONS

This volume is concerned with a key question in international political economy and international law: how transnational business governance interactions can be organized and orchestrated in a way that advances marginalized actors, promotes sound environmental, financial and social standards, while also improving regulatory capacities. The promise of hybrid governance and non-state involvement in standard-setting is greater stakeholder engagement, accountability and transparency. This promise is difficult to keep, especially when those involved may have converged on a current interest but have prospects that diverge.

The contributors to this volume point to both the opportunities and frustrations professionals, policymakers and organizations face when trying to live up to this promise. In particular, they point to four key hurdles where TBGIs produced outcomes that deviated from good intentions. These hurdles arise when:

1. There are clear gaps between policy design and implementation;
2. Standard-setting bodies become arenas for competing interests;
3. There are clear power asymmetries in the adoption of standards and best practices; and
4. The interests of professionals involved in the interaction extend beyond the standard of concern to controlling the issue more generally.

These hurdles can be identified in several of the case-based contributions to this volume. First, Sophia Carodenuto and Benjamin Cashore (Chapter 10) demonstrate that the design of timber legality assurance systems was far removed from their targets, and that domestic implementation in Cameroon had negative effects on behaviour like bribery. Phillip Paiement's study (Chapter 11) of the EU's Renewable Energy

Directive (RED) shows that the voluntary basis for the monitoring of biomass production sites has permitted non-state actors to take liberties that undermine the regime for vulnerable parties. By contrast, Jane Winn (Chapter 5) demonstrates that EU regulators have intervened in an excessive manner to force the private sector to upgrade payment systems.

Second, on how standard-setting bodies become arenas for competition, Paul Verbruggen and Tetty Havinga (Chapter 2) demonstrate that national governments have differed in their interactions with the Global Food Safety Initiative (GFSI), with some asserting a 'regulatory enrolment' strategy to pull non-state schemes into viewing issues their way. Similarly, Matthew Bach (Chapter 12) points to how the Oil & Gas Climate Initiative (OGCI) may have enrolled diverse actors to promote 'pro-innovation principles' that have regulatory effects, but its commitment as an organization is unclear – it is an arena for professional competition over the 'carbon-constrained' future of oil and gas, which allows those involved in the process to hedge against regulatory interventions while also acknowledging the need to lower their risks and uncertainties.

Third, on power asymmetries, Donal Casey (Chapter 9) shows how the retailers that formed GLOBALGAP organized and produced strategies allowing the organization to dominate the issue, hampering more democratic initiatives. Paul Foley (Chapter 14) provides an account of how alternative and more progressive bodies working on ethical eco-certifications are in a structurally weak position compared to the Marine Stewardship Council (MSC), which then blocks progressive developments. Similarly, Simin Gao and Christopher Chen (Chapter 13) illustrate how, in finance, isomorphic pressures on the governance of derivatives trading were intense, while regional variation in the governance of futures trading was more possible. This state of affairs prevailed until the global financial crisis, when international pressures led to greater conformity around a common Western model.

Fourth, on the autonomy of professionals involved in controlling issues, Graeme Auld and Stefan Renckens (Chapter 6) show how the mobility of individual assessors involved with the MSC creates tensions with the audit firms and their work. The consequence of professional mobility is a destabilization of the functioning of the transnational body, with control over assessment knowledge fragmented. Furthermore, the prominence of professional mobility in different transnational interactions is, in part, a popularity contest. As Oliver Westerwinter (Chapter 7) clearly outlines, TBGIs produce a more crowded field on popular issues, such as the environment and development. Other issues are less attractive for such coordination, such as security (where states still rule), finance (where rents are high) and human rights (where large NGOs dominate).

These hurdles point to micro, meso and macro-level phenomena that comprise the interactions in the framework for this volume (Eberlein et al. 2014). This volume adopts a broad notion of interactions to include steering mechanisms, consensus formation and relationships where actors are drawn into regulatory schemes, be it through coercion, enrolment or other means. Interactions can be both outcomes and casual factors, a notion that relaxes the idea that one always has to find the 'smoking gun' in discussing how regulation moves forward. This notion emphasizes that specifying change in the environment in which interactions take place is also important.

We suggest that our professional-organizational nexus framework can shine some light on the hurdles identified above: policy gaps, competition in standard-setting, power asymmetries and professional autonomy. Focusing on how professionals operate in two-level professional and organizational networks can provide us with some insights into why policy gaps are common, what is at stake in standard-setting beyond the content of the standard, how power asymmetries are reinforced and why professionals seek to maintain autonomy and not be beholden to particular organizations.

8.3 ISSUE PROFESSIONALS

Professionals are individuals with abstract higher-level learning and specific skill sets to address tasks (Abbott 1988). Doctors and lawyers come to mind when we characterize what is exceptional about professional work. We suggest that transnationally, professionalism is often linked more tightly to issues than to formal boundaries of professional groups (Seabrooke and Henriksen 2017). Recently scholars have noted how professionals have become more transnational and partially delinked from national professional associations (Seabrooke 2014; Carter et al. 2015; Brock 2016; Harrington 2016), while also maintaining selective ties to local networks (Dezalay and Garth 2016; Block et al. 2018; Spence et al. 2018).

We suggest that an 'issue professional' is a particular type of professional who is engaged in transnational organizing and is particularly important in determining how issues are treated and governed transnationally. Transnationality is important for issue professionals' capacity not to conform to defined jurisdictional roles common in a national context. Rather than being located in specific associations such as the

American Medical Association or the like, these professionals combine knowledge and skills to enhance their attempts at control of a specific issue. Rather than relying on the conventional link between professionals and organizations in how issues are addressed (Noordegraaf 2011a), issue professionals actively foster professional and organizational networks in their attempts at issue control.

Issue professionals are different from 'issue entrepreneurs' (Carpenter 2007). As a category, issue entrepreneur is used to provide an actor-based explanation of issue emergence. Issue professionals are not necessarily inventors of issues, but they are involved in generating, maintaining and defending attempts at issue control. There is also greater flexibility in how issue professionals determine their tasks in treating issues. Tasks include the modalities of action for professionals in how they classify, reason and take action on identified problems, or how they diagnose, infer and treat their identified problems (Abbott 1988). Changes to tasks can occur through processes of professionalization, including demands to conduct work in particular ways, according to codes of ethics. Professionalization also entails treating professionalism as a capacity to manage and organize tasks rather than the knowledge and training that inform their execution (Faulconbridge and Muzio 2008; Evetts 2013). Issue professionals have particular tasks, but they are customized for the issue of concern rather than belonging to, and being reinforced by, one particular expert discipline. On issues that are highly technical and narrow, professional tasks and transnational issue control may go hand in hand (Ban et al. 2016). Transnational organizing on the severe acute respiratory syndrome (SARS) and bird flu crises provide an example, where medical experts aligned with international organizations to diagnose and treat the problems. Here 'classic' professional tasks were closely matched to how a transnational issue was treated (see also Nilsson 2017). By contrast, the emergence of 'multi-problems' has led to dilemmas when the relevant professions and the organizations needed do not align (Noordegraaf 2011b). In a domestic context, professional coordination can be made more difficult by jurisdictional battles over tasks and who is permitted to work on what issues. Transnationality matters here in liberating issue professionals to use their career experience and differing skills in a context in which domestic jurisdictions are not relied upon, can potentially be ignored or are secondary in how issues are treated.

This is not to say that there are not struggles over who may work on what issues, but that issue professionals are not limited to the common domestic understanding of national professional jurisdictions. Issue professionals have a strong incentive to maintain their position within a network by excluding others who do not agree with their understanding of issues or threaten their resources. In some areas, such as financial reform, issue professionals behave according to prestige incentives and will be reluctant to introduce controversial ideas and topics in which they have little expertise, such as shadow banking, or political power, such as tax havens (Ban et al. 2016; Seabrooke and Wigan 2016; this dynamic may help explain the similarity of futures exchange governance design in Asia and the West: Gao and Chen, Chapter 13). Rather, they will control debates in a manner that confirms their affiliations and prestige networks (Seabrooke and Tsingou 2014). Similarly, professionals can network to ensure that knowledge production is controlled by them rather than by bureaucracies formally running the organization (Brivot 2011; this dynamic may also be at work in sustainable supply chain management [SSCM]: Meidinger, Chapter 3).

Investigating how professionals engage with their own peer networks and organizational networks is useful in considering how transnational organizing happens. We see transnational issues as organized through a professional-organizational nexus that is fruitfully conceived as a two-level network. We develop this idea further in the following section.

8.4 THE PROFESSIONAL-ORGANIZATIONAL NEXUS AS A TWO-LEVEL NETWORK

We argue that a professional-organizational nexus is the key to explaining how TBGIs play out. We provide a framework for understanding how professionals and organizations interact in transnational networks based on differentiating professional work roles and organizational types. This framework aligns closely with research that seeks to understand how professionals and other actors work in 'ecologies', be they 'linked ecologies' (Seabrooke and Tsingou 2015), 'overlapping ecologies' (Liu 2017, 2018) or 'issue ecologies' (Block-Lieb and Halliday 2017).

Professionals in our framework draw on organizational and professional networks at the same time, building alliances where they can to control how issues are treated. While others prefer to describe professionals as operating in organizational fields, we stress that both professionals and organizations have agency in forming strategies, and that neither provides a passive space for the other to operate within. As such, professionals will seek to extend their networks through common identification with other similarly trained professionals, though often not through formal professional associations, or by creating alliances with professionals with different but complementary sets of skills. By doing so they can engage in 'epistemic arbitrage' between different pools of professional knowledge and be seen as important brokers of knowledge on the issue of concern within the professional and organizational network (Seabrooke 2014). Professionals engaging in this kind of activity often do so beyond their organizations, which provide opportunities for network building but rarely oversee all activities in which those tasked with work engage.

We propose that a professional-organizational, two-level network permits us to look at relations between two different sets of actors when it comes to processes of issue control. Our two-level network consists of professional networks that are interpersonal, built throughout careers on issue-specific work, and organizational networks that exist where alliances are formed between organizations. TBGIs occur within such two-level networks.

Figure 8.1 depicts a simple two-level network that is involved in organizing a particular transnational issue. At the top are organizations (the white discs), which are networked, with the one on the far left the most isolated and the one in the centre the most connected. Below the organizations are issue professionals (the black discs), who have their own network. The professional on the far left is the least connected

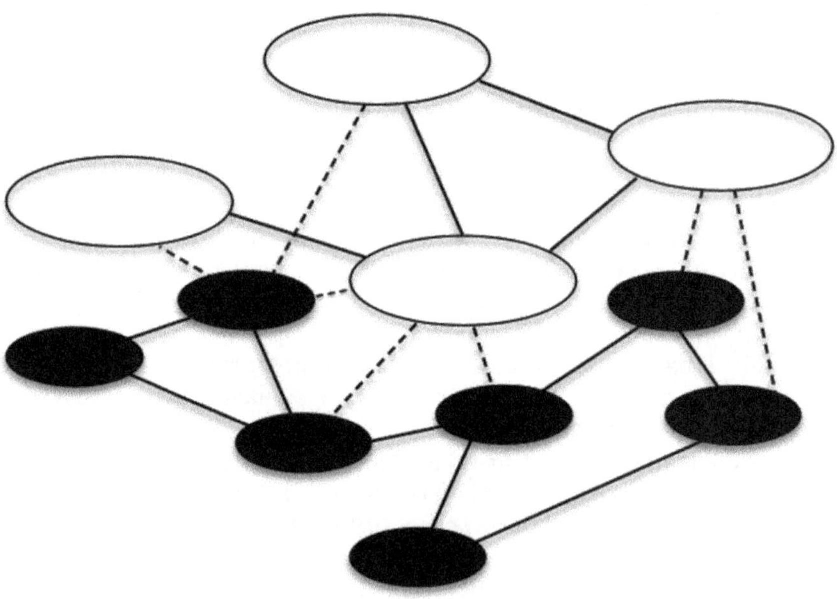

Source: Henriksen and Seabrooke 2016.

Figure 8.1 Professional-organizational, two-level network

and the professional on the centre right the most. Dashed lines between the professionals and the organizations represent ties between the two levels. In this example the professional in the upper left is linked to three organizations, while those on the far left and bottom are connected to no organizations but are connected to other professionals. On this hypothetical transnational issue the professional with three ties to organizations may have a lot of influence on how the issue is treated and how tasks are allocated.

Within such two-level networks, prominent professionals are often 'multiple insiders' (Vedres and Stark 2010) through common work teams, event attendance, involvement in expert groups and committees, and so forth, through which they build their issue-specific personal networks, but also get access to varied organizational contexts. These professionals inhabit similar 'thought worlds' across different organizational contexts (Vad Baunsgaard and Clegg 2013).

Organizations also attempt to control issues and have a range of strategies at their disposal. An obvious one is to increase the technicality of the issue to fend off competitors (Büthe and Mattli 2011). If organizations can control what is considered to be legitimate expertise on an issue, or if they coordinate professional and organizational networks tightly, then this strategy can work. Global professional service firms, for example, are highly integrated and seek to control particular issues through their knowledge management systems (Boussebaa 2009). However, if such control is not possible, then organizations need to engage in framing contests to try and control how issues are treated (Hasselbalch and Seabrooke 2018). Once there is a contest, professionals have a range of options to increase their own autonomy and propose views that run counter to organizational interests.

Describing the professional-organizational nexus as a two-level network allows us to consider how professionals and organizations take positions on particular issues relative to their peers, as well as the character of the ties between those involved in TBGIs. Our focus is on professional and organizational interaction within networks, and network theory is important in providing a foundation for understanding different types of behaviour.

A key lesson from network analysts is that the formation of social alliances in attempts to achieve control comes from patterns of interaction in which individuals and organizations are embedded (Granovetter 1985; Bearman 1993, p. 10; Emirbayer 1997; Wellmann et al. 1997). A network is a set of actors, or nodes, along with a set of ties, the relations that connect them. Relations in networks interconnect through shared points and form paths that indirectly link actors that would otherwise not be directly related. This conception enables a view of a network as a connected system, linking local behaviours to the system as a whole. A great deal of network analysis is concerned with characterizing network structures, how actors are positioned within them. Network theory makes claims about the mechanisms and processes that interact with a network structure to allow certain actors in the network to act (Borgatti and Halgin 2011). In general, a network view of strategy pays attention to the flow of knowledge and resources between professionals and organizations and the strategic behaviour emerging from their attempts to gain control over the ongoing distribution patterns within these flows.

Two-level networks also exhibit so-called 'small world' characteristics that have implications for the strategies of issue control that professionals and organizations may pursue. The idea of a small world comes from the observation that actors in a 'big world' often experience themselves as being surprisingly close to each other (Watts 1999). Transnational professional networks have large geographical distances, and the number of individuals and organizations doing work may be in the hundreds or thousands. The social distances across which organizing must be performed are complex. Creating ties to central organizations can generate what has been called 'global microstructures' (Knorr Cetina and Bruegger 2002), which often build on established frameworks that permit interpersonal ties to flourish and establish behavioural rules. Within these networks small world characteristics can emerge, with networks clustered around particular organizational alliances or professional communities. Professionals can use their skills and knowledge to shape the way organizations treat and organize issues within the network (Kroeger 2011; Seabrooke 2014).

How professionals connect is also important to understand. This may be through events, conferences, and workshops to which we normally attribute little importance, but which can be crucial for establishing how issues are treated and who controls contributing knowledge (Lampel and Meyer 2008). The use of such events to share business cards and contacts, and establish connections on social media, may seem unimportant, but can be useful in establishing 'weak ties' to actors who are at a greater social distance (Granovetter 1973). This is one of the reasons organizations value professionals who can demonstrate high job mobility, and why professionals seek out new opportunities, with many persistently 'on the market' (see Auld and Renckens, Chapter 6, for analysis of this mobility).

Professionals who change positions a lot or are not tied to particular organizations run the risk of being seen as weak but broad in their embedding strategy across two-level networks. The contrary opinion is that when this behaviour is done successfully it can contribute to 'robust action' that allows influence across networks to be greater (Padgett and Ansell 1993; Bothner et al. 2010). Studies in organizational sociology have demonstrated that those credited with good ideas are often actors occupying sparse network regions abundant with 'structural holes' (Burt 2004). Structural holes are network locations where two nodes are disconnected, which offers an opportunity for a third node to bridge the gap and gain control of the flow of information between the disconnected nodes. Where network densities are comparatively low, exploiting disconnections can be a successful strategy for organizations and professionals working to change perceptions on particular issues. Where network densities are comparatively high, organizations or professionals can exercise tighter control over how issues are treated.

Our aim here is not to provide an exhaustive account of network theories, but to demonstrate that the structural properties of networks are important in understanding how agents can behave and how transnational business governance interactions exhibit two-level dynamics.

8.5 MATCHING PROFESSIONAL AND ORGANIZATIONAL CHARACTERISTICS

Our general advice to scholars researching TBGIs is to be wary about assuming the location and form of organizational action. We agree with others who have stressed the dangers of organizational nominalism and the need for a 'relational turn' in sociology (Emirbayer 1997). Of course there are limits. Rather than everything being relational, our proposal is that understanding interactions within a two-level professional and organizational network is useful. This allows us to trace TBGIs and hybrid forms of governance while also keeping in mind the professional and organizational strategies at play.

Professional strategies will undoubtedly vary, with some aligning well with organizational strategies, while in other cases professionals will work against or around organizations. In our framework, organizational networks provide opportunities, and the scope of opportunities is also informed by organizational characteristics.

If we are to match up professionals to organizational characteristics in TBGIs, then we first need to relax some assumptions that are common in various strands of literature. First of all, the sociology of professions literature tells us that professions fight for jurisdictional control over how issues are treated, and who can work on them (Abbott 1988). This body of work also tells us that professionalism provides a 'third logic' compared to that of bureaucracy or the market (Freidson 2001). The assumption of sealed and siloed professions can be challenged when it comes to investigating TBGIs. As the contributors to this volume show, national professional associations are not commonly invoked to organize transnational standards, rules and norms. While they may be involved in select cases, such cases are the exceptions rather than commonplace.

Another assumption that must be relaxed is that the denomination of organizational types provides a useful shorthand in telling us what the organization actually does. We know from the literature in international relations that states design international organizations and give them clear mandates that dominant member states expect them to fulfil (Koremenos et al. 2001). We know that passionate norm entrepreneurs and civil society networks inform how NGOs behave (Keck and Sikkink 1998). And we know that business firms want control above all other things, including profit (Fligstein 1996). But these insights need to be investigated on an ongoing basis and should not be treated as core assumptions. This is important because organizations are rarely silos, and have internal fights. For example, sustainability managers may struggle with procurement managers to control purchasing agendas and influence C-suite executives in lead firms (Meidinger, Chapter 3). Conflicts between mandated objectives, professional norms and science are common within international organizations and NGOs, and strongly inform how policy scripts are created (Kentikelenis and Seabrooke 2017). We should expect such conflicts to exist in organizations involved in TBGIs. Our professional-organizational nexus concept helps us to identify such contests over what we refer to as issue control.

Our two-level network is a useful conceptual device here to pick apart how the hurdles identified in this book arise and what can be done about them. Understanding different types of organizational characteristics is also important in explaining how organizational form does not determine organizational behaviour within professional-organizational networks.

Organizational forms and logics can be differentiated by five characteristics that become increasingly important as competition within professional networks intensifies:

1. Scope
2. Autonomy
3. Resources
4. Staffing
5. Knowledge centralization

Scope is the narrowness or breadth of an organization's mandate. This can vary widely, with organizations such as Greenpeace, the World Bank and Unilever having wide mandates. The professional-organizational networks in which such organizations work are likely to have many structural holes for professionals to exploit. By contrast, narrower mandates of organizations such as the Bank for International Settlements (BIS) and the Tax Justice Network will require more specialized tactics from professionals seeking issue control (Ban et al. 2016; Seabrooke and Wigan 2016).

Autonomy refers to the level of independence organizations have from their principals. This is important in determining how much slack and slippage there is between the organization and its principals, where greater autonomy provides professionals internal and external to the organization greater opportunities for issue control.

Resources refers to how organizations acquire resources to fund their activities. Where organizations rely on membership subscriptions, the definition of what counts as core resources and targeted resources is important for professional and organizational activity. This definition varies widely across international organizations and NGOs. Where the organization is able to raise its own funding, professional autonomy is also likely to increase or be matched to sources other than the subscription base or principal. A contrast can be drawn between the United Nations Development Programme (UNDP) and the United Nations Office for Project Services (UNOPS); the latter is self-funding and acts very much like a firm compared to the former, which is heavily embroiled in UN bureaucratic politics.

Staffing refers to the organization's openness in hiring professionals, especially staff on ongoing as opposed to project-specific contracts. This is important in determining how departments, units and work teams are composed. This can also vary across organizational forms, with international organizations and NGOs often constrained to hire from subscribing member states or chapters, which can distort how issues are controlled within the organization (Chorev 2012). Firms are not immune to these issues either, with often a strong bias in hiring to conform to established routines and status perceptions (Lupu and Empson 2015). Even in organizations that are assumed to have tight control over their professional staff, such as the International Monetary Fund, there are cases where the use of external experts has been important in how issues are controlled (Seabrooke and Nilsson 2015).

Knowledge Centralization refers to the degree of knowledge centralization within the organization on the issue it seeks to control. This also applies to international organizations, NGOs and firms. In some cases, activist groups have in-house expertise on particular specialist issues and their professional strategies operate from that basis (Seabrooke and Wigan 2015). However, it is more common that large campaigning

NGOs do not have the expertise to produce knowledge on issues, and thus rely on external experts to produce results for them to use (Stroup and Wong 2017). This same dynamic applies to international organizations and firms, which differ strongly on whether they can produce their own knowledge on issues as they attempt to control them. Variations in this dynamic obviously provide opportunities for professionals. An increased reliance on consultants is notable across all organizational types, which has led to professional jurisdictional battles over issue control (Heusinkveld et al. 2018; Seabrooke and Sending 2019).

Finally, we suggest that thinking through these organizational characteristics helps us to identify professional strategies involved in TBGIs. This framework can be especially useful in thinking through the hurdles identified at the start of this chapter: gaps between policy design and implementation; the use of standard-setting bodies as arenas for competing interests; clear power asymmetries in standards and best practices; and the autonomy and mobility of professionals that can undermine the fidelity of standards. All of these hurdles can be understood as outcomes of professional and organizational strategies within and across their respective networks. Our professional-organizational nexus framework offers some insights into how TBGIs play out and the likely hurdles they encounter. Identifying these dynamics is important to troubleshoot where interactions deviate from their intention of advancing marginalized actors, promoting sound standards and advancing better regulation.

NOTE

1. Errol Meidinger's study of the emerging profession of sustainable supply chain management (SSCM) is a vivid illustration of this phenomenon (Chapter 3).

REFERENCES

Abbott, A. (1988), *The System of Professions: An Essay on the Division of Expert Labor,* Chicago: University of Chicago Press.

Ban, C., L. Seabrooke and S. Freitas (2016), 'Grey matter in shadow banking: international organizations and expert strategies in global financial governance', *Review of International Political Economy*, **23** (6), 1001–33.

Bearman, P. (1993), *Relations into Rhetorics: Local Elite Social Structure in Norfolk, England, 1540–1640*, New Brunswick, NJ: Rutgers University Press.

Block-Lieb, S. and T.C. Halliday (2017), *Global Lawmakers: International Organizations in the Crafting of World Markets,* Cambridge, UK: Cambridge University Press.

Blok, A., M.D. Lindstrøm, M.L. Meilvang and I.K. Pedersen (2018), 'Trans-local professional projects: re-scaling the linked ecology of expert jurisdictions', *Journal of Professions and Organization*, **5** (2), 106–22.
Borgatti, S.P. and D.S. Halgin (2011), 'On network theory', *Organization Science*, **22** (5), 1168–81.
Bothner, M.S., E.B. Smith and H.C. White (2010), 'A model of robust positions in social networks', *American Journal of Sociology*, **116** (3), 943–92.
Boussebaa, M. (2009), 'Struggling to organize across national borders: the case of global resource management in professional service firms', *Human Relations*, **62** (6), 829–50.
Brivot, M. (2011), 'Controls of knowledge production, sharing and use in bureaucratized professional service firms', *Organization Studies*, **32** (4), 489–508.
Brock, D.M. (2016), 'Professionals and their workplaces in emerging markets – a research agenda', *International Journal of Emerging Markets*, **11** (3), 460–72.
Burt, R.S. (2004), 'Structural holes and good ideas', *American Journal of Sociology*, **110** (2), 349–99.
Büthe, T. and W. Mattli (2011), *The new global rulers: The privatization of regulation in the world economy*, Princeton, NJ: Princeton University Press.
Carpenter, R.C. (2007), 'Setting the advocacy agenda: theorizing issue emergence and nonemergence in transnational advocacy networks', *International Studies Quarterly*, **51** (1), 99–120.
Carter, C., C. Spence and D. Muzio (2015), 'Scoping an agenda for future research into the professions', *Accounting, Auditing & Accountability Journal*, **28** (8), 1198–216.
Chorev, N. (2012), *The World Health Organization Between North and South*, Ithaca, NY: Cornell University Press.
Dezalay, Y. and B.G. Garth (2016), '"Lords of the dance" as double agents: elite actors in and around the legal field', *Journal of Professions and Organization*, **3** (2), 188–206.
Eberlein, B., K.W. Abbott, J. Black, E. Meidinger and S. Wood (2014), 'Transnational business governance interactions: conceptualization and framework for analysis', *Regulation & Governance*, **8** (1), 1–21.
Emirbayer, M. (1997), 'Manifesto for a relational sociology', *American Journal of Sociology*, **103** (2), 281–317.
Evetts, J. (2013), 'Professionalism: value and ideology', *Current Sociology*, **61** (5–6), 778–96.
Faulconbridge, J. and D. Muzio (2008), 'Organizational professionalism in globalizing law firms', *Work, Employment and Society*, **22** (1), 7–25.
Finnemore, M. and K. Sikkink (1998), 'International norm dynamics and political change', *International Organization*, **52** (4), 887–917.
Fligstein, N. (1996), 'Markets as politics: a political-cultural approach to market institutions', *American Sociological Review*, **61** (4), 656–73.
Freidson, E. (2001), *Professionalism, the Third Logic: On the Practice of Knowledge*. Chicago: University of Chicago Press.
Granovetter, M. (1973), 'The strength of weak ties', *American Journal of Sociology*, **78** (6), 1360–80.
Granovetter, M. (1985), 'Economic action and social structure: the problem of embeddedness', *American Journal of Sociology*, **91** (3), 481–510.
Harrington, B. (2016), *Capital Without Borders*, Cambridge, MA: Harvard University Press.

Hasselbalch, J. and L. Seabrooke (2018), 'Professional strategies and enterprise in transnational projects', in Mike Saks and Daniel Muzio (eds), *Professions and Professional Service Firms: Private and Public Sector Enterprises in the Global Economy*, Abindgon, UK and New York: Routledge, pp. 46–64.

Henriksen, L.F. and L. Seabrooke (2016), 'Transnational organizing: issue professionals in environmental sustainability networks', *Organization*, **23** (5), 722–41.

Heusinkveld, S., C. Gabbioneta, A. Werr and A. Sturdy (2018), 'Professions and (new) management occupations as a contested terrain: redefining jurisdictional claims', *Journal of Professions and Organization*, **5** (3), 248–61.

Kentikelenis, A.E. and L. Seabrooke (2017), 'The politics of world polity: script-writing in international organizations', *American Sociological Review*, **82** (5), 1065–92.

Koremenos, B., C. Lipson and D. Snidal (2001), 'The rational design of international institutions', *International Organization*, **55** (4), 761–99.

Knorr Cetina, K. and U. Bruegger (2002), 'Global microstructures: the virtual societies of financial markets', *American Journal of Sociology*, **107** (4), 905–50.

Kroeger, F. (2012), 'Trusting organizations: the institutionalization of trust in interorganizational relationships', *Organization*, **19** (6), 743–63.

Lampel, J. and A.D. Meyer (2008), 'Field-configuring events as structuring mechanisms: how conferences, ceremonies, and trade shows constitute new technologies, industries, and markets', *Journal of Management Studies*, **45** (6), 1025–35.

Liu, S. (2017), 'Overlapping ecologies: professions and development in the rise of legal services in China', *Sociology of Development*, **3** (3), 212–31.

Liu, S. (2018), 'Boundaries and professions: toward a processual theory of action', *Journal of Professions and Organization*, **5** (1), 45–57.

Lupu, I. and L. Empson (2015), 'Illusion and overwork: playing the game in the accounting field', *Accounting, Auditing and Accountability Journal*, **28** (8), 1310–40.

Nilsson, A. (2017), 'Making norms to tackle global challenges: the role of Intergovernmental organisations', *Research Policy*, **46** (1), 171–81.

Noordegraaf, M. (2011a), 'Remaking professionals? How associations and professional education connect professionalism and organizations', *Current Sociology*, **59** (4), 465–88.

Noordegraaf, M. (2011b), 'Risky business: how professionals and professional fields (must) deal with organizational issues', *Organization Studies*, **32** (10), 1349–71.

Padgett, J.F. and C.K. Ansell (1993), 'Robust action and the rise of the Medici, 1400–1434', *American Journal of Sociology*, **98** (6), 1259–1319.

Seabrooke, L. (2014), 'Epistemic arbitrage: transnational professional knowledge in action', *Journal of Professions and Organization*, **1** (1), 49–64.

Seabrooke, L. and L.F. Henriksen (eds) (2017), *Professional Networks in Transnational Governance*, Cambridge, UK and New York: Cambridge University Press.

Seabrooke, L. and E.R. Nilsson (2015), 'Professional skills in international financial surveillance: assessing change in IMF policy teams', *Governance*, **28** (2), 237–54.

Seabrooke, L. and O.J. Sending (2019), 'Contracting development: managerialism and consultants in intergovernmental organizations', *Review of International Political Economy*, forthcoming.

Seabrooke, L. and E. Tsingou (2014), 'Distinctions, affiliations, and professional knowledge in financial reform expert groups', *Journal of European Public Policy*, **21** (3), 389–407.
Seabrooke, L. and E. Tsingou (2015), 'Professional emergence on transnational issues: linked ecologies on demographic change', *Journal of Professions and Organization*, **2** (1), 1–18.
Seabrooke, L. and D. Wigan (2015), 'How activists use benchmarks: reformist and revolutionary benchmarks for global economic justice', *Review of International Studies*, **41** (5), 887–904.
Seabrooke, L. and D. Wigan (2016), 'Powering ideas through expertise: professionals in global tax battles', *Journal of European Public Policy*, **23** (3), 357–74.
Spence, C., A. Sturdy and C. Carter (2018), 'Professionals with borders: the relationship between mobility and transnationalism in global firms', *Geoforum*, **91**, 235–44.
Stroup, S.S. and W.H. Wong (2017), *The Authority Trap: Strategic Choices of International NGOs*. Ithaca, NY: Cornell University Press.
Vad Baunsgaard, V. and S. Clegg (2013), '"Walls or boxes": the effects of professional identity, power and rationality on strategies for cross-functional integration', *Organization Studies*, **34** (9), 1299–1325.
Vedres, B. and D. Stark (2010), 'Structural folds: generative disruption in overlapping groups', *American Journal of Sociology*, **115** (4), 1150–90.
Watts, D.J. (1999), 'Networks, dynamics, and the small-world phenomenon', *American Journal of Sociology*, **105** (2), 493–527.
Wellman, B., R.Y.L. Wong, D. Tindall and N. Nazer (1997), 'A decade of network change: turnover, persistence and stability in personal communities', *Social Networks*, **19** (1), 27–50.

PART II

Advancing the interests of marginalized actors

9. Interactions, iteration and early institutionalization: Competing lessons of GLOBALGAP's legitimation

Donal Casey

9.1 INTRODUCTION

As non-state regulatory organizations emerge and develop, they respond to anticipated and actual governance interactions to build, maintain and repair their legitimacy. These interactions span not just cooperation, enrolment and co-optation, but also antagonistic interactions characterized by provocation and conflict (Eberlein et al. 2014). This chapter examines the emergence and subsequent development of GLOBALGAP, a retailer-led transnational business governance (TBG) organization that regulates good agricultural practices (GAP) in the areas of crops, livestock and aquaculture. GLOBALGAP develops GAP standards and oversees a system of implementation based on third-party certification and benchmarking (Casey 2017). In this chapter, I foreground GLOBALGAP's interactions with market, state and civil society actors in order to document and provide an original reading of the role that these interactions play in the legitimation of TBG organizations.

What would eventually become GLOBALGAP began in 1996 as an informal grouping of fresh-produce quality managers, technical managers and purchasers from 13 European retailers (Möller 1998a, p. 71). The grouping was driven by three significant changes in the legal landscape of European food retailing. Firstly, at the national and European Union (EU) level, governments shifted regulatory responsibility from the state to food business operators. The United Kingdom's Food Safety Act 1990 was the starting point for this devolved responsibility (Scott 1990). Under this 'benchmark piece of devolutionist legislation', primary responsibility for ensuring the safety of all branded food products and fresh unpacked (unbranded) products rested on the final supplier

(Campbell et al. 2006, p. 71). Following the bovine spongiform encephalitis (BSE) crisis, the EU adopted a similar approach (ibid.). Regulation 178/2002 placed the primary responsibility for ensuring compliance with food law, particularly in relation to food safety, on food business operators.[1] Secondly, EU product liability rules were extended in the wake of the BSE crisis to include primary agricultural products. Finally, the EU reduced Maximum Residue Levels (MRLs) for pesticides. These changes created risks and incentives that drove the development of new forms of regulation of food safety and quality.

The 13 retailers called themselves the Euro-Retailers Produce Working Group (EUREP) and established a formal membership model to finance the group (Hofmans 1999, p. 6). EUREP described itself as a 'technical working party aimed at promoting and encouraging best agricultural practice in the fruit and vegetable production industry' (Garbutt 1999, p. 5). Over subsequent years, EUREP engaged in a process of enrolment and sought to expand its membership (Bell and Shelman 2009, p. 3). In 2007, EUREPGAP re-branded itself GLOBALGAP (GLOBALGAP 2007). For the sake of simplicity, I will refer to the organization as GLOBALGAP throughout this chapter, even when discussing the period before the rebranding. By the end of 2015, GLOBALGAP's membership had expanded to 47 retailer members, 190 producer and supplier members, 153 associate members and over 150 000 certified producers worldwide.

In this chapter, I argue that an iterative process of legitimation, interactions and the anticipation of interactions with state, market and civil society actors led GLOBALGAP to enhance the representation and participation of structurally weaker parties such as smallholders, and to address concerns about the exclusionary effects of its standards. State, market and civil society actors sought to shift GLOBALGAP towards accommodating both a 'logic of control' and a 'logic of empowerment' (Auld et al. 2015). A logic of control places TBG organizations on a path that prioritizes the integrity of the regulatory system and the creation of mechanisms that effectively regulate behaviour and ensure compliance. A logic of empowerment, by contrast, prioritizes the participation in governance organizations of actors that are marginalized in supply chains. However, early institutionalization confers power on particular stakeholders and crystallizes a dominant logic (ibid.). I contend that the enduring nature of early institutionalization shaped GLOBALGAP's responses to legitimacy demands from state, market and civil society actors, and, in so doing, tempered the potential for these governance interactions to advance democracy, justice and fairness within the organization.

The chapter proceeds in four parts. Part 2 presents the theoretical framework. Part 3 analyses the ways in which GLOBALGAP managed its legitimacy in its early years by anticipating legitimacy demands and learning from past experience. Part 4 examines how the structures, practices and processes developed in its early years were challenged as GLOBALGAP expanded, and its interactions with state, market and civil society organizations increased. Finally, Part 5 sheds light on the enduring nature of the structures, practices and processes that GLOBALGAP developed in its early years, and explores how early institutionalization tempers the inherently iterative nature of legitimacy management.

9.2 LEGITIMACY AND LEGITIMATION

Legitimacy has long been recognized as 'an important resource that organizations need to actively gain and maintain through interaction with their environment to be successful' (Richardson and Eberlein 2011, p. 221). As such, legitimacy is one of the main drivers for TBG interactions, and the conferral of legitimacy is one of the key effects of such interactions (Eberlein et al. 2014). In what follows, I outline my understanding of GLOBALGAP's legitimation and the role that governance interactions play in this process (Casey 2017).

9.2.1 Embedded Regulators

The key to understanding the legitimating dynamics of non-state regulatory organizations lies in the recognition of their embeddedness in an environment that constrains and empowers the adoption of particular structures, practices and processes. The notion of embeddedness rests upon a theoretical shift in the study of organizations from a closed, rational approach to an open systems model (Meyer 2008, p. 453). While a closed systems perspective viewed organizations as hermetically sealed from their environment, open systems approaches focus attention on organizations' interaction with and interdependence on their environments (Scott 1998, pp. 112–7). Scholars have carried forward these insights in an attempt to understand the actions and interactions of TBG organizations. TBG schemes, David Doorey explains, 'are a function of developments in the broader social environment' as the social forces within an organization's environment shape its 'interactions, strategies and outputs' (2015, p. 464). Further, as Bernstein argues, 'what constitutes legitimacy results from the interaction of the community of actors affected by the regulatory institution . . . with the broader institutionalized norms . . . that prevail in the relevant issue area' (2011, p. 19). As such, legitimacy demands stem from pressures by the stakeholders and the rules, norms and cognitions that occupy the environment within which non-state regulators are embedded.

The legitimacy of TBG organizations is rooted in the evaluations and assessments of their sources of legitimacy – their legitimacy communities (Black 2008, p. 144). The acceptance and legitimacy of a regulator flows from congruence between a regulator's structures, practices, processes and outputs and its legitimacy communities' 'beliefs or expectations or . . . interests' (ibid.). As Gulbrandsen emphasizes, 'a non-state standards organization must obtain legitimate rule-making authority and accept answerability to salient constituencies in its organizational field' (2008, p. 568). For legitimacy to be granted, therefore, organizations must be cognizant of and responsive to the legitimacy demands of those actors whose behaviour they seek to shape, or from whom they seek support (Tyler 2006, p. 392).

Identifying GLOBALGAP's legitimacy communities starts in the agricultural supply chain. This supply chain 'directs and frames political struggle of the external audience' as, at each of its stages, market actors choose whether they are willing to support GLOBALGAP's activities (Cashore 2002, p. 512). Here, we must distinguish between supply-side actors such as producers and demand-side actors such as retailers (Cashore et al. 2004, pp. 23–6). It is also important to recognize actors operating in the verification market, including inspection, certification and accreditation bodies, as important legitimacy communities for GLOBALGAP, as well as other non-state governance organizations such as the Global Food Safety Initiative (GFSI) (Tamm Hallström and Gustafsson 2014; Verbruggen and Havinga, Chapter 2).

State actors represent another significant legitimacy community for GLOBALGAP. States have a direct economic interest in the trade of agricultural products and develop national food safety and quality standards that interact and compete with non-state standards (see Verbruggen and Havinga, Chapter 2 for an example). At the intergovernmental level, the United Nations Conference on Trade and Development (UNCTAD), the United Nations Food and Agricultural Organization (FAO) and the United Nations Industrial Development Organization (UNIDO) are three of the most prominent intergovernmental organizations with interests in the regulation of agricultural value chains, particularly in developing countries. The World Trade Organization (WTO), Codex Alimentarius Commission (Codex), the World Organisation for Animal Health (OIE) and the International Plant Protection Convention (IPPC) are also significant. The latter three organizations develop international standards that interact and compete with GLOBALGAP standards, making these organizations a potential source of legitimacy for GLOBALGAP at the international level.

Civil society actors shape non-state regulatory organizations such as GLOBALGAP through interactions such as enrolment, collaboration, provocation and conflict (Bartley 2007, p. 310). Civil society actors include campaign-based, non-governmental organizations (NGOs) such as Greenpeace, OXFAM, Friends of the Earth and the Pesticide Action Network. Other civil society actors are certification-based NGOs, such as the Worldwide Fund for Nature (WWF) and the meta-regulator the ISEAL Alliance and its members. Finally, civil society actors may also take the form of representative organizations such as Bureau Européen des Unions de Consommateurs (BEUC).

It is necessary, however, to look beyond the demands of legitimacy communities and to examine legitimacy demands that take the form of institutionalized norms that structure the environment in which TBG organizations are embedded (Djelic and Sahlin-Anderson 2006b, p. 21). As Wood and others have observed:

> Theoretical frameworks . . . that analyse strategic action in isolation from the social structures in which it occurs, will fail to grasp all the dynamics of governance interactions (2015, p. 350).

Scholars have begun to explore the norms that constrain and empower contemporary TBG organizations (Djelic and Sahlin-Anderson 2006a, pp. 382–3; Bernstein 2011; Auld 2014; Auld et al. 2015). Perhaps the most pertinent of these for this chapter is democratization. This norm exerts pressure by promoting a model of governance that provides structures and procedures that advance transparency, openness, representation, participation, deliberation and consensus.

9.2.2 Managing Legitimacy

Early scholars' suggestions that organizations were passive to the uniform pressures exerted within institutional environments neglected the possibility for organizations to act strategically in their reaction to such pressures, and the role of choice, agency and interests in such actions (Child 1972, p. 4; DiMaggio 1988, pp. 3–22). Given the complexity of environments that impose diverse and potentially conflicting legitimacy demands, seams of latitude emerge from the tension created by the inability to integrate all legitimacy demands and the bounded nature of possible action if a regulator is to survive (Suchman 1995, pp. 585–6). Within this setting, organizations 'can and do formulate strategies for fostering legitimating perceptions of desirability, proprietary and appropriateness' (ibid., p. 577). Given the multitude of legitimacy demands and the potential for conflict among them, non-state regulatory organizations must decide which sources of legitimacy to respond to (Scott 1987, p. 502).

It has been argued that this decision, which lies at the heart of legitimacy management, is shaped by the actors making legitimacy demands and the content of those demands (Oliver 1991, p. 161; see Wood, Chapter 16 for further elaboration of this theme). Organizations have central and peripheral legitimacy communities (Suddaby et al. 2007). These legitimacy communities exert different degrees of influence, which change over time (ibid.). A legitimacy community may have influence over an organization for a number of reasons. Regulatory organization may be dependent upon certain actors for important resources such as capital, expertise, endorsements or personnel (Oliver 1991, p. 164). Further, legitimacy communities may be represented within an organization or have the power to determine its response given the organization's decision-making and membership structure (Pache and Santos 2010, pp. 160–61). Indeed, a regulatory organization's governance structure acts as a 'filter' for legitimacy demands (Greenwood et al. 2011, pp. 342–6).

The content of legitimacy demands and the means by which they are imposed are also significant for understanding organizations' management of legitimacy (Oliver 1991, pp. 167–70). An organization's identity, goals and objectives may temper its response to legitimacy demands, as conformance to these demands may interfere with the organization's ability to fulfil its core mission or may jar with its identity (Oliver 1991, pp. 164–7; Pache and Santos 2010, pp. 459–60; Greenwood et al. 2011, p. 347). In this context, Auld and colleagues speak about challenges to the particular logic of a TBG organization and the willingness of organizations such as the Forest Stewardship Council (FSC) to accommodate demands that seek to shift the organization from one logic to another (Auld et al. 2015).

Legitimacy is 'always problematic', as social values and expectations are often ambiguous, contradictory and ever evolving (Ashforth and Gibbs 1990, p. 177). What constitutes legitimate structures, practices and processes is not stable and is difficult to anticipate in advance (Boström and Tamm Hallström 2013, p. 102). Non-state regulatory organizations must build, revise and recast themselves in order to manage their legitimacy. While legitimation is inherently iterative, the early institutionalization of structures, practices and processes have a significant impact on legitimacy by cementing the distribution of power within an organization and crystallizing a dominant organizational logic (Tamm Hallström and Boström 2010, p. 111). The enduring nature of early institutionalization thus tempers the potential for governance interactions to advance democracy, justice and fairness within non-state regulatory organizations.

9.3 ANTICIPATION AND LEARNING

Individuals involved in the emergence of non-state regulators cannot know clearly in advance what actors the organization will interact with, or indeed the legitimacy demands that will be made of the organization. GLOBALGAP's management of legitimacy in its early years was anticipatory and relied on its founders' prior learning and experience. The anticipatory nature of legitimacy management in an organization's infancy is central to the iterative nature of legitimation.

9.3.1 Anticipating Demands

While retailers were the driving force behind GLOBALGAP, the organization sought support from producers and suppliers in 1999 and opened the organization to associate members, including producers, suppliers, certification bodies, agricultural consultancies and other organizations. Through this process of enrolment, associate members could participate in the organization's technical sub-committees and contribute to the development of the GLOBALGAP protocol (Hofmans 1999, p. 6). Although GLOBALGAP had little interaction in its early years with stakeholders beyond this associate membership constituency, it sought to anticipate legitimacy demands from both state and civil society organizations.

An important change in GLOBALGAP's governance occurred in 2000 when the organization adopted a three-tier membership structure, which still exists today, comprising retail members (tier 1), supplier and producer members (tier 2), and other associate members (tier 3). It also proposed to create a formal supply chain partnership of retailers, producers and suppliers (EUREPGAP 2001a). The retailer, producer and supplier members adopted the proposal for a formalized supply chain partnership at a joint meeting in January 2001 (EUREPGAP 2001a). They created a Steering Committee and a Technical and Standards Committee, constituted by retail and supplier members only, as GLOBALGAP's core decision-making bodies (EUREPGAP 2001c, EUREPGAP 2001d). Interestingly, there was also an ambition to establish a broader multi-stakeholder Council composed of state and civil society actors, which would have had a consultative role (EUREPGAP 2001b; van der Grijp 2008, p. 127).

The opening up of GLOBALGAP's membership and the establishment of the supply chain partnership signalled to broader stakeholders that GLOBALGAP had support from the entire supply chain and was not just a retail-led initiative. Furthermore, in expanding its membership, GLOBALGAP anticipated and responded to possible demands of civil society and state actors to legitimate its governance and standard setting (EUREPGAP 2000; Möller 2006, p. 26). A GLOBALGAP representative opined that a governance structure 'involving all supply chain stakeholders' would lead 'to a high acceptance throughout the sector including Governments and NGOs' (EUREPGAP 2000). The organization also noted that '[a]cceptance by NGOs and Consumer organizations as well as governments and their organizations can be achieved by including them in the advising and standard setting structures' (EUREPGAP 2001e, p. 16).

The anticipatory nature of GLOBALGAP's legitimation extended beyond its governance and standard setting to the organization's system of implementation. Third-party certification was not commonly used to implement food safety and quality standards when GLOBALGAP was established. The organization's development of a system of implementation based on accredited third-party certification was a response to demands from accreditation bodies, but also an attempt to gain acceptance from civil society, state and market actors by anticipating a variety of potential legitimacy demands from these stakeholders (Casey 2017). In 2000, following recommendations from accreditation bodies, the retail members of GLOBALGAP decided that certification by third parties accredited in accordance with International Organization for Standardization (ISO) Guide 65 would be required for all grower options (Möller 2000; Casey 2017). Once GLOBALGAP established an implementation system based on accreditation to ISO Guide 65, the chairperson of GLOBALGAP's Technical and Standards Committee emphasized that '[t]he key to all stakeholder and government recognition of . . . schemes is an ISO accreditation' (EUREPGAP 2001e, p. 16). Furthermore, a GLOBALGAP representative observed that accredited third-party certification would 'also help guarantee transparency towards media and challenges from non-governmental organizations' (Garbutt and Möller 1999, p. 32). Thus, GLOBALGAP anticipated that accredited third-party certification would provide broad acceptance from state and civil society actors, along with the support the organization received from market actors.

9.3.2 Learning and Past Experience

The establishment of the supply chain partnership and a system of implementation based on accredited third-party certification were responses to actual legitimacy demands from market actors and anticipated demands from state and civil society actors. However, the prior learning and experience of the GLOBALGAP's founders heavily influenced the organization's legitimation and responses to these demands. As Philip Schleifer (2015, pp. 6–7) notes: 'Institutional entrepreneurs and their choices are often informed by the lessons they draw from their experiences and the experiences of others.'

GLOBALGAP's founders drew on their prior experience and learning from other regulatory organizations in their attempt to legitimate GLOBALGAP's governance and standard setting. Initially, they gained an understanding of the importance of producer and supplier participation through previous experience in establishing a beef labelling scheme in Germany (Wise 1998, p. 96; Möller 1998b). Prior learning also led to a governance structure featuring industry control of key decision-making bodies along with a broader stakeholder consultative council. A number of GLOBALGAP's founding members participated in the UK's Assured Produce Scheme. Inspiration for the supply chain partnership model came from GLOBALGAP's initial study of the Assured Produce Scheme's partnership between the National Farmers Union and retailers (ibid.). Furthermore, the Marine Stewardship Council (MSC) developed a similar broad stakeholder consultative body in July 2001 (Gulbrandsen 2008, pp. 571–2). As such, the supply chain partnership and the proposed GLOBALGAP Council exemplify conscious mimicry of existing institutional models and conformance with the institutional force of democratization (see also Bach, Chapter 12 and Gao and Chen, Chapter 13, for discussion of mimicry, modelling and mimetic isomorphism).

Prior learning influenced not only standard setting and governance but also GLOBALGAP's approach to the implementation of its standards. Reflecting upon the experience of the Assured Produce Scheme, a GLOBALGAP report noted that:

> [A]n independent verification system is an essential part of any credible and transparent assurance scheme. Experience shows that consumers and opinion formers place little reliance on self-regulation. (Wise 1998, p. 96)

Thus, while GLOBALGAP's move to accredited third-party certification was a response to anticipated and actual legitimacy demands, the decision was informed by the experience and lessons learned by its founders.

GLOBALGAP had very little interaction with state and civil society actors in its early years and remained largely under their radar as it emerged (EUREP 1999). During this period, GLOBALGAP focused on enrolling market actors such as retailers, producers and suppliers, as well as certification and inspection bodies. Nevertheless, it is striking the extent to which GLOBALGAP sought to anticipate the legitimacy demands of state and civil society actors, and the degree to which prior learning and experience informed its legitimacy management. However, non-state regulatory organizations cannot know in advance exactly with whom they will interact, or what demands stakeholders will make of them. Indeed, 'legitimacy cannot be a stable condition but is something fluid that must be repeatedly created, recreated, and conquered' (Boström and Tamm Hallström 2013, p. 102).

9.4 INTERACTIONS AND RESPONSES

Managing legitimacy becomes particularly problematic as non-state regulatory organizations expand in scope, scale and complexity, and are subjected to conflicting demands from an increasing number of legitimacy communities (Ashforth and Gibbs 1990, p. 177). This section examines GLOBALGAP's inability to fully anticipate and satisfy the legitimacy demands of market, state and civil society actors as its governance, standard setting and implementation systems initially developed. In response, GLOBALGAP iteratively rebuilt, revised and strengthened its governance, standard setting and implementation activities in order to manage its legitimacy.

9.4.1 Increased Interaction and Demands

The years following 2001 saw increased criticism of GLOBALGAP's governance and standard setting. Producers and suppliers challenged the extent to which the supply chain partnership gave them sufficient influence and voice within the organization (Leighton 2002, 2003, 2006). Civil society and state actors demanded that GLOBALGAP open up to wider stakeholder representation. For example, during the 2001 GLOBALGAP conference in Bologna, an FAO representative stressed that GLOBALGAP must 'undertake greater consultation with stakeholders to ensure that it responds to diversity' (Tallontire et al. 2008, p. 15). State actors also requested direct consumer representation within the organization (EUREPGAP 2003, p. 4). UNCTAD and the European Commission called for wider stakeholder involvement in

GLOBALGAP's governance to ensure representation of all stakeholders' views and interests (Hoffmann and Vossenaar 2007, p. 19; Interview). In 2002, the Commission observed that GLOBALGAP did not have an open, public and documented consultation process, and that there were limited mechanisms for the participation of interested parties (European Commission 2002). The report concluded that GLOBALGAP failed to meet the participation requirements found in ISO standard-setting guidelines. Civil society actors also demanded that GLOBALGAP provide stakeholder participation beyond market actors within its governance and standard setting, and expressed concerns about the organization's openness and transparency. Indeed, an interviewee stressed that NGOs shared the concern for multi-stakeholder participation and transparency within non-state regulators' governance and standard setting (see also Greenpeace International 2010, p. 3).

One of the more prominent criticisms of GLOBALGAP has been the limited participation of smallholders within its governance and standard setting. An interviewee explained that the German semi-state development agency Deutsche Gesellschaft für Technische Zusammenarbeit (GTZ) requested that GLOBALGAP 'open up some representation space' for smallholders within its governance structure. Further, UNCTAD reported in 2006 that GLOBALGAP standards did not 'adequately take into account local conditions of developing countries' and that there was 'a need for more dialogue between representatives of private-sector standard-setting organizations, governments and producers/exporters in developing countries' (Hoffmann and Vossenaar 2007, p. 18).

Concerns about participation in and transparency of GLOBALGAP's standard-setting procedure were voiced loudly within the WTO Committee on Sanitary and Phytosanitary Measures (SPS Committee). The chairperson of GLOBALGAP, Nigel Garbutt, attended a side event during the 2007 WTO SPS Committee meeting (World Trade Organization, Committee on Sanitary and Phytosanitary Measures 2007d). During the main meeting, St. Vincent and the Grenadines, the Bahamas and Egypt called for non-state, standard-setting organizations such as GLOBALGAP to 'ensure the involvement of producers in developing the standards' (ibid., p. 10). Further, state actors argued that 'proliferation of private standards' raised concerns about the lack of transparency in the manner that the standards were set (ibid., p. 10). An interviewee noted that the concerns raised within the SPS Committee had a significant influence on how GLOBALGAP responded to concerns relating to the participation of smallholders within its governance and standard setting.

GLOBALGAP's system of implementation was also the subject of criticism. While stakeholders recognized the cost of implementation borne by producers as an issue, this issue became increasingly vocalized as GLOBALGAP expanded. Producers, state and civil society actors communicated concern to GLOBALGAP about the cost of implementation and the exclusionary impact of these costs on producers in both developed and developing countries (see for example COLEACP/PIP 2003; World Trade Organization, Committee on Sanitary and Phytosanitary Measures 2005, 2007a, p. 11, 2007b, 2007c, p. 4; UNCTAD 2005; European Fresh Produce Association 2006). An interviewee explained that, like many states, civil society actors viewed the cost implications for producers negatively and had communicated these concerns to GLOBALGAP. The interviewee stressed that GLOBALGAP's certification practices meant that 'there was no element of equity at the bottom of the value chain', and that there was 'nothing in the structural arrangements of GLOBALGAP to deal with such inequity in relation to the cost of compliance'.

9.4.2 Continued Learning and Responding to Legitimacy Demands

In developing certain standards, GLOBALGAP engaged in a process of co-optation, cooperation and enrolment of actors within the standard-setting process. For example, to develop the GLOBALGAP Risk Assessment on Social Practices standard (GRASP, a voluntary add-on module that assesses the social practices in primary production process), GLOBALGAP and the retailer COOP sought cooperation through a public-private partnership with GTZ between June 2005 and April 2007 (Heise et al. 2007). In developing the shrimp base of its aquaculture standard, GLOBALGAP engaged directly with the NGOs Oxfam Novib and the International Union for Conservation of Nature (IUCN) (van Mulekom and Parr 2007). The standard-setting process for both the GRASP add-on module and the aquaculture shrimp standard provided not just broader consultation than previous GLOBALGAP standard setting, but also introduced novel participatory mechanisms such as stakeholder workshops (Heise et al. 2007; Garbutt 2008). Anne Tallontire and others note that '[t]he aquaculture standard development process . . . appear[ed] to mark a significant change in stakeholder engagement, demonstrating a new openness' (2008, p. 17). The learning that took place in the development of these standards, and through GLOBALGAP's cooperative interactions with state and civil society actors such as GTZ and Oxfam Novib, carried forward into

GLOBALGAP's general approach to standard setting and its response to the concerns relating thereto.

The 2006 GLOBALGAP conference in Prague, which was part of a standard revision process ending in 2007, sought to provide not only greater transparency about the revision process, but also more space for participation in it (EUREPGAP 2006). UNCTAD noted that the 2007 revision process was 'an indicator of progress' towards greater transparency and participation (World Trade Organization, Committee on Sanitary and Phytosanitary Measures 2007c, p. 9). By the end of 2006, GLOBALGAP also began to draw upon the transparency and participation requirements contained in international standards to legitimate its standard revision process and respond to increasing concerns raised by market, state and civil society actors (Casey 2017).

In 2011, GLOBALGAP began to introduce new Stakeholder Committees to formalize wider stakeholder participation in its governance structures. An interviewee noted that, due to the limited success of previous efforts to integrate wider stakeholder participation within the organization, a more focused attempt was employed to target specific stakeholder groups. Membership of the Stakeholder Committees consisted of individuals from retail, producer, supplier, certification body, research, NGO, governmental, standard setting, consultant and information technology organizations (GLOBALGAP 2012). The Stakeholder Committees have since been transformed into focus groups. The establishment of the Stakeholder Committees and focus groups suggests GLOBALGAP's continued perception of the importance of wider stakeholder participation within its governance for the acceptance of the organization by certain market, state and civil society actors.

From 2007, GLOBALGAP responded to the increasing criticism of the closed nature of the supply chain partnership by acknowledging 'that there are particular issues to be considered with regard to smallholders, especially those in Africa and other parts of the developing world' (Tallontire et al. 2008, p. 15). The creation of an Africa Observer project and a Smallholder Task Force in 2007 and 2008, respectively, sought to integrate smallholders within GLOBALGAP's governance and standard setting. These initiatives, developed in cooperation with GTZ and the UK Department for International Development (DFID), were designed to represent African smallholders at both Sector Committee and Board levels (Africa Observer 2007a, b).

The Africa Observer project and many of the developments discussed previously are part of a trend to open GLOBALGAP to wider participation and consultation (Tallontire et al. 2013, p. 8). TBG organizations 'have to adjust and evolve to meet changing and growing expectations around their democratic and inclusive character' (Auld et al. 2015, p. 118). Wood and others prompt us to look beyond interactions with actors to incorporate interactions with structural features such as norms and discourses into the study of transnational business governance interactions (TBGIs) (2015, p. 350). In understanding this move towards opening up GLOBALGAP, we must also pay attention to the important role that that dominant discourse of democratization plays in this process (Djelic and Sahlin-Anderson 2006a, pp. 382–3).

GLOBALGAP also responded to key legitimacy demands in relation to its system of implementation. It recognized the cost of implementation as an important issue at an early stage and introduced the option of group certification as a means to reduce the costs for smallholders (Hofmans and Garbutt 2001, Supplement, p. 3). Between 2004 and 2006, GLOBALGAP cooperated with UNCTAD in a project aimed at understanding how smallholders in developing countries could comply with food safety standards and gain access to export markets (Garbutt and Coetzer 2005). In so doing, GLOBALGAP representatives focused their attention on the ability of national producer organizations and states to benchmark national GAP schemes against the GLOBALGAP standard. GLOBALGAP also cooperated with GTZ to develop a GLOBALGAP Smallholder Manual and engaged in stakeholder consultation in relation to the development of a more effective means of group certification (EUREPGAP 2005, p. 40; Africa Observer 2008; Tallontire et al. 2008, p, 17; GTZ 2010).

GLOBALGAP built, revised and recast itself in an iterative, trial-and-error manner in order to manage its legitimacy. The anticipatory nature of legitimacy management in a non-state regulatory organization's early years can lead to the creation of institutional structures that do not meet the later expectations of the organization's legitimacy communities. Further, as non-state regulatory organizations expand, they attract new legitimacy communities whose demands may conflict with the organization's extant structures, practices and processes. As GLOBALGAP's legitimacy communities expanded beyond market actors such as large retailers and producers with key concerns relating to food safety, to include both state and civil society actors, the demands made against GLOBALGAP moved beyond food safety to concerns relating to the marginalization of smaller producers and the inclusiveness of its governance and standard setting.

9.5 EARLY INSTITUTIONALIZATION

The structures, practices and processes established during a non-state regulatory organization's early years have an enduring quality (Tamm Hallström and Boström 2010, p. 111). As Graeme Auld observes: '[E]arly design choices can generate hard-to-overcome inertia shaping subsequent developments' (2014, p. 17). Indeed, 'depending on their starting points', TBG organizations such as the FSC and MSC have responded to legitimacy demands 'in different ways and with varying effects on actors' regulatory capabilities and the distribution of power' (Auld et al. 2015, p. 118). GLOBALGAP's early institutionalization conferred power on particular legitimacy communities and crystallized a dominant logic within the organization. As such, early institutionalization is crucial for our understanding of how and why GLOBALGAP has managed its legitimacy in the way it has.

9.5.1 Institutionalization of Power, Internal Cohesion and Shared Commitment

Membership categories confer powers on particular actors and withhold them from others. GLOBALGAP's adoption of the supply chain partnership and three-tiered membership structure (retailer, supplier/producer and other) was a process of both inclusion and exclusion, with implications for the power and roles of particular actors within the organization (Tamm Hallström and Boström 2010, Chapter 8). It solidified power within particular constituencies, namely retailers, suppliers and large producers.

Further, the institutionalization of the supply chain partnership positioned GLOBALGAP as an industry-led organization and provided internal cohesion and commitment within the organization. The central legitimacy communities of the supply chain partnership were industry actors that shared reputational and legal risks, and prioritized a logic of control within the organization.

In managing its legitimacy, GLOBALGAP strongly resisted attempts to undermine the supply chain partnership at its core and left intact the three-tiered membership structure and the resulting allocation of power to market actors. In GLOBALGAP's early years, retailers, producers and suppliers kept power within the Steering Committee and the Technical and Standards Committee, and proposed to give a weaker consultative role to a multi-stakeholder Council (Tamm Hallström and Boström 2010, p. 148). While the development of Stakeholder Committees more recently within the organization represented a trend towards the democratization of GLOBALGAP, they did not undermine the supply chain partnership's power in the organization's core decision-making bodies. Indeed, the Stakeholder Committees' terms of reference stated that '[t]he relationship to NGOs should remain unchanged' (GLOBALGAP 2012). In addition, although GLOBALGAP's standard-setting procedure evolved to enhance transparency, openness and participation, the role of the Sector Committees and the supply chain partnership in setting standards was not undermined. Rather, the formalized standard-setting procedure was superimposed upon the existing supply chain partnership model of standard-setting.

Supply chain actors thus defended challenges to their power in GLOBALGAP's key decision-making bodies (Bell and Shelman 2009, p. 9). Wider stakeholder involvement threatened not only the existing distribution of power within the organization, but also the internal cohesion and commitment built up at the organization's core. This internal cohesion and commitment flowed from the shared reputational and legal risks of GLOBALGAP's central legitimacy communities represented in the supply chain partnership. One interviewee explained that:

> [T]he industry feels that they need to have the responsibility where it belongs. When they have financial and legal accountability, they would like to take the decisions. And that means that when we talk about whether we have NGOs, civil society or government organizations in our decision-making roles. No!

Indeed, a civil society representative emphasized that any discussion of broader multi-stakeholder participation within GLOBALGAP's governance was a 'no-go area'. As Auld and colleagues note in their discussion of the FSC, MSC and Fairtrade International (FLO): '[T]he participation of more stakeholders with varying interests can threaten internal cohesion and established positions of internal dominance' (2015, p. 119).

The institutionalization of the supply chain partnership at its core framed GLOBALGAP's response to demands to embed wider stakeholder participation within its governance structure. GLOBALGAP has largely resisted legitimacy demands targeted at the power vested in the supply chain partnership, which are seen to challenge not only the current balance of power within the key decision-making bodies, but also the internal cohesion and shared commitment that the supply chain partnership provided. The emergence of GLOBALGAP as a retailer-led initiative and the subsequent establishment of the supply chain partnership crystallized the identity of GLOBALGAP as an industry-led regulatory organization. The creation of three membership categories made a clear statement regarding which actors constituted the core and which the periphery of the organization. This distinction is reflected in GLOBALGAP's key decision-making bodies.

9.5.2 Protecting the Logic of Control

Early institutionalization not only confers powers upon particular legitimacy communities, it also lays the foundations for the achievement of the organization's goals and objectives. Reflecting a logic of control, one of GLOBALGAP's founding objectives is a regulatory system based on a single robust standard implemented through third-party verification.

While GLOBALGAP representatives recognized that the standard's stringency and third-party certification costs were at the heart of critics' concerns, they dismissed demands that would undermine the core objectives of the organization and its dominant logic of control institutionalized in its early years. As I noted above, GLOBALGAP responded to the increased criticism in relation to the cost of implementation for smallholders in a number of ways. Firstly, it continued its cooperation with GTZ to develop a smallholder manual to facilitate the implementation of the standard (GTZ 2010). Secondly, it engaged in stakeholder consultation in relation to the development of a more effective means of group certification (Africa Observer 2008). While these responses sought to accommodate and address concerns relating to the cost of implementation, they did so in a manner that did not undermine either GLOBALGAP's standard or third-party certification, which are two of the core features that underpin the organization's initial and dominant logic of control.

A GLOBALGAP representative stressed that 'the value of the reference standard is that it's the same for everybody' and that GLOBALGAP's 'position is obviously that "the standard is the standard" and that it wouldn't be appropriate to have one standard for one part of the world and a standard for another' (COLEACP/PIP 2004, p. 4). In addition, the representative highlighted that the cost of certification is determined by the market, and that in 'a competitive market for certification' it is up to producers to negotiate and 'shop around' (ibid.). GLOBALGAP's strategic manoeuvring around the concerns from state, market and civil society actors in relation to the cost of implementation reveals the importance of a non-state regulator's goals and dominant logic in determining how they manage legitimacy demands (Oliver 1991, pp. 164–7; Pache and Santos 2010, pp. 459–60).

9.6 CONCLUSION

GLOBALGAP's structures and processes became increasingly complex as it managed its legitimacy and responded to legitimacy demands. Indeed, non-state regulatory organizations expand 'in all directions: centrally, de-centrally, and horizontally' as they seek to manage their legitimacy (Tamm Hallström and Boström 2010, p. 167). The complexity of non-state regulatory organizations in turn reflects the power and underlying logic of those organizations. Beyond my empirical analysis of GLOBALGAP, this chapter sought to make two key contributions to broader discussions in regulatory governance scholarship about the legitimation of TBG organizations, and the role played by interactions with state, market and civil society actors in this process.

Firstly, I argue that legitimation is an inherently iterative process that drives and shapes TBGIs. My analysis suggests that in the early years of TBG organizations, legitimacy management is anticipatory and often informed by founders' prior learning and experience. The anticipatory nature of legitimacy management can lead to the creation of institutional structures that do not meet, or indeed conflict with, legitimacy communities' later expectations. In responding to these legitimacy demands, TBG organizations must iteratively rebuild, revise and strengthen their governance, standard setting and implementation activities. Through this iterative process of legitimation, interactions and the anticipation of interactions with state, market and civil society actors led GLOBALGAP to enhance the representation and participation of structurally weaker parties within the organization and address concerns relating to the exclusionary effects of its standards. While these findings are grounds for optimism in terms of the potential positive effects of TGBIs, this optimism is somewhat dulled by my further findings.

Secondly, I contend that early institutionalization of an organization's structures, practices and processes significantly influences how they manage their legitimacy. Early institutionalization not only confers power on particular legitimacy communities, it also crystallizes a dominant logic within TBG organizations. In this chapter, the enduring nature of early institutionalization shaped GLOBALGAP's responses to legitimacy demands from state, market and civil society actors. In so doing, early institutionalization tempered the potential for governance interactions to advance democracy, justice and fairness within the organization.

NOTE

1. Regulation (EC) No 178/2002 of the European Parliament and of the Council of 28 January 2002 laying down the general principles and requirements of food law, establishing the European Food Safety Authority and laying down procedures in matters of food safety [2002] OJ L31/1.

REFERENCES

Africa Observer (2007a), *About the Africa Observer*, archived version accessed 9 April 2019 at http://web.archive.org/web/20080820231944/http://www.africa-observer.info/about.html.

Africa Observer (2007b), *Smallholder Task Force: Background and Objective*, archived version accessed 9 April 2019 at http://web.archive.org/web/20100705042612/http://www.globalgap.org/cms/upload/About_Us/Smallholder-Involvement/Smallholder-Taskforce-Members.pdf.

Africa Observer (2008), GLOBALGAP *Group Certification: A Challenge for Smallholders in Europe and Developing Countries 28-29 April 2008: Workshop Report*, archived version accessed 9 April 2019 at http://web.archive.org/web/20080820231934/http://www.africa-observer.info/documents/Report_GLOBALGAP_workshop.pdf.

Ashforth, Blake E. and Barrie W. Gibbs (1990), 'The double edge sword of organizational legitimation', *Organizational Science*, **1** (2), 177–94.

Auld, Graeme (2014), *Constructing Private Governance: The Rise and Evolution of Forest, Coffee, and Fisheries Certification*, New Haven and London: Yale University Press.

Auld, Graeme, Stefan Renckens and Benjamin Cashore (2015), 'Transnational private governance between the logics of empowerment and control', *Regulation & Governance*, **9** (2), 108–24.

Bartley, Tim (2007), 'Institutional emergence in an era of globalization: the rise of transnational private regulation of labour and environmental conditions', *American Journal of Sociology*, **113** (2), 297–351.

Bell, David E. and Mary L. Shelman (2009), *GLOBALGAP: Food Safety and Private Standards, Harvard Business School Case Study 9-509-004*, Boston: Harvard Business Publications.

Bernstein, Steven (2011), 'Legitimacy in intergovernmental and non state global governance', *Review of International Political Economy*, **18** (1), 17–51.

Black, Julia (2008), 'Constructing and contesting legitimacy and accountability in polycentric regulatory regimes', *Regulation & Governance*, **2** (2), 137–64.

Boström, Magnus and Kristina Tamm Hallström (2013), 'Global multi-stakeholder standard setters: how fragile are they?', *Journal of Global Ethics*, **9** (1), 93–110.

Campbell, Hugh, Geoffrey Lawrence and Kiah Smith (2006), 'Audit culture and the antipodes: the implications of EurepGAP for New Zealand and Australian agri-food industries', in T. Marsden and J. Murdoch (eds), *Between the Local and the Global: Confronting Complexity in the Contemporary Agri-Food Sector*, Bingley, West Yorkshire: Emerald, pp. 69–93.

Casey, Donal (2017), 'Structuring private food safety governance: GLOBALGAP and the legitimating role of the state and rule intermediaries', in P. Verbruggan and T. Havinga (eds), *Hybridization of Food Governance: Trends, Types and Results*, Cheltenham, UK and Northampton, MA: Edward Elgar, pp. 31–53.
Cashore, Benjamin (2002), 'Legitimacy and the privatization of environmental governance: how non-state market-driven (NSMD) governance systems gain rule-making authority', *Governance: An International Journal of Policy, Administration and Institutions*, **15** (4), 503–29.
Cashore, Benjamin, Graeme Auld and Deanna Newsom (2004), *Governing Through Markets: Forest Certification and the Emergence of Non-State Authority*, New Haven, CT: Yale University Press.
Child, John (1972), 'Organizational structure, environment and performance: the role of strategic choice', *Sociology*, **6** (1), 1–22.
COLEACP/PIP (2003), 'EUREPGAP conference: PIP details problems of ACP exporters,' *PIP Magazine: Magazine of the Pesticides Initiative Programme*, No. 2, December, p. 2, accessed 9 April 2019 at https://www.coleacp.org/en/e-bibliotheque/pip-magazine-ndeg2-0.
COLEACP/PIP (2004), 'Interview with Nigel Garbutt, Chairman Eurepgap', *PIP Magazine: Magazine of the Pesticides Initiative Programme,* No. 4, September, p. 4, accessed 9 April 2019 at https://www.coleacp.org/en/e-bibliotheque/pip-magazine-ndeg4-0.
DiMaggio, Paul J. (1988), 'Interest and agency in institutional theory', in Lynne G. Zucker (ed.), *Institutional Patterns and Organizations: Culture and Environment*, Cambridge, MA: Ballinger, pp. 3–22.
Djelic, Marie-Laure and Kerstin Sahlin-Anderson (2006a), 'Institutional dynamics in a re-ordering world', in M.-L. Djelic and K. Sahlin-Anderson (eds), *Transnational Governance: Institutional Dynamics of Regulation*, Cambridge, UK: Cambridge University Press, pp. 375–97.
Djelic, Marie-Laure and Kerstin Sahlin-Anderson (2006b), 'Introduction: a world of governance: the rise of transnational regulation', in M.-L. Djelic and K. Sahlin-Anderson (eds), *Transnational Governance: Institutional Dynamics of Regulation*, Cambridge, UK: Cambridge University Press, pp. 1–28.
Doorey, David J. (2015), 'Mapping the ascendance of the "living wage" standard in non-state global labour codes', *Transnational Legal Theory*, **6** (2), 435–65.
Eberlein, Burkard, Kenneth W. Abbott, Julia Black, Errol Meidinger and Stepan Wood (2014), 'Transnational business governance interactions: conceptualization and framework for analysis', *Regulation & Governance*, **8** (1), 1–21.
EUREP (1999), *EUREPGAP Verification 2000 Official Launch Conference: List of Represented Countries and Companies*, archived version accessed 9 April 2019 at http://web.archive.org/web/20010212101438/http://www.eurep.org/arbeitskreise/seiten/eurep-ak-eurep-Part_Org.htm.
EUREPGAP (2000), 'EUREPGAP implementation 2000 plus conference: supplement', in K. Möller (ed.), *EUREPGAP Implementation 2000 Plus*, Cologne: EHI EuroHandelsinstitut.
EUREPGAP (2001a), *1st EUREPGAP/FOODPLUS Steering Committee Meeting*, archived version accessed 9 April 2019 at http://web.archive.org/web/20010623150547/http://www.eurep.org/arbeitskreise/seiten/news-sc-meeting_5-4-01.htm.

EUREPGAP (2001b), *Council: Statutes, Members and Decisions*, archived version accessed 9 April 2019 at http://web.archive.org/web/20021220143950/http://www.eurep.org/sites/Council-members.html.

EUREPGAP (2001c), *EUREPGAP/FoodPLUS GmbH Steering Committee Terms of Reference*, Cologne: EUREPGAP/FoodPLUS, archived version accessed 9 April 2019 athttp://web.archive.org/web/20031018002318/http://www.eurep.org/downloads/SC-TERMS-of-Reference-5-4-01.pdf.

EUREPGAP (2001d), *Terms of Reference for EUREPGAP Technical and Standards Committee: Fruit and Vegetables*, Cologne: FoodPLUS.

EUREPGAP (2001e), 'Understanding EurepGAP certification', in N. Garbutt (ed.), *EUREPGAP: The Global Partnership for Safe and Sustainable Agriculture – Partnership 2001 Plus*, Cologne: FoodPLUS.

EUREPGAP (2003), *EUREPGAP News Update June 2003*, Cologne: FoodPLUS.

EUREPGAP (2005), *EUREPGAP Global Report 2005*, Cologne: FoodPLUS, accessed 9 April 2019 at http://www2.globalgap.org/documents/webdocs/E-book-Globalreport.pdf.

EUREPGAP (2006), *Prague Conference Report September 2006*, Cologne: FoodPLUS, accessed 9 April 2019 at http://www2.globalgap.org/documents/webdocs/EurepGAP_Newsletter_All-scopes_web.pdf.

European Commission (2002), *Final Report: Evaluation of Environmental Product Declaration Schemes*, DG Environment, September, B4-3040/2001/326493/MAR/A2.

European Fresh Produce Association (2006), *Suppliers Statement at the EUREPGAP Conference: 21 September – Prague*, 22 September, accessed 9 April 2019 at http://www.forumphyto.fr/wp-content/uploads/2011/07/060921EGStatementEng.pdf.

Garbutt, Nigel (1999), 'Why EUREP?', in K. Möller (ed.), *EUREPGAP Verification 2000*, Cologne: EHI EuroHandelsinstitut.

Garbutt, Nigel (2008), 'GLOBALGAP aqua culture certification', slides presented at FAO/NACA/SCA/DFID Expert Workshop on Guidelines for Aquaculture Certification, London, 28-29 February, accessed 9 April 2019 at http://library.enaca.org/certification/london08/05_globalgap.pdf.

Garbutt, Nigel and Elmé Coetzer (2005), *Options for the Development of National/Sub-regional Codes of Good Agricultural Practice for Horticultural Products Benchmarked to EurepGAP: Consultation Draft*, Geneva: UNCTAD.

Garbutt, Nigel and Kristian Möller (1999), 'Pathway to independent verification', in K. Möller (ed.), *EUREPGAP Verification 2000*, Cologne: EHI EuroHandelsinstitut.

GLOBALGAP. (2007), *Harmonization of Farm Assurance Systems: EUREPGAP now GLOBALGAP*, Press Release, 7 September, Cologne: GLOBALGAP, archived version accessed 9 April 2019 at http://web.archive.org/web/20100705061108/http://www.GLOBALGAP.org/cms/upload/Documents/070907_press_release_GLOBALGAP_ENG-KM.pdf.

GLOBALGAP. (2012), *Sector Committees*, archived version accessed 9 April 2019 at http://web.archive.org/web/20100705040648/http://www.globalgap.org/cms/front_content.php?client=1&changelang=1&parent=&subid=&idcat=17.

Greenpeace International (2010), *Assessment of the GLOBALGAP Aquaculture Certification Programme*, January, Amsterdam: Greenpeace International, archived version accessed 9 April 2019 at http://web.archive.org/web/20150922101813/http://www.greenpeace.org/international/PageFiles/42959/GlobalGap%20assessment%20briefing%20FINAL.pdf.

Greenwood, Royston, Mia Raynard, Farah Kodeih, Evelyn R Micelotta and Michael Lounsbury (2011), 'Institutional complexity and organizational responses', *Academy of Management Annals*, **5** (1), 317–71.

GTZ (2010), *GLOBALGAP Smallholder QMS Set-up Guide: How to establish a QMS in your group*, Eschborn, Germany: Deutsche Gesellschaft für Technische Zusammenarbeit (GTZ).

Gulbrandsen, Lars H. (2008), 'Accountability arrangements in non-state standards organizations: instrumental design and imitation', *Organization*, **15** (4), 563–83.

Heise, Jenni, Kerstin Uhlig and Laurent Vonwiller (2007), *The Grasp Project Report: Towards Good Social Practices in Agriculture*, Eschborn, Germany: Deutsche Gesellschaft für Technische Zusammenarbeit (GTZ).

Hoffmann, Ulrich and Rene Vossenaar (2007), *Codes for Good Agricultural Practices: Opportunities and Challenges for Fruit and Vegetable Exports from Latin American Developing Countries: Experiences of Argentina, Brazil and Costa Rica*, UNCTAD/DITC/TED/2007/2, Geneva: UNCTAD.

Hofmans, Willem (1999), 'EUREP's accomplishments to date', in K. Möller (ed.), *EUREPGAP Verification 2000*, Cologne: EHI EuroHandelsinstitut.

Hofmans, Willem and Nigel Garbutt (eds) (2001), *EUREPGAP: The Global Partnership for Safe and Sustainable Agriculture – Partnership 2001 Plus*, Cologne: FoodPLUS.

Leighton, Tommy (2002), 'Krasemann questions Eurep gap: Kai Krasemann, president of Freshfel, has hit out at the commercial integrity of Eurep Gap', *Fresh Produce Journal*, 10 November, accessed 9 April 2019 at http://www.fruitnet.com/fpj/article/102803/krasemann-questions-eurep-gap.

Leighton, Tommy (2003), 'EurepGAP must deliver on promises', *Fresh Produce Journal*, 19 September, accessed 9 April 2019 at http://www.fruitnet.com/fpj/article/132200/eurepgap-must-deliver-on-promises.

Leighton, Tommy (2006). 'Garbutt call for EurepGAP unity', *Fresh Produce Journal*, 6 October, accessed 9 April 2019 at http://www.fruitnet.com/fpj/article/139927/garbutt-call-for-eurepgap-unity.

Meyer, John W. (2008), 'Reflections on institutional theories of organizations', in R. Greenwood, C. Oliver, R. Suddaby and K. Sahlin-Andersson (eds), *Sage Handbook of Organizational Institutionalism*, Thousand Oaks, CA: Sage, pp. 790–811.

Möller, Kristian (ed.) (1998a), *Integrated Production of Fruit and Vegetables*, Cologne: EHI EuroHandelsinstitut.

Möller, Kristian (1998b), 'The Euro-retailer produce working group EUREP', in K. Möller (ed.), *Integrated Production of Fruit and Vegetables*, Cologne: EHI EuroHandelsinstitut.

Möller, Kristian (2000). *EUREP Info E-Mail 02/2000*, archived version accessed 9 April 2019 at http://web.archive.org/web/20010706041838/http://www.eurep.org/arbeitskreise/seiten/eurep-info-email-2-2000.htm.

Möller, Kristian (2006), 'Economics of standard owners: competition as barrier to global harmonisation of food assurance systems', in L. Theuvsen, A. Spiller, M. Peupert and G. Jahn (eds), *Quality Management in Food Chains*, Wageningen, NL: Wageningen Academic Publishers, pp. 23–8.

Oliver, Christine (1991), 'Strategic responses to institutional processes', *Academy of Management Review*, **16** (1), 145–79.

Pache, Anne-Claire and Filipe Santos (2010), 'When worlds collide: the internal dynamics of organizational responses to conflicting institutional demands', *Academy of Management Review*, **35** (3), 455–76.

Richardson, Alan J. and Burkard Eberlein (2011), 'Legitimating transnational standard setting: the case of the international accounting standards board', *Journal of Business Ethics*, **98**, 217–45.
Schleifer, Philip (2015), *Creating Legitimacy for Private Rules: Explaining the Choice of Legitimation Strategies in Transnational Non-State Governance*, Robert Schuman Centre for Advanced Studies Research Paper No. RSCAS 2015/62, accessed 9 April 2019 at http://cadmus.eui.eu/handle/1814/36815.
Scott, Colin (1990), 'Continuity and change in British food law', *Modern Law Review*, **53** (6), 785–801.
Scott, W. Richard (1987), 'The adolescence of institutional theory', *Administrative Science Quarterly*, **32** (4), 493–511.
Scott, W. Richard (1998), *Organizations: Rational, Natural and Open Systems*, 4th edn, Upper Saddle River, NJ: Prentice-Hall.
Suchman, Mark (1995), 'Managing legitimacy: strategic and institutional approaches', *Academy of Management Review*, **20** (3), 571–610.
Suddaby, Roy, David J. Cooper and Royston Greenwood (2007), 'Transnational regulation of professional services: governance dynamics of field level organizational change', *Accounting, Organizations and Society*, **32** (4), 333–62.
Tallontire, Anne, Valerie Nelson, Adrienne Martin and Maggie Opondo (2008), 'Governance and agency in the global horticulture chain: the case of global GAP', paper presented at European Association of Development Institutes General Conference: The Need For Policy Coherence and New Partnerships, Geneva, 24–28 June.
Tallontire, Anne, Maggie Opondo and Valerie Nelson (2013), 'Contingent spaces for smallholder participation in GlobalGAP: insights from Kenyan horticulture value chains', *Geographical Journal*, **180** (4), 353–64.
Tamm Hallström, Kristina and Magnus Boström (2010), *Transnational Multi-Stakeholder Standardization: Organizing Fragile Non-State Authority*, Cheltenham, UK and Northampton, MA: Edward Elgar.
Tamm Hallström, Kristina and Ingrid Gustafsson (2014), 'Value-neutralizing in verification markets: organizing for independence through accreditation', in S. Alexius and K. Tamm Hallström (eds), *Configuring Value Conflicts in Markets*, Cheltenham, UK and Northampton, MA: Edward Elgar.
Tyler, Tom R. (2006), 'Psychological perspectives on legitimacy and legitimation', *Annual Review of Psychology*, **57**, 375–400.
UNCTAD (2005), *Division on International Trade in Goods and Services, and Commodities: Activity Report 2004, Major Outputs and Lessons Learnt, Note by the UNCTAD Secretariat*, 14 March, UNCTAD/DITC/MISC/2004/24, accessed 9 April 2019 at https://unctad.org/en/Docs/ditcmisc200424_en.pdf.
van der Grijp, Nicolien (2008), 'Regulating pesticide risk reduction: the practice and dynamics of legal pluralism', PhD thesis, Vrije Universiteit, Amsterdam.
van Mulekom, Leo and Mathew Parr (2007), 'Oxfam and IUCN NL: Pursuing responsible policies and practices in the supply chain of tropical shrimps', slides presented at GLOBALGAP Conference, Bangkok, 6–7 September, archived version accessed 9 April 2019 at http://web.archive.org/web/20100705054616/http://www.globalgap.org/cms/upload/Resources/Presentations/Bangkok/4_L_vanMulekom.pdf.
Wise, Christopher (1998), 'The NFU-retailer partnership's "assured produce" scheme', in K. Möller (ed.), *Integrated Production of Fruit and Vegetables*, Cologne: EHI EuroHandelsinstitut.

Wood, Stepan, Kenneth W. Abbott, Julia Black, Burkard Eberlein and Errol Meidinger (2015), 'The interactive dynamics of transnational business governance: a challenge for transnational legal theory', *Transnational Legal Theory*, **6** (2), 333–69.

World Trade Organization, Committee on Sanitary and Phytosanitary Measures (2005), *Summary of the Meeting Held on 29–30 June 2005: Note by the Secretariat*, 18 August, G/SPS/R/37/Rev.1.

World Trade Organization (2007a), *Summary of the Meeting of 11–12 October 2006: Note by the Secretariat*, 3 January, G/SPS/R/43.

World Trade Organization (2007b), *Specific Trade Concerns: Note by the Secretariat: Addendum, Issues Considered in 2006*, 6 February, G/SPS/GEN/204/Rev.7/Add.1.

World Trade Organization (2007c), *Private Sector Standards and Developing Countries Exports of Fresh Fruit and Vegetables: Communication from the United Nations Conference on Trade and Development (UNCTAD)*, 26 February, G/SPS/GEN/761.

World Trade Organization (2007d), *Summary of the Meeting of 28 February –1 March 2007: Note by the Secretariat*, 30 May, G/SPS/R/44.

10. Can non-state regulatory authority improve domestic forest sustainability? Assessing interactive pathways of influence in Cameroon

Sophia Carodenuto and Benjamin Cashore

10.1 INTRODUCTION

Ever since international efforts failed to achieve a legally binding agreement on forests at the 1992 United Nations Conference on Environment and Development, a plethora of targeted interventions has emerged to address key challenges surrounding sustainable forest management. Two of the most important problem definitions with significant repercussions in tropical forest countries such as Cameroon include: (1) tropical deforestation and associated climate impacts; and (2) the proposition that the international timber trade, especially owing to demand in consumer countries, contributes to illegal forest activities in (sub)tropical forests. These two problem definitions have led to the development of two policy approaches.

To address climate change, negotiators working under the auspices of the United Nations Framework Convention on Climate Change (UNFCCC) have proposed the mitigation-focused policy approach, Reducing Emissions from Deforestation and Forest Degradation, sustainable management of forests, and the conservation and enhancement of forest carbon stocks in developing countries (REDD+). The main incentives for REDD+ are financial: developing countries are compensated for verified forest-related carbon emission reductions. In parallel, the European Union's Forest Law Enforcement, Governance and Trade (FLEGT) Action Plan applies demand- and supply-side trade measures to address illegal forest activities. Responding to customer and consumer demand, the European Union Timber Regulation (EUTR) creates incentives for legal logging by prohibiting the importation of illegally harvested timber and wood products. By weeding out illegal supply, this prohibition is expected to secure markets for legally produced timber. The EU also enters into Voluntary Partnership Agreements (VPAs) with timber-exporting countries as a way to formalize legality requirements and guarantee access to the European market. As a result, much attention is focused, through VPAs, on helping develop national timber tracing and legality assurance systems.

Architects of both REDD+ and FLEGT embrace increasing complexity (Rayner et al. 2010) by turning to non-state actors and domestic firms to foster behavioural changes (Bernstein and Cashore 2012). Hence, they are part of the transnational business governance (TBG) phenomenon that Eberlein et al (2014, p. 3) define as 'systematic efforts to regulate business conduct that involve a significant degree of non-state authority in the performance of regulatory functions across national borders'. REDD+ and FLEGT involve the exercise of both state and non-state authority, including multilateral funding programs, international non-governmental organizations, aid organizations, and multinational forestry and agribusiness firms, to name a few (McDermott et al. 2012).

Given the increasing use of TBG to address what used to be the subject of international negotiations and treaties, we turn our attention to understanding the effects of these global efforts on influencing the complex governance challenges at the domestic level. We shed light on this broad quest by posing the following question: Do the domestic-level governance interactions brought about by global TBG initiatives such as REDD+ and FLEGT lead to durable sustainability impacts on the ground?

To address this question we take a closer look at the precise way in which these policy instruments are influencing Cameroon's domestic forest challenges. Cameroon is a relevant case because of the important ecological, economic and social contributions of its forests (Lescuyer et al. 2016) and the attention that global elites have placed on REDD+ and legality verification to improve practices on the ground. Over 40 per cent of Cameroon's land is covered by dense humid forest, forming an important part of the Congo Basin tropical forest biome. The country exports timber to the EU and is home to large areas of tropical forest viewed as critical for potential REDD+ projects (Wasseige et al. 2012; Bourges et al. 2014). National policymakers have identified deforestation and illegal forest activities as critical problems that increasingly place the country's forest at risk. Roughly a decade ago, Cameroon became engaged in REDD+ by submitting an initial funding application to the Forest Carbon Partnership Facility (FCPF) and, around the same time, entered preliminary VPA negotiations with the EU. Cameroon was one of the pioneer FLEGT countries, possibly because early studies on illegal logging suggested that the majority of illegally harvested tropical timber found on EU markets originated in or passed through Cameroon (Hirschberger 2008). Cameroon is the transit country for timber from neighbouring countries such as the Central African Republic and the Republic of Congo, and the timber's country of origin is often indistinguishable due to weak supply chain tracking (Lawson and MacFaul 2010, p. 113).

10.2 ANALYTICAL FRAMEWORK

Consistent with social science research on policy cycles or stages in general (Lerner and Lasswell 1951; deLeon 1999) and the TBGI framework in particular, we place attention on what is commonly referred to as the implementation phase of the policy cycle: where attention turns to the types of specific calibrations, mechanisms and policy settings that are often determined following the formal adoption of policy goals, objectives and instruments (Hall 1993). To unpack these complex processes that unfold over time, we draw on Bernstein and Cashore's 'pathways of influence' framework to disentangle distinct causal mechanisms through which global policy measures influence the domestic level (Bernstein and Cashore 2012).

We draw on a meta-analysis of five empirical case studies conducted during the course of multiple research stays in Cameroon from 2011 until 2015. Two case studies focus on different elements of FLEGT/VPA implementation (Carodenuto and Cerutti 2014; Carodenuto and Ramcilovic-Suominen 2014), two concentrate on REDD+ implementation (Carodenuto et al. 2015; Carodenuto and Kalame 2015), and the fifth links the analysis of the two policies (Carodenuto 2016). The data for the first two case studies are 24 semi-structured interviews with representatives of Cameroon's private forestry sector. The purpose of the interviews was to better understand and empirically assess the benefits of and barriers to FLEGT/VPA implementation. The first case on REDD+ examined the analytical process of developing Cameroon's REDD+ strategy by proposing and testing a methodology for assessing the causes of deforestation and forest degradation to be addressed by the future national REDD+ strategy. The other case on REDD+ studied Cameroon's social safeguards approach through a legal review combined with participant observation of the national process of developing free, prior and informed consent (FPIC) guidelines for REDD+. The final case study included ten semi-structured interviews with civil society representatives from environmental and social organizations based in Cameroon's Southwest Region. This case study analysed the potential of the information transparency instruments proposed by REDD+ and FLEGT to achieve improved accountability in Cameroon's forest governance.

10.2.1 Pathways of Influence

Bernstein and Cashore's work on pathways of influence (2000, 2012) was designed to conceptualize and assess the role of non-domestic factors in shaping domestic policy-making processes. This approach is highly relevant because the FLEGT/VPA and REDD+ in Cameroon epitomize internationalization trends in environmental policy-making characterized by a shift from government regulations dominating forest decision-making to a more complex governance environment marked by interactions introduced by multiple governance mechanisms, international institutions and transnational actors (Rayner et al. 2010; Buttoud 2011). The pathways of influence framework (Figure 10.1) helps to reveal the underlying assumptions and expectations about a policy's trajectory, potentially explaining why support for an intervention might occur (Cashore et al. 2015). We argue that unpacking the dominant paradigm or discourse underpinning a given policy intervention, that is, the assumed causal logic, is helpful in better understanding policy implementation.

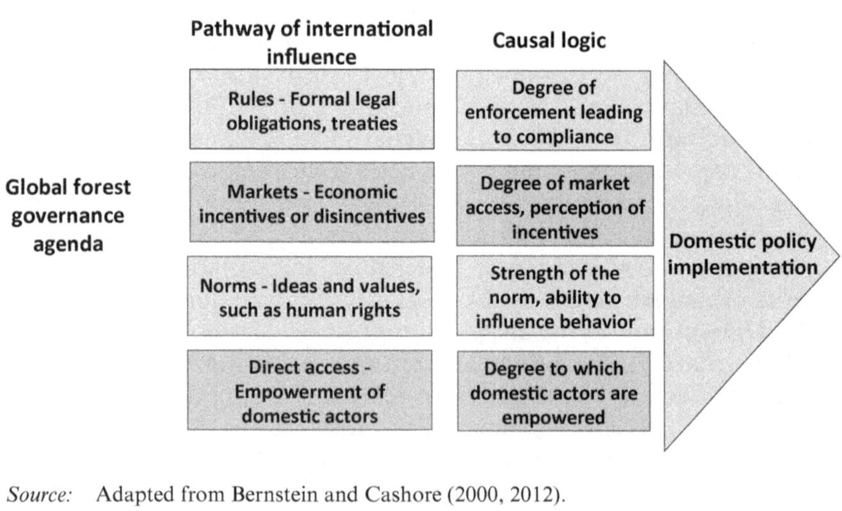

Source: Adapted from Bernstein and Cashore (2000, 2012).

Figure 10.1 Transnational business governance pathways of influence

Each pathway turns attention to different causal explanations as to why TBG processes have influence within a given domestic setting. The rules pathway turns attention to formal legal obligations, such as international treaties translated into laws ratified at the national level. The causal logic relevant here reflects a 'command and control' approach, wherein the TBG regime's traction can be judged by the degree to which compliance to the rule is mandatory, for example through enforcement or penalties. Ultimately, this pathway is considered influential not simply when rules exist, but when these rules are adhered to. The markets pathway focuses on 'economic incentives for firms, managers and individuals to behave in ways that improve environmental stewardship and foster social values' (Cashore et al. 2016, p. 45). This pathway's causal logic is based on economic theories that portray individuals and organizations as rational and narrowly self-interested agents whose ultimate aim is to maximize financial gain, that is, *homo economicus*. The norms pathway refers to the influence of broadly accepted principles such as respect for the sovereignty of nation states and – in the environmental sphere – the importance of preserving biodiversity and respecting the human rights of affected groups. Finally, the direct access pathway refers to the use of finance and technology transfer to empower public and private domestic actors. Influence along this pathway can occur through direct funding, education and capacity building, including through attempts at co-governance via partnerships between domestic and international actors. Bernstein and Cashore (2012) explain that the logic underlying this pathway is the degree to which marginalized groups are empowered.

10.2.2 Policy Implementation: A Nuanced Look at Ends, Means and Settings

Consistent with the TBGI framework, we expand the more targeted emphasis that usually accompanies a discussion of implementation to review: 1) the overarching *goals* that guide policy in a particular field; 2) the *techniques or policy instruments* used to attain those goals; and 3) the *precise settings* of these instruments (Hall 1993, p. 278). Disaggregating FLEGT/VPA and REDD+ can help identify which logics of influence emerge as dominant and, thereby, where policy implementation, and hence influence, are hampered (Cashore and Howlett 2007).[1] This analytical perspective highlights an important set of mechanisms often overlooked in the TBG literature: the tools and techniques of regulatory governance.

The empirical research conducted for this chapter identified two main types of policy instruments currently employed for REDD+ and FLEGT/VPA implementation in Cameroon: 1) highly technical information transparency instruments related to timber tracking and legality verification, for example, the Timber Legality Assurance System (TLAS)[2]; and 2) procedural tools that aim to broaden the number and type of actors engaged in REDD+ and FLEGT/VPA, for example, multi-stakeholder consultations and FPIC as a standard for engaging marginalized actors.

10.3 ANALYSIS: FLEGT/VPA AND REDD+ PATHWAYS OF INFLUENCE IN CAMEROON

10.3.1 Unpacking FLEGT/VPA

The EU FLEGT Action Plan's main policy goal is to reduce illegal logging and related trade. However, the Action Plan also aims to foster forest sector growth and economic development and to improve forest governance.[3] These overarching goals are taken up by VPA countries, with Cameroon's VPA emphasizing socioeconomic development as a main desired outcome of the VPA process. Thus, Cameroon's VPA intends not only to satisfy the timber legality requirements of the EUTR, but also to foster sustainable forest sector growth and 'encourage economic opportunities for resident local communities and local enterprises'.[4]

The Timber Legality Assurance System (TLAS) is the dominant policy instrument for implementing FLEGT/VPA in Cameroon. This system aims to verify the legality of all pertinent wood products circulating in Cameroon, including those sold on the domestic market, as this is thought to reduce the risk of leakage of non-compliant timber into export markets. In many VPA countries, including Cameroon, the amount of timber traded domestically is roughly equal in volume to that exported (Cerutti and Lescuyer 2011; Hansen et al. 2013). Once operational, the TLAS will allow EU-exporting forest enterprises to receive FLEGT licenses, thereby granting them automatic access to EU markets. Cameroon's TLAS has been designed to give the government the final say in whether a batch of timber receives a FLEGT legality certificate or not, as a government-based 'licensing authority' is designated by Cameroon to issue and validate FLEGT licenses for each timber shipment (Fripp et al. 2013).[5]

In the case of Cameroon, the precise settings of the TLAS instrument have focused on formal law, or written rules: state legislation that prescribes the official documentation a timber operator must obtain in order to comply with FLEGT legality. Because the TLAS as currently proposed applies to all timber circulating in Cameroon, VPA implementation risks harming local timber operators because the domestic market is based on informal rules and procedures, falling entirely outside formal law (Cerutti and Lescuyer 2011). Small-scale loggers operating informally were not directly represented as a stakeholder during the VPA negotiations when such fundamental elements of the TLAS were agreed (Woodshow et al. 2016).

10.3.2 Unpacking REDD+

Similar to FLEGT/VPA, REDD+ in Cameroon encompasses a number of overarching global goals that have been translated into specific objectives at the national level. To mitigate climate change, REDD+ aims to transfer funds to compensate developing countries for their sustainability efforts. Similar to many REDD+ countries, Cameroon has integrated social and environmental safeguards as a mechanism not only to avoid harm, but also to improve the status quo, specifically in relation to biodiversity conservation and respect for the human rights of marginalized forest communities (Visseren-Hamakers et al. 2012). Similar to the Cameroon-EU VPA, REDD+ in Cameroon aims to improve forest governance and increase information transparency, thereby allowing a broader range of stakeholders, including marginalized groups, to participate in decision-making processes surrounding forests.

The dominant policy instruments currently perceptible in Cameroon in connection with REDD+ are procedural instruments such as awareness raising, information dissemination, and multi-stakeholder consultation. This is largely explained by the fact that Cameroon remains in the so-called 'readiness' phase of REDD+, in which institutions and stakeholders prepare REDD+ strategies to be implemented in the future. At the time of writing, Cameroon had not yet succeeded in transferring international climate finance to land-based investments to reduce forest-related emissions as a result of REDD+. Nonetheless, REDD+ has raised significant expectations, especially among highly vocal civil society groups advocating respect for the interests and rights of local communities in the national REDD+ policy process (Somorin et al. 2014, p. 91). Social safeguards advocacy is driven not only by the campaign for protecting the rights of marginalized indigenous communities, but also by the long-standing struggle to demand political reform towards more democratic institutions (Assembe-Mvondo et al. 2014). An exemplary policy instrument in this case (and analysed more in detail in this chapter) is the development of national FPIC guidelines for REDD+ activities that take place where indigenous and other forest communities live. The aim of FPIC in the context of REDD+ is to support the right to self-determination, specifically with regard to the rights of indigenous peoples to determine whether, and what type of, development occurs on their traditionally held land.

In contrast to the TLAS, the precise settings of the FPIC guidelines for REDD+ are based on informal norms, defining consent as 'the collective decision made by rights-holders and reached through the customary decision-making processes of the affected peoples or communities' (Cameroon Ministry of the Environment, Nature Protection and Sustainable Development 2014, p. 39). These FPIC guidelines are not legally binding, as they have yet to be converted into specific regulations that guide practices on the ground and render them enforceable (Carodenuto and Kalame 2015). Further, the state agency tasked with enforcing adherence to such guidelines, the Ministry of Environmental Protection and Sustainable Development, does not currently possess the manpower or resources required to effectively enforce these FPIC guidelines (ibid.).

10.3.3 Direct Access: the Dominant Pathway

Table 10.1 summarizes the potential pathways of influence by which the TBG processes of REDD+ and FLEGT/VPA might affect domestic policy settings in Cameroon, and the evidence for each pathway. Although REDD+ and FLEGT/VPA may have originally employed the rules, markets and norms pathways, their translation into Cameroon's domestic policy implementation is dominated by the direct access pathway, especially with regard to the policy instruments through which both TBG processes are being implemented. Again, this may be explained by the fact that both TBG processes remain in the preparation phase, dominated by significant financial and technical support, and the policy mechanisms exerting influence via markets or rules have not yet materialized. The causal logic of the direct access pathway – the degree to which marginalized groups are empowered – explains the support for information transparency systems, multi-stakeholder deliberations, and local training and capacity building to facilitate broad stakeholder participation.

10.3.4 Implications for FLEGT/VPA

Delivering FLEGT legality certificates appears to be the most pressing short-term goal for VPA implementation in Cameroon. This requires an operational TLAS. However, Carodenuto and Ramcilovic-Suominen (2014) find that understanding the complexity of the current TLAS requires specialized knowledge held only by select experts, which works to limit the participation and influence of non-expert officials within the forest

Table 10.1 Pathways of influence for FLEGT/VPA and REDD+ in Cameroon

Pathway	Potential influence	Evidence of influence
Markets	FLEGT/VPA: 'green lane' access to EU markets for timber with FLEGT legality certificate	Weak: FLEGT legality certificates have not yet been produced as proposed through the TLAS
	REDD+: access to international climate finance markets and performance-based payments	Weak: Performance-based payments have not yet materialized and no REDD+ carbon-based transactions
Rules	FLEGT/VPA: VPA ratification into national law renders the FLEGT legality criteria legally enforceable	Weak: Law enforcement and rule of law remain weak in forest sector, difficulty in verifying the compliance underlying legal 'papers'
	REDD+: FPIC becomes legally enforceable through passing of regulatory decree	Weak: FPIC guidelines remain legally unenforceable
Norms	FLEGT/VPA: Non-state actors in Cameroon bring about change as a result of their governance, transparency and accountability agenda	Moderate: Financial and technical support provided to numerous non-state actors, but the change in business as usual remains difficult to assess
	REDD+: Safeguards advocacy brings about improved recognition of the rights of marginalized indigenous people and forest communities	Weak: The impact of national FPIC guidelines remains limited without the government officially recognizing certain groups that have self-identified as indigenous
Direct Access	FLEGT/VPA: Marginalized actors are empowered to demand that the forestry sector in Cameroon provide equitable and sustainable development	Substantial: Significant transfer of technology and finance, which is helping civil society and other actors to become more vocal
	REDD+: Marginalized actors are empowered to ensure that REDD+ supports equitable and sustainable rural development	Substantial: Significant transfer of technology and finance, which is helping civil society and other actors to become more vocal

Note: The elements listed in this table are not exhaustive. The examples used do not aim to demonstrate all goals and instruments of the VPA and REDD+, but rather to summarize the key findings of this chapter's meta-analysis.

administration and the forestry sector. The impact of technical knowledge in excluding, rather than empowering, stakeholders is a common theme within contemporary scholarship on environmental governance. Gupta and Mason (2016) suggest that 'governance by disclosure' for environmental sustainability is increasingly based on a technocratic rationale. This, in turn, involves implementing information transparency instruments that develop elaborate systems of professional auditing and legality certification that only those with time and expertise can fully comprehend. Hence, and somewhat ironically, the transformative potential of transparency is often reduced as the resulting technocracy can counteract originally intended democratization objectives of using disclosure to enhance accountability, participation and citizens' right to know (ibid.). This means that policy instruments must be designed and specified carefully in ways that develop technical procedures that empower, rather than detract from, inclusive governance. This may be achieved by involving non-experts in the design and implementation of these technically complex instruments.

The TLAS's highly technical approach has led to the involvement of numerous financial and technical partners that provide significant training and capacity building to support TLAS operationalization. Thus, the direct access pathway emerges as dominant, which implies that the causal logic for successful FLEGT/VPA implementation is the empowerment of marginalized actors. While it is too early to draw conclusions about the ability of the VPA to have this type of positive impact, Carodenuto and Cerutti (2014) indicate that the EU market-access benefits resulting from VPA/TLAS will not diffuse to the majority of Cameroon's private forestry operators, who operate informally and serve local timber markets. Rather, multinational forestry companies that enjoy niche export markets through pre-existing Forest Stewardship Council (FSC) certification appear positioned to reap the most benefits. In fact, many timber operators believe that the informal sector will be eliminated as a result of VPA implementation while multinational forestry companies operating on an industrial scale expect VPA implementation to increase their market share (Carodenuto and Cerutti 2014).

10.3.5 Implications for REDD+

Similar to other transnational forest governance processes, REDD+ influences domestic policy largely through capacity building, characterized by the provision of financial resources to assist existing civil society organizations or to help create new organizations (Bernstein and Cashore 2012, p. 594). Procedural instruments dominate, such as the multi-stakeholder consultation process conducted to develop the national FPIC guidelines, or the consultation process underway at the time of writing to develop the national REDD+ strategy. These reflect the widely accepted paradigm shift in forest policy-making (and policy implementation) from top-down management by professionals to more inclusive governance approaches involving a broad range of stakeholders. The input legitimacy that arises from effective participatory processes has long been considered essential for maintaining societal support in liberal democracies and is considered an important contributing factor to successful policy implementation (Buttoud 1999). What remains unclear, however, is the extent to which capacity building and stakeholder learning through consultative fora can effect the kind of transformational change required to effectively allow for REDD+ to stimulate socially equitable rural development.

As with FLEGT/VPA, much of the domestic influence of REDD+ has occurred through the direct access pathway. Specifically, decisions to implement REDD+ focused on the provision of financial resources for capacity building. The instrument logic was that this would empower marginalized stakeholders and, as a result, enhance domestic good forest governance by improving the legitimacy of the system. Although influence through the provision of finance 'can help shift the balance of power in domestic policy processes', broader contextual factors such as 'democracy, openness and accountability are prerequisites for the successful use of this strategy' (Bernstein and Cashore 2012, p. 594). The REDD+ process in Cameroon produced FPIC guidelines that ultimately aim to enshrine adequate mechanisms for the meaningful participation of indigenous and other communities whose customarily owned land and forests are affected by REDD+. However, these guidelines are not legally enforceable and stem from a Ministry that does not have the resources nor the presence on the ground required to support their interpretation and application (Carodenuto and Kalame 2015). Therefore, the REDD+ process has to date emphasized procedural efforts with less attention to policy specification such as the passing of legally binding regulations, budget allocations, or policy adjustments to foster compliance with or mainstreaming of REDD+, including safeguards standards. This seems problematic for REDD+'s long-term influence, since provision of finance may facilitate initial uptake domestically, but is often less effective in influencing policy and legal frameworks (Bernstein and Cashore 2012).

10.3.6 Interaction: State and Non-State Regulatory Authority

The direct access pathway's causal logic is that through capacity building and additional resources, marginalized communities and other stakeholders are more likely to influence the domestic policy process, shaping outcomes and (potentially) impacts. The hypothesis is that policy solutions that travel this pathway are more durable as they influence the political economy of the given national context. For example, building non-state actors' capacity could better enable civil society to access, digest, and use information for the purpose of independent monitoring of forestry operations, which is a key component of VPA implementation.[6]

The direct access pathway is often travelled by those advancing 'new governance' approaches that take a richer set of actors into account for operationalizing policy on the ground (Melish and Meidinger 2012). In this context, the interaction between state and non-state actors aims to empower marginalized actors, specifically in terms of their ability to influence regulatory governance. However, consistent with the literature (Bartley 2014; Cashore and Stone 2014) the findings generally indicate that neither REDD+ nor timber legality verification have been designed in a way that will accomplish this type of empowering process. Instead, policies reinforce national sovereignty and the substantive duty of states to enforce compliance. For example, the TLAS is designed in such a way that the government and its line authorities have the sole authority to input data into the TLAS, and ultimately the government has full discretion over what is considered legal timber (Carodenuto and Cerutti 2014; Carodenuto and Ramcilovic-Suominen 2014). This corroborates other scholarship that finds that legality verification efforts 'that seek to identify and label legal products along global supply chains are designed to champion and reinforce existing government policies' (Cashore et al. 2016) rather than create new and potentially more empowering policy reforms. With regard to REDD+, Carodenuto and Kalame (2015) review how the FPIC guidelines – in line with international laws that recognize FPIC as a legal norm imposing clear affirmative duties on states – place ultimate responsibility on the state to ensure that REDD+ project implementers obtain FPIC. Further, these guidelines do not properly address the issue of the absence of formal recognition of customary land tenure rights.

Given that our findings suggest that both REDD+ and FLEGT/VPA aim to reinforce the regulatory authority and capacity of the state, the perceived legitimacy of the state may have implications for policy implementation. Private sector operators across the board (from both the formal and informal sectors) cite government corruption as the most important barrier to VPA implementation (Carodenuto and Ramcilovic-Suominen 2014). This is corroborated by other studies highlighting that trust and accountability are lacking, especially in the forest sector (Cerutti et al. 2013). The VPA seeks influence by building trust and accountability through building the capacity of the national forest control authorities and introducing timber tracing and legality verification through the TLAS.

10.3.7 Outlook: Linking Pathways of Influence and TBGIs

The pathways of influence framework helps to better understand the explanatory logics underpinning TBG processes and the resulting interaction between state and non-state actors in domestic policy settings. The case of Cameroon suggests that REDD+ and FLEGT rely largely on the direct access pathway, implying that they build on the assumption that empowering marginalized groups will foster more durable policy solutions. However, the current structure and legal framework of the forest sector excludes smallholder artisanal loggers from reaping the potential benefits of VPA implementation as they are not able to export to the EU. Further, the current technical complexity of the FLEGT policy instrument employed for on-the-ground operationalization is not likely to result in the desired outcomes in terms of effectively influencing the interaction between state and non-state actors.

An important contextual factor affecting policy implementation is the openness of the policy process, that is, the degree to which non-state actors influence decision-making and are able to exercise regulatory authority (Wu 2010). Building on the proposition that REDD+ and FLEGT/VPA exemplify international and transnational efforts to influence domestic practices, these policies can be further defined as increasingly relevant not only for the behaviour of states, but also for the non-state actors active within those states – civil society and domestic firms. Cameroon's forest and environmental sectors have been described as not open to non-state actors (Dkamela et al. 2014; Korhonen-Kurki et al. 2014). REDD+ and FLEGT/VPA directly attempt to redress this situation. Our analysis in this chapter aims to convey the knowledge generated by the cumulative findings of the embedded case studies regarding interaction between state and non-state regulatory authority. This then allows for theorizing how such interactions can be better designed to ratchet up standards in the pursuit of the public goods of justice and sustainability.

The ability of REDD+ and FLEGT/VPA to influence on-the-ground behaviour may be related to the potentially sensitive issues of sovereignty that may arise when travelling along the direct access pathway (Bernstein and Cashore 2012). In the context of Cameroon, numerous scholars have attributed the lack of effective forest policy implementation to weak national commitment, considered symptomatic of post-colonial states (Dkamela et al. 2014, citing Kapoor 2002). Further, 'internationally driven national forest policy processes tend to encounter massive implementation challenges' simply due to the fact that they stem from global priorities that may not reflect national policy agendas (Dkamela et al. 2014, p. 3). Cameroon's overarching economic development objectives as outlined in its Vision 2035 focus on investments in agro-industry, infrastructure and manufacturing, with less emphasis on sustainable forest management (Cameroon Ministry of Economy, Planning and Regional Development 2009).

In Cameroon, scholars and practitioners present different findings related to the relevance of multi-stakeholder engagement in the REDD+ policy processes. Some criticize REDD+ for being based on externally driven policy reforms, paralleling the failure of the 1994 forest law reform process (Dkamela et al. 2014). These scholars argue that the lack of national ownership of the policy process fundamentally limited the inclusiveness of the 1994 forest law reform, stating 'civil society and forest-dwelling communities had little or no involvement in the debates on the law', which resulted in 'the law's basis in technical information and foreign ideologies, and its omission of forest-dwelling communities' knowledge and opinions', making implementation of the law 'highly likely to fail' (ibid., p. 6). The documented concentration of REDD+ technical knowledge, information and resources in international actors explains why these authors believe REDD+ risks implementation failure similar to the 1994 forest law (ibid.). On the other hand, Cameroon's VPA negotiations have been praised for providing the first instance of government and civil society representatives sitting around the same table (Bollen and Ozinga 2013; Wodschow et al. 2016). Since the negotiations closed, however, the ability of non-state actors to influence policy-making related to VPA implementation has been considerably weakened (Wodschow et al. 2016, p. 7).

An analysis of the barriers to VPA implementation reveals that decisions made about different types of policy levels – especially objectives, mechanisms/calibrations and settings – can explain whether, when and how global interventions reinforce or alter domestic state-societal relations and problem solving on the ground. Overall, the technical policy choices made to advance the VPA in Cameroon do not seem well equipped to lead to significant and durable change on the ground. This is owed in large part to Cameroon's informal sector being ill-suited to the formalization approach of the VPA. Rather, it seems that significant reforms of the underlying structural dynamics – both in the forest administration as well as the legal framework governing how forest resources are distributed between international and domestic market-oriented enterprises – are needed before the VPA's proposed TLAS can benefit the domestic sector. Such reforms, in turn, require that those making decisions about policy objectives, settings and calibrations take into account, and more clearly incorporate, domestic historical practices and controversies. This also means making sure that choices over calibrations are consistent with broader policy goals and objectives, rather than working at cross purposes. For instance, a formal goal of the VPA process was to enhance socioeconomically equitable development. Yet this goal seems to be overshadowed by more narrow tasks, such as the delivery of FLEGT licenses for timber exports to the EU. While important as a short-term step, this narrower focus on TLAS implementation to generate FLEGT licenses for EU timber exports risks missing or even undermining the broader governance and socioeconomic objectives of the FLEGT Action Plan.

To be sure, the case of Cameroon demonstrates how the translation of international forest policies through the direct access pathway has resulted in technological solutions as a procedural means for tackling the complex governance challenges inhibiting effective legality. Cameroon's forest sector – like those of many tropical forest countries suffering from so-called resource curses – suffers from weak rule of law (Cerutti et al. 2013). Acknowledging the magnitude of the problem, it becomes clear that governance reform in Cameroon requires drawing on technical data-collection systems as a means rather than an end. Failure to do so raises the risk that the TLAS will exacerbate the informal collection of payments (Carodenuto and Cerutti 2014). This is because timber legality in Cameroon is based on the sector's pre-existing, paper-based system whereby companies require various official papers proving that they have paid different taxes, respected various norms and so on. These papers are generally obtained through bribes. Especially in the domestic market, the rules are very unclear, allowing various administrative agents from different government agencies to demand 'papers' or 'official stamps' on an ad hoc basis (Cerutti et al. 2013). The risk with FLEGT/VPA is that now these papers, especially the FLEGT legality certificate itself, have even more value. Proving the underlying legality of any paper is extremely complex, however.

We also see several positive opportunities emerging from this analysis. A more nuanced look at instrument choice and design may provide a window of opportunity for policy learning efforts that focus on generating multi-stakeholder attention and knowledge about the causal processes through which global interventions might influence on-the-ground problems, and the strategic implications of these processes. This type of effort focuses greater attention on linking decisions about policy mechanisms, calibrations and settings to the causal pathways that might be unleashed by those decisions. This means, for example, that promoting the implementation process on the basis of its participatory nature means taking a closer look at the governance context, which may further entrench existing power relations rather than fostering equitable socioeconomic development. Refocusing the agenda on developing policy instruments that are operational and meet policy aims may help to move forward with effective policy implementation.

This research helps to better unpack the actual effects of policy instruments and to recognize when unintended consequences may undermine the basic purpose of the policy itself. With regard to FLEGT, the expected forest governance reforms relating to reducing corruption and improving law enforcement that are brought about by VPA implementation should benefit all timber operators, domestic and international. However, the policy means, the TLAS, is designed so that there is a significant risk that Forestry Ministry officials will seek more or higher bribes for the papers required by the TLAS, with the most valuable paper being the FLEGT license itself. Further, given that the TLAS is based on formal law, it is highly likely that the informal domestic market will be excluded from the main benefits resulting from VPA implementation while power will be increasingly concentrated in the hands of concession-owning forestry industries. The TLAS demonstrates how technology can act as a channel through which to achieve policy goals, but also as a tool for further exploitation of existing power imbalances (Cashore et al. 2015). Taken together, two observations stand out. First, it is clear that policymakers must carefully identify, and understand, the causal processes through which choices about mechanisms, calibrations, and settings in TBG systems might influence domestic processes. Second, they must also expand their attention to a range of causal pathways, rather than focusing so much attention on market logics. Social norms, informal institutions and historical contexts all play important roles in influencing how specific policy instruments become influential and effective.

NOTES

1. Cashore and Howlett expand Hall's typology to identify six, not three, ways to classify policy choices: ends-focused goals, objectives and settings; and means-focused instrument logics, mechanisms and calibrations. We use these distinctions to guide our broad analysis, rather than probe deeply into each one, which is beyond the scope of a single chapter. Rather, we simply make the point that distinguishing different types of policy choices can help better understand the pathways through which TBG instruments may have shaped, or failed to shape, domestic policy.

2. As explained in detail by Gupta and Mason (2016), REDD+ Measurement, Reporting and Verification (MRV) – the national forest monitoring systems that are required for REDD+ countries to access REDD+ payments – have characteristics similar to the TLAS in terms of being an expert-led, problem-solving approach mired by technical complexity. A review of the design and implementation of Cameroon's proposed MRV system is not included in this chapter.
3. Communication from the Commission to the Council and the European Parliament: Forest Law Enforcement, Governance and Trade (FLEGT) – Proposal for an EU Action Plan, COM (2003) 251 final.
4. Voluntary Partnership Agreement between the European Union and the Republic of Cameroon on Forest Law Enforcement, Governance and Trade in Timber and Derived Products to the European Union (FLEGT) (Cameroon-EU) (adopted 6 May 2010, entered into force 1 December 2011), [2011] OJ L92/4 (Cameroon-EU VPA), Article 2(2)(d). The other objectives are: '(a) to promote trade in timber and derived products; (b) to establish a basis for dialogue and cooperation; (c) to promote the development of the forest industries in Cameroon and to thereby improve the competitiveness of the sector; . . . [and] (e) to strengthen the capacities of actors in Cameroon by encouraging the creation of a favourable climate for investment in the sustainable management of forests' (ibid.).
5. Ibid., Article 5.
6. Ibid., Article 16.

REFERENCES

Assembe-Mvondo, S., C.J.P. Colfer, M. Brockhaus and R. Tsanga (2014), 'Review of the legal ownership status of national lands in Cameroon: a more nuanced view', *Development Studies Research*, **1** (1), 148–60.

Bartley, T. (2014), 'Transnational governance and the re-centered state: sustainability or legality?', *Regulation & Governance*, **8** (1), 93–109.

Bernstein, S. and B. Cashore (2000), 'Globalization, four paths of internationalization and domestic policy change: the case of ecoforestry in British Columbia, Canada', *Canadian Journal of Political Science/Revue canadienne de science politique*, **33** (1), 67–99.

Bernstein, S. and B. Cashore (2012), 'Complex global governance and domestic policies: four pathways of influence', *International Affairs*, **88** (3), 585–604.

Bollen, A. and S. Ozinga (2013), *Improving Forest Governance: A comparison of FLEGT VPAs and their impact*, Brussels: FERN.

Bourges, M.J., S. Carodenuto, M. Nguemadji, C. Njomaha and M. Tolo (2014), Mission d'appui à l'identification de projets pilotes REDD+ au Cameroun: Etude préparatoire pour la mise en œuvre du R-PP, Rapport pour la GIZ au Cameroun, Berlin: GIZ.

Buttoud, G. (1999), 'Principles of participatory processes in public decision making', in Anssi Niskanen and Johanna Väyrynenn (eds), *Regional Forest Programmes: A Participatory Approach to Support Forest Based Regional Development*, Joensuu, Finland: European Forest Institute, pp. 11–28.

Buttoud, G. (ed.) (2011), 'Special issue: change in forest governance as a collective learning process', *Forest Policy and Economics*, **13** (2), 87–154.

Cameroon Ministry of Economy, Planning and Regional Development (2009), *Cameroon Vision 2035*, Yaoundé, Cameroon: Ministry of Economy, Planning and Regional Development.

Cameroon Ministry of the Environment, Nature Protection and Sustainable Development (2014), *Operational Guidelines for Obtaining Free, Prior and Informed Consent (FPIC) in REDD+ Initiatives in Cameroon: Including Principles, Criteria and Indicators*, Yaoundé, Cameroon: Ministry of the Environment, Nature Protection and Sustainable Development.

Carodenuto, S. (2016), 'Access to information and non-state regulatory authority: a case study of REDD+ and FLEGT/VPA access to information in Cameroon', unpublished working paper (on file with author).

Carodenuto, S. and P.O. Cerutti (2014), 'Forest law enforcement, governance and trade (FLEGT) in Cameroon: perceived private sector benefits from VPA implementation', *Forest Policy and Economics*, **48**, 55–62.

Carodenuto, S. and F. Kalame (2015), 'Operationalizing free, prior and informed consent (FPIC) for REDD+: insights from the national FPIC guidelines of Cameroon', *Carbon & Climate Law Review*, **9** (2), 156–67.

Carodenuto, S., E. Merger, E. Essomba, M. Panev, T. Pistorius and J. Amougou (2015), 'A methodological framework for assessing agents, proximate drivers and underlying causes of deforestation: field test results from Southern Cameroon', *Forests*, **6** (1), 203–24.

Carodenuto, S. and S. Ramcilovic-Suominen (2014), 'Barriers to VPA implementation: a case study of Cameroon's private forestry sector', *International Forestry Review*, **16** (3), 278–88.

Cashore, B., C. Elliott, E. Pohnan and M. Stone (2015), 'Achieving sustainability through market mechanisms,' in R. Panwar, R. Kozak and E. Hansen (eds), *Forests, Business and Sustainability*, Abingdon, UK and New York: Routledge, pp. 59–83.

Cashore, B., C. Elliot, E. Pohnan, M. Stone and S. Jodoin (2016), 'Achieving sustainability through market mechanisms', in Rajat Panwar, Robert Kozak and Eric Hansen (eds), *Forests, Business and Sustainability*, Abingdon, UK and New York: Routledge, pp. 45–70.

Cashore, B. and M. Howlett (2007), 'Punctuating which equilibrium? Understanding thermostatic policy dynamics in pacific northwest forestry', *American Journal of Political Science*, **51** (3), 532–51.

Cashore, B. and M.W. Stone (2014), 'Does California need Delaware? Explaining Indonesian, Chinese, and United States support for legality compliance of internationally traded products', *Regulation & Governance*, **8** (1), 49–73.

Cerutti, P.O. and G. Lescuyer (2011), 'The domestic market for small-scale chainsaw milling in Cameroon: present situation, opportunities and challenges, CIFOR Occasional Paper No. 61, Bogor, Indonesia: Centre for International Forestry Research, accessed 28 March 2019 at http://webdoc.sub.gwdg.de/ebook/serien/yo/CIFOR_OP/61.pdf.

Cerutti, P.O., L. Tacconi, G. Lescuyer and R. Nasi (2013), 'Cameroon's hidden harvest: commercial chainsaw logging, corruption, and livelihoods', *Society & Natural Resources*, **26** (5), 539–53.

deLeon, P. (1999), 'The stages approach to the policy process: what has it done? Where is it going?' in P. Sabatier (ed), *Theories of the Policy Process*, Boulder, CO, Westview Press, pp. 19–34.

Dkamela, G.P., M. Brockhaus, F. Kengoum Djiegni, J. Schure and S. Assembe Mvondo (2014), 'Lessons for REDD+ from Cameroon's past forestry law reform: a political economy analysis', *Ecology and Society*, **19** (3), Article

No. 30, accessed 28 March 2019 at https://www.ecologyandsociety.org/vol19/iss3/art30.

Eberlein, B., K.W. Abbott, J. Black, E. Meidinger and S. Wood (2014), 'Transnational business governance interactions: conceptualization and framework for analysis', *Regulation & Governance*, **8** (1), 1–22.

Fripp, E., S. Carodenuto and L. Culliane (2013), *Voluntary Partnership Agreements (VPAs): An Opportunity to Address Corruption in the Forest Sector*, GIZ Forest Governance Programme Working Document, Berlin: GIZ.

Gupta, A. and M. Mason (2016), 'Disclosing or obscuring? The politics of transparency in global climate governance', *Current Opinion in Environmental Sustainability*, **18**, 82–90.

Hall, P.A. (1993), 'Policy paradigms, social learning, and the state: the case of economic policymaking in Britain', *Comparative Politics*, **25** (3), 275–96.

Hansen, C.P., J. van Brussels, T. Tuomasjukka and M. Shannon (2013), *Governance Research Agenda for FLEGT: Towards Global Forest Governance Research and Action*, Joensuu, Finland: European Forest Institute.

Hirschberger, P. (2008), *Illegal Wood for the European Market: An Analysis of the EU Import and Export of Illegal Wood and Related Products*, Frankfurt am Main: WWF-Germany.

Kapoor, I. (2002), 'Capitalism, culture, agency: dependency versus postcolonial theory', *Third World Quarterly*, **23** (4), 647–64.

Korhonen-Kurki, K., J. Sehring, M. Brockhaus and M. Di Gregorio (2014), 'Enabling factors for establishing REDD+ in a context of weak governance', *Climate Policy*, **14** (2), 167–86.

Lerner, D. and H.D. Lasswell (eds) (1951), *The Policy Sciences: Recent Developments in Scope and Method*, Stanford, CA: Stanford University Press.

Lawson, S. and L. MacFaul (2010), *Illegal Logging and Related Trade: Indicators of the Global Response*, London: Chatham House.

Lescuyer, G., R. Eba'a Atyi, R. Nasi and T. Fomete Nembot (2016), 'Editorial: valuing the cameroonian forest', *International Forestry Review*, **18**, Supplement 1, 1–3.

McDermott, C.L., L. Coad, A. Helfgott and H. Schroeder (2012), 'Operationalizing social safeguards in REDD+: actors, interests and ideas', *Environmental Science & Policy*, **21**, 63–72.

Melish, T. and E. Meidinger (2012), 'Protect, respect, remedy and participate: "New Governance" lessons for the ruggie framework', in Radu Mareș (ed.), *The UN Guiding Principles on Business and Human Rights: Foundations and Implementation*, Leiden and Boston: Brill Nihjoff, pp. 303–36.

Rayner, J., A. Buck and P. Katila (eds) (2010), *Embracing Complexity: Meeting the Challenges of International Forest Governance*, IUFRO World Series, vol. 28, Vienna: International Union of Forest Research Organizations, accessed 28 March 2019 at https://www.iufro.org/publications/series/world-series/article/2011/01/24/world-series-vol-28-embracing-complexity-meeting-the-challenges-of-international-forest-governa.

Somorin, O.A., I.J. Visseren-Hamakers, B. Arts, D.J. Sonwa and A. Tiani (2014), 'REDD+ policy strategy in Cameroon: actors, institutions and governance', *Environmental Science & Policy*, **35**, 87–97.

Visseren-Hamakers, I.J., C. McDermott, M.J. Vijge and B. Cashore (2012), 'Trade-offs, co-benefits and safeguards: current debates on the breadth of REDD+', *Current Opinion in Environmental Sustainability*, **4** (6), 646–53.

Wasseige, C. de, P. de Marcken and N. Bayol (2012), *The Forests of the Congo Basin: State of the Forest 2010*, Luxembourg: Publications Office of the European Union.
Wodschow, A., I. Nathan and P. Cerutti (2016), 'Participation, public policy-making, and legitimacy in the EU voluntary partnership agreement process: the Cameroon case', *Forest Policy and Economics*, **63**, 1–10.
Wu, X. (2010), *The Public Policy Primer: Managing the Policy Process*. London: Routledge.

11. Transnational delegation, accountability and the administrative governance of biofuel standards

Phillip Paiement

11.1 INTRODUCTION

In 2009, the European Parliament and Council revised the Renewable Energy Directive (RED), establishing a target for Member States of at least 10 per cent renewable energy sources for transport fuels by 2020.[1] The RED included criteria for 'sustainable' biofuels, which aimed to conserve lands with high biodiversity value, limit greenhouse gas (GHG) emissions, and avoid carbon stock losses related to biofuel production.[2] However, as much of the European Union's biofuels are imported, monitoring the sustainability of biofuel production beyond EU borders presents an extraterritorial governance challenge to manage the risk of inadvertently transitioning to biofuels that might be unsustainable and potentially even more harmful than current energy sources.

The European Commission recognized certain non-state voluntary schemes whose standards ensure compliance with the sustainability criteria,[3] thereby acknowledging the role private supply chain governance can play in its environmental and energy policies. The assemblage of EU institutions and voluntary schemes constitutes a type of transnational business governance interaction (TBGI) between state and non-state bodies. Delegating monitoring roles to voluntary schemes gives the EU a transnational extension to implement its policies concerning global biofuel production, but by diverging from the 'New Approach' to production standards (Pelkmans 1987) it invites criticism about participation, transparency and accountability in this new transnational governance assemblage.

This chapter examines the effect of the EU's reliance on voluntary schemes in the RED on the administrative governance of biofuel production. It assesses, first, the challenges this delegation presents to the EU's oversight mechanisms; and second, this delegation's organizational effects on the field of non-state sustainable biofuel standards. The chapter is concerned with the effects of this delegation assemblage on the administrative practices of both the voluntary schemes and the EU as they relate to participation, transparency and accountability, with an ultimate concern for the consequences faced by structurally disempowered economic actors in the assemblage.

The chapter begins with the background of the 2009 RED revision (Part 2), followed by an elaboration of assemblage theory (Part 3). Next, it describes the two-step delegation comprising the RED assemblage, including the associated accountability concerns (Part 4). It then assesses the resulting changes to the field of sustainable biomass standards and their accountability mechanisms (Part 5), and explores the consequences for marginalized stakeholders in biomass production (Part 6).

11.2 THE EU AND BIOFUEL SUSTAINABILITY

11.2.1 The Sustainability Controversy Surrounding Biofuels

The EU's 2003 Biofuels Directive established initial targets for the proportion of biofuels usage in Member States.[4] Before the 2009 revisions increased the renewable energy target to 20 per cent by 2020,[5] the European Council emphasized the need to consider the sustainability (in addition to renewability) of biofuels, including the impacts of biofuel production on agriculture and broader 'environmental and social consequences of the production and consumption of biofuels'.[6]

The Council turned its attention to the sustainability of biofuel production during a period of worldwide discussion about the desirability of biofuels as a source of renewable energy. Both the United States (US) and the EU had emphasized the growing importance of biofuels in their economies, for both energy independence and environmental concerns. Yet, there was a growing concern that biofuels were not inherently more sustainable than conventional energy sources due to the social and environmental side effects of biofuel production.

First, the concentration of biofuel production in the tropics gave rise to concerns about tropical deforestation driven by growing US and EU demand for biofuels. Secondly, biofuels came under criticism due to their impacts on the price and availability of food crops for human consumption. In 2008, large fluctuations in world commodity prices that caused localized food crises were attributed to growing demand for biofuels (Mitchell 2008). This 'food versus fuel' controversy flared as the European Parliament was discussing revisions of the Directive (Mol 2007; Partzsch 2009; Bailis and Baka 2011). Jean Ziegler, the UN Special Rapporteur on the right to food, argued in a 2007 press conference that it is 'a crime against humanity to convert agricultural [sic] productive soil into soil which produces food stuff that will be turned into biofuel', and insisted on a five-year moratorium on biofuels (UN 2007). The controversy made it necessary for the EU to ensure that biofuels included in the EU's energy policies were not implicated in conversions of food-producing land or other environmentally harmful practices.

11.2.2 Sustainability in the 2009 Renewable Energy Directive

The RED sustainability criteria constituted an essential piece of the 2009 revision. To be included in the renewable energy targets, biofuels must generate GHG emissions savings of at least 35 per cent (increasing to 50 per cent by 2017 and 60 per cent by 2018) and must not be made from materials produced from peatland with a high biodiversity value or land with a high carbon stock.[7] Additionally, the Commission must report to the Parliament and Council every two years regarding the social sustainability of global biofuel markets and production, and foodstuff affordability in developing countries.[8]

The Directive obligates Member States to require independent auditing of economic operators producing and trading biofuels within the EU.[9] To address biofuels produced outside the EU, the Directive authorizes the Commission to recognize voluntary schemes that provide standards to demonstrate compliance with the sustainability criteria, effectively delegating monitoring to these non-state bodies.[10] Such schemes must meet 'adequate standards of reliability, transparency and independent auditing'.[11]

In 2011, the Commission recognized an initial group of seven voluntary schemes (European Commission 2011), later expanding to 19. While this delegation of monitoring to voluntary schemes provides a key tool for transnational implementation of the RED, it also introduced a number of questions about how this new hybrid governance assemblage operates. In particular, there are significant concerns about the accountability and transparency of the monitoring that these voluntary schemes provide to the Commission, and questions as to where complaints about their compliance decisions should be heard.

11.3 THE TRANSNATIONAL BUSINESS GOVERNANCE INTERACTIONS ASSEMBLAGE

The European Commission engaged in a new type of delegation when it recognized voluntary schemes under the RED. The Commission had relied on voluntary schemes as one of numerous enforcement tools in its 2003 Forest Law Enforcement, Governance and Trade (FLEGT) Action Plan, but the RED elevated the use of voluntary sustainability schemes to a new level (Overdevest and Zeitlin 2014). The TBGI literature has accomplished an extensive mapping of theories of interactions in transnational governance, serving as a helpful starting point (Eberlein et al. 2014; Wood et al. 2015). The TBGI framework provides a comprehensive analytic perspective for studying governance assemblages involving public-public, private-public, private-private and other types of hybrid relationships (Zumbansen 2011).

This study is a meso-level analysis focused on 'interactions among TBGI schemes, and between them and state-based regulators' (Eberlein et al. 2014, p. 8). Furthermore, it is concerned with 'conditional referencing' mechanisms, insofar as the Commission makes compliance with the RED sustainability criteria conditional on certification of a product's supply chain and production methods in accordance with a recognized voluntary standard scheme. This study interrogates the character of these interactions to assess whether they exhibit competition, coordination, co-optation or chaos. Finally, this study is concerned with the effects of the interaction, including increases in regulatory capacity and performance, 'races to the top' and 'races to the bottom', as well as 'homogenization' of voluntary standards (Eberlein et al. 2014, pp. 11–13).

Abbott and Snidal's theory of regulatory orchestration, which plays a formative role in TBGI scholarship, arises from the observation that transnational new governance – characterized by high decentralization of regulatory activities, fragmentation of regulatory expertise and capacities, and the extensive use of voluntary codes – could be improved through greater orchestration by states and intergovernmental organizations (Abbott and Snidal 2009; Abbott et al. 2015). The current study could certainly be approached from the perspective of the EU's orchestrating role. In fact, Philip Schleifer provides a compelling account of the RED as a partial failure of orchestration insofar as 'EU regulators have failed to establish a level playing field among biofuel certification schemes', facilitating forum shopping and negative forms of competition among standards bodies (Schleifer 2013, p. 542).

While many of Schleifer's findings will be echoed below, some aspects of orchestration theory are problematic for studying the delegation interactions comprised in the RED. First, the orchestration theory treats the state as a single homogenous entity. This approach would force analysis of the EU as a unitary actor, overlooking nuanced dynamics between competing EU organs. In addition, orchestration theory views the state's engagement in transnational regulatory spaces as a new phenomenon breaking with historical practices of 'old governance'. This assumption overlooks the lengthy history of states engaging with transnational business governance (for example Cutler 2003). Finally, the theory approaches orchestration as a normatively desirable state practice aimed at achieving effectiveness, transparency and empowerment of marginalized groups in transnational governance (Abbott and Snidal 2009, pp. 564–77). This is what allows Schleifer to speak in terms of 'success' and 'failure' of orchestration. However, such an approach presumes normative agreement on the ends of orchestration, a contentious issue in itself. Instead, it would be more beneficial to orient analysis towards the question of what kind of regulatory work the EU's orchestration is producing, rather than immediately assessing its desirability.

Another way to look at this arrangement is as a regulatory 'assemblage' of public actors (the Commission and Parliament), non-state voluntary schemes and private companies (Mol 2010; Ponte and Daugbjerg 2015). The concept of assemblages arises from the social-ontological work of Deleuze and Guattari (1987, p. 88; Delanda 2006a). Assemblages are scalar relationships between smaller parts assembled into a greater large-scale entity (Delanda 2006b). The interacting parts of an assemblage are often themselves assemblages of lower-level parts. The large-scale entity is engaged in constituting its parts by empowering them with resources and constraining them with limitations (Delanda 2006b, pp. 251–2). Finally, assemblages are characterized by contradictory territorialization and deterritorialization processes that stabilize and destabilize the assemblage's identity (Delanda 2006b, p. 253). The concept of a regulatory assemblage is comparable to Oren Perez's notion of 'ensemble regulation' in that they both emphasize networks of various types of actors (Perez 2011). However, Perez's focus on positive externalities produced by networks that are oriented around shared principles contrasts sharply with the internal contradictions and tensions presupposed in the regulatory assemblage framework.

Saskia Sassen's (2006, 2008) historical analysis of territory, authority and rights postulates that transnational or global assemblages of public authorities and private market actors from seemingly contradictory and competing levels (national versus transnational) and sources of authority (state versus market) asymmetrically empower particular elements of each competing authority and level. Sassen describes how national executives have frequently been empowered, at the expense of legislatures and courts, in their engagement with transnational market authorities (ibid.; see also Sullivan 2014; Valverde 2015).

Viewing transnational governance arrangements as assemblages emphasizes the inter-related spatial and temporal dimensions of governance. The assemblage framework focuses on the dynamics of contradictory processes of globalization that territorialize and de-territorialize in the form of globalized localisms and localized globalisms (de Sousa Santos 2002). Lastly, it emphasizes interdependent and polycentric governance architectures rather than privileging the formal authority of states and international organizations (Ponte and Daugbjerg 2015).

An assemblage framework is thus more appropriate than orchestration for assessing the EU as a multi-interested, complex actor in the transnational delegation constructed in the RED. It opens up the possibility of seeing particular entities in the EU and biofuel production being (dis-)empowered in different ways as a result of their interactions. This approach is further premised on the assumption that different actors pursue multiple, competing and conflictual visions of biofuel sustainability in their engagement with the governance assemblage. Assemblage theory also embeds the analysis within the spatio-temporal dimensions of biofuel sustainability. As Stefano Ponte and Carsten Daugbjerg note, the problem of biofuel sustainability governance is premised on the fact that the sustainability of a biofuel cannot be measured by the end product. The RED thus serves to build connections among the fragmented spaces and moments of biofuel supply chains that implicate biofuel sustainability (Ponte and Daugbjerg 2015, p. 104).

Ultimately, assemblages offer a useful concept for capturing the extensive layers of actors, norms and processes with contradictory interests and purposes that are brought into relationship with each other because of the RED (Zumbansen 2012). It does this without presupposing what would constitute a 'success' or 'failure', but rather in terms of empowerment and disempowerment. With this framework of TBGI assemblages in mind, the next section assesses the relationship between the Commission and the voluntary schemes and compares it to the Commission's more common relationships with standard setting and monitoring bodies.

11.4 THE COMMISSION'S DELEGATION TO VOLUNTARY SCHEMES

The European Commission has a long history of delegating tasks to private organizations responsible for technical standards, but this delegation occurs within the context of the delegation of legislative power from the Council to the Commission. In this sense, the Commission's relationship with standard-setting bodies must be assessed within a two-step process of delegation.

The Council frequently delegates legislative powers to the Commission (Craig and de Búrca 2008, p. 118; Bergström 2005). The European Court of Justice (ECJ) affirmed the validity of this type of delegation in the *Köster* decision.[12] Article 290 of the Treaty on the Functioning of the European Union authorizes the Council and Parliament to give the Commission the power to adopt 'non-legislative acts of general application', and Article 291 provides for delegation of 'implementing powers' to the Commission. While the distinction between these two types of powers has its grey margins, the inclusion of these provisions in the treaty has been widely considered a positive step towards further institutionalizing historically common delegation practices (Craig 2008; Ponzano 2008).

This delegation of powers occurs within the tension between the democratic and national accountability provided by the Parliament and Council and the effective implementation provided by the Commission. Yet, as the Council and Parliament delegate power, they simultaneously include constraint mechanisms. In the case of the RED, these include mandatory consultation with third countries, producers, consumers and civil society, and the establishment of a Committee on the Sustainability of Biofuels and Bioliquids for Member States to provide input and direction to the Commission.[13] In this respect, this delegation in the RED follows a well-established pattern in the EU's institutions.

A second, more problematic delegation step frequently occurs within the Commission's own implementing measures. It is difficult to maintain accountability when the Commission delegates authority to other actors such as EU agencies. EU committees and agencies are not formally subject to the jurisdiction of the ECJ, and it is difficult for courts to review their actions (Curtin 2007, p. 535). Despite these concerns, in its 1958 *Meroni* decision the ECJ upheld the Commission's delegation of powers to third parties, even private actors.[14] The validity of delegation is contingent on a series of provisos established in that decision, including that the delegated powers must be powers of the Commission, clearly defined and strictly executive, subject to the same conditions as if they had been exercised by the Commission, and subject to Commission supervision.[15] More than half a century later, these criteria remain influential in the ECJ's reasoning (Dehousse 2002).

11.4.1 The Commission's 'New Approach' to Standards

Since 1985, the New Approach has structured the Commission's delegation to non-state standards bodies. It requires that Directives on issues such as product safety and building safety provide only 'essential requirements'

(Pelkmans 1987),[16] leaving details to be set out in technical standards issued by European standards bodies. Conformity with the standards, while formally voluntary, is equivalent to compliance with the essential requirements (Schepel 2005, pp. 227–8). This approach allows the EU to generate technical specifications efficiently but does not delegate powers fully to standards bodies, as compliance remains possible without the standards. Importantly, the Commission itself does not substantively review the standards (Schepel 2005, pp 235–9). As Harm Schepel notes, there are clear inconsistencies between the 'New Approach' and the *Meroni* decision in that '[t]he powers of the European standards bodies go far beyond "implementation"; there is no control or supervision of the Commission or possibilities of judicial review' (Schepel 2005, p. 227). Admittedly, the Council strengthened the accountability of the delegation procedure with legislation requiring greater transparency, qualified majority decision-making and the involvement of different types of stakeholders (Schepel 2005, pp. 242–6).[17] Yet, it has become more apparent that the 'New Approach' constitutes a more significant delegation of powers than once believed, requiring more attention to the decision-making procedures of delegated bodies. It is worth noting that the recent decisions in the *Fra.bo* and *Elliott James* cases have further complicated the status of the New Approach and opened the doors to a substantive review of private standards by the ECJ (Schepel 2013).[18]

11.4.2 A 'Different Approach' in the RED

The RED's approach to voluntary schemes is rather different from the New Approach to technical standards. The New Approach is generally limited to issues that affect product characteristics, while the RED voluntary schemes monitor production processes that go well beyond visible or traceable effects on the quality or nature of the product.[19] For example, whether or not palm oil originates from palms grown in former tropical forests would not affect the character or quality of the palm oil. Whereas New Approach technical standards originate from national and European standards bodies, the voluntary schemes involved in the RED arise from bodies that operate transnationally and are generally delineated by industry sectors. The Commission's comprehensive list of national standardization bodies excludes the RED voluntary schemes (European Commission 2019a). The International Organization for Standardization (ISO) also distinguishes between national and so-called 'private' standards bodies (ISO 2010). In other words, the voluntary schemes embraced by the RED constitute a new genus of standards for the EU. The EU has diverged from the New Approach in other notable fields of standardization such as food quality and safety standards, which also include transnationally oriented standards composed by industry actors, multi-stakeholder platforms and other organizations, in addition to recognized national standard-setting bodies (Verbruggen and Havinga 2017; Verbruggen and Havinga, Chapter 2).

The delegation of monitoring and enforcement roles to voluntary schemes constitutes an ad hoc form of conditional referencing governed by an equally ad hoc set of measures in the RED. In July 2010, the Commission announced the procedure and requirements for recognizing voluntary schemes for purposes of compliance with sustainability criteria (European Commission 2010). The RED allows the Commission to recognize voluntary schemes only if they meet 'adequate standards of reliability, transparency and independent auditing'.[20] This trio of reliability, transparency, and independent auditing provide the ad hoc accountability structure for delegation between the Commission and voluntary schemes.

The Commission's recognition guidelines provide thorough requirements for assessing the reliability and independent auditing of voluntary schemes. They require that schemes 'have an auditable system for the evidence related to the claims they make or rely on, keep any evidence for a minimum of five years, and accept responsibility for preparing any information related to the auditing of such evidence' (European Commission 2010, section 2.2.1). They include requirements for ensuring sophisticated audits, including tailoring audit procedures to the particular risks posed by the economic operator, establishing verification plans appropriate to the scope and complexity of the audited operations, and obtaining missing documentation or explanations before finishing audits. The Commission also requires that audits be independent insofar as they must be performed by someone other than the economic operator and the voluntary scheme (ibid.).

The Commission's communication is silent about the transparency of voluntary schemes. Its 2015 Assessment Protocol, however, requires that voluntary schemes make available a list of current and previously certified economic operators, 'the latest version of scheme documents including the guidelines for audits', certification bodies accepted by the voluntary scheme, and contact details of the organization responsible for the voluntary scheme (European Commission 2015b). Thus, while the Commission rarely addresses this third dimension of its accountability structure, its assessment procedure at least contains minimal requirements.

Between 2011 and 2017, the Commission recognized 19 voluntary schemes for monitoring compliance with the Directive's sustainability criteria (with attrition, there were 15 recognized schemes in August 2019). The Commission recognized all of the schemes before the 2015 Assessment Protocol template, with its section on transparency, were in use (European Commission 2015b). Not a single assessment conducted by the Commission as of the date of writing includes any review of the transparency of the voluntary schemes.

The Commission introduced the heightened transparency evaluation measures in reaction to the 2015 Indirect Land-Use Change Directive, which amended the 2009 RED (European Commission 2015a, c).[21] This Directive further entrenched the trio of principles concerning reliability, independent auditing and transparency of voluntary schemes. It requires the Commission to report to the Parliament and Council on the transparency of voluntary schemes, including 'the accessibility of the scheme, the availability of the translations in the applicable languages of the countries and regions from which raw materials originate, the accessibility of a list of certified operators and relevant certificates, and the accessibility of auditor reports'.[22] Furthermore, the amendments introduced additional requirements for the involvement of stakeholders, including vulnerable groups such as indigenous and local communities, in decision-making processes during the drafting and revision of voluntary schemes. These changes introduced a more thorough accountability regime for the delegation of monitoring to voluntary schemes, which had not yet been used when the research for this chapter was completed. Eventually, all recognized schemes will have to be re-evaluated using the more stringent procedure.

In summary, while transparency, independent auditing and reliability were supposed to comprise the accountability structure for the conditional referencing of voluntary schemes under the RED, for the first four years the Commission completely ignored transparency. Confirmation that the scheme's requirements and measurement processes met the RED sustainability criteria was the overriding priority, while the Commission eschewed any serious review of organizational transparency and public participation in standard setting.

Having provided this descriptive account of the delegation interactions between the EU institutions and voluntary schemes, the next section will shift focus to the effects of the interaction on the field of voluntary schemes.

11.5 TRANSFORMATIONS IN THE FIELD OF TRANSNATIONAL STANDARDS FOR BIOMASS SUSTAINABILITY

This section evaluates the impacts of the conditional referencing interaction on the field of transnational sustainability standards. It first addresses the proliferation effects created by the possibility of conditional referencing, and then the variation in administrative formats among the voluntary schemes that arose with this proliferation.

As this chapter is concerned with the transnational dimensions of the RED, the analysis is limited to the ten schemes operating outside the EU: International Sustainability and Carbon Certification (ISCC), Bonsucro EU, Round Table on Responsible Soy (RTRS) EU Red, Roundtable on Sustainable Biofuels (RSB) EU RED, Biomass Biofuel Sustainability Voluntary Scheme (2BSvs), Abengoa's RED Bioenergy Sustainability Assurance (RBSA), Greenergy, Roundtable on Sustainable Palm Oil (RSPO) RED, Neste Oil's hydrotreated vegetable oil (HVO) Renewable Diesel Scheme, and the NTA 8080 standard of the Netherlands Standardization Institute (NEN).[23] The other nine schemes recognized by the Commission either operate only within the EU or are limited to a GHG calculation tool rather than a fully fledged sustainable biofuels standard.

11.5.1 The Proliferation of a Standards Market for Sustainable Biomass

An initial effect of the RED was a proliferation of sustainable biomass standard-setting schemes (Reinecke et al. 2012). Of the ten schemes recognized by the Commission, only seven operated sustainable biomass standards before the revised RED came into effect: ISCC, Bonsucro, RTRS, RSB, RSPO, NEN and Greenergy. The other three schemes – 2BSvs, RBSA and Neste Oil's HVO scheme – were all created in response to the RED. NEN's NTA 8080 standard pre-dated the revised RED but was likely written with it in mind. Hence, the introduction of the RED's conditional referencing possibility drove at least three transnational standard-setting organizations to enter the field of biomass sustainability standards.

In addition to the proliferation of standard-setting *schemes*, the conditional referencing possibility was also responsible for the proliferation of *standards* in the field of sustainable biomass. Of the seven schemes already operating standards for sustainable biomass, four created add-ons to their pre-existing standards to meet the RED criteria. This approach, taken by RTRS, RSB, Bonsucro and RSPO, introduced an additional layer of complexity to each organization's standards. Each has a baseline standard applicable to all certified operators, plus an EU RED add-on for those seeking RED compliance. Hence, the conditional referencing possibility is also responsible for four new standards from pre-existing bodies. In this sense, the RED has contributed to a proliferation of standards for biomass sustainability.

Both homogenization and fragmentation dynamics arose from the proliferation of schemes and standards. The fact that the majority of recognized schemes were created either explicitly with the RED in mind or as add-on options for already existing standards suggests that there was some homogenization towards more stringent requirements, although this was limited to specific issues. For instance, it was common for pre-existing schemes to add provisions regarding historic land-use change restrictions and a GHG emissions calculation tool to their standards in order to integrate the EU's sustainability criteria, as RSPO did for its RED standard. These changes were intended to exclude biofuels produced on recently converted forestland or peatland, the conversion of which to agro-industrial plantations results in excessive carbon emissions. Strikingly, only one recognized scheme (NEN's NTA 8080) created an 'opt-out' version of their standard that allowed for pre-existing standard users to opt for a less stringent standard if they were interested in compliance with the standard only for the purpose of gaining recognition as a sustainable biofuel under RED. Thus, looking narrowly at the specific issues for which new criteria were added into standards (land conversion and GHG emissions calculations), the RED requirements contributed to a degree of upward harmonization. However, as Schleifer rightly points out, the general trend was that the new standards were overall less stringent than pre-existing ones and there was no trend towards homogenization in any comprehensive sense (Cashore et al. 2007; Schleifer 2013). For example, the 2BSvs and Neste Oil HVO standards covered only the substantive areas required by the RED: conservation of land with high biodiversity, limitation of GHG emissions and the avoidance of carbon stock losses in biofuel production. In contrast, the pre-existing RSPO and RSB standards included a much wider array of environmental issues, such as soil erosion and fertility, pesticide use and storage, and waste reduction strategies. They also included social standards pertaining to labour rights and the land rights of local communities. The extensive considerations in these pre-existing standards did not appear in the standards created after the introduction of the RED.

The Directive also caused a degree of fragmentation regarding standardization bodies' organizational formats. Four of the seven organizations pre-dating the RED self-identified as multi-stakeholder initiatives (RSB, RSPO, RTRS and Bonsucro), while another is considered an industry-dominated body (ISCC), and the last was the Dutch national standardization body (Ponte 2014, p. 268). The schemes developed in response to the RED introduced considerably more diversity into this field. Some were in-house schemes created by individual corporations for their value chains (Neste Oil's HVO scheme and Abengoa's RBSA scheme), while others were created by trade associations and other groups of economic operators (for example 2BSvs). This fragmentation raises concerns about the accountability, transparency and legitimacy of these new standard-setting bodies, which will be addressed in the following sections.

11.5.2 (Un)accountability in Diverse Administrative Structures

This section focuses on the organizational formats of the voluntary schemes recognized by the Commission, including variations in the actors involved in decision-making, the possibilities for public participation in standard setting and governance, and institutional transparency. In other words, it is concerned with their administrative governance structures.

The six recognized schemes that were already active in sustainable biomass standard setting before the Commission began its recognition assessments had relatively stringent and comprehensive administrative governance practices. At the time, RSB was a Full Member and Bonsucro an Associate Member of the ISEAL Alliance (ISEAL), a non-state umbrella group that sets meta-standards for sustainability standard-setting bodies. ISEAL is an influential voice in defining credible and legitimate standard setting for sustainability governance (Reinecke et al. 2012, p. 33; Loconto and Fouilleux 2014). RSPO became an Associate Member in 2012 – a process that must have begun prior to the Commission's initial recognition of schemes in 2011. These organizations' ISEAL membership signifies their use of stringent procedural standards for their governance, which Errol Meidinger likens to the US Administrative Procedure Act (Meidinger 2006, p. 69). ISEAL maintains Codes of Good Practice for standard setting, assurance and impacts, which provide robust requirements for the governance and implementation of sustainability standards. The Standard-setting Code requires that participation in governance bodies creating standards should be open to all stakeholders and be composed of a 'reasonable balance' of stakeholders, that standards creation and revision should include public notice and comment procedures, that standards should be publicly available online, and that the procedures of standards development and revision should be transparent (ISEAL Alliance 2014; Paiement 2016; Wood 2016). RSPO, Bonsucro and RSB must have been compliant with ISEAL's Standard-setting code when the RED was revised in 2009, as both full and associate membership requires compliance with it. Compliance is initially verified by ISEAL staff and subsequently monitored through peer evaluations by other ISEAL members. In light of Bonsucro's, RSPO's and RSB's ISEAL membership, their performance regarding the actors involved in decision-making, public participation in standard creation and institutional transparency can be considered strong. For example, all three had a primary governance body composed of representatives from various trade sectors, as well as environmental and social NGOs. Likewise, they used public notice and comment periods in the revision of their standards. In summary, their administrative governance demonstrated high levels of transparency, public participation and multi-stakeholder decision-making and was held to these high levels by an independent organization, ISEAL.

RTRS is an ISEAL 'subscriber' and has a multi-stakeholder governance format comparable to RSB, RSPO and Bonsucro. Its primary governance body is composed of voting members representing producers, industry, trade and finance, and civil society sectors. Its most recent standard revision process featured three public notice and comment periods, generating more than 250 comments (RTRS 2017). The technical bodies that drafted the current and earlier versions of its standards included balanced participation by representatives of producers, trade and civil society (ibid.; RTRS 2013). As such, RTRS's administrative governance was similar to that of the ISEAL members, albeit without the extra guarantee of independent verification by ISEAL. Consequently, four of the pre-existing standards were developed in accordance with the most concrete and robust global administrative norms for standardization in sustainability governance.

NEN, responsible for NTA 8080, is the Netherlands' national standards body. As the Dutch ISO member body, NEN is bound by ISO's requirements concerning transparency and stakeholder participation in the standard-setting process (ISO/IEC 1994). For example, NTA 8080 was initially written by a technical committee of 25 individuals representing universities, environmental NGOs, trade associations, businesses (including Shell) and public authorities (the Dutch Ministry of Economic Affairs) (NEN 2009). While this entailed a broad representation of stakeholders, they were all based in the Netherlands notwithstanding that the standard was explicitly developed for global utilization. Furthermore, while NEN's standard-setting process was fairly transparent, there is no evidence that stakeholders outside the Netherlands were able to provide input to NTA 8080 (NEN 2017). As such, the NTA 8080 standard could be said to perform at a moderate level in terms of transparency and the actors involved in decision-making, and at a low level for public participation.

The remaining pre-existing standard, ISCC, had a less exemplary administrative governance structure at the time. It was criticized for having close ties to biomass and biofuel traders (Ponte 2014). Only after having produced its standard did it proclaim itself a multi-stakeholder organization. It later introduced a General Assembly of stakeholders to participate in the standard development process for future revisions, although unlike ISEAL members, the Assembly does not have balanced representation for different classes of stakeholders (ISCC 2011). The ISCC Board reflects a tripartite representation of producers, traders and others (NGOs, researchers, and public sector organizations) (ibid.). Despite participation from organizations like the WWF, the General

Assembly is comprised overwhelmingly of downstream industry actors. Of the roughly 100 members listed on their website as of 2017, no more than ten were identifiable as civil society organizations (ISCC 2017a). In terms of transparency and public participation, ISCC utilizes public comment periods for their standards. Audit reports for producing entities certified by ISCC are not publicly available, although there is currently a working group to improve this issue of transparency (ISCC 2017b). In summary, despite having improved on a number of governance concerns, ISCC still performs at only a moderate level for public participation, transparency and the actors involved in decision-making.

The four new organizations created following the introduction of the RED scheme demonstrate remarkably less extensive governance systems. Neste Oil developed its own standard for use within its supply chain, despite also using both ISCC and RSPO for different operations within its corporate family. There is no account of how their standard was written and whether external stakeholders participated. The 2BSvs Consortium is composed of collectives of economic operators in biomass industries, and there is scarce public information about the process by which the standard was created and whether stakeholders participated (Association 2BS 2016). Furthermore, much of the administrative work surrounding the standard was contracted out to the auditing firm Bureau Veritas. Abengoa Bioenergy's RBSA standard was developed primarily for use within its own value chains. Aside from brief yearly reports, there is no transparency as to the standard writing procedures or stakeholder participation possibilities. In its Annual Report for 2013–14, the company stated that '[a] team takes care of the continuous keeping and improvement of the management system as far as objectives, contents and management are concerned', without providing further information about the team (Abengoa Bioenergy 2014, p. 10). The fourth organization, Greenergy, was no longer listed as a recognized scheme after its recognition lapsed in June 2017. It also appears from its website that it no longer maintains a standard for sustainable biofuel production. In any event, Greenergy is a UK-based private limited liability company that supplies fuel throughout the EU. There is no indication that external parties were involved in the creation of the standard, and it appears to have been used only within Greenergy's supply chain (Greenergy 2011). In short, all four of these new organizations perform at low levels for public participation, transparency and multi-stakeholder decision-making processes.

One possible theory of the RED's effect on biofuel standards is that the RED offered a platform for public exchange of biofuel sustainability standards and their associated governance processes. This theory could lead to the hypothesis that newer standards bodies simply took organizational shortcuts and borrowed from existing standards bodies without the thorough development procedures exercised by earlier standards. This hypothesis can be considered on two levels. In terms of the substantive content of biofuel standards, the hypothesis might have some purchase, but it would need to be demonstrated by a substantive review of the standards' policies, which goes beyond the scope of this chapter. In terms of the development and administration of the standards, the primary concern here, this hypothesis does not hold water. As I have shown, the RED led to a diversification of dispute procedures, transparency standards and accountability mechanisms. Whether the less accountable and less transparent formats of the new schemes were chosen for strategic purposes related to the biofuel controversy or simply to save time and costs is difficult to say and a moot question insofar as the Commission has tolerated these practices that derogate from the requirements set forth in the RED.

In summary, the RED led to a decrease in accountability, transparency and participatory opportunities for stakeholders in the field of sustainable biomass standards. The Commission's choice to forego assessments of transparency undoubtedly facilitated this development. Breaking this regulatory assemblage down into constituent elements illustrates the asymmetrical dynamics of empowerment. Industry-led standards and the Commission's interest in increasing biofuel trade were empowered by the assemblage. The accountability concerns of the Parliament and Council, as well as the position of multi-stakeholder standards, lost out. Rather than speaking of 'success' or 'failure', the assessment of the RED as an assemblage demonstrates, in all its contradictions, how pursuit of the goal of increasing transparency and accountability in global supply chains paradoxically facilitated the development of unaccountable private governance. Next, I identify what is at stake for marginalized stakeholders in this increase of unaccountable administrative structures of private governance.

11.6 THE FATE OF STAKEHOLDERS WHEN THE EU'S SUSTAINABLE TRADE POLICIES GO GLOBAL

The EU's recognition of voluntary schemes has raised a number of criticisms. Criticisms related to environmental and social effects of the RED are connected to the above analysis of the character of the interaction and its consequences for biomass sustainability standards and their administrative governance structures. In drawing these relationships, this last section discusses the significance of this particular manifestation of

TBGIs and reflects on the governance work that it accomplishes from the perspective of disempowered stakeholders.

Critics have pointed to the possible negative consequences of a more crowded field of standards. Some have argued that the proliferation of standards 'may become a major barrier to trade in the absence of harmonization of standards or of mutual recognition of conformity assessment reports' (Zezza 2012, p. 47). Others have noted that there is considerable diversity among the multiple greenhouse gas calculation tools recognized by the Commission, and that producers can enhance their emissions performance on paper by as much as 20 to 35 per cent simply by using different calculation tools (Hennecke et al. 2013). Hence, the multiplicity of recognized standards, combined with a lack of harmonization mechanisms, raises concerns about the ability of this governance interaction to achieve the climate change mitigation goals of the RED by incentivizing trade in sustainably sourced biomass.

More disturbing, however, are accounts of how this interaction works to introduce the EU's climate change mitigation goals as priorities within biomass production sites across the Global South, while ignoring and overriding local and national natural resource and socio-economic development interests of producer countries (German and Schoneveld 2012, p. 776). One study remarked that the EU's policies and the recognized schemes often approach natural resource and socio-economic issues from very different perspectives than those of local communities, resulting in 'frictional encounters' between global biofuel value chains and these communities (Franco et al. 2010). For example:

> treating land as 'marginal' can justify its appropriation for agro-industrial biofuels, but may provoke protest from local poor people being dispossessed. Meanwhile, agro-industrial plantations may create 'employment' but then also degrade its conditions and readily undermine other livelihoods in the informal economy. (Franco et al. 2010, p. 691)

A key concern is balancing the pursuit of globally applicable governance frameworks for sustainable biomass with sensitivity to the local heterogeneity of environmental and socio-economic interests. This may also include differentiation among governance mechanisms to make it easier for low-risk smallholders and informal producers to enter sustainable biomass markets while high-risk, agro-industrial producers are still held to stringent standards (Schut and Florin 2015).

The ability of the EU's energy policies to override local and national interests in producing countries is all the more problematic given the accountability structures defining the EU's delegated interactions. As argued above, the Commission's recognition process was unclear and neglected any substantial review of the transparency of schemes (Romppanen 2013, p. 343). The accountability concerns raised here spread even further into the interaction assemblage. Seita Romppanen (ibid., p. 349) has criticized the dual public and private roles that the verifiers of conformity to the schemes' standards play in this assemblage: 'As delegated agents, verifiers are required to apply central demands of good administration and answer to the legal requirements set for the sustainability of biofuels. As business actors, verifiers are to be competitive and respond to the needs of the biofuels market.' Their conflicting interests could lead to a form of capture in which their public function is neglected and their commercial competitiveness is prioritized instead, a familiar concern in private verification scenarios (Lytton and McAllister 2014; Verbruggen and Havinga, Chapter 2).

Furthermore, as demonstrated above, the majority of the schemes developed in response to the RED have opaque decision-making procedures and limited or no opportunities for public participation. This poses problems for local communities affected by biomass production. For example, affected communities in a palm-oil–producing region of Indonesia's Central Kalimantan province, 'despite multiple performance standards and sources of authority, still do not have access to functioning recourse mechanisms and remedies' (Larsen et al. 2012). The lack of transparency and public participation mechanisms, in both the Commission's recognition of schemes and the schemes' own internal governance, has resulted in systemic unaccountability.

A two-decades–long land dispute in Malaysia tied to the global trade pressures of renewable biofuels illustrates the significance of unaccountability in the RED interactions. Since 1996, the indigenous community of Long Teran Kanan has been in a dispute with the palm oil production company Rinwood-Pelita and its successor, IOI-Pelita Plantations (Colchester et al. 2013; Lucas 2013). The local community claims native customary rights to a section of land planted and harvested by IOI. The local courts initially ruled that the community was entitled to these customary rights but that the state could limit them and issue leases affecting them. The appeals court overturned the judgment in 2010, leading to a new wave of protests by the community. Meanwhile, the production of palm oil continued with little interruption.

This example connects with the RED due to IOI's membership in RSPO. Despite the ongoing dispute, IOI became a certified RSPO producer in 2004. This gave the indigenous community an alternative venue to raise concerns about the alleged dispossession, which auditors did not find to violate RSPO's requirement for free, prior and informed consent (FPIC) to be obtained in contested land acquisitions. After

2013, the local community worked with RSPO's Dispute Settlement Facility to assess whether it was in their interests to pursue resolution via the RSPO. In this case, the transparency of the RSPO's certification activities and decision-making procedures, and the presence of a dispute-resolution mechanism provided this community with a new venue to contest their rights in a national context in which trade interests benefit from overlooking such rights and courts have opted against protecting them.

In April 2016, the RPSO suspended IOI's membership for reasons unrelated to this dispute after the consultancy Aidenvironment complained that IOI was expanding plantations in Indonesia using techniques prohibited by the RSPO (RSPO 2016a). In response, IOI filed a lawsuit in Zurich, claiming that the RSPO did not have the right to suspend its membership and that IOI was 'unfairly affected' (Vaughn 2016). The lawsuit was dropped a month later (Mathiesen 2016). In August 2016, RSPO lifted its suspension of IOI's membership after IOI demonstrated initial steps towards compliance (RSPO 2016b). In response, Greenpeace blocked IOI facilities in the port of Rotterdam. IOI maintained its RSPO membership as of the time of writing. Immediately following IOI's suspension in 2016, Unilever announced that it would no longer source palm oil from IOI and maintained this ban on IOI's products well after RSPO lifted its suspension. But in August 2017, Unilever announced that it had seen sufficient improvements to re-establish business ties with IOI (Unilever 2017). Nestlé also stopped sourcing palm oil from IOI upon its RSPO suspension, and at the time of writing had yet to change its policy. In the meanwhile, the Long Teran Kanan dispute was still being mediated in the RSPO Dispute Settlement Facility.

This example demonstrates the potential and limitations of transnational actions to discipline poor corporate behaviour. For example, in the formal complaints submitted to RSPO that led to IOI's suspension, resolution of the Long Teran Kanan dispute was included in the list of actions that Aidenvironment expected IOI to take in order to retain its RSPO certification (Aidenvironment 2015). This reference was included notwithstanding that the complaints that ultimately led to IOI's suspension targeted IOI subsidiaries in Indonesia. In this manner, the RSPO complaint and dispute-resolution procedures allowed affected parties to draw together dispersed transboundary violations of social and environmental standards into a cumulative targeted action. The transparency of audit reports, and thus corporate performance, allowed civil society actors to contest the business activities of IOI's subsidiaries in seven different states and provinces in Indonesia and Malaysia in a single critical strategy of dispute resolution.

At the same time, this example demonstrates how the market-driven and collaborative character of RSPO allows businesses to resume their sustainable images quickly (within one month in this case) if they are willing to initiate a process of dispute resolution. RSPO could have maintained IOI's suspension until its business activities were independently audited and found to be in compliance. Yet this would have frozen IOI palm oil out of the supply chains of RSPO's downstream members (Unilever, Nestlé, etc.) and also out of the EU RED framework as a consequence of the RSPO suspension.

This example illustrates how the RED's influence on the accountability and transparency of biofuel standards can manifest in concrete opportunities for stakeholders to contest possible rights violations arising from biofuel production. Biofuel standards with non-transparent and industry-driven governance bodies that lack public participation mechanisms in standard setting and dispute resolution pose a challenge to these kinds of transnational actions by dispersed affected communities. The four new biofuel standards created in light of EU RED (2BSvs, Abengoa, Neste Oil and Greenergy) all lacked essential components that would make these actions possible, including publicly available audit reports, public complaint procedures, and transparent dispute-resolution mechanisms. In other words, the EU RED led to a lower quality of administrative governance in biofuel standards, making it more difficult to hold large palm oil producers publicly accountable for poor environmental and social performance. This rise in unaccountable governance resulting from RED empowered agri-industry producers through their access to the EU market for sustainable biofuel, at the expense of already marginalized communities whose opportunities to use biofuel standards as a basis for contestation are curtailed by opaque and publicly unaccountable standard-setting organizations (see also Veitch 2007).

11.7 CONCLUSION

The current assemblage of the Parliament, Council, Commission and non-state schemes constitutes a globally influential series of governance interactions. In its transnational delegation to voluntary schemes, the Commission avoided any systematic review of the schemes' administrative governance structures and instead emphasized functionality. By emphasizing the ability of schemes to implement and monitor the RED's sustainability goals, the Commission initiated a proliferation of new biomass standards that had less robust administrative governance structures than their precursors. This is problematic for already marginalized communities lacking venues to raise their grievances tied to global biofuel value chains. In other words, the RED assemblage 'allows energy security priorities of affluent nations to put local livelihoods in peril and benefit already privileged market actors' (Larsen et al. 2012, p. 302).

Approaching the RED through assemblage theory illustrates how transnational interactions manifest in differentiated ways for the diverse actors and interests involved in and affected by them. In this case, it illustrates how interactions can foster unaccountability at the expense of competing trade interests. Suspending judgment on the success or failure of this interaction makes it possible to see the more intricate dynamics between competing and contradictory interests that compose the assemblage. Lastly, the assemblage approach demonstrates how this interaction itself became a constituent element of the broader assemblage of institutions and procedures by which marginalized communities draw attention to perceived injustices related to biofuel production.

NOTES

1. Directive 2009/28/EC of 23 April 2009 on the promotion of the use of energy from renewable sources and amending and subsequently repealing Directives 2001/77/EC and 2003/30/EC [2009] OJ L140/16 (hereafter 'Renewable Energy Directive').
2. Ibid., articles 17–19.
3. Ibid., article 18(4).
4. Directive 2003/30/EC of 8 May 2003 on the promotion of the use of biofuels or other renewable fuels for transport [2003] OJ L123/42. See also Directive 2001/77/EC of 27 September 2001 on the promotion of electricity produced from renewable energy sources in the internal electricity market [2001] OJ L283/33.
5. Renewable Energy Directive, article 3(1).
6. Ibid., preamble, paragraph 9.
7. Ibid., article 17(2–6).
8. Ibid., article 17(7).
9. Ibid., article 18(3).
10. Ibid., article 18(4).
11. Ibid., article 18(5).
12. Case 25/70 *Einfuhr- und Vorratsstelle für Getreide und Futtermittel v. Köster et Berodt & Co* [1970] ECR 1161.
13. Renewable Energy Directive, article 23(2), 25(2); see also article 21.
14. Case 9/56 *Meroni & Co., Industrie Metallurgiche, S.p.A. v. High Authority of the ECSC* [1957–58] ECR 133.
15. Ibid., p. 152.
16. Council Resolution of 7 May 1985 on a new approach to technical harmonization and standards, [1985] OJ C136/1.
17. Council Resolution of 18 June 1992 on the role of European standardization in the European economy [1992] OJ C173/1. See Regulation (EC) 1025/2012 of 25 October 2012 on European Standardisation, [2012] OJ L316/12 (hereafter 'European Standardisation Regulation'), articles 3-6.
18. Case C-171/11 *Fra.bo SpA v. Deutsche Vereinigung des Gas- und Wasserfaches eV (DVGW) — Technisch-Wissenschaftlicher Verein*, Judgment of 12 July 2012; Case C-613/14 *James Elliott Construction Limited v. Irish Asphalt Limited*, Judgment of 27 October 2016.

19. European Standardisation Regulation, article 2(4)(b).
20. Ibid., article 18(5).
21. Directive 2015/1513 of 9 September 2015 amending Directive 98/70/EC relating to the quality of petrol and diesel fuels and amending Directive 2009/28/EC on the promotion of the use of energy from renewable sources [2015] OJ L239/1.
22. Ibid., article 2(6)d.
23. Between 2017 and 2019, the Commission's recognition decisions for Abengoa, Greenergy, Neste HVO and NTA 8080 schemes expired and had not been renewed as of September 2019.

REFERENCES

Abbott, Kenneth W., Philipp Genschel, Duncan Snidal and Bernhard Zangl (eds), (2015), *International Organizations as Orchestrators*, Cambridge, UK: CUP.

Abbott, Kenneth W. and Duncan Snidal (2009), 'Strengthening international regulation through transnational new governance: overcoming the orchestration deficit', *Vanderbilt Journal of Transnational Law*, **42**, 501–78.

Abengoa Bioenergy (2014), *Annual Report of the Application of the RSBA Standard (2013–2014)*, Seville: Abengoa S.A.

Aidenvironment (2015), 'Response to the IOI Group-Aksenta verification of Aidenvironment's RSPO complaint', 25 June, accessed 29 August 2019 at https://www.rspo.org/files/download/f7ecb5d2ad2041e.

Association 2BS (2016), *Government and Management of 2BS Voluntary Scheme, Version 1.9*, Paris: Association 2BS.

Bailis, Robert and Jennifer Baka (2011), 'Constructing sustainable biofuels: governance of the emerging biofuel economy', *Annals of the Association of American Geographers*, **101**, 827–38.

Bergström, Carl Frederik (2005), *Comitology: Delegation of Powers in the European Union and the Committee System*, Oxford, UK: OUP.

Cashore, Benjamin, Graeme Auld, Steven Bernstein and Constance McDermott (2007), 'Can non-state governance "ratchet up" global environmental standards? Lessons from the forest sector', *Review of European Community and International Environmental Law*, **16**, 158–72.

Colchester, Marcus, Thomas Jalong and Wong Meng Chuo (2013), 'Sarawak: IOI-Pelita and the community of Long Teran Kanan', in Marcus Colchester and Sophie Chao (eds), *Conflict or Consent: The Oil Palm Sector at a Crossroads*, Moreton-in-Marsh, UK, Bogor, Indonesia and Jakarta Selatan, Indonesia: Forest Peoples Programme, Perkumpulan SawitWatch and Transformasi untuk Keadilan Indonesia, pp. 28–53.

Cutler, A. Claire (2003), *Private Power and Global Authority: Transnational Merchant Law in the Global Political Economy*, Cambridge, UK: CUP.

Craig, Paul (2008), 'The role of the European Parliament under the Lisbon Treaty', in Stefan Griller and Jacques Ziller (eds), *The Lisbon Treaty: EU Constitutionalism Without a Constitutional Treaty?*, Vienna: Springer, pp. 109–34.

Craig, Paul and Gráinne de Búrca (2008), *EU Law: Texts, Cases, and Materials,* 4th edn, Oxford, UK: OUP.

Curtin, Deirdre (2007), 'Holding (quasi-)autonomous EU administrative actors to public account', *European Law Journal*, **13**, 523–41.

Dehousse, Renaud (2002), 'Misfits: EU law and the transformation of European governance', in Christian Joerges and Renaud Dehousse (eds), *Good Governance in Europe's Market*, Oxford, UK: OUP, pp. 207–29.

Delanda, Manuel (2006a), *A New Philosophy of Society: Assemblage Theory and Complexity*, London: Continuum.

Delanda, Manuel (2006b), 'Deleuzian social ontology and assemblage theory', in Martin Fuglsang and Bent Meier Sorensen (eds), *Deleuze and the Social*, Edinburgh: Edinburgh University Press, pp. 250–66.

Deleuze, Gilles and Félix Guattari (1987), *A Thousand Plateaus,* Minneapolis: University of Minnesota Press.

de Sousa Santos, Boaventura (2002), *Toward a New Legal Common Sense: Law, Globalization, and Emancipation,* 2nd edn, London: Butterworths LexisNexis.

Eberlein, Burkard, Kenneth Abbott, Julia Black, Errol Meidinger and Stepan Wood (2014), 'Transnational business governance interactions: conceptualization and framework for analysis', *Regulation & Governance,* **8**, 1–22.

European Commission (2010), 'Communication from the commission on voluntary schemes and default values in the EU biofuels and bioliquids sustainability scheme', OJ C 160/01.

European Commission (2011), 'First EU sustainability schemes for biofuels get the go-ahead', IP/11/901, 19 July, accessed 29 August 2019 at http://europa.eu/rapid/press-release_IP-11-901_en.htm.

European Commission (2015a), 'Update of Commission website, notifications and transparency measures', 12 March (copy on file with author).

European Commission (2015b), 'Assessment Protocol template', 11 November, accessed 29 August 2019 at https://ec.europa.eu/energy/sites/ener/files/documents/Assessment%20Protocol%20template_111115.pdf.

European Commission (2019a), *Key Players in European Standardisation*, accessed 29 August 2019 at https://ec.europa.eu/growth/single-market/european-standards/key-players_en.

European Commission (2019b), *Voluntary Schemes*, accessed 29 August 2019 at https://ec.europa.eu/energy/en/topics/renewable-energy/biofuels/voluntary-schemes.

Franco, Jennifer, Les Levidow, David Fig, Lucia Goldfarb, Mireille Hönicke and Maria Luisa Mendonça (2010), 'Assumptions in the European Union biofuels policy: frictions with experiences in Germany, Brazil and Mozambique', *Journal of Peasant Studies*, **37**, 661–98.

German, Laura and George Schoneveld (2012), 'A review of social sustainability considerations among EU-approved voluntary schemes for biofuels, with implications for rural livelihoods', *Energy Policy,* **51**, 765–78.

Greenergy (2011), 'Greenergy sustainability programme for Brazilian bioethanol becomes first voluntary scheme to gain approval under the EU Renewable Energy Directive', press release, 19 July, accessed 29 August 2019 at https://www.greenergy.com/press_archives/2011/Greenergy_gets_RED_approval.pdf.

Hennecke, Anna M., Mireille Faist, Jürgen Reinhardt, Victoria Junquera, John Neeft and Horst Fehrenbach (2013), 'Biofuel greenhouse gas calculations under the European Renewable Energy Directive: a comparison of the BioGrace tool vs. the tool of the Roundtable on Sustainable Biofuels', *Applied Energy*, **102**, 55–62.

ISCC (International Sustainability & Carbon Certification) (2011), *ISCC Statutes, Version 1.14*, Cologne: ISCC System GmbH.

ISCC (International Sustainability & Carbon Certification) (2017a), *ISCC Members*, accessed 20 December 2017 at https://www.iscc-system.org/stakeholders/iscc-association/membership-list.

ISCC (International Sustainability & Carbon Certification) (2017b), *Governance*, accessed 20 December 2017 at https://www.iscc-system.org/about/governance-and-transparency.

ISEAL Alliance (2014), *Standard-Setting Code of Good Practice: Setting Social and Environmental Standards, Version 6.0*, London: ISEAL Alliance.
ISO/IEC (International Organization for Standardization/International Electrotechnical Commission) (1994), *ISO/IEC Guide 59: 1994, Code of Good Practice for Standardization*, Geneva: ISO/IEC.
ISO (International Organization for Standardization) (2010), *International Standards and 'Private Standards'*, Geneva: ISO.
Larsen, Rasmus Kløcker, Norman Jiwan, Arie Rompas, Johanes Jenito, Maria Osbeck and Abetnego Tarigan (2012), 'Towards 'hybrid accountability' in EU biofuels policy? Community grievances and competing water claims in the Central Kalimantan oil palm sector', *Geoforum*, **54**, 295–305.
Loconto, Allison and Eve Fouilleux (2014), 'Politics of private regulation: ISEAL and the shaping of transnational sustainability governance', *Regulation & Governance*, **8**, 166–85.
Lucas, Jake (2013), 'Forest people "disillusioned" in battle to protect land', *Thomas Reuters Foundation News,* 26 November, accessed 29 August 2019 at http://news.trust.org//item/20131126101312-463ag/.
Lytton, Timothy D. and Lesley K. McAllister (2014), 'Oversight in private food safety auditing: addressing auditor conflict of interest', *Wisconsin Law Review*, 289–335.
Mathiesen, Karl (2016), 'Malaysian palm oil giant IOI drops lawsuit against green group', *The Guardian*, 7 June, accessed 29 August 2019 at https://www.theguardian.com/sustainable-business/2016/jun/07/palm-oil-ioi-rspo-unilever-nestle-kelloggs-mars-deforestation-indonesia.
Meidinger, Errol (2006), 'The administrative law of global private-public regulation: the case of forestry', *European Journal of International Law*, **17**, 47–87.
Mitchell, Donald (2008), 'A note on rising food prices', The World Bank Development Prospects Group, Policy Research Working Paper No. 4682, July.
Mol, Arthur P.J. (2007), 'Boundless biofuels? Between environmental sustainability and vulnerability', *Sociologia Ruralis*, **47**, 297–315.
Mol, Arthur P.J. (2010), 'Environmental authorities and biofuel controversies', *Environmental Politics*, **19**, 61–79.
NEN (Netherlands Standardization Institute) (2009), *NTA 8080:2009, Netherlands Technical Agreement 8080: Sustainability Criteria for Biomass for Energy Purposes*, Delft, Netherlands: NEN.
NEN (Netherlands Standardization Institute) (2017), *NEN Schemabeheer, Version 4.0*, Delft, Netherlands: NEN.
Overdevest, Christine and Jonathan Zeitlin (2014), 'Assembling an experimentalist regime: transnational governance interactions in the forest sector', *Regulation and Governance*, **8**, 22–48.
Paiement, Phillip (2016), 'ISEAL Alliance and the administrative governance of transnational sustainability standards', *Tilburg Law Review*, **21**, 144–68.
Partzsch, Lena (2009), 'The legitimacy of biofuel certification', *Agriculture and Human Values*, **28**, 413–25.
Pelkmans, Jacques (1987), 'The new approach to technical harmonization and standardization', *Journal of Common Market Studies*, **25**, 249–69.
Perez, Oren (2011), 'Private environmental governance as ensemble regulation: a critical exploration of sustainability indexes and the new ensemble politics', *Theoretical Inquiries in Law*, **12**, 543–79.
Ponte, Stefano (2014), '"Roundtabling" sustainability: lessons from the biofuel industry', *Geoforum*, **54**, 261–71.

Ponte, Stefano and Carsten Daugbjerg (2015), 'Biofuel sustainability and the formation of transnational hybrid governance', *Environmental Politics*, **24**, 96–114.
Ponzano, Paolo (2008), '"Executive" and "delegated" acts: the situation after the Lisbon Treaty', in Stefan Griller and Jacques Ziller (eds), *The Lisbon Treaty: EU Constitutionalism Without a Constitutional Treaty?* Vienna: Springer, pp. 135–41.
Reinecke, J., S. Manning and O. von Hagen (2012), 'The emergence of a standards market: multiplicity of sustainability standards in the global coffee industry', *Organization Studies*, **33**, 791–814.
Romppanen, Seita (2013), 'The role and relevance of private actors in EU biofuel governance', *Review of European Community & International Environmental Law*, **22**, 340–53.
RSPO (Roundtable on Sustainable Palm Oil) (2016a), 'Notice to RSPO members on the suspension of IOI group's certification', 1 April, accessed 29 August 2019 at http://www.rspo.org/news-and-events/announcements/notice-to-rspo-members-on-the-suspension-of-ioi-groups-certification.
RSPO (Roundtable on Sustainable Palm Oil) (2016b), 'RSPO statement on IOI and the Greenpeace actions in Rotterdam', 28 September, accessed 29 August 2019 at https://rspo.org/news-and-events/news/rspo-statement-on-ioi-and-the-greenpeace-actions-in-rotterdam.
RTRS (2013), *RTRS Standard for Responsible Soy Production, Version 2.0*, Zurich: RTRS.
RTRS (Round Table on Responsible Soy) (2017), *RTRS Standard for Responsible Soy Production, Version 3.1*, Zurich: RTRS.
Sassen, Saskia (2006), *Territory, Authority, Rights: From Medieval to Global Assemblages*, Princeton, NJ: Princeton University Press.
Sassen, Saskia (2008), 'Neither global nor national: novel assemblages of territory, authority and rights', *Ethics & Global Politics*, **1**, 61–79.
Schepel, Harm (2005), *The Constitution of Private Governance: Product Standards in the Regulation of Integrating Markets*, Oxford and Portland, OR: Hart.
Schepel, Harm (2013), 'The new approach to the new approach: the juridification of harmonized standards in EU law', *Maastricht Journal of European and Comparative Law*, **12**, 521–33.
Schleifer, Philip (2013), 'Orchestrating sustainability: the case of European Union biofuel governance', *Regulation & Governance*, **7**, 533–46.
Schut, Marc and Madeleine J. Florin (2015), 'The policy and practice of sustainable biofuels: between global frameworks and local heterogeneity. The case of food security in Mozambique', *Biomass and Bioenergy*, **72**, 123–35.
Sullivan, Gavin (2014), 'Transnational legal assemblages and global security law: topologies and temporalities of the list', *Transnational Legal Theory*, **5**, 81–127.
Unilever (2017), 'Unilever responds to the RSPO decision to lift suspension of the IOI group', 30 August, accessed 29 August 2019 at, https://www.unilever.com/news/Press-releases/2016/Unilever-reacts-to-palm-oil-suppliers-suspension-from-RSPO.html.
UN (United Nations) (2007), 'UN independent rights expert calls for five-year freeze on biofuel production', 26 October, accessed 29 August 2019 at https://news.un.org/en/story/2007/10/237362-un-independent-rights-expert-calls-five-year-freeze-biofuel-production.
Valverde, Mariana (2015), *Chronotopes of Law: Jurisdiction, Scale and Governance*, Abingdon, UK: Routledge.
Vaughn, Adam (2016), 'Top palm oil producer sues green group over deforestation allegations', *The Guardian*, 9 May, accessed 29 August 2019 at https://www.

theguardian.com/environment/2016/may/09/top-palm-oil-producer-sues-green-group-over-deforestation-allegations.

Veitch, Scott (2007), *Law and Irresponsibility: On the Legitimation of Human Suffering*, Abingdon: Routledge Cavendish.

Verbruggen, Paul and Tetty Havinga (eds) (2017), *Hybridization of Food Governance: Trends, Types and Results*, Cheltenham, UK and Northampton, MA: Edward Elgar.

Wood, Stepan (2016), 'Exploring the relationship between administrative norms and competence in transnational governance: ISO, ISEAL and sustainability standards', *Tilburg Law Review*, **21**, 193–229.

Wood, Stepan, Kenneth W. Abbott, Julia Black, Burkard Eberlein and Errol Meidinger (2015), 'The interactive dynamics of transnational business governance: a challenge for transnational legal theory', *Transnational Legal Theory*, **6**, 333–69.

Zezza, Annalisa (2012), 'Creating a sustainable market for biofuels: some governance issues', *EuroChoices*, **11**, 41–8.

Zumbansen, Peer (2011), 'Neither "public" nor "private", "national" nor "international": transnational corporate governance from a legal pluralist perspective', *Journal of Law and Society*, **38**, 50–75.

Zumbansen, Peer (2012), 'Defining the space for transnational law: legal theory, global governance and legal pluralism', *Transnational Law and Contemporary Problems*, **21**, 305–35.

12. Capturing climate: Tracking nascent transnational business governance interactions around the Oil and Gas Climate Initiative

Matthew Bach

Our shared ambition is for a 2°C future. It is a challenge for the whole of society. We are committed to playing our part.

OGCI CEO Declaration (OGCI 2015c)

12.1 INTRODUCTION: A SHIFTING LANDSCAPE

The oil and gas sector has traditionally been reluctant to involve itself in global efforts to address climate change, treating climate change as a risk and hesitating to accept its share of responsibility. Yet over the past several years, this strategy has slowly given way to more active involvement as firms recognize the value of assuming a constructive role in climate governance. Senior managers describe the industry as gradually adopting a more strategic outlook in which climate change is seen as an opportunity – whether in terms of portfolio optimization, neutral or negative emissions technologies, or carbon pricing instruments.[1] This shift can be traced to macro-level changes both within and outside the climate regime (Bach 2017).

At the international level, states are taking on growing levels of commitment, for instance by agreeing to a two-degree Celsius (2°C) pathway in Paris. This has effectively created a normative boundary beyond which actors could expose themselves to sanctions. The importance of states has, however, declined as other actors have taken up calls for climate action. Nor have firms been absent from this bottom-up movement. Some have committed to ambitious emissions reduction strategies, while others have banded together in support of climate change mitigation and adaptation (Chan et al. 2015; GGCA 2015; UNEP 2015; Pattberg and Widerberg 2016). Another development has been increasing support for a low-carbon future, in which energy is primarily generated from renewable sources such as wind, solar and hydro. The mainstreaming of renewable energy technologies as part of what has been called an energy transition makes a low-carbon future a distinct possibility (Cherp et al. 2011; Verbong and Loorbach 2012; DDPP 2015).

The scale of this transition has already prompted an overhaul of corporate strategies. In 2016, German energy firm E.ON finished splitting off its fossil assets (Timperley 2016), French energy utility Engie announced that it would aim to derive 90 per cent of its earnings from low-carbon sources within three years (Froley 2016), and Danish oil and gas firm DONG Energy announced that it would follow suit (Skydsgaard et al. 2016). Discursive changes are also afoot that place climate change at the centre of decision-making. Concepts such as the carbon bubble and stranded assets have pushed large institutional investors to divest their fossil energy holdings (Mathieu 2015). Symbolically, the 2016 decision by the Rockefeller Foundation to divest from fossil fuels made waves (RFF 2016).

In this context, the potential costs of inaction by the oil and gas industry increasingly speak against avoidance as a strategy. There is a very real possibility that oil and gas need no longer play a central role in energy systems. Industry is having to reverse its position in order to avoid being locked out of a low-carbon future. The Oil and Gas Climate Initiative (OGCI) exemplifies the intersection of these developments and the response of industry actors to them. It gathers ten of the largest producers, accounting for nearly one fifth of global oil and gas production. The majority of these firms are 'carbon majors', the 90 entities responsible for 63 per cent of historical carbon dioxide and methane emissions (Heede 2014). OGCI members have committed to a 2C pathway, endorsed current climate policy and science, and begun to reimagine themselves within a new energy landscape. The initiative was founded in 2014, and governance interactions are emerging around it that will reveal much about the role that it and its members might play in global climate governance and, by extension, the future of the sector.

Any study of nascent governance efforts by the oil and gas industry in the context of climate change necessarily inscribes itself within the broader landscape of non-state governance. As states increasingly govern in conjunction with other actors, governance configurations have taken more varied, experimental, bottom-up and polycentric forms (Hoffmann 2011; Pattberg 2016). This growth in institutional and organizational diversity has opened a Pandora's box of interactions, connecting, shaping and fuelling global governance.

Much has been written about transnational business governance (TBG) schemes in sectors such as forestry and fisheries that have seen a high degree of uptake of forms of governance crossing actor categories and state borders (Bartley 2007; Auld et al. 2008; Gulbrandsen 2010; Auld 2014). More recently, there has been a rise in TBG initiatives in extractive industries (Bach 2016). Though proponents of TBG initially had doubts about the value of such efforts in relation to non-renewable resources, even meta-standard-setters such as the ISEAL Alliance have come to adopt a 'content-neutral' approach (ISEAL Alliance 2013). The vast majority of TBG initiatives in this area target mining and metals, though some work with coal (for example, Better Coal) or oil and gas (for example, Equitable Origin).

The OGCI fits well with Burkard Eberlein and others' (2014) definition of TBG: it features the exercise of substantial authority by non-state actors in the performance of regulatory governance; it seeks to address the climate impacts of the oil and gas sector; and it exists within a transnational space, beholden to no single nation state. Yet its nascent institutions and lack of track record mean that research into it must rely in large part on statements made by its members and other stakeholders. This reliance raises the ubiquitous question of whether such schemes in the end amount to anything more than greenwashing. Taken from another perspective, the study of an early-stage TBG initiative poses a challenge to the transnational business governance interactions (TBGI) analytical framework (Eberlein et al. 2014; Wood et al. 2015), as the interactions in question are limited largely to agenda-setting.

To address these limitations, I link the TBGI framework to mid-level theoretical propositions from John Braithwaite and Peter Drahos (2000) concerning global business regulation. Their mid-range theory seeks to understand how principles, norms, standards and rules emerge, diffuse and interact in a globalized world. By examining a broad range of economic sectors, they identify mechanisms and pathways through which actors generate changes in the regulation of business on a global scale. This theory provides some indications of how the OGCI's agenda-setting efforts might achieve wider influence and, perhaps, alter the ways in which the oil and gas sector engages with climate change and its governance.

Little research has been done on the involvement of the oil and gas industry in climate governance and none has examined the OGCI. This is therefore a preliminary, exploratory study. I begin with an overview of TBG in the oil and gas sector, before examining the OGCI and its interactions (Part 2). I then turn to the theory of global business regulation put forward by Braithwaite and Drahos (2000) to tease out broader implications of this study (Part 3). In the conclusion (Part 4), I turn my attention to normative considerations and question the motivations underlying the initiative.

12.2 A STUDY IN NASCENT INTERACTIONS

12.2.1 TBG in the Oil and Gas Sector

The oil and gas sector has been particularly challenging to regulate since extraction is conducted under many circumstances and by only a few powerful actors. These are public (national oil companies or NOCs) and private (multinational oil companies or MOCs). At times they compete, at others they join forces. The sector as a whole has tended to resist oversight, instead advocating self-regulation. For the most part, oil and gas companies have not subscribed to TBG schemes.

Some initiatives, such as Equitable Origin, have modelled themselves after TBG schemes in other sectors by embracing a multi-stakeholder ethos in targeting the social and environmental costs of extraction. However, these efforts have mostly failed to enrol major oil and gas actors. The Extractive Industries Transparency Initiative (EITI), which seeks to foster a higher degree of transparency in dealings between extractive companies and governments, is a striking exception in this regard. Other initiatives, including the World Bank's Global Gas Flaring Reduction (GGFR) partnership, have taken a more technical approach and enjoyed a higher degree of industry uptake. This pattern of weak involvement from the oil and gas sector extends to wider non-state climate governance efforts. The UN's NAZCA Portal on Global Climate Action gathers data on climate commitments from non-state actors, including 77 TBG or 'cooperative' initiatives (UN 2019). By my calculation, oil and gas firms accounted for barely four per cent of the 1270 commitments made by companies at the time of writing.

Though the oil and gas industry lags behind its peers in terms of TBG and climate governance, it has recently multiplied the number of initiatives to which it subscribes. These include: the Zero Routing Flaring by 2030 initiative; the Oil & Gas Methane Partnership; the Low Carbon Technology Partnership initiative (LCTPi); the Energy Transitions Commission (ETC); and the OGCI. All have been established since 2014, corroborating interviewees' claims that a real shift is occurring in the oil and gas sector.[2]

I focus exclusively on the OGCI in this chapter for two reasons: first, it is the only initiative both by and for industry; and second, its members account for nearly a quarter of the world's oil and gas production and almost 12 per cent of all historical greenhouse gas (GHG) emissions. As such, the OGCI should provide a clear picture of early attempts by the industry to engage in climate governance.

12.2.2 A Brief History of the OGCI

In January 2014, the chief executives of some of the world's largest oil and gas firms gathered on the sidelines of the World Economic Forum in Davos, Switzerland. They were increasingly concerned about the risks posed by climate change and wanted to position themselves as 'recognized and ambitious provider[s] of practical solutions for climate change mitigation' (OGCI 2015a). In short, they wanted to be on the right side of a carbon-constrained future. Led by the Chairman of Saudi Aramco and the CEOs of Total and Eni, the conversation grew into a set of commitments from major national and multinational oil companies,[3] most notably to support a two-degree target. In September 2014, the OGCI was officially announced at the UN Climate Summit in New York as an example of how a 'diverse group of national and international oil companies, which compose a significant share of global oil and gas production, [are] committed to be "part of the climate solution"' (UN 2014).

The veil was first lifted on the inner workings of the OGCI at a technical workshop in Paris in May 2015. Led by Gerard Moutet, chair of the OGCI executive committee and vice-president of Total for climate and energy, the event gathered views from member companies and invited stakeholders in support of the initiative's development. It also solicited feedback on a draft report detailing its agenda. Further, three work streams were initiated at this meeting: long-term solutions; the role of natural gas; and instruments and tools for carbon reduction. The workshop sought to link the OGCI to more established actors in climate governance, notably by securing attendance by two of the UN's highest climate change officials: the Executive Secretary of the UN Framework Convention on Climate Change (UNFCCC) and the Assistant UN Secretary General on Climate Change. The head of the OECD's International Energy Agency (IEA) also attended.[4] Other policymakers and civil society representatives were reportedly present, though I was unable to uncover any details since the meeting was held under the Chatham House Rule.[5]

The OGCI emerged into the public eye in October 2015, when the CEOs of its member companies gathered in Paris ahead of the UNFCCC's 21st Conference of the Parties (COP) to present the initiative and a first report setting out its ambitions (OGCI 2015b). This was an occasion for strong and optimistic statements on behalf of some of the world's largest GHG emitters, as shown by some quotes taken from the day's press conference (Politiques énergétiques 2015; my transcription):

> What is the most important today [. . .] is that you have here in Paris eight CEOs recognizing that trying to stay below 2°C is the right track [. . .]. We are committing our companies by making these statements. I think it is quite an important step. (Patrick Pouyanné, CEO, Total)

> Well, we've done a lot in just a year and a half getting ten big companies together, I think we'll get more, but I think the first thing for us is we all recognize the problem, we all have a sense of commitment, a sense of urgency about it. (Bob Dudley, CEO, BP)

The OGCI is intended as a 'bottom-up, voluntary, industry-driven initiative' that will serve as a 'platform to address climate change concerns, to share industry best practices, advance technological solutions, and to catalyze meaningful action and coordination on climate change' (OGCI 2014). Member companies must make five commitments: to '[s]hare best practices to enhance overall standards and environmental performance'; 'develop common methodologies to measure climate-related impacts and contributions to solutions'; 'design a reporting process that enables the voluntary pooling of efforts and the communication of progress as a group to external stakeholders'; 'facilitate and deepen engagement in international multi-stakeholder specific solutions and initiatives as well as the design of shared roadmaps'; and 'engage with other industries to identify and build climate-related synergies' (OGCI 2015d). It is still too early to judge whether these commitments are being implemented. For the moment, there is evidence of work on the first three, and the last two remain somewhat more on the sidelines.

Much of the work done by the OGCI in 2016 focused on internal coordination between the member companies. The major announcement of the year came ahead of the UNFCCC COP in Marrakech, in the form of a commitment by OGCI members to invest USD 1 billion in low-emissions technologies. The majority of this fund will be used to accelerate the deployment of carbon capture, use and storage (CCUS) in gas-fired power plants, while also tackling the issue of methane leakage, which contributes significantly to climate change (Solsvik and Fouche 2016). A spokesperson for the group noted that the initiative would consider increasing its investment upon review (Sampathkumar 2016).

Responses from outside the sector were muted. One specialist climate and energy website highlighted a lack of outreach.[6] Neutral or positive stories dominated news coverage of the OGCI, possibly due to access to primary material (Blas 2015; Scott 2015; Stothard and Clark 2015);

others mostly used OGCI press releases (Willsher 2015; King 2016). In general, business-friendly groups lauded the initiative and environmentalists depicted it as pure talk. On Twitter, the 'We Mean Business' industry coalition for a low-carbon transition asked in a non-committal way if the OGCI goes far enough, while Greenpeace tweeted that 'OGCI = Oil Generates Climate Instability', and digital advocacy consultant Alice Stollmeyer dismissed it as 'empty words' with the warning: 'Arsonists don't make good firefighters.'

More recently, the OGCI began to collaborate with additional stakeholders, including the Environmental Defense Fund (EDF), a leading US-based environmental NGO, and the Massachusetts Institute of Technology's Joint Program on the Science and Policy of Global Change. The former supported the OGCI's efforts to identify gaps in methane monitoring. The latter was enlisted to 'bring academic rigor to the discussion of how to help reduce greenhouse gas emissions in alignment with the 2°C goal' (Dwortzan 2016).

In spite of scepticism surrounding its launch, the OGCI moved rapidly over little more than three years to establish itself as an alternative model for oil and gas involvement in climate governance. Drawing on this brief history of the initiative, I now turn to the TBGI framework, which I will use to map the governance interactions emerging around the OGCI.

12.2.3 Applying the TBGI Framework

The TBGI analytical framework proposes a six-by-six matrix of the components of regulatory governance and the dimensions of interaction (Eberlein et al. 2014). Given that the OGCI is a nascent initiative that has undertaken little beyond goal and agenda-setting, I focus exclusively on the first component of regulatory governance, agenda-setting. While this might be considered a thin application of the TBGI framework, it allows for a greater unpacking of this portion of the matrix. As for the dimensions of the interactions, I limit myself to the first four questions posed by Eberlein et al. (2014: 7): '(i) who or what is interacting; (ii) what drives and shapes the interactions; (iii) what are the mechanisms and pathways of interaction; [and] (iv) what is the character of the interactions', since it remains too early to draw longitudinal conclusions. Table 12.1 provides an overview of the interactions that will be described below.

I do not approach each element of the matrix separately, however, as the drivers and shapers of interaction have already been briefly discussed in the previous sections, and I integrate the remaining three

Table 12.1 The TBGI matrix applied to the OGCI

Component of regulatory governance	Goal / Agenda-setting
Who/what interacts?	Micro: firms, CEOs, managers, shareholders (for MOCs), states (for NOCs) Micro-meso: oil and gas industry trade organizations (IPIECA, American Petroleum Institute (API), Fuels Europe); World Economic Forum Meso: states (directly through NOCs; indirectly through MOCs); international organizations (World Bank, UN, OECD/IEA) Meso: other TBG initiatives (the World Bank's GGFR/Zero Routine Flaring by 2030 initiative; Sustainable Energy for All; the UN Global Compact's Caring for Climate initiative; the Climate & Clean Air Coalition's Oil & Gas Methane Partnership (CCAC OGMP); the Global Methane Initiative; the Carbon Sequestration Leadership Forum; and the World Business Council for Sustainable Development's Low Carbon Technology Partnerships Initiative) Meso: civil society (World Resources Institute; The Shift Project)
Drivers and shapers	UNFCCC process; growth of renewables; discourses (carbon bubble, stranded assets); climate action social movements; scientific consensus from IPCC
Mechanisms	Modelling
Interaction character	Cooperation inside OGCI and with other TBGs; competition with IPIECA; hybrid of cooperation and competition with non-member firms

elements into a discussion of interactive mechanisms. Mechanisms serve as instruments through which actors can enact the regulatory principles they support (see Part 3). Modelling, one of the mechanisms identified by Braithwaite and Drahos (2000), is particularly relevant here, although I take some liberties in its interpretation. Other mechanisms are also at play, such as reciprocal adjustment, where regulatory actors modify practices in response to one another's changes, but these remain beyond the scope of this chapter.

12.2.3.1 Modelling

Modelling is a process of observational learning in which actors display, symbolically interpret and emulate regulatory models (ibid., pp. 580–81). It can be an important mechanism of governance interaction because busy decision-makers who have limited time and resources to develop their own regulatory solutions can be led by regulatory entrepreneurs to adopt pre-packaged models from elsewhere (ibid., pp. 30, 589). The OGCI used this mechanism in three ways: modelling from others; modelling for others; and hybrid modelling.

Braithwaite and Drahos understand modelling *from others* as emulation of regulatory models. I argue here for a broader understanding of this mechanism, as we are dealing with an early-stage initiative rather than a mature instance of TBG. Thus, the OGCI drew on the work of other initiatives, aligning itself with their goals. In this sense, the OGCI adopted 'models from the centre for reasons of legitimacy, in order to harness the identitive power of being perceived as modern, civilized and progressive' (ibid., p. 585). While Braithwaite and Drahos imply a geographical distinction, I view centre and periphery in terms of distance from the climate regime, in which the oil and gas sector has been a peripheral actor. The OGCI was remarkably candid in detailing the TBG initiatives that it sought to interact with, learn from and model itself after (OGCI 2015c) (see Figure 12.1 and Table 2.2).

Table 12.2 'Modelling from': examples of initiatives from which the OGCI drew inspiration

Initiative	Modelling
The IPIECA is the global oil and gas trade association for social and environmental issues and the main link between the industry and the UN system.	The OGCI drew on IPIECA's methodology for GHG reporting.
The GGFR partnership is led by the World Bank and brings together states, firms, international organizations and the EU to agree concrete measures to limit flaring. The Zero Routine Flaring by 2030 initiative was launched in 2015 to broaden stakeholder engagement.	The OGCI collaborated with the GGFR, CCAC and OGMP to adopt their approaches to methane management and develop joint standards.
The Oil & Gas Methane Partnership (OGMP) of the UN's Climate & Clean Air Coalition (CCAC) seeks to enrol industry in efforts to reduce methane emissions throughout the oil and gas value chain. While the CCAC is a multi-stakeholder forum including states, international organizations and NGOs, the OGMP focuses exclusively on firms.	

Several motivations underpinned the OGCI's selection of initiatives to emulate. First, it tried to 'build on, rather than duplicate, the work of others' (Moutet 2015). In practice, the OGCI borrowed materials from the GGFR partnership on flaring, from the Climate & Clean Air Coalition's Oil & Gas Methane Partnership (CCAC OGMP) on methane, and the International Petroleum Industry Environmental Conservation Association (IPIECA, the industry's leading voice on environmental and social issues) on GHG measurement methodologies.[7] A second apparent motivation was a desire to tap into and replicate the broader networks and legitimacy of existing initiatives. Third, the OGCI wished to do business with actors open to a future for oil and gas; the targeted initiatives have all taken neutral or positive stances towards the industry.

Modelling *for others* implies taking on a more innovative role within the oil and gas sector by spearheading a progressive agenda and experimenting

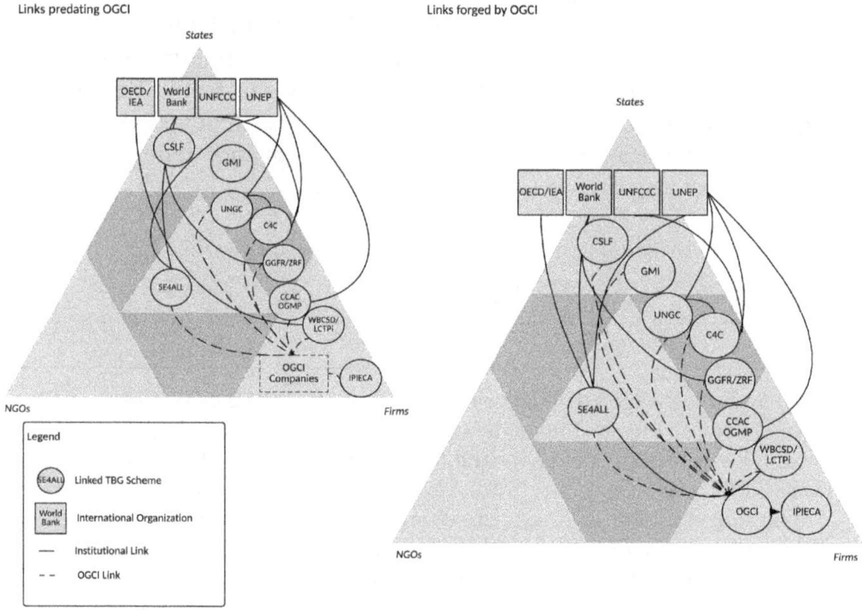

Note: The left-hand triangle represents links pre-dating the formation of the OGCI, whereas the right-hand one displays those forged by the OGCI. The dotted lines in the former represent pre-existing links between OGCI members and specific TBG schemes; those in the latter represent links established directly between the OGCI and these TBG schemes. Whereas solid lines refer to formal links between international organizations and TBG schemes (for example, membership or ownership), dotted ones include broader relationships (for example, cooperation or adoption of similar norms).

Source: Governance triangle adapted from Abbott 2012.

Figure 12.1 Linkages between the OGCI and other TBG schemes

with models for a low-carbon industry. By altering the frame of reference from the broader climate regime to the oil and gas sector, the OGCI sought to position itself as a progressive element, as a model for others. In particular, it pursued this through its interactions with trade organizations, which themselves could be characterized as TBG initiatives.

Although numerous trade organizations exist in the oil and gas sector, the OGCI firms are especially linked to three of the most prominent ones. As shown in Figure 12.2, nearly all companies involved in the OGCI have long-standing links with IPIECA, the American Petroleum Institute (API) and Fuels Europe.[8] These are key industry forums – each targeting specific polities, gathering diverse memberships, and pursuing different issues. The lines drawn between associations and firms in Figure 12.2 indicate membership ties, whereas the arrowed lines between trade associations indicate unilateral membership.

IPIECA has until now acted as the main link between industry and the UN system, having been founded in 1974, two years after the UN Environment Programme (UNEP). On climate, it works in four areas: understanding the latest policy and science; acting as a forum for industry at the UN; developing good practices; and facilitating industry-internal communications and strategy.[9] API represents the interests of the oil and gas industry in the US. It also acts as a standard setter, publishing technical standards and guidance for its members. This role has helped

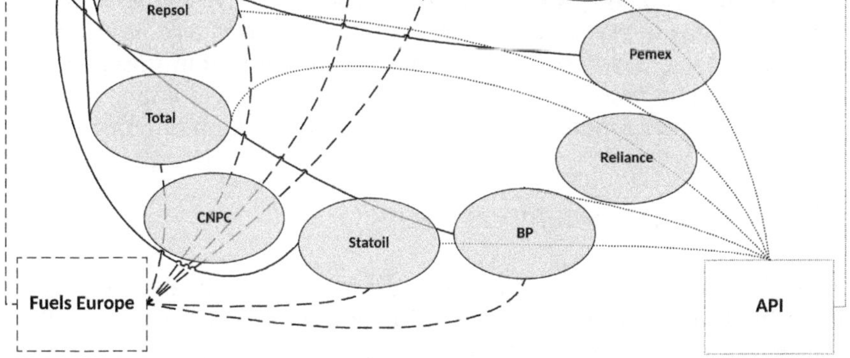

Figure 12.2 OGCI firms–trade association links

it achieve influence beyond its members, in some cases setting *de facto* industry-wide standards. In relation to climate change, it has mostly established itself as a sceptic. Fuels Europe is the trade association of producers and refiners in the EU. It seeks to influence EU policy-making in their favour. It has adopted a more proactive position on climate change, recognizing the problem and the need for solutions.

During the press conference of the October 2015 OGCI event, the CEO of Total stated in response to a question concerning lobbying and his firms' membership of Fuels Europe and API that 'it is better for climate change that we can advocate inside [these associations], being around the table' (Politiques énergétiques 2015, my transcription). And speaking purely on behalf of Total: 'Today I'm committed and I'm committing the full company [to the goals of the OGCI] – all lobbyists from Total in all organizations have the same position' (ibid.). It therefore seems that the OGCI, or at the very least its member Total, intends to use its membership in oil and gas trade associations to lobby for the initiative's goals.

In spite of the OGCI's apparent desire to foster climate action within the oil and gas sector, as evidenced by the above statements, the situation is somewhat more nuanced. This leads me to introduce a third type of modelling, which was not included in the original theory of Braithwaite and Drahos, in spite of their claim that global business regulation involves 'many kinds of actors which regulate while being regulated themselves' (Braithwaite and Drahos 2000, p. 10). Hybrid modelling captures the idea that actors can simultaneously fashion themselves after others and present themselves as a model for others to follow.

The OGCI draws on the work of IPIECA regarding climate reporting and advocates the use of its guidelines, while also seeking to influence this organization's positions towards climate change.[10] Historically, IPIECA has been the sector's primary mandate holder for climate issues, linking member firms and the UNFCCC process. In practice, however, IPIECA has been limited in its ability to play a proactive part in climate governance, as its diverse membership and consensus decision-making prevent it from engaging with more contentious issues.[11] This has given rise to a dual relationship, in which IPIECA is at once a model for the OGCI and a target for its ambitions.

12.3 THEORIZING FUTURES

Though the flexibility of the TBGI framework makes it suitable for capturing a broad range of phenomena and interactions, it is less successful in sharpening analytical efforts. When it comes to the OGCI, only the agenda-setting portion of the matrix is engaged. Agenda-setting is an amorphous element compared to other components of regulatory governance such as sanctioning or monitoring, which imply relatively well-delineated sets of activities. Agenda-setting might be evidenced by a CEO's statement, a report, a meeting between key stakeholders or even the launch of a new governance initiative. The diversity of actions that can be entered under this category is a double-edged sword: integrating broad-ranging material at an early stage strengthens the analysis, yet also dilutes its clarity and focus.

Such pitfalls might be avoided by asking who is seeking to influence whose or which agenda? OGCI member firms sought to influence the agenda of the UN-led climate process and those of national governments by inviting key representatives to events. They sought to influence their peers' agendas through their pre-existing ties to industry associations, and their own agendas by seeking to recast themselves as pro-climate actors. At the same time, there have been some indications that other actors, including governments and civil society organizations, are keen to influence the agendas of the OGCI and its member companies. Agenda-setting may very well be characterized as a two-way street.

New initiatives may not provide the wealth of empirical details found in more mature cases, but they have the advantage of providing an early glimpse into governance innovations that might come to define how a problem is addressed. Analysis of the OGCI's interactions reveals how it has positioned itself within the climate change regime, how it has formed a vision of the oil and gas sector in a low-carbon world, and how it is attempting to influence climate policy in ways compatible with this vision.

The TBGI framework is somewhat more limited in understanding the significance of these nascent interactions, especially since we are not able to track their evolution and outcomes over time. Turning to theory therefore offers greater interpretative possibilities, as it allows us to go beyond inductive methods and tease out how emerging phenomena might develop based on existing knowledge of similar cases and conditions (Wood et al. 2015). This is particularly important given that path dependencies accrue with time and gradually constrain the types and range of actions open to an initiative.

Braithwaite and Drahos's (2000) mid-range theory of global business regulation is helpful in situating the OGCI within contests of regulatory principles, webs of influence and micro-macro sequences and, in so doing, making visible some wider implications. There are clear commonalities between this theory and the TBGI framework. Not only do they share similar concepts (for example, mechanisms) and a similar understanding of regulatory governance, they also examine how transnational actors initiate and effect changes in the norms and rules that govern our lives, as well as the production and consumption on which they depend.

I consider two specific aspects of the theory in this section. The first is the role of principles in non-state governance and how actors deploy them in attempts to enact regulatory change. The second concerns potential pathways for actors to influence global business governance, including how dialogic webs can accelerate norm diffusion and spur voluntary compliance, and how micro-macro sequences can act as pathways for far-reaching regulatory change.

12.3.1 Contesting Principles

For Braithwaite and Drahos, principles and rules form a two-tiered structure with rules at the lower level and principles above. Principles are 'abstract prescriptions that guide conduct' (ibid., p. 9) and that 'evolve from the values and practices of a given community of actors' (ibid., p. 18) who employ them to incorporate changes into regulatory and social systems. Principles 'set the direction for regulatory change' (ibid., p. 522) and are the elements through which regulatory contests operate.

Of the many principles identified by Braithwaite and Drahos, the pro-innovation principles of world's best practice and continuous improvement appear most relevant here. The former concerns economic activity that operates based on rules that exceed requirements from current practice and regulation. The latter relates to efforts to post better (environmental) performance year on year, regardless of whether minimum standards have been exceeded.

The OGCI draws strongly on the world's best practice, in seeking to assume industry leadership and establish new technologies and practices for climate-compatible oil and gas production. Following the announcement of the $1 billion fund for low-carbon technologies, the OGCI stated that their ambition was to help 'develop and demonstrate innovative technologies' (OGCI 2017). This marked an apparent shift away from the respective competing principles of deregulation and rule compliance, which industry has traditionally pursued and in some cases continues to pursue. A shadow of doubt nevertheless lingers, as a rhetoric based on principles might in fact cloak opposing practices (Braithwaite and Drahos 2000, p. 517), amounting to what is more commonly known as greenwashing (Wood 2003).

It is nonetheless significant that the OGCI firms were putting their weight behind progressive principles. Though they are by no means strangers to the language of innovation, they had generally called for the preservation of the status quo in relation to climate change and its governance – arguing for industry self-regulation and against greenhouse gas emissions limits and carbon pricing. Their embrace of pro-innovation principles also carries with it broader implications, as such principles are not only markers of regulatory change, but can create upward or downward dynamics across regulatory systems. In particular, what is known as a ratchet can emerge from such situations. Ratchets are dynamics that can either increase or decrease standards across the board. For this to happen, Braithwaite and Drahos theorize that three conditions need to be fulfilled: (i) the entrenchment of a minimum standard; (ii) the use of principles encouraging innovation; and (iii) the presence of a feedback loop between (i) and (ii) so that with each new innovation the minimum standard goes up or down (Braithwaite and Drahos 2000, p. 519).

So far, it would appear that the OGCI has laid the groundwork for a ratchet by setting a minimum standard – staying below a two-degree increase – and adopting proactive principles. Should a feedback loop arise between its minimum standards and the outcomes of its innovation, a ratchet could be set in motion. This could alter the direction taken by industry and, more generally, responses to climate change. Allowing for some speculation, one could imagine that through its interactions with trade associations and other firms, the OGCI could effectively push the diffusion of its commitments across the industry and that, through its interactions with states and international organizations, it could then support their adoption as a new, higher minimum standard.

Examining the principles that actors draw on and contest provides us with insights into the dynamics underpinning the governance interactions identified in the previous section. In this sense, attention to conflicting principles can enrich the TBGI framework by bringing into focus the driving forces behind interactions and thereby enhance our understanding of why they take on specific characteristics.

12.3.2 Pathways of Influence

The value of Braithwaite and Drahos's theory of global business regulation in relation to the OGCI lies largely in its ability to consider the effects of TBGI on macro-level regulatory change, which unfolds in two ways: by developing dialogic webs, through which agendas can be moved forward; and by initiating sequences.

12.3.2.1 Weaving webs of dialogue

Building on Bruno Latour's (1986) concept of enrolment, Braithwaite and Drahos (2000, p. 556) argue that the globalization of business regulation takes place through webs of influence. Webs may be of dialogue, coercion or reward. Dialogic webs, they argue, are particularly effective in fostering norm diffusion and voluntary compliance by: (i) defining problems; (ii) fostering issue linkages and interdependencies; (iii) leading to normative commitments; (iv) institutionalizing compliance; and (v) institutionalizing praise and shame. Moreover, the mechanisms discussed in Part 2.3 form an integral part of these webs; dialogue enables actors to (re-)define their interests and thereby creates opportunities for mechanisms to be set in motion (ibid., p. 553). This approach seems helpful in two ways. First, as the OGCI has rapidly tied itself into webs of dialogue with a multitude of powerful actors, there seems to be a very real possibility that it could influence the direction of climate policies by enrolling others in its vision of a low-carbon future. This can be seen in its involvement of leading figures from international organizations (see Figure 12.3). Second, webs

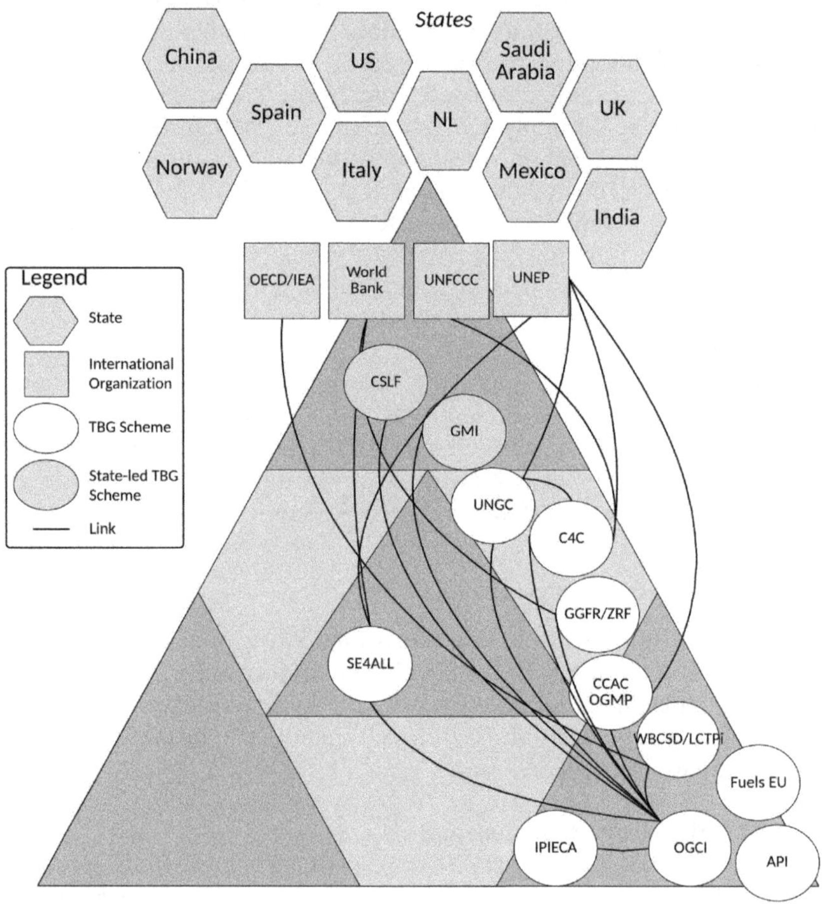

Note: This figure shows the range of actors enrolled within the OGCI's web of dialogue. The states listed are either the OGCI members' owners or the seat of their headquarters. The links between the TBG schemes listed within the triangle are discussed in relation to Figure 12.1.

Figure 12.3 The web of dialogue around the OGCI

of dialogue are more effective in delivering compliance than webs of reward or coercion, and are available to all actors. Though the absence of the latter could be taken as a weakness of the OGCI, it may well be that networks are sufficient for members to make good on their commitments.

12.3.2.2 Initiating sequences

Braithwaite and Drahos also lay out potential pathways through which the OGCI would be able to impact global regulation. Though largely speculative at this stage, it is helpful to think of the OGCI and its governance interactions as part of wider-reaching processes, including proactive and reactive chains and forum shifting. Proactive and reactive sequences illustrate how actors tend to act or react in relation to major events such as disasters (Braithwaite and Drahos 2000, p. 562). The oil and gas industry has tended to take a more reactive approach to regulatory issues, adopting higher operating standards in response to disasters and the ensuing mass public criticism. Events such as the Deepwater Horizon oil spill or the Brent Spar (Grabosky 2013) are textbook examples in this regard. The OGCI reveals what might be a more proactive approach, in which regulatory change is not reactive or disaster-driven. Though speculative, this hypothesis is supported by the efforts of the OGCI to enrol key actors from the climate regime in its vision of a role for the oil and gas sector in a warming world, as well as by a push for higher standards in methane management or carbon pricing, which would effectively contribute to spreading the costs while giving them a first mover advantage. This could also be seen as a cooperative effort aimed at stemming the long-term damage, whether financial or reputational, that generally results from reactive sequences.

Forum shifting could also be at work here. It takes place when actors consider that they cannot achieve their goals within a given setting. Such strategies are restricted primarily to the powerful, whose withdrawal of support can generate significant costs – financial or symbolic – for the sidelined actors and institutions. The emergence of the OGCI could be seen as an instance of forum shifting, in which its members are dissatisfied with climate governance in other organizations, but are unable to sway them in their favour. In this instance, the move is primarily away from IPIECA, which has traditionally held the industry's mandate for climate change. A senior manager from a major international oil and gas firm indicated that IPIECA carries too much 'baggage' in terms of its membership to allow it to play a progressive role in this area.[12] Considering the OGCI as an element of a forum-shifting sequence could therefore help to better understand the reasons for its emergence, as well as its relationship to other initiatives and, ultimately, its potential significance.

12.3.3 Theorizing Nascent TBGIs

At the time of writing this chapter, the OGCI was very much in a nascent state, having restricted its activities to agenda-setting. Though this fact provides for a somewhat limited use of the TBGI framework, there are plenty of signs that the OGCI and its member firms have made a concerted effort to promote their vision of a climate-compatible oil and gas sector and link themselves to already established and legitimate actors across the climate regime.

Interesting as this is as a standalone finding, I have used Braithwaite and Drahos's theory of global business regulation to point to potential pathways by which the OGCI and the governance interactions surrounding it could take on greater significance and lead to larger-scale regulatory change. Three elements of the theory have been particularly helpful in this regard, the first being that the OGCI is deploying pro-innovation principles, which have the potential to set in motion regulatory ratchets – feedback loops that can raise or lower standards across the board. Then, it became apparent that the OGCI was weaving what Braithwaite and Drahos term dialogic webs, as a means of enrolling diverse actors from across the climate regime. The last element of immediate relevance is a set of micro-macro sequences, through which the actions of individual actors can be placed within a broader context of regulatory change.

Bringing these theory-driven insights back to the TBGI framework offers a new vantage point from which to reflect on its value for the analysis of nascent governance interactions. An initial observation is that systematically mapping the interactions surrounding the OGCI via the framework – not only in terms of the actors involved, but also in terms of the mechanisms through which they take place – provides a solid analytical foundation from which to consider the potential effects of these interactions. Another observation is that Braithwaite and Drahos's theory strengthens the TBGI framework by offering interpretative possibilities. Indeed, the framework on its own says little regarding what the various governance interactions might mean; a well-matched and well-developed theoretical lens becomes necessary for meaningful results. A further thought on the relevance of the theory for the framework – and vice versa – returns to this chapter's central question, which is how the relevance of nascent TBG initiatives and their interactions can be better understood. By pointing to specific dynamics and pathways through which the OGCI enrols actors in both the climate and oil and gas regimes, and highlighting the initiative's potential to set in motion path-breaking regulatory change, the theory sounds a cautionary note regarding the potential for capture.

12.4 REFLECTING RESPONSIBILITIES

While the OGCI was nascent and undertook little beyond goal and agenda-setting over the first three years of its existence, we would be remiss to neglect the potential impact of such an initiative in the longer term. This is very much the underlying message from this chapter's analysis of the OGCI through the TBGI framework and the global business regulation theory of Braithwaite and Drahos (2000). Whether the initiative's attempts to enrol actors from across the climate regime for its vision of a climate-compatible oil and gas industry or its efforts to speed up the development and adoption of low-carbon technologies and practices amount to leadership or capture remains a matter of perspective.

This uncertainty is linked to the elephant in the room, the question of motivations. What are the true motives of the OGCI and its member firms in engaging with climate governance? Should their statements and actions be taken at face value or should more opaque strategies be uncovered? While it is rarely possible to fully shed light on the motivations of actors in any context, this becomes all the more difficult here, as so many of the discussions are held behind closed doors. It is also unlikely that a fundamental truth might be exposed, because this assumes unitary and coherent actors; the reality is far messier with a range of positions and motivations taking hold within and across organizations. It is unlikely that Total and Saudi Aramco fully share the same motivations in joining the OGCI and in placing their weight behind it.

Some contextual hints can nevertheless be found that might offer a rough answer to these questions. As noted in the introduction, the oil and gas industry is no longer the only show in town. While this does not mean that the end of the road is around the corner, it nevertheless signals a significant modification of the landscape within which the OGCI and its member firms operate. This sense has been reinforced by the adoption of the Paris Agreement, which can be seen as defining a politically acceptable degree of warming, as well as a rise in efforts to phase out fossil fuels, whether from cities, investors or civil society groups. Taking this situation into account, the main motivation underlying the formation of the OGCI is to put forward a renewed vision for the oil and gas industry as an industry that can continue to operate within a carbon-constrained world. However, it is fundamentally unclear whether this is driven by a desire to head off potential reputational and regulatory risks, to seize emerging opportunities, to simply 'do the right thing', or a combination thereof.

NOTES

1. Interviews IND-1, IND-2 and IND-4. I conducted key informant interviews with individuals employed by OGCI member companies (four interviews), individuals otherwise involved in the oil and gas sector (two interviews), and a representative of a civil society organization critical of the OGCI (one interview). The interviews were intended to supplement the limited publicly available materials on the Oil & Gas Climate Initiative. Interviews with industry respondents are designated by the code IND; with international organizations by INT; and civil society organizations by CSO.
2. Interviews IND 1–5. See Table 12.2 for further details of these initiatives.
3. National oil companies (NOCs) are state-led and include Saudi Aramco (Saudi Arabia), China National Petroleum Corporation (CNPC), Pemex (Mexico) and Statoil (Norway). By contrast, multinational oil companies (MOCs), such as BP, Shell and Total, are private businesses. Though both face similar challenges, their agendas and relationship to regulation can differ significantly.
4. Interview INT-6.
5. The Chatham House Rule states that 'participants are free to use the information received, but neither the identity nor the affiliation of the speaker(s), nor that of any other participant, may be revealed' (Chatham House 2017).
6. Interview CSO-1.
7. Interview IND-6.
8. CNPC and Reliance Industries are the main exceptions.
9. Interview IND-3.
10. Interview IND-6.
11. Interviews IND 1–3.
12. Interview IND-1.

REFERENCES

Abbott, K.W. (2012), 'The transnational regime complex for climate change', *Environment and Planning C: Government and Policy*, **30** (4), 571–90.

Auld, G. (2014), *Constructing Private Governance: The Rise and Evolution of Forest, Coffee, and Fisheries Certification*, New Haven, CO: Yale University Press.

Auld, G., L.H. Gulbrandsen and C.L. McDermott (2008), 'Certification schemes and the impacts on forests and forestry', *Annual Review of Environment and Resources*, **33** (1), 187–211.

Bach, M. (2016), 'Shale gas "evolution": is environmental and social certification an option?', *National Geographic Voices*, 5 April 2016, accessed 5 September 2017 at https://voices.nationalgeographic.org/2016/04/05/shalegas.

Bach, M. (2017), 'Is the oil and gas industry serious about climate action?', *Environment: Science and Policy for Sustainable Development*, **59** (2): 4–15.

Bartley, T. (2007), 'Institutional emergence in an era of globalization: the rise of transnational private regulation of labor and environmental conditions', *American Journal of Sociology*, **113** (2), 297–351.

Blas, J. (2015), *How the European Oil Industry Decided to Save the Climate*, Bloomberg, 23 June 2015.

Braithwaite, J. and P. Drahos (2000), *Global Business Regulation*, Cambridge, UK: Cambridge University Press.

Chan, S. et al. (2015), 'Reinvigorating international climate policy: a comprehensive framework for effective nonstate action', *Global Policy*, **6**(4), 466–73.

Chatham House (Royal Institute of International Affairs) (2017), *Chatham House Rule*, accessed 31 October 2017 at https://www.chathamhouse.org/about/chatham-house-rule.
Cherp, A., J. Jewell and A. Goldthau (2011), 'Governing global energy: systems, transitions, complexity', *Global Policy*, **2** (1), 75–88.
DDPP – Deep Decarbonization Pathways Project (2015), *Pathways to Decarbonization*, Paris: Sustainable Development Solutions Network and Institute for Sustainable Development and International Relations.
Dwortzan, M. (2016), *Engaging Industry in Addressing Climate Change*, News item on MIT Energy Initiative website, accessed 5 September 2017 at http://energy.mit.edu/news/engaging-industry-addressing-climate-change.
Eberlein, B., K.W. Abbott, J. Black, E. Meidinger and S. Wood (2014), 'Transnational business governance interactions: conceptualization and framework for analysis', *Regulation & Governance*, **8** (1), 1–21.
Froley, A. (2016), 'Engie launches 3-yr transition plan', *Natural Gas World*, 26 February, accessed 4 October 2019 at https://www.naturalgasworld.com/engie-launches-3-yr-transition-plan-28377.
GGCA (Galvanizing the Groundswell of Climate Actions) (2015), *Lima-Paris Action Agenda Independent Assessment Report*.
Grabosky, P. (2013), 'Beyond responsive regulation: the expanding role of non-state actors in the regulatory process', *Regulation & Governance*, **7** (1), 114–23.
Gulbrandsen, L.H. (2010), *Transnational Environmental Governance: The Emergence and Effects of the Certification of Forest and Fisheries*, Cheltenham, UK and Northampton, MA, USA: Edward Elgar Publishing.
Heede, R. (2014), 'Tracing anthropogenic carbon dioxide and methane emissions to fossil fuel and cement producers 1854–2010', *Climatic Change,* **122** (1–2): 229–41.
Hoffmann, M.J. (2011), *Climate Governance at the Crossroads*, Oxford: Oxford University Press.
ISEAL Alliance (2013), 'A sustainability renaissance? The role of standards in the extractives sector' (webinar slides), 25 June, accessed 4 October 2019 at https://www.responsiblejewellery.com/files/Standards-for-the-Extractives-Sector-Presentation.pdf.
King, E. (2016), 'Oil majors vague on climate plans post Paris deal', Climate Home, 12 January 2016.
Latour, B. (1986), 'The powers of association', in J. Law (ed.), *Power, Action and Belief: A New Sociology of Knowledge?* Sociological Review Monograph 32. London and Boston: Routledge & Kegan Paul.
Mathieu, C. (2015), 'Carbon risk and the fossil fuel industry', Actuelles de l'Ifri: Paris, France.
Moutet, G. (2015), 'We commit ourselves', *Oil Magazine* (30), December 2015, 7–11.
OGCI (2014), 'Industry leaders, including energy companies, forge partnerships to advance climate solutions and reduce short-lived climate pollutants', press release, 23 September.
OGCI (2015a), Report of workshop, 22 May (copy on file with author).
OGCI (2015b), 'More energy, lower emissions: Catalyzing practical action on climate change', October, accessed 7 October 2019 at https://oilandgasclimateinitiative.com/wp-content/uploads/2017/10/ogci-report-2015-news.pdf.

OGCI (2015c), 'Oil & Gas Climate Initiative Joint Collaborative Declaration', 16 October, accessed 7 October 2019 at https://oilandgasclimateinitiative.com/wp-content/uploads/2017/10/ogci-ceo-Declaration-2015.pdf.

OGCI (2015d), 'OGCI CEOs jointly declare action on climate change', press release, 16 October, accessed 7 October 2019 at https://oilandgasclimateinitiative.com/oil-gas-ceos-jointly-declare-action-climate-change/.

OGCI (2017), 'OGCI climate investments', accessed 2 September 2017 at http://www.oilandgasclimateinitiative.com/climateInvestments.html.

Pattberg, P. (2016), 'Environmental governance in the anthropocene: complexity, fragmentation and the role of transnational institutions', VU Amsterdam.

Pattberg, P. and O. Widerberg (2016), 'Transnational multistakeholder partnerships for sustainable development: conditions for success', *Ambio*, **45**, 42–51.

Politiques énergétiques (2015), Video of the 16 October 2015 CEO press conference: https://www.politiques-energetiques.com/logci-paris-quand-les-petroliers-se-mobilisent-pour-le-climat.

RFF (2016), *RFF's Decision to Divest. Rockefeller Family Fund,* accessed 23 August 2016 at http://www.rffund.org/divestment.

Sampathkumar, M. (2016), 'Oil and gas companies pledge $1 billion to reduce emissions—but they won't give up on fossil fuels', ThinkProgress on Medium, 17 November 2016.

Scott, M. (2015), *Can Oil Companies Really Be Part of the Transition to a Low-Carbon Future?,* Forbes, 29 September 2015.

Skydsgaard, N. et al. (2016), *Denmark's DONG Energy to Get Out of Oil and Gas Business,* Reuters, 8 November 2016.

Solsvik, T. and G. Fouche (2016), *Big Oil Pledges $1 Billion for Gas Technologies to Fight Climate Change,* Reuters, 4 November 2016.

Stothard, M. and P. Clark (2015), *Energy Groups Pledge to Tackle Climate Change*, The Financial Times, 16 October 2015.

Timperley, J. (2016), 'E.ON completes split of fossil fuel and renewable operations', *The Guardian*, 4 January 2016.

UN (2014), *Press Release: Industry Leaders, including Energy Companies, Forge Partnerships to Advance Climate Solutions and Reduce Short-Lived Climate Pollutants*, Climate Summit 2014, 23 September 2013.

UN (2019), *Global Climate Action NAZCA Portal*, accessed 5 April 2019 at http://climateaction.unfccc.int.

UNEP (2015), *Climate Commitments of Subnational Actors and Business: A Quantitative Assessment of Their Emission Reduction Impact,* Nairobi: UNEP.

Verbong, G. and D. Loorbach (2012), *Governing the Energy Transition: Reality, Illusion or Necessity?* New York: Routledge.

Willsher, K. (2015), 'Oil companies deny that joint climate pledge is lip service', *The Guardian*, 16 October 2015.

Wood, S. (2003), 'Green revolution or greenwash? Voluntary environmental standards, public law and private authority in Canada', in Law Commission of Canada (ed.) *New Perspectives on the Public-Private Divide*, Vancouver and Toronto: UBC Press, pp. 123–65.

Wood, S., K.W. Abbott, J. Black, B. Eberlein and M. Meidinger (2015), 'The interactive dynamics of transnational business governance: a challenge for transnational legal theory', *Transnational Legal Theory*, **6** (2), 333–69.

13. Transnational business governance interactions and financial regulation change: A case of Asian financial markets

Simin Gao and Christopher (Chao-Hung) Chen

13.1 INTRODUCTION

This chapter argues that transnational business governance interactions (TBGI) play an important role in the two main competing schemes that govern global derivatives markets. On the one hand, the over-the-counter (OTC) market has developed a single monopolistic transnational business governance (TBG) scheme in the form of standard documentation published by the International Swaps and Derivatives Association (ISDA), which governs over 90 per cent all of derivatives trading (Henderson 2010a, 803). On the other hand, the market for exchange-traded products (for simplicity, 'futures'[1]) has seen multiple exchanges created around the world since the nineteenth century, offering multiple poles in the global governance of futures trading. While each futures exchange has a similar business and governance model, there is no monopoly like the ISDA in the market for exchange-traded derivatives.

The governance schemes of the global derivatives market have several levels of interactions. On the one hand, the ISDA scheme and the futures schemes interact with one another. For example, some OTC trades are cleared in a clearing house that underlies the futures scheme. On the other hand, the global derivatives governance system interacts with state and supranational regulators, especially as the global financial system was reformed and regulation of derivatives trading – in particular of OTC derivatives – was tightened in the wake of the global financial crisis.

This chapter considers these interactions and adds another angle: the interaction between East and West. We use these terms as shorthand for East and Southeast Asia, on one hand, and Europe, the UK, North America and Australia on the other. The futures schemes and ISDA scheme both originated in and reflect the social and economic conditions of the advanced Western capitalist world. The futures schemes in both West and East have largely the same governance model. In addition, the ISDA standard documentation has become a global script. Even countries that do not share the common law tradition of London or New York adopted the essence of these contractual norms from the 1980s onward. Since the financial crisis of 2008, Asian markets have, to various degrees, adopted regulatory reform proposals aimed at Western derivatives markets and market participants. This chapter asks why similar governance regimes are adopted across the globe for derivatives trading, whether on futures exchanges or the OTC market. In particular, we examine the implementation of the ISDA and futures schemes in Asia and the associated interaction between the West and East in a market dominated by American, British and European banks.

In other words, our key question is why there seems to be a high degree of convergence of norms governing derivatives markets. This chapter will focus on the techniques and strategies adopted in some East Asian countries in light of TBG schemes originating in the West. The chapter considers what drives East Asian markets to implement the same futures and ISDA schemes to govern their derivatives market (Eberlein et al. 2014, pp. 9–10). We examine the isomorphic forces behind the global convergence (and, to a lesser degree, divergence) of governance regimes of futures exchanges and the OTC market from the angle of markets in the East. Applying the theory of institutional isomorphism, this chapter illustrates different forces that drive regulators and market operators in the East to adopt governance schemes created in the West, and examines factors that may cause some degree of divergence.

Part 2 introduces the drivers of isomorphism and explores the general character of interactions among TBG regimes. Part 3 examines the parallel schemes governing the global futures and OTC derivatives markets. In addition to describing the derivatives market generally, we identify the isomorphic forces that drove the convergence of governance norms. Part 4 concludes.

13.2 CONVERGENCE OR DIVERGENCE OF GLOBAL BUSINESS GOVERNANCE NORMS

13.2.1 Drivers of Isomorphism

Isomorphism is a concept in organizational theory that captures the 'process of homogenization' that forces 'one unit in a population to resemble other units that face the same set of environmental conditions' (DiMaggio and Powell 1983, p. 149). In an environment with multiple organizations, some organizations' responses to the environment may lead others to respond similarly (Schelling 1978). Isomorphism is a process by which an organization comes to resemble others due to the same environmental conditions (Hawley 1968). There are three kinds of isomorphism: coercive isomorphism 'stems from political influence and the problem of legitimacy'; mimetic isomorphism results from 'standard responses to uncertainty'; and normative isomorphism 'associates with professionalization' (ibid., p. 150). Coercive isomorphism is driven by the pressures of powerful actors. Transnational institutional convergence is possible 'if existing institutions have been thoroughly discredited, morally or functionally, and, at the same time, if there is a powerful external actor who is able to enforce a new institutional design' (Beckert 2010, p. 153). In other words, the advanced institutional design of powerful states can be adopted by marginal states when existing institutions in the latter need changing.

Professionals play an important role in isomorphism. According to Kevin Leicht and Craig Jenkins (1998, p. 1327):

> Competing states are subject to normative isomorphic pressure through the professional networks of state managers. These states are also pressured to imitate or mimic policies of other states to keep up in the competition for private investment and economic development.

The media for mimetic isomorphism may be 'in-service educational programs, consultant arrangements, employer professional school networks, and trade journals' (DiMaggio & Powell 1983, p. 74). Normative isomorphism can also be used to interpret the roles of professionals and trade associations in driving the convergence of rulemaking by different states in derivative markets. An example is the operation of ISDA, the professional association of derivatives traders, which we discuss in Part 3. The initial goal of ISDA was to create standard documentation to facilitate trading. For professionals in derivatives markets, using standard documents for trading can minimise the risk of legal uncertainty. That is why we observe that ISDA, as representative of trading professionals, plays a very active role in lobbying lawmakers in different jurisdictions to recognize the legitimacy of the key mechanisms built by ISDA standard contracts, and to adopt the ISDA standard forms globally, including in Asian markets.

Gaining legitimacy with external constituents is a force behind isomorphism when those constituents expect an organization to function. The driving force behind mimetic isomorphism is 'the legitimation that an institutional regulation finds within an organizational field' (Beckert 2010, p. 158) against the uncertainty of solutions (Cyert & March, 1963). Convergence in rulemaking becomes possible because an institution in some countries becomes a successful model for other countries to follow to reduce the uncertainty of creating their own rules (Trampusch 2000; Beckert 2010, p. 158). Innovation by one organization to decrease uncertainty may be copied by other organizations (Alchian, 1950). Therefore, the direction of convergence of financial rules is usually from successful and powerful markets to marginal ones. The governance model of Asian derivatives exchanges demonstrates this phenomenon of mimetic isomorphism. For market operators in emerging markets, the simplest way to create a futures exchange is to follow a well-established model from developed countries, which has proved to be successful and efficient. With large Western exchanges and central counterparties (CCPs, or clearing houses) seeming to run well, mimicking the Western model is perhaps the safest approach. This may explain why futures exchanges in Asia all adopted the same governance model.

As we will elaborate further in Part 4, different isomorphic forces operate in the global derivatives market. For example, we have seen mimetic and normative isomorphism in the way modern futures exchanges are modelled around the world. In the early stage of development of the OTC market, we also saw the force of mimetic isomorphism as global market dealers helped to spread the ISDA standard forms to Asian markets. In the post-financial crisis era, we gradually saw more coercive isomorphism as market reforms were proposed by the US and EU before gradually being implemented in major Asian markets. In 2009, the G20 declared a commitment to strengthening the international financial regulatory system, with three major reform proposals for derivatives trading: the trading mandate to force OTC trades to move to exchanges, the clearing mandate to require centralized clearing of OTC trades, and the reporting mandate to require trading parties to report information about a trade to a trade repository. To gain legitimacy in the global clearing market and compete for a bigger share, some Asian markets started to clear OTC trades even before the implementation of the clearing mandate. However, some divergence of rules persisted where Asian national interests were not aligned with those of major markets like the US or EU. Asian countries have been relatively slow to implement the trading and clearing mandates, though the reporting mandate has been largely implemented, at least in Hong Kong and Singapore (Gao and Chen 2017).

13.2.2 The Substance and Character of Interactions

13.2.2.1 The substance of interaction

We can further consider in general terms the norms in financial law underlying the global derivatives market and how they might interact with each other on the global level. The substance of global business regulation is a hybrid of domestic and international law (Koh 2006), which can include both state and non-state norms and can be applied across more than one country or jurisdiction (Friedman 1996). Non-state norms, including non-binding standards, the *lex mercatoria,* model laws, and common approaches or standards for institutional monitoring, are elements of the international business order. This hybrid normativity is particularly interesting in the arena of financial law, which involves not only territory-based regulations but also international and non-state regulatory norms. For example, the governance schemes of the global derivatives market include not only national law in each market but also transnational regulatory norms.

The ISDA master agreement operates as a non-state norm regulating the bilateral relationship of trading parties for the vast majority of OTC derivatives transactions. In addition to the ISDA standard documentation, the regulatory regime for the OTC market consists of state regulations, private practices, regulatory standards set by international organizations and the 'best practices' of other jurisdictions. On the international level, the three mandates for OTC derivatives market regulation (that is, the trading, clearing and reporting mandates) were prescribed by the G20 in 2009 and are monitored by the Financial Stability Board (FSB). The mandates must be implemented by national laws (for example, the Dodd-Frank Act[2] in the US, along with subsidiary rules issued by the Commodity Futures Trading Commission).

In contrast, regulation of futures exchanges is rooted in national law, though the governance model is similar around the world. In addition, especially after the global crisis, some global norms have been created to improve the regulatory standards and legal infrastructure of the OTC market, such as the G20's reporting, clearing and trading mandates. The hybrid substance of transnational financial law illustrates the 'multiple centrifugal tendencies' (Teubner 2004, p. 3) of global society, which is an essential condition for transnational interaction.

13.2.2.2 The directions of interaction

Market forces play an important role in driving the transnational interaction of business governance norms. The direction of flow of business governance norms is determined by asymmetric market power, namely from central to marginal markets. Countries with sophisticated markets can make the rules and export them to other countries through ongoing business communications. Such legal norms can also originate from a leading country's legislature, and such state authorization may have great influence for encouraging other countries to adopt or transplant foreign rules. For example, the US Sarbanes-Oxley Act of 2002[3] became a model for a number of other states (Weber 2010).

In the arena of derivatives, the US and UK are the dominant markets (Bank for International Settlements 2013). Laws made in these core markets are widely regarded as models for smaller players to follow. Business law-making in the most powerful countries has both domestic and international consequences due to these transnational interactions. Considering the potential effect of their rules in international society, the most powerful markets are generally more conscious and deliberate in their rulemaking (Coffee 2014).

Marginal markets are not simply passive receivers, however. They may actively adopt the best practices and international standards that are beneficial for their countries. As Andrew Walter shows, domestic politics in Asian countries play an important role in the adoption of financial standards set by international organizations such as the G7 (Walter 2008, p. 173). For example, the Asian market (even in countries following the civil law tradition) embraces the ISDA master agreement as the governing contractual norm since it facilitates trading with global market dealers, even though it is largely structured on New York and English law. The degree of acceptance of the G20's three mandates also varies, reflecting national concerns. We have seen a higher degree of adoption and convergence of rules around the reporting mandate, which requires traders to report derivatives trades to a repository in order to improve transparency. Nonetheless, major Asian markets such as Hong Kong and Singapore have lagged behind in implementation of the mandatory clearing requirement for OTC derivatives due to some national interests and concerns about the solvency of clearing houses (Gao and Chen 2017). Thus, marginal markets might not adopt central governance norms wholesale if countervailing national interests affect their strategies in adopting certain norms.

13.2.3 What Determines the Effects of Interactions?

The effects of TBGIs can differ. Some interactions may directly influence the local legislature and may even promote isomorphism of business rules in different jurisdictions. Some interaction may have no significant effects. What determines these effects?

One important factor is the norms that are the subject of interaction. Gregory Shaffer (2012) finds that legal norms that interact with one another usually have certain common characteristics (such as legitimacy, clarity and coherence) that can produce domestic legal and institutional changes. In addition, a receiving state's relation to the transnational legal order and its own domestic context are also critical factors in determining the effects of downloading legal norms (ibid.). These effects depend partly on the norms' degree of fit with the receiving country's law and political economy. As Hideki Kanda and Curtis Milhaupt (2003, p. 891) point out, there are two kinds of fit: 'Micro-fit is how well the imported rule complements the pre-existing legal infrastructure in the host country. Macro-fit is how well the imported rule complements the pre-existing institutions of the political economy in the host country.' For example, as the ISDA form is constructed upon English and New York law, its fit is higher in Singapore and Hong Kong than in other Asian markets because of their common law heritage and the presence of many international banks in both markets.

With this background in mind, we turn now to the TBG schemes governing global derivatives, and their interactions. In addition to a general discussion on the interactions between different schemes and how the interactions evolve, we also focus on how the schemes flow from core markets in the West to some Asian markets.

13.3 EAST-WEST INTERACTIONS IN TRANSNATIONAL BUSINESS GOVERNANCE SCHEMES FOR GLOBAL DERIVATIVES MARKETS

13.3.1 Characteristics of Derivatives Markets

The futures and OTC markets are both global and each represents a kind of TBG scheme. The futures market has a far longer history. Since the establishment of the Chicago Board of Trade in the mid-nineteeth century, the futures market blossomed as a trading forum for many agricultural products before expanding into financial futures (for example, interest rate or index futures) and energy products (for example, crude oil futures) from the 1970s onwards. In contrast, the rise of OTC derivatives is fairly recent. The market kicked off in the 1980s and grew at an exponential rate.

The development of governance regimes of the two market sectors followed different paths. American and European giants dominated the futures market. According to the Bank for International Settlements (BIS), the total open interests in all futures exchanges in North America amounted to US$ 15.705 trillion at the end of 2015, with the amount in Europe being US$7.08 trillion and US$1.775 trillion in Asia and the Pacific (Bank for International Settlements 2016). However, many Asian markets still create their own futures exchanges. For example, the Shanghai Futures Exchange was created in 1999, offering a range of metal-linked contracts.

Trading volumes in the OTC market are much larger than those of all futures exchanges combined. Pursuant to statistics provided on the BIS website, the total notional amount outstanding in the first half of 2017 was US$ 542.435 trillion (Bank for International Settlements 2018b), in contrast with the total open interests worth US$ 33.694 billion in June 2017 for exchange-traded futures and options (Bank for International Settlements 2018a).

Like the futures market, the OTC market also has two clear power centres. According to the BIS, the daily average of OTC interest rate derivatives in the UK amounted to US$ 1,347.74 trillion, followed by the US (US$ 628.15 trillion), France (US$ 202.21 trillion) and Germany (US$ 101.34 trillion). In Asia, the biggest market is Japan (US$ 67.14 trillion, fifth in the world) with Singapore (US$ 37.14 trillion) in eighth position and Hong Kong (US$ 27.90 trillion) in twelfth. Thus, both the futures and OTC derivatives markets are dominated by traders in the Western world. This has a profound effect on how the norms and governance schemes are designed and implemented on the global level.

13.3.2 Mimetic and Normative Isomorphic Forces Shaping the Futures Schemes

Forces of mimetic and normative isomorphism influence the way Asian markets adopt governance schemes regulating the exchange-traded futures market. The fact that an exchange has to be situated physically in a particular country (even in the age of electronic trading) generates multiple TBG schemes regarding futures, with each futures exchange being a TBG scheme. This multiplicity leads to multilateral interactions of governance schemes. However, the governance structure of a futures exchange is built largely on the same pattern around the world, though details vary.

The hallmark of futures trading is that all exchange-traded contracts (whether futures contracts or options) are standardized to the point that price is the only issue that requires negotiation. This feature allows market participants to buy and sell multiple contracts at the same time. A typical futures market is run by an exchange operator (for example, Chicago Mercantile Exchange [CME]), which sets out trading rules and specifies the types of contracts that are available for trading. To trade directly in an exchange, a market participant must become an exchange member. Members are usually large banks, financial institutions or fund management firms. Other traders must have a contract with a member or a clearing house to enjoy trading and clearing services. In large exchanges, there can be multiple layers of members with different rights and obligations.

Typically, the making of a contract between two traders sets off a chain of novation of contracts until a central counterparty (CCP, or clearing house) becomes the ultimate counterparty to all contracts. The standardization of contracts then allows the CCP to calculate any profit or loss incurred by a trader. To secure payment obligations from trading positions incurred by a market participant, the market has developed the margin system, under which a trader must pay a certain sum of money (or liquid asset) to a CCP or clearing member as collateral. The value of the margin account is marked to the market on a daily basis to reflect profits or losses incurred by the trader, who must post more collateral if the value of the margin account drops below a certain level (the margin call). Otherwise, the trader's trading positions can be closed out to stop losses. This is an essential feature to ensure the solvency and soundness of the futures market and the clearing system. It operates through a pyramid structure of governance from national regulatory rules at the apex, down through exchange and clearing rules to contractual terms and membership agreements.

The same model (exchange trading with trades cleared by a CCP) has been applied in virtually all major futures exchanges in the world, though details may differ (for example, the exact margin rate or acceptable instruments for margin). This raises an interesting question: why does a generic model of governance scheme govern domestic and international trading activities? We argue that there could be two isomorphic forces behind the phenomenon.

On the one hand, this could be a case of mimetic isomorphism. For market operators in emerging markets, the simplest way to create a futures exchange is to follow a well-established model in developed countries, which is relatively transparent and rarely fails – there have only been three incidents of CCP insolvency in the past half century (Wendt 2015, p. 11, note 7). With large Western exchanges and CCPs seemingly running very well, mimicking the Western model is perhaps the safest approach. This may explain why most (if not all) futures exchanges in Asia adopt the same governance model. For example, in both the Singapore and Hong Kong exchanges, direct participation in trading and clearing is controlled by membership (HKEX 2018b; SGX 2018) with different margin requirements for different products, the same model adopted in leading futures exchanges in the West (HKEX 2018a; SGX 2018).

On the other hand, we also observe signs of normative isomorphism. The network of international banks and professionals might help to spread the use of the same governance model to emerging markets, as they are more familiar with the trading and clearing process if futures markets in different countries are largely running on the same governance platform. Large financial institutions, as market-makers, should prefer a new exchange in an emerging market to operate on the same governance model so that they might reduce compliance and transaction costs. It might also benefit the local market operator if the governance scheme is similar to those in the West so as to attract Western traders to trade in the local market. In addition, advisers who help to set up a new futures exchanges are most likely professionals or bankers who are familiar with the Western model. Those factors might explain why the governance schemes of the futures around the world seem to converge.

However, globalization and the interconnection of financial markets could offer some challenges to the governance of futures schemes, given that futures schemes are still largely regulated by the national law of the jurisdiction where an exchange or CCP is situated. The worst-case scenario is when a CCP goes bankrupt. It may be less of a problem when two or more CCPs are in the same jurisdiction governed by the same laws. However, when they are situated in different jurisdictions (especially in places with different legal systems), there could be complications. A country may be more inclined to ring-fence local assets in the case of bankruptcy, making it more challenging to maintain cross-margin in a case where a large participant or a CCP becomes insolvent. This may explain why cross-exchange trading among different countries has not reached a larger scale. It is hard to predict how legal issues will be resolved. To resolve such issues, harmonization of laws regarding security interests and enforceability of collateral as well as insolvency rules may be the ultimate solution. If so, it would lead to less polycentrism in the underlying regulatory structure of futures schemes in the world.

Consolidation of exchange and clearing businesses provides an additional angle of interactions between governance schemes. For example, the US has seen the creation of the CME group, the merger of the two Chicago giants – the Chicago Mercantile Exchange and Chicago Board of Trade – in 2007. The Eurex, a large futures exchange based in Europe, created a trading platform in Singapore in 2009, while the Intercontinental Exchange acquired the New York Stock Exchange in 2012. These mergers may create a new range of regulatory issues (Kokkoris and Olivares-Caminal 2007, 2008; Schammo 2008).

In contrast, in most Asian markets, it is still very common to have a national monopoly or duopoly of futures exchanges. In terms of ownership, some exchanges in Asia are still more or less owned and controlled by the state (for example, in Taiwan or China), while some exchanges are publicly traded companies (for example, the Singapore Exchange [SGX] in Singapore and Hong Kong Exchange [HKEx] in Hong Kong). This creates a different environment of interactions among futures exchanges or CCPs in Asia compared to those in the US or Europe. If we consider that an exchange and CCP are fundamental financial infrastructure in a country, it is natural that the national interest is often an important concern, especially when foreign ownership is involved.

A higher level issue concerns the regulation of exchanges and CCPs. In many markets in Asia, a futures exchange and CCP are bundled together. This is the traditional 'vertical silo' approach, in which contracts traded on an exchange must be assigned to a specific CCP for clearing. This is still the case in most futures exchanges in Asia. Adopting the silo approach, a CCP in theory may be a separate body from an exchange (for example, LCH [formerly London Clearing House] in relation to the London International Financial Futures Exchange) or may be in-house (for example, the clearing arm of SGX or HKEx being part of the exchange group).

However, in the twenty-first century, the EU's Markets in Financial Instruments Directive opened up the market to more competition in terms of trading venue and clearing services.[4] The EU has abandoned the traditional vertical silo approach so that trades conducted on an exchange may be cleared in different CCPs (Financial Times 2008). This development in Europe offers another layer of interactions (between exchanges and CCPs) and more interactions for cross-border trading and clearing in the future for Asian traders.

There is no clear prospect of Asian markets adopting the EU model at the time of writing. Countries in the Asia Pacific region are not as integrated as the EU, even considering the Association of South-East Asian Nations (ASEAN) economic community. With the market and regulatory framework fragmented by national borders, it is understandable that national regulators would prefer the vertical silo model, which is also easier for the regulator to control. It remains to be seen whether any major Asian market is willing to break up the vertical silo model to accommodate more competition for trading and clearing services. This also means that the path of development of the futures scheme as a whole might diverge to a certain degree in the future between the East and West depending on the development of the market and regulatory environment.

13.3.3 Signs of Mimetic Isomorphism in the OTC Market

The OTC market developed a monopolistic governance regime in the ISDA master agreement to the point that it was virtually the only TBG scheme for the OTC derivatives market, at least before the global financial crisis

(Porter 2014). The OTC market also shows emerging signs of polycentrism as national regulators have sought to regulate it since the global financial crisis. One observer estimates that approximately 90 per cent of the USD $600 trillion aggregate notional amount of OTC derivatives are processed under one or another of the ISDA forms (Henderson 2010a; Rauterberg and Verstein 2013). Given the size of the global OTC derivatives market, it is notable that the market has developed such a singular and dominant documentation system. The rise of the ISDA master agreement system as the dominant contract form governing the OTC derivatives markets could be seen as a result of normative isomorphism.

ISDA's initial goal was to create standard documentation to facilitate trading. As one observer noted, the 'ISDA's limited early role was to standardize documentation, a role which quickly expanded into lobbying to create greater legal certainty in derivatives' (Henderson 2010b, p. 20). As OTC derivatives grew exponentially in the 1980s, the market needed a standard set of documentation to provide a contractual platform for trading (Porter 2014). ISDA, as the association of international banks and dealers operating in the OTC derivatives market, filled the gap.

International banks were the main drivers and vehicle to spread the use of the ISDA standard form to other areas of the world, indicating a sign of normative isomorphism. On the one hand, a trader in smaller markets most likely had to trade with major global dealers, who were accustomed to the ISDA form and would probably prefer to use it to reduce compliance costs. On the other, even without trading with major global dealers, derivatives traders outside the US, UK and Europe still benefit from adopting the ISDA form because it is easier to apply a form that has been created and tried out in established markets, similar to the adoption of the futures exchange governance model discussed above. Even without transacting with a Western bank as a counterparty, using a form that has been proven in larger markets is a safer choice than writing a new contract from scratch. Moreover, if an Asian bank enters into back-to-back transactions with a foreign bank to hedge a domestic derivative transaction, there should be less legal risk if all contracts are governed by the same set of contractual norms.

It is not that no one tried to offer a different version of documentation. China had its own version of standard documentation developed by the National Association of Financial Market Institutional Investors (NAFMII) (Ong and Hsiao 2013). However, this initiative was not a real competitor to ISDA. On the one hand, although the NAFMII form claims to be 'presented in a more succinct manner to accommodate the unique situation of the Chinese market', it incorporates key ideas of the ISDA standard form, including the single-contract approach and close-out netting (ibid., p. 78). Thus, the NAFMII form was essentially a copy of the ISDA form in a different language. On the other hand, as we explain below, the most critical factor perhaps is that China is not the epicentre of global derivatives trades, with trading volume falling far behind other Asian financial centres. With Chinese traders playing a minor role in global OTC derivatives trading, it is not a surprise that the NAFMII did not have an impact in the end. Conversely, the ISDA scheme prevailed largely because the ISDA form was widely adopted by major market dealers.

In sum, in the OTC market, we have seen the rise of the ISDA standard documentation as the predominant governing norm. Similar to the futures scheme, normative isomorphism through major market dealers is the driving force behind the adoption of the ISDA scheme in the Asian market. Combined with the fact that the derivatives market grew at lightning speed, the use of the ISDA form soon achieved a scale that is hard to reverse.

It is worth noting that the adoption of the ISDA scheme in Asia followed a different path to that of the futures scheme. Asian futures exchanges are typically established under existing legal and regulatory frameworks and are often national monopolies. Each country virtually copies the whole governing mechanism from the West. In contrast, the rise of the ISDA scheme occurred without a specific legal mandate. The ISDA scheme prevails in the context of the dominance of Western markets and market-makers. Asian countries played more of a reactive role when receiving the ISDA scheme.

13.3.4 Towards Coercive Isomorphism and Divergence after the Global Financial Crisis?

Before the global financial crisis, the futures scheme and the ISDA scheme seemed to follow two parallel lines, each governing its own domain. However, the global financial crisis changed the scene and forced more interactions between the two governing mechanisms. Between West and East, we suggest that there are not only signs of coercive isomorphism but also the potential for divergence in the governance of derivatives markets.

In 2009, the G20 declared a commitment to strengthening the international financial regulatory system. In particular, the G20 decided that '[a]ll standardized OTC derivative contracts should be traded on exchanges or electronic trading platforms . . . and cleared through central counterparties by end-2012 at the latest' (University of Toronto 2018). Moreover, 'OTC derivatives contracts should be reported to trade repositories'; otherwise they 'should be subject to higher capital requirements' (ibid.). In short, the G20 adopted three main regulatory reform proposals: the trading mandate (mandatory trading on an exchange); the clearing mandate (mandatory clearing through a CCP); and the reporting mandate (mandatory reporting to a trade repository). The primary goals were to control counterparty risk, improve transparency and prevent systemic risk via the derivatives market.

One result of these reforms was more interactions between the futures schemes and the ISDA scheme. With the clearing mandate, more OTC derivatives must be cleared by a CCP. According to ISDA, about 82 per cent of the total notional amount of OTC derivatives were cleared as of early April 2016 (ISDA SwapsInfo 2018). This makes major CCPs the ultimate counterparties for trillions of dollars of trades. In this way, many OTC trades are governed partly by the ISDA scheme (before clearing) and partly by the futures scheme (after entering into the clearing system). To compete for a bigger share in the global clearing market, some Asian markets started to clear OTC trades even before the implementation of the clearing mandate. For example, the SGX started to clear OTC derivatives as early as 2010, and the HKEx launched its OTC clearing services in 2013, before implementing the clearing mandate. To facilitate the migration, ISDA has actively offered solutions by offering standard documents to complement existing ISDA master agreements (for example, the ISDA/FIA Cleared Derivatives Execution Agreement and the ISDA/FIA Client Cleared OTC Derivatives Addendum).

However, if we take a larger view, Asian countries have been relatively slow to implement the trading and clearing mandates compared with the US and Europe, though the reporting mandate was largely implemented in at least Hong Kong and Singapore (Chen 2016; Gao and Chen 2017). What could be delaying the implementation of the clearing and trading mandates in Asia? We suggest that the delay in implementing the clearing mandate may reflect conflicting driving forces behind the interactions of governance schemes. The global financial crisis was clearly the single dominant event that drove the regulatory reforms. However, since it took place mainly in the West, the reforms aimed at Western market infrastructure. Since it might not be that difficult to move trading activities outside the US or Europe, major Western markets pushed major Asian markets like Singapore and Hong Kong to accept the new regulatory norms (the three mandates) through international organizations such as the FSB and the BIS.

While many Asian markets, especially financial centres such as Hong Kong and Singapore, would like to gain more market share in global derivatives trading (or even in clearing services), the ability of Asian countries to compete with Western giants through different regulatory or governance regimes is restrained by laws in the Western markets. For example, there is a clear concern in the US and EU to prevent their traders from circumventing American and European regulations. Thus, a US trader may not simply clear a trade in any CCP outside the US. To meet the local clearing obligation by submitting a trade to a foreign CCP (so-called 'substituted compliance'), the foreign market must have similar regulatory infrastructure to that in the US.[5] The EU has a similar rule.[6] As major derivatives dealers are mostly in the US or Europe, rules restraining substituted compliance have induced major Asian market regulators to adopt rules similar to those in the US or EU. Thus, Asian countries have little choice but to accept the mandates if they wish to create or maintain a prosperous derivatives market. The SGX was the first Asian market to be recognized by the US Commodity Futures Trading Commission, in 2013 (Grant 2013). Both Singapore and Hong Kong obtained recognition from the EU as 'equivalent' CCPs in 2014 (European Commission 2018). Whether such uniformity is good or bad for the market is another question (Griffith 2014). Therefore, we suggest that Asian markets were, in a way, coerced to adopt the mandates to force trade reporting and centralized clearing before mandatory exchange trading of derivatives, showing signs of coercive isomorphism that we did not see before the global financial crisis.

However, in the case of centralized clearing, there are obvious national concerns that would affect the strategies adopted by Asian markets to implement the mandates, which could produce a certain degree of divergence. For example, Asian markets still need to maintain financial stability and the solvency of their own clearing system. For the clearing mandate to succeed, a CCP, as the ultimate risk taker of cleared contracts, must stay solvent and have enough opposing trades to reduce risk exposure. Large CCPs in the West enjoy some competitive advantage as they are bigger, have a larger volume of trades and might have a better pool of liquid assets as collateral. Thus, Asian regulators would face a dilemma. On the one hand, an insistence on local clearing may drive traders away if their home countries do not allow substituted compliance, or may increase systemic risk if liquidity is limited. If they allow substituted compliance, Asian regulators may face a strong extraterritorial effect of US or European regulations and the risk of negative externalities because they do not have the power to regulate US or European CCPs, whose failure would have wide repercussions and spill-over effects for Asian traders who clear their local trades in the West. Those factors might explain why both Hong Kong and Singapore adopted the clearing mandate but delayed its implementation.

In contrast, such national concerns do not necessarily affect the reporting mandate, as transparency and data protection – the mandate's major concerns – do not have implications for solvency or national economic policy. Even if a trade is reported to a trade repository in a foreign territory through substituted compliance, a local regulator might still acquire trading information through regulatory cooperation. As mandatory trade reporting generally improves market transparency, Asian regulators have fewer concerns about implementing the reporting mandate for local market participants.

The trading mandate provides the strongest form of forced interactions. By forcing trades to be conducted in an organized exchange, it attempts to shift trades from more flexible OTC markets to more organized exchange markets. If implementing the clearing mandate is already difficult, it is obvious why Asian regulators are not keen to implement the trading mandate. After all, the rule favours large Western exchange operators over Asian exchange operators, who are still more nationally based and less consolidated than those in the US or Europe.

However, one point worth noting is that the reforms of the OTC derivatives markets have led to a proliferation of trading platforms outside existing gigantic exchange operators like CME and Eurex. Those platforms flourish not as a formal large exchange operator but as a 'swap execution facility'[7] in the US or an 'organized trading facility' in Europe.[8] These are platforms that offer trading information (such as price) and a mechanism to execute trades for parties. They are not futures exchanges but operate on a smaller scale. It is also uncertain whether these trading platforms run on a common governance model like a futures exchange. The co-existence of large exchange operators and smaller trading platforms on top of CCPs may provide a further study of interactions of TBG schemes in the future.

13.4 CONCLUSION

The governance of the global derivatives market is polycentric, with norms generated at both national and transnational levels. There are some isomorphic forces behind the interactions of schemes governing this market. Those forces affect rulemaking processes across national borders, resulting in different degrees of interaction between different regulatory regimes and governance schemes.

There are two main areas of TBGI between West and East in our case study: the multiple futures schemes governing the futures markets, contrasted with the single and monopolistic ISDA scheme governing the

OTC derivatives market. The governance structure of a futures scheme has been successfully copied into Asian markets, showing signs of mimetic and normative isomorphism. In addition, the rise of the ISDA scheme is a product of economic power, and it prevails even in Asian markets through professionals and major market dealers, again suggesting the power of mimetic isomorphism. After the global financial crisis, new regulations forced more interactions between the two schemes by prescribing mandatory centralized clearing and exchange trading, showing not only the polycentric structure of regulation of the derivatives market but also a certain degree of coercive isomorphism. However, we have seen Asian countries delay implementation of those two mandates. In this case, the economic power behind the transnational flow of norms is complicated by national interests and other local economic concerns. Those are areas worth looking into in the future for further interactions between futures exchanges and the OTC market.

NOTES

1. The futures markets trade not only futures (standardized forward contracts) but also options and other standardized products. For simplicity, we use the term 'futures' to identify the exchange-traded market.
2. Dodd-Frank Act Wall Street Reform and Consumer Protection Act, Pub. L. 111–203, H.R. 4173.
3. Sarbanes-Oxley Act of 2002, Pub. L. 107–204.
4. Directive 2004/39/EC of 21 April 2004 on markets in financial instruments amending Council Directives 85/611/EEC and 93/6/EEC and Directive 2000/12/EC of the European Parliament and of the Council and repealing Council Directive 93/22/EEC [2004] OJ L145/1.
5. See 17 CFR § 50.52(b)(4) (2013).
6. Regulation (EU) 648/2012 of 4 July 2012 on OTC derivatives, central counterparties and trade repositories, [2012] OJ L201/1, Recitals 7 and 8.
7. 7 USC § 1a(50).
8. Regulation (EU) 600/2014 of 15 May 2014 on markets in financial instruments and amending Regulation (EU) No 648/2012, [2014] OJ L173/84, Article 2(1)(15).

REFERENCES

Alchian, Armen (1950), 'Uncertainty, evolution, and economic theory', *Journal of Political Economy,* **58**, 211–21.

Bank for International Settlements (2013), *Triennial Central Bank Survey: Interest Rate Derivatives Market Turnover in 2013*, Basel: Bank for International Settlements.

Bank for International Settlements (2016), 'Exchange-Traded Derivatives Statistics', accessed 1 June 2016 at https://www.bis.org/statistics/extderiv.htm.

Bank for International Settlements (2018a), *Exchange-Traded Futures and Options, by Location of Exchange*, accessed 1 June 2018 at http://stats.bis.org/statx/srs/table/d1.

Bank for International Settlements (2018b), *Global OTC Derivatives Market*, accessed 1 June 2018 at http://stats.bis.org/statx/srs/table/d5.1.
Beckert, Jens (2010), 'Institutional isomorphism revisited: convergence and divergence in institutional change', *Sociological Theory,* **28** (2), 150–66.
Chen, Christopher (2016), 'Over-the-counter derivatives regulation in Hong Kong and Singapore', *Brill Perspective on International Banking and Securities Law,* **1** (4), 1–50.
Coffee, John C. (2014), 'Extraterritorial financial regulation: why E.T. can't come home', *Cornell Law Review,* **99**, 1259–302.
Cyert, Richard M. and James G. March (1963), *A Behavioral Theory of the Firm,* Englewood Cliffs, NJ: Prentice-Hall.
DiMaggio, Paul J. and Walter W. Powell (1983), 'The iron cage revisited: institutional isomorphism and collective rationality in organizational fields', *American Sociological Review,* **48** (2), 147–60.
Eberlein, Burkard, Kenneth W. Abbott, Julia Black, Errol Meidinger and Stepan Wood (2014), 'Transnational business governance interactions: conceptualization and framework for analysis', *Regulation and Governance,* **8** (1), 1–21.
European Commission (2018), *Post-Trade Services,* accessed 1 June 2018 at http://ec.europa.eu/finance/financial-markets/derivatives/index_en.htm#maincontentSec4.
Financial Times. 2008. 'Clearing the way'.
Friedman, Lawrence M. (1996), 'Borders: on the emerging sociology of transnational law', *Stanford Journal of International Law,* **32**, 65–90.
Gao, Simin and Christopher Chen (2017), 'Financial transnationalism and financial regulation change: a case study for derivatives markets', *European Business Organisation Law Review,* **18**, 193.
Grant, Jeremy (2013), 'SGX approved for US derivatives clearing', *Financial Times*, 29 December.
Griffith, Sean J. (2014), 'Substituted compliance and systemic risk: how to make a global market in derivative regulation', *Minnesota Law Review,* **98**, 1291–373.
Hawley, Amos H. (1968), 'Human ecology', in David L. Sills (ed.), *International Encyclopedia of the Social Sciences*, New York: Macmillan, pp. 328–37.
Henderson, Schuyler K. (2010a), *Henderson on Derivatives,* 2nd edn, LexisNexis.
Henderson, Schuyler K. (2010b), *Henderson on Derivatives,* 2nd edn, London: LexisNexis.
HKEX (2018a), *Hang Seng Index Futures*, accessed 1 June 2018 at http://www.hkex.com.hk/Products/Listed-Derivatives/Equity-Index/Hang-Seng-Index-(HSI)/Hang-Seng-Index-Futures?sc_lang=en#&product=HSI.
HKEX (2018b), *Participantship/Membership*, accessed 1 June 2018 at http://www.hkex.com.hk/Services/Rules-and-Forms-and-Fees/Forms/Listed-Derivatives/Clearing/Participantship-Membership?sc_lang=en.
ISDA SwapsInfo (2018), *ISDA SwapsInfo*, accessed 1 June 2018 at http://www.swapsinfo.org.
Kanda, Hideki and Curtis J Milhaupt (2003), 'Re-examining legal transplants: the director's fiduciary duty in Japanese Corporate Law', *American Journal of Comparative Law,* **51**, 887–901.
Koh, Harold Hongju (2006), 'Why transnational law matters', *Penn State International Law Review,* **24**, 745–53.
Kokkoris, Ioannis and Rodrigo Olivares-Caminal (2007), 'Some issues on cross-border stock exchange mergers', *University of Pennsylvania Journal of International Law,* **29**, 455–526.
Kokkoris, Ioannis and Rodrigo Olivares-Caminal (2008), 'Lessons from the recent stock exchange merger', *Journal of Competition Law & Economics,* **4**, 837–69.

Leicht, Kevin T. and J. Craig Jenkins (1998), 'Political resources and direct state intervention: the adoption of public venture capital programs in the American states, 1974–1990', *Social Forces,* **76** (4), 1323–45.
Ong, Kingsley T.W. and Mark W.H. Hsiao (2013), 'From ISDA to NAFMII: insolvency stalemate and PRC bankruptcy jurisprudence', *Capital Market Law Journal,* **8** (1): 77–88.
Porter, Tony (2014), 'Technical systems and the architecture of transnational business governance interactions', *Regulation and Governance,* **8** (1): 110–25.
Rauterberg, Gabriel V. and Andrew Verstein (2013), 'Assessing transnational private regulation of the OTC derivatives market: ISDA, the BBA, and the future of financial reform', *Virginia Journal of International Law*, **54**, 9–50.
Schammo, Pierre (2008), 'Regulating Transatlantic stock exchanges', *International and Comparative Law Quarterly,* **57** (4), 827–62.
Schelling, Thomas C. (1978), *Micromotives and Macrobehavior.* New York: Norton.
SGX (2018), *Singapore Exchange*, accessed 1 June 2018 at https://www.sgx.com.
Shaffer, Gregory (2012), 'Transnational legal process and state change', *Law & Social Inquiry,* **37**, 229–64.
Teubner, Gunther (2004), 'Global private regimes: neo-spontaneous law and dual constitution of autonomous sectors?', in Karl-Heinz Ladeur (ed.), *Public Governance in the Age of Globalization*, London: Ashgate, pp. 71–87.
Trampusch, Christine (2000), 'Grenzen der diffusion: Die formative phase der arbeitsmarktpolitik in den Niederlanden', in *Sozialmodell Europa: Konturen eines Phänomens,* Wiesbaden: Springer, pp. 153–77.
University of Toronto (2018), *G20 Leaders Statement: The Pittsburgh Summit*, accessed 1 June 2018 at http://www.g20.utoronto.ca/2009/2009communique0925.html.
Walter, Andrew (2008), *Governing Finance: East Asia's Adoption of International Standards.* Ithaca, NY: Cornell University Press.
Weber, Rolf H. (2010), 'Multilayered governance in international financial regulation and supervision', *Journal of International Economic Law,* **13**, 683–704.
Wendt, Froukelien (2015), 'Central counterparties: addressing their too important to fail nature', WP/15/21.

14. A Coxian perspective on transnational business governance interactions: Counter-hegemonic certification movements in fisheries

Paul Foley

14.1 INTRODUCTION

This chapter contributes to the study of transnational business governance interactions (TBGIs) by focusing on the role and interests of producers in patterns of proliferation and competition in transnational governance.[1] Such patterns are widespread in sectors such as coffee (Raynolds and Wilkinson 2007; Raynolds et al. 2007), forestry (Cashore et al. 2004; Gale 2014), aquaculture (Havice and Iles 2015), and fisheries (Foley and Havice 2016). Proliferation and competition are a core focus of the TBGI research agenda, but questions remain in terms of how and why competition has emerged in some sectors and not in others and the causes and consequences of competition (Büthe 2010, p. 15; Smith and Fischlein 2010; Auld 2014; Eberlein et al. 2014). This chapter suggests that new insight can be gained by utilizing a 'production and power' perspective to analyse transnational business governance (TBG) proliferation and competition. The targets of most TBG initiatives are producers (Büthe 2010), but implications for producers and social development are not well understood or theorized (Bartley et al. 2015). While some TBG initiatives have yielded notable achievements, researchers have raised fundamental questions about their impacts for producer livelihoods, empowerment, and local development (Reed and Mukherjee-Reed 2012; Utting 2012). This chapter puts questions of production, power and social development at the forefront. It proposes that we conceptualize the interactive dynamics of TBG in terms of the inter-relations between production and power, including how principles and relations of production and development interact with governance institutions at state and international levels.

This chapter examines the relationship between TBGIs and producers by utilizing the critical international political economy (IPE) approach to 'production and power' developed by Robert Cox, a pioneer in the development of neo-Gramscian international relations (IR) scholarship and a novel perspective on hegemony in IR. Unlike conventional IR theory, which reduces hegemony to a single dimension of dominance based on the economic and military capabilities of states, Cox's critical theory broadens the inquiry to include the 'basic processes at work in the development of social forces [of production] and forms of state, and in the structure of global political economy' (Cox 1996, p. 91). Hegemony is understood not as the dominance of one powerful nation state, but as a socialization process with material, cultural and ideological dimensions. Cox's approach is useful because it theorizes not only production and power but also the interactions between transnational governance and the social relations of production in efforts to foster hegemony in the global political economy:

> This means starting at the beginning with production so as to consider how the diversity of ways in which production is carried on and the variety of social relationships generated in production processes condition the social forces that can become bases of power in state and world order. It also means following the reverse course to consider how power institutionalized in world order and in the state shapes and controls the development of production relations. (Cox 1987, p. 4)

This chapter applies Cox's approach to the study of proliferating certification systems in the global capture fisheries sector. As Graeme Auld suggests in a study of the Marine Stewardship Council (MSC), 'it is critical to assess the MSC in relation to other fisheries' governance instruments and that efforts are undertaken to enhance attention to the needs of small and marginalized fishers, particularly if development goals are to be advanced' (Auld 2012, p. 148; see also Auld and Cashore 2013, p. 154). The chapter argues that the MSC's lack of engagement with and support for political economies of production and development facilitated the emergence of two forms of producer-oriented counter-hegemonic movements, conceptualized below as territorial and ethical eco-certification initiatives.

Part 2 introduces Cox's approach. Part 3 uses this approach to examine factors that facilitated the emergence of alternatives to the MSC. Parts 4 and 5 examine prominent examples of territorial and ethical eco-certification initiatives, emphasizing how principles and relations of production and development interact with governance institutions at state and international levels. Part 6 reflects on the implications of the analysis for TBGI. The conclusion considers the extent to which competing visions of eco-certification in the fisheries sector contain counter-hegemonic potential.

14.2 THE APPROACH: APPLYING COXIAN IPE TO THE STUDY OF TBGIs

The TBGI literature advocates the development of middle-range theoretical tools that can accommodate the multiplicity of interacting entities and scales of interaction, and the co-evolution of social agency and structure (Wood et al. 2015). Robert Cox developed a middle-range method of historical structure as a conceptual tool and heuristic device designed around three interacting spheres of activity and interaction on which hegemony is built: the social relations of production, which more specifically refer to the *social forces* that are generated by the production process; *forms of state*, which are historically contingent state-civil society complexes; and *world orders*, consisting of the particular assemblage of forces that sequentially define phases of stability or conflict for the state system (Cox 1996, pp. 135–8).

Within each sphere, three further categories of power interact: material capabilities; ideas (of which there are two kinds); and institutions. Material capabilities refer to productive and destructive power potentials, such as technological and organizational capabilities (Cox and Schechter 2002, p. 98). The first type of ideas consists of *intersubjective* meanings, defined by Cox as 'those shared notions of the nature of social relations which tend to perpetuate habits and expectations of behaviour', while the second are collective images of social order held by different groups. These include collective views as to what constitutes the legitimacy of prevailing power relations and the meaning of justice. Institutions are the means through which a particular order is stabilized and perpetuated (ibid., p. 99).

This approach can be adapted to TBGI research. As illustrated in Figure 14.1,[2] the sphere of social forces of production can be translated into the social forces of production in TBG eco-certification formations, such as the various social forces that facilitate and regulate the production process. The sphere of forms of state can be translated into national and subnational, or territorial, eco-certification formations. The world order level of activity can be translated into transnational or global eco-certification formations, including formal transnational certification initiatives (for example, MSC and ethical eco-certification initiatives) as well as the broader ideas and institutions in which these are embedded. It

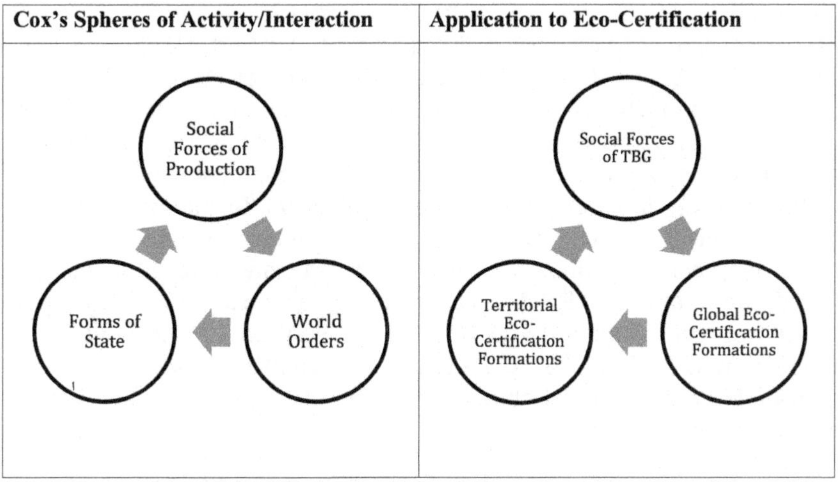

Source: Adapted from Cox 1987, 1996.

Figure 14.1 The Coxian approach to historical structures and its application to eco-certification

is important to note that this framework does not imply that actual eco-certification initiatives exist isolated within one of the three spheres. The spheres interact and are mutually constitutive. Actual eco-certification initiatives, this heuristic framework suggests, will tend to interact with and integrate ideas and institutions of the other spheres of activity/interaction.

Each sphere is, in turn, shaped by the interaction of categories of power: ideas, material capabilities, and institutions. In the eco-certification context, these include, respectively: 1) the near-hegemonic commitment by various social forces (for example, various corporations, environmental NGOs, and small-scale producers) to ideas of good governance, transparency, sustainability, and market mechanisms; 2) the material, technological, organizational, and wealth resource capacity for developing knowledge and strategies for assessing production, changing practices, and reorganizing supply chains; and 3) the institutions of multi-stakeholder collaboration, and the tools and techniques of standardization, certification, traceability, labelling, and branding.

The degree to which actual eco-certification initiatives reflect the ideas, interests, and material capabilities associated with particular spheres of activity will depend on the interactions among the forces of power. For example, in the cases below, including the MSC and alternatives, all eco-certification initiatives integrate specific production-focused standards (institutions) defined by specific ideas (principles) of sustainable or responsible fishing. Across the cases, there is also a trend of creating ideational, discursive, and technical links to state and international-based norms and institutions of fisheries management. The eco-certification approaches differ, however, in terms of scalar and social development emphasis.

From a Coxian perspective, eco-certification formations can also be distinguished into three contrasting strategic governance models of development: neoliberal, embedded liberal, and alter-globalization (Reed and Mukherjee-Reed 2012). The programs examined below tend to fall between neoliberal and embedded liberal governance and development models. None of the programs currently embraces a strong alter-globalization model that might form the basis of a progressive counter-hegemonic movement.

14.3 EXPLAINING THE EMERGENCE AND PROLIFERATION OF TBG IN FISHERIES

In the 1990s, in response to the perceived failure of international and national fisheries management, environmental non-governmental organizations (NGOs) and industry collaborators pioneered the development of voluntary market-based instruments to encourage change in buyers' or consumers' decisions and in fishing practices (Gulbrandsen 2010; Kalfagianni and Pattberg 2013). While a plethora of eco-certification initiatives emerged in fisheries (Parkes et al. 2010), the starting point for most analyses of TBGIs in the fisheries sector is the MSC. Created in the late 1990s through a partnership between Unilever and the WWF, the MSC's integrated third-party certification, eco-labelling, and traceability program has become the most influential TBG initiative in the sector by securing commitments from large North American and European buyers (for example, retailers and food service companies) to source MSC-certified seafood (Ponte 2012). By 2017, over 300 fisheries in more than 30 countries, accounting for about 10 per cent of the world's wild capture harvest, were certified to the MSC's standard for 'sustainable and well managed' fisheries (MSC 2017). However, new certification, eco-labelling, and traceability programs proliferated in the wake of the rise of the MSC, particularly in the late 2000s and early 2010s. While a wide range of small and large producers have enrolled in MSC certification, with geographic concentration in the Global North, the MSC's fragile relationship with political economies of production facilitated territorial and ethical eco-certification counter-movements.

Four production-related factors, including issues involving the interaction between social forces of production and the MSC/global eco-certification formation, have contributed to the proliferation of territorial and ethical eco-certification initiatives. The first two factors concern the relationship between the MSC standard and political economies of production. First, the lack of sensitivity to existing national fisheries management contexts provides some of the impetus for producers and their state and non-state sponsors embedded in particular jurisdictions to resist the MSC and initiate alternatives that better suit their interests and aspirations (Foley and Havice 2016; Potts et al. 2016). Unlike the MSC, the Forest Stewardship Council (FSC) mandates the development of context-sensitive national or subnational standards that are consistent with the FSC principles and criteria. This grants a measure of authority and legitimacy to local initiatives and political economies (Auld and Cashore 2012). The MSC, however, relies on strategic outreach offices to interact with state management regimes and producer interests, with no formal incorporation of national contexts in its standard-setting or institutional designs.

Second, the MSC's standard for sustainable and well-managed fisheries does not include principles and criteria related to social development. It is focused on ecological principles and criteria, with an emphasis on assessing target fish stock health and fisheries' impacts on ecosystems. It does not cover human rights, labour rights, employment conditions and benefits, or workers' health and safety (Potts et al. 2016, p. 85). Nor does it incorporate economic indices such as complying with local minimum wage laws, paying workers a living wage, or paying producers a premium over the conventional price of a product (ibid., p. 89). The MSC also has no institutional mechanism to distinguish between models of production. Unlike 'shade coffee' labels and similar certification systems (Golden et al. 2010), MSC certification and labelling do not provide consumers with information about whether the fish was caught by large industrial fisheries or small-scale fisheries, nor does the MSC distinguish fishing technologies and methods. This is a primary motivation for various producer-oriented social forces of production (such as small-scale fisheries and grassroots NGOs) to engage in certification initiatives that endorse alternative modes of production.

The third and fourth factors – lack of material rewards and inequity in access – focus on the social development consequences of certification for producers. As for the third factor, as noted above, the MSC does not include a direct benefit mechanism such as requiring buyers to pay fishers a price premium to generate economic rewards for certified producers. Some fisheries have received price premiums as a result of market changes, others have not (Morgan 2004; Mathew 2011), while for others the impact of certification on price change remains unclear relative to other factors (Roheim et al. 2011). Where price premiums exist, they are typically captured by retailers, who do not pass them along to producers (Asche et al. 2015, p. 90; Potts et al. 2016, p. 149). MSC certification can provide producers with a point of difference for product differentiation, which can in theory improve fishers' positions relative to competitors (Morgan 2004; Roheim and Seara 2009), but the advantages of differentiation are often lost as competitors become certified (Goyert et al. 2010; May 2012). At the level of production, evidence suggests that it was not the promise of material rewards but the threat of losing access to existing – mainly North American and European – retail markets that drove much of the early producer interest in MSC certification. Certification can help fisheries access new markets, but it is more commonly sought to maintain access to existing markets controlled by big buyers such as retailers and food service companies that adopt purchasing policies requiring suppliers to have certification (Roheim and Seara 2009; Goyert et al. 2010; Potts et al. 2011).

Finally, and related, for producers, a lack of direct economic rewards from MSC certification is particularly problematic relative to costs of achieving and maintaining certification. While the MSC has attempted to make its certification system relevant and more accessible to small-scale fisheries, particularly those in developing countries, the direct and indirect costs of certification remain a major problem from the producers' perspective. The financial and human resource demands of acquiring and maintaining MSC certification suggest that a relatively high level of capacity is required for marginalized producers to engage in the program. External financial support for small-scale producers will likely remain a common feature in MSC certification as it has for FSC certification (Parkes et al. 2010; Tikina et al. 2010). Larger-scale industrial producers have scale advantages and often have larger data sets that are critical in certification assessments (Potts et al. 2011, p. 62), but even they remain concerned about certification costs (Foley and Havice 2016). A result is that producers often put pressure on states to subsidize the material costs of acquiring and maintaining certification, thus generating interactions with states. Nevertheless, in the absence of more equitable access, initiatives such as the MSC 'may well be leading to deeper isolation of many of the poorest would-be providers to international markets' (Potts et al. 2016, p. 150).

The stark contrast between a key rationale for MSC certification – that producers will benefit and be rewarded for sustainable practices – and the actual problematic outcomes of certification is indicative of more fundamental contradictions in global elite justifications for market-based interventions as empowering marginalized groups (Carodenuto and Cashore, Chapter 10). This is partly why the MSC can be understood as relying on and reinforcing a neoliberal model of governance and development. The MSC's model of implementation and development is characterized by a strong commitment to market forces. Ideationally, it places faith in the neoliberal values of the market, individualism (with consumers as key agents), NGO-corporate partnerships, and devolution of authority (Konefal 2012). The MSC's tenuous relationship to principles and outcomes of social development is a primary cause for the emergence of ethical eco-certification initiatives that seek to alter the terms and conditions under which some producers interact with the global economy.

14.4 TERRITORIAL ECO-CERTIFICATION FORMATIONS

The discussion above highlighted the MSC's lack of formal engagement with national fisheries production and management contexts. Despite this failure, in some situations, internal relations between producers and states are being adjusted to the global market imperatives of the MSC (Gale and Haward 2011; Foley 2013; Gulbrandsen 2014) and of sustainability verification and assurance more generally. In other situations (sometimes simultaneously), new territorial eco-certification formations are emerging as social forces of production resist the MSC and incorporate global market norms and institutions into their domestic or local strategies (Foley and Havice 2016). By territorial eco-certification, I refer to a process similar to what Cox theorized as the internationalization of the state, whereby national policies and practices have been adjusted to the exigencies of the world economy (Cox 1987, p. 253). But rather than focus on state institutions, this analysis focuses on external pressures and realignments of internal power relations between producers and states in the development of territorial but not necessarily state-administered eco-certification.

At the supra-national scale, an example includes the unsuccessful Nordic eco-certification initiatives initiated while the MSC was under development in the late 1990s (Gulbrandsen 2009). Other new national and subnational eco-certification initiatives have been institutionalized since 2007, in part because of the absence of local flexibility in MSC standard definition and development (Potts et al. 2016, p. 108). These include the Marine Eco-Label Japan, which was established in 2007; the Iceland Responsible Fisheries eco-label and certification program, which was developed between 2007 and 2009; the Alaska Responsible Fisheries Management Certification program, which was created in 2010; and a Canadian pilot project that was initiated in 2011 but failed to materialize (Foley and Hébert 2013; Foley and Havice 2016). All of these programs were motivated by influential and relatively powerful domestic producer associations' interests in developing an alternative to the MSC so as to reassert control over the regulatory relations of production, to enhance control over communication of production and regulatory practices, and to assert a territorial brand of eco-certification (Foley and Havice 2016). None of these programs are administered by governments, however.

Yet interactions with state and international ideas and institutions are critical to each initiative. The state interacts with and facilitates the development of each by supporting the establishment of programs, providing the institutional setting through which programs are established, providing stakeholder representation on new programs, and providing research and technical capacity (Foley and Havice 2016). Internationally, all established initiatives are designed to meet the specifications outlined in the United Nations Food and Agriculture Organization Code of Conduct for Responsible Fisheries (FAO Code of Conduct) (FAO 1995) and Guidelines for Ecolabelling of Fish and Fishery Products from Marine Capture Fisheries (FAO Guidelines) (FAO 2005). Thus, these initiatives are not only embedded in territorial social relations of production but also in international governance norms and institutions, demonstrating the deep interactions among social forces of production, state-civil society complexes and world order spheres in the territorial eco-certification movement (Foley 2017).

While territorial eco-certification challenges the MSC, most existing cases nevertheless currently constitute neoliberal models of governance and development that share important similarities with the MSC. Like the MSC, these initiatives focus largely on stock-centric and ecosystem notions of sustainable or responsible fishing. Like other forms of non-state and intergovernmental standardization (Wood 2012), both the MSC and most territorial eco-certification initiatives are devoid of substantive social principles and criteria that might support social development purposes. Like the MSC, moreover, alternatives developed at national and subnational levels also reflect the hope that compliance with, and transparency of, the sustainable and responsible fishing messaging enabled by certification and labelling standards will afford producers advantages through market forces.

14.5 ETHICAL ECO-CERTIFICATION FORMATIONS

Unlike the fair trade certification movement, fisheries certification was not born out of a movement for social justice. While certified fair trade farming movements gained momentum as a development strategy for small-scale Southern producers rooted in North-South trade solidarity, the MSC developed a narrow focus on environmental sustainability (Boström et al. 2015). Although social issues have not been a major driver in seafood standards, particularly in the wild caught sector (Potts et al. 2016, p. 87), a number of eco-certification initiatives emerged in the Global North in the early 2010s in the wild capture sector that seek to empower structurally disadvantaged producers in both the Global North and South.

For the creators of some emerging eco-certification initiatives, standards and principles of sustainable fishing ought to include producer-oriented economic and social dimensions of sustainability. For example, in 2007, Naturland announced its intention to develop a standard designed to improve the livelihoods of fishers anywhere in the world (Auld 2014, p. 212). Its standard includes social responsibility provisions, including those for human rights, freedom to accept or reject employment, freedom of association and access to trade unions, children's rights, health and safety, and general employment conditions (Naturland 2015, 2016). Fair Trade USA announced plans to create the first Fair Trade Capture Fisheries Standard in 2014 to remedy the absence of social criteria in fisheries certification. It aimed to incorporate social accountability and industrial health and safety requirements and would be limited to small-scale, artisanal fisheries (Fair Trade USA 2014). Another initiative released in 2014, the Artysanal standard and label, is also limited to artisanal, coastal, and smaller scale fisheries. This France-based initiative distinguishes fishing methods and technologies and includes social and economic considerations (Artysanal 2014). These certification programs promote specific ethics of production with the aim of distinguishing, recognizing, and rewarding particular social relations of production and of empowering structurally disadvantaged social forces of production.

A related approach, not formally involving certification, makes the social relations of production visible through independent traceability standards. New collaborations between small-scale producers and NGOs have also emerged to endorse not only specific modes of production but also groups and individuals who engage in small-scale production methods. In an effort to raise its profile, for example, the Artysanal program collaborated with the ThisFish traceability program, which is administered by the NGO EcoTrust Canada (ThisFish 2014). This program uses a fish tagging and tracking system that enables consumers to learn about who caught the fish they buy and communicates information to individual harvesters through a website. EcoTrust shares the Artysanal program's triple bottom line approach with a mission around integrating economic, social, and environmental values, and seeks to explore ways to empower producers to extract more value out of supply chains.

These ethical eco-certification initiatives have limited interactions with states but substantial interactions with international (non-state and state-based) ideas and institutions. Examples of interactions with the state include Artysanal standard's decision not to define small-scale fisheries but instead to rely on the definitions of particular jurisdictions where fisheries operate. Another is the Fair Trade USA standard's requirement of compliance with national law and local legislation as a minimum baseline (Fair Trade USA 2014). Initiatives also interact with non-state and international institutions. One example of interaction with non-state institutions is provided by Naturland, a German-based organic certifier that is accredited by IFOAM – Organics International (formerly the International Federation of Organic Agriculture Movements). Fair Trade USA represents another example: some of its environmental criteria will be based on MSC criteria, and fisheries that are already MSC-certified will automatically pass certain parts of the assessment focusing on ecological criteria. The France-based Artysanal program was developed through an international collaboration between SMART Association, the World Forum of Fish Harvesters and Fish Workers, and Eurofins Certification, the authorized certification body for Artysanal. ThisFish administers a traceability data standard, but it does not develop its own rules around the sustainability of fisheries or seafood. It instead shows eco-ratings of various other programs such as the MSC, Ocean Wise, SeaChoice and Seafood Watch on its system as a way of communicating environmentally relevant information to buyers such as retailers, chefs, and consumers.

Like the MSC and territorial eco-certification initiatives, interactions with international institutions such as the FAO and the International Organization for Standardization (ISO) appear important for ethical eco-certification initiatives. The Fair Trade USA capture fisheries standard claims that its standard follows the FAO Code of Conduct, the FAO guidelines, and a number of International Labour Organization conventions (Fair Trade USA 2014). The Artysanal standard claims it is distinct from other prominent labels by integrating environmental, economic, and social criteria as recommended in the FAO Code of Conduct. The ThisFish program interacts with international norms by distinguishing itself from other standards, including an ISO standard (ISO 12875) for the traceability of finfish released in 2011 and the European Union's 'catch certificate' regulation requiring validation from governments of exporting countries that imported seafood came from a legal fishery (ThisFish 2012). Like the MSC and in contrast to territorial eco-certification initiatives, these ethical eco-certification initiatives are also internationalized in the sense of supporting producers from different jurisdictions. The Fair Trade USA approach is limited in that it will assess and certify only US companies and their international suppliers. The Artysanal standard is more ambitious as it was created to 'drive development in the fishing industry toward responsible fishing from artisanal, small-scale, coastal fisheries worldwide' (Artysanal 2014, p. 14). Its aim is 'to become internationally recognized, and it is open to any fishery (both from developing and developed countries) that complies with the related specification requirements' (ibid.). Thus, while ethical eco-certification initiatives are oriented toward supporting specific social relations of production, the programs interact with international and transnational institutions and norms. And although ethical eco-certification initiatives interact less with states than territorial eco-certification initiatives, the varied interactions with state-civil society and, more importantly, world order spheres of activity suggest that Cox's 'production and power' approach has analytical and explanatory value.

These ethical eco-certification initiatives have fundamental goals to transform power relations in the social and economic arenas so as to render visible, and provide more opportunities for, structurally disadvantaged producers and workers. The initiatives embrace an approach more attentive to questions of social development for marginalized producers and promote alternative versions of what constitutes relevant knowledge about production processes and how and to whom to communicate that knowledge (Parlee and Wiber 2011). However, while these approaches explicitly privilege structurally disadvantaged producers, they also contain elements of a neoliberal model of governance and development by taking the prevailing consumption structures as given and placing substantial faith in the capacity and willingness of institutional and corporate buyers and consumers to deliver material value and benefits to producers. Like both the MSC and territorial eco-certification approaches, these ethical eco-certification initiatives place faith in market mechanisms and do not have the capacity for, or a strategy to achieve, structural transformation. While Fair Trade USA includes an institutional mechanism to require buyers to pay fishers a fair trade premium, the impact of the premium depends on the fluctuations of market-driven prices. There is no mechanism for general structural change or an alteration of prevailing power relations. Each ethical eco-certification initiative shares the MSC's faith in the power of transparency and market mechanisms. The programs, in other words, are more akin to embedded liberalism than alter-globalization.

14.6 DISCUSSION: TRANSNATIONAL BUSINESS GOVERNANCE INTERACTIONS

This section reflects on the implications of the analysis above for the 'dimensions of interaction' in the TBGI framework, in particular drivers and shapers, mechanisms and pathways, characters and effects of interaction (Eberlein et al. 2014). In terms of drivers and shapers of interactions, a key feature driving proliferation and competition in the fisheries sector is the effort of social forces of production to re-embed political economic interests and values in eco-certification initiatives and in trade relations more generally. This embedding emphasizes specific and competing political economies of eco-certification, which I have theorized as territorial and ethical eco-certification initiatives. These trends demonstrate not only how industry characteristics drive key aspects of TBGIs in the fisheries sector, but also how multi-faceted and contested producer interests specifically drive competition and proliferation. The distinction between large-scale industrial and small-scale artisanal fisheries, though complex and blurred in many contexts, provides a key wedge in the global politics of fisheries certification and distinguishes ethical eco-certification initiatives from both the MSC and most territorial eco-certification programs.

Cultures, discourses, mentalities, epistemic communities, and ideational factors also drive TBGIs in the sector. The cultural politics of neoliberal globalization and faith in market mechanisms constitute a meta-ideational and institutional 'world order' driving force that operates across all spheres of interaction and in all eco-certification initiatives. The development of some territorial eco-certification initiatives was driven by deeply cultural and nationalistic politics of nationally and sub-nationally embedded seafood producers. For ethical eco-certification initiatives, we observe a different set of cultural discourse committed to small-scale, artisanal fish workers who are often situated in vulnerable rural coastal communities where there are few economic development alternatives to fish production.

Mechanisms and pathways of interaction include various tools and techniques of governance. The MSC, territorial, and ethical eco-certification formations constitute hybrid governance through which non-state and state norms, practices, tools, and techniques are enrolled in influencing conditions of production and market access. Rule referencing and conditional rule referencing were observed across cases and scales of interaction as various initiatives seek to enhance legitimacy, capacities, and symbolic resources. The FAO is the most significant international rule reference point.

In terms of the character of interactions, we also observe competition, coordination, and co-optation, often simultaneously. We observe competition for authority over key terms such as who and what defines sustainable and responsible fisheries. We also observe competition over regulatory turf, reputation, and legitimacy in the rise of territorial eco-certification initiatives. Territorial eco-certification initiatives created as distinct alternatives to the MSC nevertheless adopt policies and procedures shared with the MSC, with most claiming compliance with FAO fisheries management norms, many of which were developed before the emergence of the MSC. Ethical eco-certification initiatives coordinate by 'carving out' niches (Eberlein et al. 2014, p. 22) in the sector as they seek to fill a perceived gap in social principles and criteria. Competition and coordination also exist together, which is particularly salient with the trend across the cases to incorporate FAO norms and guidelines. This trend is important evidence of the value of applying Cox's approach, which anticipates that the most promising hegemonic or counter-hegemonic strategies will integrate ideas and institutions of the social forces of production, state-civil society complexes and world order.

The effects of interactions within and between eco-certification formations are both competitive and mutually reinforcing. Patterns of emulation around the FAO guidelines on eco-labelling enhance legitimacy and credibility in the increasingly competitive field (Foley and Havice 2016). The continuities of market-orientation have also created a mutually reinforcing legitimacy dynamic (Meidinger 2009, p. 249) around faith in the idea that voluntary eco-certification initiatives will generate win-win governance and economic outcomes. However, even initiatives that include more explicit principles of social sustainability and responsibility for producers do not necessarily have a greater direct impact on social development. As Magnus Boström and others argue with reference to an inquiry into the concept of social sustainability in standards more broadly, 'even in the most contrasting case – Fairtrade – social sustainability is shaped and narrowed through processes of bureaucratization, translation, and adoption into local settings' (Boström et al. 2015, p. 151). Ultimately, they conclude, 'integrating the social and the environmental in policy, administration, and management will require a long-term learning process' (ibid., p. 152). The impacts of proliferation and interaction ultimately remain an open question, though the patterns of interaction and change do not appear fundamentally transformative at present.

14.7 CONCLUSION: TOWARD COUNTER-HEGEMONIC MOVEMENTS?

Producer interests and identities are not homogenous. The proliferation of territorial and ethical fisheries eco-certification initiatives in the last decade reflects not only the agency and interests of producers, but also the varied relations and interests of production and divergent producer visions of development. Territorial and ethical eco-certification initiatives reflect different strategies to distinguish and reward different political economies of production and different models of (sustainable or responsible) development. The strategies of governance and development constitute, in effect, differing visions not just of production but also of social reproduction: the relationship between the human and ecological conditions of livelihood and survival and the historical structures that depend on those social and ecological conditions (Bakker and Gill 2003).

While the integration of producer interests with new eco-certification initiatives can be interpreted as enhancing participatory governance through local or 'stakeholder' ownership, it also creates competition, fragmentation and confusion (Potts et al. 2016, p. 109). The general response of each alternative is to integrate internationally recognized norms and institutions into eco-certification, particularly the fisheries management principles and eco-labelling guidelines of the FAO. By translating Cox's 'production and power' approach to an analysis of these dynamics, we can see that territorial and ethical eco-certification initiatives compete with the MSC in terms of representing and recognizing different social relations of production, but share the MSC's commitment to world order norms and institutions such as the FAO and, more generally, to neoliberal forms of governance and development.

The relationship between fisheries eco-certification and hegemony is ambiguous. Like the forestry eco-certification movement, fisheries eco-certification initiatives are products of the historical forces of neoliberal global political economy. The FSC has been conceptualized as a product of neoliberal world order but with counter-hegemonic potential relative to eco-certification alternatives developed collaboratively by industrial producers and states (Bloomfield 2012). Its counter-hegemonic potential lies mainly in its institutional structure as an open multi-stakeholder forum (ibid.) and in its inclusion of social principles and criteria. The MSC, however, uses a more closed multi-stakeholder institutional structure and lacks a social category of principles and criteria (Gulbrandsen 2010). Territorial eco-certification initiatives tend to share the MSC's core focus on ecological sustainability, while ethical eco-certification initiatives tend to offer competing visions of (sustainable or responsible) development that seek to empower structurally disadvantaged producers and workers. As currently constituted, the most significant potential of ethical eco-certification initiatives is their ability to influence ideas (including values and principles of sustainable or responsible fisheries) and institutional contexts in global fisheries governance debates. This influence might help shift policy debates away from conceptions of sustainable and responsible fisheries consistent with a neoliberal globalization model of development to conceptions that challenge existing power structures by including ethical and social justice considerations. It might help shift the agenda, in other words, away from neoliberal models of governance and development toward embedded liberal or alter-globalization models of governance and development. However, while ethical eco-certification initiatives can pose ideational and institutional challenges to prevailing power relations that privilege industrial producer and corporate interests, the counter-hegemonic potential of existing approaches is significantly constrained by the structural and material disadvantages of the initiatives and by the passive approach of voluntary, market-oriented eco-certification.

To be counter-hegemonic in the sense used by Cox, initiatives will likely need to integrate social relations of production with state and world order ideas and institutions in a way that can meaningfully challenge the prevailing power relations and systematically support structurally disadvantaged producers. An important constraint, a Coxian perspective tells us, is that states and international organizations will tend 'to develop governance strategies based on particular types of economic development models that reflect the interests of the actors that constitute their basis of support' (Reed and Mukherjee-Reed 2012, p. 369). This partly explains why existing territorial eco-certification initiatives tend to reflect the interests of large, industrial-dominated national or sub-national producer associations (Foley and Havice 2016) and why many states tend to support domestic industry efforts to achieve MSC certification. Another constraint includes 'new constitutionalist' institutions, like the World Trade Organization, which facilitate market-driven and 'trade-friendly' voluntary mechanisms of governance but make it difficult for governments to formally endorse or institutionalize voluntary standards (Gill 1995, 1998). It is important to enhance our understanding of these constraints through further research in order to understand the challenges of, and opportunities for, supporting eco-certification as a counter-hegemonic movement.

What is needed is a new historic bloc of collaborations (or public-private partnerships) between political and civil society that can overcome these constraints to form the basis of a new global fisheries governance regime committed to a form of sustainable and responsible development that meaningfully includes social and economic principles and that generates material protections and security for disadvantaged and vulnerable producers and workers. Two paths to such a counter-hegemonic eco-certification movement are conceivable from a Coxian perspective. A first might involve the MSC transforming its approach by integrating social standards of sustainability and engaging more formally with state-civil society complexes and international institutions (such as the FAO) as a strategy for expanding embedded liberalism in fisheries. Since its inception, some producers and civil society actors have pressured the MSC to incorporate social principles into its standard, but the MSC has resisted such moves. While some industry actors continue to pressure the MSC to incorporate social dimensions of sustainability into its standard, producers are divided on the issue of whether and how to engage the social question (Kearns 2017). For this reason and given that the MSC is already deeply embedded in industrial and corporate structures, even if the MSC incorporates social principles into its approach, it will more likely develop an approach that remains neoliberal or a soft embedded liberal approach.

A second, more bottom-up approach might involve the strategic coalescing of an ethical eco-certification initiative (most of which currently operate transnationally) with a territorial eco-certification approach. For this approach to challenge the prevailing power relations in the global political economy of fisheries, social movements from civil society, including producers and progressive environmental NGOs, will need to foster new identities of shared interests between seafood workers and transnational economic interests, from financial and trading interests to service workers and consumers. To develop further hegemonic potential, additional political action and organization within nation state and international institutions and structures will then be required to institutionalize an integrated and ethically based alter-globalization model of governance and development.

NOTES

1. The author would like to thank Stepan Wood, Derek Hall, and Sophia Carodenuto for helpful comments and suggestions on earlier drafts of this paper. This research was supported by the Social Sciences and Humanities Research Council of Canada.
2. This adaptation draws parallels to a recent study by Westermann, who adapts the neo-Gramscian approach to the study of migration systems (Westermann 2013).

REFERENCES

Artysanal (2014), *Artysanal® Standard: For Artisanal, Coastal and Small-Scale Fisheries,* Montélimar, France: SMART Association.

Asche, F., T.A. Larsen, M.D. Smith, G. Sogn-Grundvåg and J.A. Young (2015), 'Pricing of eco-labels with retailer heterogeneity', *Food Policy*, **53**, 82–93.

Auld, G. (2012), 'The Marine Stewardship Council', in Darryl Reed et al. (eds), *Business Regulation and Non-State Actors: Whose Standards? Whose Development?* New York: Routledge, pp. 178–89.

Auld, G. (2014), *Constructing Private Governance: The Rise and Evolution of Forest, Coffee, and Fisheries Certification*. New Haven, CT: Yale University Press.
Auld, G. and B. Cashore (2012), 'The Forest Stewardship Council', in Reed, Utting and Mukherjee-Reed (eds), *Business Regulation and Non-State Actors: Whose Standards? Whose Development?* New York: Routledge, pp. 134–47.
Auld, G. and B. Cashore (2013), 'Mixed signals: NGO campaigns and non-state market-driven (NSMD) governance in an export-oriented country', *Canadian Public Policy*, **39**, 143–56.
Bakker, I. and S. Gill (2003), *Power, Production and Social Reproduction: Human in/Security in the Global Political Economy*, Basingstoke, Hampshire: Palgrave MacMillan.
Bloomfield, M.J. (2012), 'Is forest certification a hegemonic force? The FSC and its challenges', *Journal of Environment & Development*, **21** (4), 391–413.
Boström, M., A.C. Vifell, M. Klintman, L. Soneryd, K.T. Hallström and R. Thedvall (2015), 'Social sustainability requires social sustainability: procedural prerequisites for reaching substantive goals', *Nature and Culture*, **10** (2), 131–56.
Büthe, T. (2010), 'Global private politics: a research agenda', *Business and Politics*, **12** (3), article 12.
Cashore, B., G. Auld and D. Newsom (2004), *Governing Through Markets: Forest Certification and the Emergence of Non-State Authority*. New Haven, CN: Yale University Press.
Cox, R.W. (1987), *Production, Power, and World Order*, New York: Columbia University Press.
Cox, R.W. (1996), 'Social forces, states, and world orders', in Robert W. Cox with Timothy J. Sinclair (eds), *Approaches to World Order*, New York, NY: Cambridge University Press, pp. 85–124.
Cox, R.W. with M.G. Schechter (2002), *The Political Economy of a Plural World: Critical Reflections on Power, Morals and Civilization*. London: Routledge.
Eberlein, B., K.W. Abbott, J. Black, E. Meidinger and S. Wood (2014), 'Transnational business governance interactions: conceptualization and framework for analysis', *Regulation & Governance*, **8** (1), 1–21.
Fair Trade USA (2014), *Fair Trade USA Capture Fisheries Standard: Draft Version 1.0*, Oakland, CA: Fair Trade USA.
FAO (United Nations Food and Agriculture Association) (1995), *Code of Conduct for Responsible Fisheries*, Rome: FAO.
FAO (2005), *FAO Guidelines for the Ecolabelling of Fish and Fisheries Products from Marine Capture Fisheries*, Rome: FAO.
Foley, P. (2013), 'National government responses to Marine Stewardship Council (MSC) certification: insights from Atlantic Canada', *New Political Economy*, **18** (2), 284–307.
Foley, P. (2017), 'The territorialization of transnational sustainability governance: production, power and globalization in Iceland's fisheries', *Environmental Politics*, **26** (5), 915–37.
Foley, P. and E. Havice (2016), 'The rise of territorial eco-certifications: new politics of transnational sustainability governance in the capture fisheries sector', *Geoforum*, **69** (February), 24–33.
Foley, P. and K. Hébert (2013), 'Alternative regimes of transnational environmental certification: governance, marketization, and place in Alaska's salmon fisheries', *Environment and Planning A*, **45** (11), 2734–51.
Gale, F. (2014), 'Australian forest governance: a comparison of two certification schemes', *Australian Journal of Environmental Management*, **21** (4), 396–412.

Gale, F. and M. Haward (2011), *Global Commodity Governance: State Responses to Sustainable Forest and Fisheries Certification*, Houndmills, Basingstoke, Hampshire: Palgrave Macmillan.

Gill, S. (1995), 'Globalisation, market civilisation, and disciplinary neoliberalism', *Millennium: Journal of International Studies*, **24** (3), 399–423.

Gill, S. (1998), 'New constitutionalism, democratisation and global political economy', *Pacifica Review*, **10** (1), 23–38.

Golden, J.S., K.J. Dooley, J.M. Anderies, B.H. Thompson, G. Gereffi and L. Pratson (2010), 'Sustainable product indexing: navigating the challenge of ecolabeling', *Ecology and Society*, **15** (3), article 8.

Goyert, W., R. Sagarin and J. Annala (2010), 'The promise and pitfalls of Marine Stewardship Council certification: Maine lobster as a case study', *Marine Policy*, **34** (5), 1103–09.

Gulbrandsen, L. (2009), 'The emergence and effectiveness of the Marine Stewardship Council', *Marine Policy*, **33**, 654–60.

Gulbrandsen, L. (2010), *Transnational Environmental Governance: The Origins and Effects of the Certification of Forests and Fisheries,* Cheltenham, UK and Northampton, MA, USA: Edward Elgar.

Gulbrandsen, L. (2014), 'Dynamic governance interactions: evolutionary effects of state responses to non-state certification programs', *Regulation & Governance*, **8** (1), 74–92.

Havice, E. and A. Iles (2015), 'Shaping the aquaculture sustainability assemblage: revealing the rule-making behind the rules', *Geoforum*, **58**, 27–37.

Kalfagianni, A. and P. Pattberg (2013), 'Fishing in muddy waters: exploring the conditions for effective governance of fisheries and aquaculture', *Marine Policy*, **38**, 124–32.

Kearns, M. (2017), 'Urged by industry, MSC weighs adding social sustainability standards', *SeafoodSource*, 27 April, accessed 2 September 2019 at https://www.seafoodsource.com/news/environment-sustainability/how-should-certifiers-approach-social-sustainability--sanford-ceo-top-industry-panel-weighs-in.

Konefal, J. (2012), 'Environmental movements, market-based approaches, and neoliberalization: a case study of the sustainable seafood movement', *Organization & Environment*, **26** (3), 336–52.

Mathew, S. (2011), 'The costs of certification', *SAMUDRA Report*, **58**, 41–5.

May B. (2012), 'What Alaska's pullout tells us about the Marine Stewardship Council', *Robertsbridge*, 31 January, accessed 2 September 2019 at https://www.robertsbridgegroup.com/our-views/alaska-pullou.

Meidinger, E. (2009), 'Private import safety regulation and transnational new governance', in Cary Coglianese, Adam Finkel, and David Zaring (eds), *Import Safety: Regulatory Governance in the Global Economy*, Philadelphia: University of Pennsylvania Press, pp. 233–53.

Morgan, G. (2004), 'Report into the Marine Stewardship Council Re-certification of the Western Rock Lobster Fishery', Prepared for the Western Australian Fishing Industry Council (WAFIC), 27 August.

MSC (Marine Stewardship Council) (2017), *MSC in Numbers*, accessed 31 December 2017 at https://www.msc.org/global-impacts/key-facts-about-msc.

Naturland (2015), *Naturland: Welcome to Naturland, Version 05/2015*. Gräfelfing, Germany: Naturland.

Naturland (2016), *Naturland Standards for Sustainable Capture Fishery, Version 05/2016*. Gräfelfing, Germany: Naturland.

Parkes, G., J.A. Young, S.F. Walmsley, R. Abel, J. Harman, P. Horvat, A. Lem, A. MacFarlene, M. Mens and C. Nolan (2010), 'Behind the signs: a global review of fish sustainability information schemes', *Reviews in Fisheries Science*, **18** (4), 344–56.

Parlee, C.E. and M. Wiber (2011), 'Who is governing food systems? Power and legal pluralism in lobster traceability', *The Journal of Legal Pluralism*, **43**, 121–48.

Ponte, S. (2012), 'The Marine Stewardship Council (MSC) and the making of a market for "sustainable fish"', *Journal of Agrarian Change*, **12** (2–3), 300–315.

Potts, T. (2011), *Sustainable Seafood and Eco-Labelling Research Report: The Marine Stewardship Council, UK Consumers, and the UK Fishing Industry*, Oban, UK: Scottish Association for Marine Science.

Potts, J., A. Wilkings, M. Lynch and S. McFatridge (2016), *State of Sustainability Initiatives Review: Standards and the Blue Economy*, Winnipeg: International Institute for Sustainable Development.

Raynolds, L.T., D. Murray and A. Heller (2007), 'Regulating sustainability in the coffee sector: a comparative analysis of environmental and social certification and labeling initiatives', *Agriculture and Human Values*, **24** (2), 147–63.

Raynolds, L.T. and J. Wilkinson (2007), 'Fair trade in the agriculture and food sector: analytical dimensions', in L.T. Raynolds, D.L. Murray and J. Wilkinson (eds), *Fair Trade: The Challenges of Transforming Globalization*, London and New York: Routledge, pp. 33–48.

Reed, D. and A. Mukherjee-Reed (2012), 'From non-state regulation to governance? Shifting the site of contestation', in Reed, Utting and Mukherjee-Reed (eds), *Business Regulation and Non-State Actors: Whose Standards? Whose Development?* New York: Routledge, pp. 356–67.

Roheim, C. and T. Seara (2009), *Expected Benefits of Fisheries Certification: Results of a Survey of MSC Fisheries Clients*, Narragansett, RI: URI Sustainable Seafood Initiative.

Roheim, C., F. Asche and J. Insignares (2011), 'The elusive price premium for ecolabelled products: evidence from seafood in the UK market', *Journal of Agricultural Economics*, **62** (3), 655–68.

Smith, T.M. and M. Fischlein (2010), 'Rival private governance networks: competing to define the rules of sustainability performance', *Global Environmental Change*, **20**, 511–22.

ThisFish (2012), *ThisFish Traceability Data Standard 1.0: Draft Document for Public Consultation*', Vancouver: Ecotrust Canada (also online, accessed 2 September 2019, at http://thisfish.info/generic/article/37).

ThisFish (2014), *World's First Small-Scale Fishery Certification Uses ThisFish Traceability*', accessed 2 September 2019 at http://thisfish.info/generic/article/artysanal-iceland

Tikina, A.V., J.L. Innes, R.L. Trosper and B.C. Larson (2010), 'Aboriginal peoples and forest certification: a review of the Canadian situation', *Ecology and Society*, **15** (3), 33.

Utting, P. (2012), 'Introduction: multistakeholder regulation from a development perspective', in Reed, Utting and Mukherjee-Reed (eds), *Business Regulation and Non-State Actors: Whose Standards? Whose Development?* New York: Routledge, pp. 31–48.

Westermann, R. (2013), 'The Neogramscian approach: using "critical" theories to explain migration systems', paper presented at the THEMIS conference, Examining Migration Dynamics: Networks and Beyond, University of Oxford, 24–26 September.

Wood, S. (2012), 'The International Organization for Standardization', in Reed, Utting and Mukherjee-Reed (eds), *Business Regulation and Non-State Actors: Whose Standards? Whose Development?* New York: Routledge, pp. 81–94.

Wood, S., K. Abbott, J. Black, B. Eberlein and E. Meidinger (2015), 'The interactive dynamics of transnational business governance: a challenge for transnational legal theory', *Transnational Legal Theory*, **6** (2), 333–69.

15. Private ordering and transnational social justice: The Forest Stewardship Council's advocacy of free, prior and informed consent

Natalie Oman

15.1 INTRODUCTION

The question of whether the burgeoning human rights commitments of private transnational actors could impact public governance of social justice issues opens a new vista of dangers and empowering possibilities. On one hand, worries about private standard-setting often relate to the absence of traditional rule of law requirements that legitimize government rule-making, such as checks and balances, accountability and transparency. Concerns also relate to promotion of a social justice agenda that may not align with local values and could be regarded as reflecting alien and inappropriate priorities. On the other hand, rights-enhancing possibilities can flow from the establishment of a popular mandate for a locally appropriate social justice agenda, and from the opportunities for the empowerment of marginalized actors that could result.

This chapter examines a phenomenon at the intersection of these dangers and possibilities: the adoption and development of an emerging customary international legal norm by a transnational hybrid actor. It surveys the promotion by the Canadian chapter of the Forest Stewardship Council (FSC) of the norm of free, prior and informed consent (FPIC). The FSC recently revisited its early interpretation of FPIC and advocated a strengthened version of the norm that compares favourably with its most robust readings by international organizations and states and situates the FSC, and especially FSC Canada, at the leading edge of indigenous rights norm development in transnational governance.

The FSC's recent history reveals how transnational business governance interactions (TBGIs) can offer a means to develop, import and apply elements of the powerful international discourse of human rights to strengthen domestic standards and empower weaker actors. Additionally, it offers insight into the potentially influential role in these interactions of an often neglected class of non-state actor – the transnational indigenous peoples' movement.

The chapter argues that private transnational actors' human rights commitments can impact public governance of social justice issues indirectly, by contributing to the evolution of customary international law (CIL). It explores three hypotheses that emerged from the author's research, which included interviews with members and officials of FSC Canada, FSC International and indigenous forestry initiatives:

1. By changing the frame of reference used to assess the human rights and ecosystem impacts of forestry in accordance with emerging CIL norms, FSC Canada's standard-setting process offers an alternative non-state route to establishing a de facto indigenous veto over forestry projects in Canada.
2. FSC Canada and FSC International's development of a robust FPIC norm is a manifestation of a broader campaign by the global indigenous peoples' movement to use international human rights law to advocate indigenous rights, drawing in part on indigenous legal norms.
3. This movement has the potential to impact the core meaning of indigenous rights in CIL, widening the acceptance of 'penumbral' (Hart 1958, p. 607) interpretations of FPIC.

This chapter examines two types of TBGIs: (1) interactions between an emerging CIL norm (FPIC) and a transnational private governance institution (the FSC); and (2) interactions within FSC International and FSC Canada. This examination sheds light on two issues central to the TBGI project: (1) how TBGIs are impacted by, and perhaps in turn impact, processes of CIL formation; and (2) what conditions within a transnational private governance institution enable marginalized actors to exploit interactions strategically to improve social justice outcomes. The chapter argues that private transnational actors' human rights commitments impact public governance of social justice issues indirectly, through their contributions to the evolution of CIL. This study is part of a larger project to reconceptualize the sources of international law to align better with practice – a project that owes much to critical and Third World Approaches to International Law.

To theorize interactions among international legal norms, private governance norms and domestic state law, I turn to the work of H.L.A. Hart. The impact of these mutually ramifying processes of norm consolidation on the content of FPIC is illuminated by Hart's conception of core and penumbra. Hart argued that words and concepts have 'a core of settled meaning' that shades into more ambiguous cases. He termed this zone of contested interpretations the penumbra (Hart 1958, p. 607). Applying Hart's concepts and contemporary international legal theory to the case of the FSC and FPIC, this chapter offers insights into promising mechanisms for empowering marginalized interests through TBGIs, including:

1. The FSC's participatory governance features play a key role in facilitating marginalized actors' creation of opportunities for norm entrepreneurship within the organization;
2. Successful intra- and inter-organizational norm entrepreneurship employed an international legal norm and leveraged the moral suasive force of the international discourse of human rights through an alignment of interests and values; and
3. This may have strengthened the international legal norm of FPIC itself.

15.2 THE FSC'S TRANSNATIONAL BUSINESS GOVERNANCE INTERACTIONS

FSC International is a hybrid civil society-business NGO established in 1993, following the 1992 Rio Earth Summit. The FSC sets voluntary transnational standards for forest management, chain of custody and traceability. Compliant forestry firms are eligible for FSC certificates that provide evidence of social and environmental responsibility. Auditing and certification are performed by third-party organizations accredited by the FSC. The FSC is funded largely by corporate and private charitable funds, along with certification fees. As of April 2019, there were about 198 million hectares of FSC-certified forests in 84 countries. Of these, 50.7 million hectares were in Canada, representing 15 per cent of all Canadian forests and 26 per cent of the total FSC-certified area (FSC International 2019a). The total certified area in Canada grew from 30 569 hectares in 1998 to 50.7 million hectares in early 2019 (FSC International 2019a, 2019b).

The core elements of the FSC's certification scheme are contained in its ten (originally nine) FSC Principles and accompanying Criteria (P&C) (FSC International 2015). The Principles constitute the fundamental rules of forest stewardship. The Criteria elaborate and contextualize the principles. Indicators for each criterion provide performance direction to FSC certificate applicants and auditors. The P&C apply globally and may not be altered at the national or subnational levels. They are elaborated through international generic indicators (IGIs). National forest management standards have been developed in many countries to customize the application of the global P&C and IGIs to fit local conditions. This is accomplished through the development of additional indicators, verifiers and norms, as well as guidance documents and interpretations. All of these bespoke elements that tailor the international P&C and IGIs to particular national contexts are subject to approval by FSC International's Policy and Standards Unit and the FSC International Board's Policy and Standards Committee.

The FSC has continued to develop the P&C through a recursive process involving substantial grassroots input. All aspects of the FSC framework are subject to periodic review and revision, with extensive field testing, public and stakeholder consultations, and educational and consensus-building discussions. The aim of this inclusive system of adaptive improvement is effective implementation and increasing uptake of the FSC framework.

FSC International has a participatory, multi-chambered governance structure involving environmental, economic and social representatives from the Global South and North. The highest-order legislative body is FSC International's General Assembly, which meets roughly triennially. It votes on policy resolutions and elects the FSC's nine-person Board of Directors. The Board is the FSC's executive branch. Its membership is balanced with respect to both the three chambers (economic, social and environmental) and Global North and South. The social chamber has responsibility for indigenous issues; in addition, since 2011 the three chambers have been complemented by the Permanent Indigenous Peoples Committee at the international level.

Uniquely in Canada, a fourth Aboriginal Peoples chamber participates equally alongside the standard three chambers. The FSC Canada General Assembly meets annually, and an executive director reports to the chamber-balanced FSC Canada Board of Directors. At both the international and national levels, a small secretariat assists the executive branch. Should differences of interpretation arise concerning any aspect of the FSC's forest management framework, there is a sophisticated system of dispute resolution that includes rapid resolution requirements at every stage and emphasizes consensual outcomes. This system provides for appeals to FSC International, as well as (in recent years) culturally sensitive dispute resolution mechanisms for indigenous peoples and local communities.

FSC Canada, like the FSC's other national organizations, is involved in both international standard-setting and the generation and refinement of national and local implementation guidelines. This bottom-up institutional governance process has enabled the enhancement of the

FPIC requirement and the deepening of the emphasis on the connection between the FSC's recognition and enforcement of FPIC on the one hand, and the international legal norms discussed below on the other.

15.3 EVOLUTION OF THE FSC'S POLICY ON INDIGENOUS CONSULTATION

From its inception, the FSC committed itself to developing its standard for forest management to reflect evolving environmental, social, legal and economic circumstances. This commitment has been expressed both through FSC International's revisions of the P&C, and the development of customized local standards that adapt the P&C to local conditions.

FSC International's P&C, in their original form, asserted that '[t]he legal and customary rights of indigenous peoples to own, use and manage their lands, territories, and resources shall be recognized and respected' and that 'indigenous peoples shall control forest management on their lands and territories unless they delegate control with free and informed consent to other agencies' (Principle 3 and Criterion 3.1, as originally adopted). This language mirrored the Rio Earth Summit's Forest Principles and Agenda 21, which were cited as the Principle's inspiration. In turn, national and regional FSC standards tailored the international P&C to local circumstances. The FSC British Columbia (FSC BC) standard is an example of the latter process (Tollefson et al. 2008). The FSC BC standard and the people involved in its development had a major influence on subsequent revision of FSC International's and FSC Canada's approaches to indigenous rights.

Between 1996 and 2005, FSC BC developed a regional standard that included a robust interpretation of Criterion 3.1's original requirement to attain the 'free and informed consent' of indigenous peoples (FSC International 2002, Criterion 3.1). The interpretation of free and informed consent advocated by the FSC BC steering committee and advisory teams, which included indigenous actors, reinforced the expectation that forest managers were to exceed existing legal requirements. The FSC BC regional standard states: 'Under no circumstances should certification proceed in the face of dissatisfaction of the affected First Nation(s) regarding management activities within the Management Unit' (FSC Canada 2005, p. 13). The standard also included a strong commitment to ecosystem-based management that reflected the approach employed by indigenous communities in northwestern BC.[1]

This doubling-down on FSC's commitment to recognize indigenous peoples' rights occurred in a climate of increasing indigenous activism in BC. Litigation and protests opposing old-growth logging during the 1970s and 1980s led to judicial recognition of the continuing existence of aboriginal title and rights,[2] which were then affirmed in the 1982 Canadian Constitution.[3] In this rapidly transforming context, the government of BC launched a treaty negotiation process to address the claims of indigenous peoples whose land had never been ceded to the Crown. Previously, the province had steadfastly refused to address indigenous land claims, partly on the ground that this would undercut the province's resource economy by creating an uncertain investment climate.

FSC BC proposed reversing the flow of interpretive authority regarding indigenous claims by beginning with the presumption that claims were legitimate, in line with ILO Convention 169 on Indigenous and Tribal Peoples (ILO C169)[4] and the then-draft United Nations Declaration on the Rights of Indigenous Peoples (UNDRIP). FSC BC used the draft UNDRIP as a guide in formulating the pivotal definitions of 'legal and customary rights' and 'land, territories and resources', thereby endorsing a strong reading of two concepts crucial for the application of FPIC. FSC BC also included an explanatory note in the standard's guidance document indicating that forest managers were expected to respect 'all [relevant] binding international agreements', even those not ratified by Canada (FSC Canada 2005, p. 18). The document then listed ten treaties, including ILO C169, that contained international legal norms that were binding on FSC-certified organizations. In this way, FSC BC established that certificate holders should comply with the highest international norms, even if they exceeded domestic legal requirements for indigenous rights protection. FSC BC did not, however, detail how specific international legal provisions impacted the responsibilities of forest managers. Thus, the elements for a justificatory narrative grounded in international law were present in FSC BC's standard, but not yet positioned to support the shift to free, *prior* and informed consent (FPIC).

Key indigenous players in the BC process, along with more recent FSC Canada members and allies subsequently sought to make more explicit these international legal grounds for recognition of indigenous rights generally and FPIC specifically. The achievements and lessons of the FSC BC process were transmitted by a committed group of actors through the participatory governance structures of the FSC. They were further developed through outreach initiatives created in partnership with the National Aboriginal Forestry Association (NAFA) and an Indigenous Advisory Council jointly appointed by NAFA and the FSC (Tollefson et al. 2008, p. 234). These developments eventually shaped the revision of FSC International's P&C and IGIs between 2009 and 2012.

This dramatic reimagining of FSC International's approach to indigenous rights was signalled by the creation of the Permanent Indigenous Peoples Committee in 2011, and the addition of a single word to the P&C. 'Free and informed consent' in the original P&C became 'free, prior and informed consent' (FSC International 2012b, Criteria 3.2, 3.3, 3.6, 4.2, 4.8), reproducing the UNDRIP terminology. This was the tip of the iceberg: the new standard expanded FPIC requirements to five Criteria under two Principles. It emphasized the significance of engagement and consultation with indigenous peoples, clearly distinguished these from consent and underscored the expectation of consent. To ensure that stakeholders understood these changes, FSC International produced new IGIs and a guide on implementing FPIC, which included an expanded definition of and justification for the indigenous consent requirement and articulated the international legal grounds for the right to FPIC (FSC International 2012a).

Since 2012, FSC Canada has taken the lead on 'mainstreaming' FPIC, comprehensively revising all its standards and policies to align with the FPIC requirements in the new international standard (which was updated in 2015) and adapting them to the complex legal landscape of aboriginal rights in Canada. This included development of the first national FPIC guidance, which identifies 23 FPIC-relevant indicators across four Principles in the draft FSC Canada National Standard and provides an appendix of 25 applicable UNDRIP articles and 13 applicable ILO C169 articles (FSC Canada 2016b, pp. 25, 27, 28). The development of the new national standard entailed an exhaustive process including extensive consultation with stakeholders and donors and 23 trials in public and private forests across the country, both FSC-certified and non-certified, with significant indigenous community participation (FSC Canada 2018a, p. 4). As a result, the new Canadian national standard changed substantially from one draft to the next. It was finalized and submitted to FSC International for approval in 2018 (FSC Canada 2018b). After resolution of FSC International's outstanding concerns, the new standard was launched in June 2019.

This process introduced two key changes: the restriction of FPIC to indigenous peoples, and the introduction of the 'indigenous cultural landscapes' (ICLs) concept. The first change was a reaction to developments at FSC International. The revised P&C of 2012 expanded the scope of FPIC, provided criteria for determining when consent is required and emphasized the need to obtain consent before commencing management activities (FSC International 2012b). FSC International's FPIC implementation guide of the same year asserted that FPIC 'is a right under international law and is an expression of indigenous peoples' collective right to self-determination' and, in some cases, national legislation (FSC International 2012a, p. 16). Crucially, the revised P&C and the FPIC implementation guide extended FPIC beyond indigenous peoples to encompass local communities whose interests might be impacted by forest management (FSC International 2012a, p.6; 2012b, pp. 15–16). The decision to apply FPIC to local communities was not grounded in any intrinsic legal right of such groups in international or domestic law.

This broadening of the scope of FPIC aligned with the *UN-REDD Guidelines on Free, Prior and Informed Consent* (UN-REDD Programme Secretariat 2013), the authoritative source on FPIC at the time. However, in consultation with members, FSC Canada's national standard development group rolled back this change definitively, underscoring the uniquely indigenous character of FPIC in the Canadian context. On the grounds that local communities already possess legal rights rooted in 'general human rights and access to public land' and that no customary rights have been identified for Canadian local communities to date, FSC Canada's December 2016 summary of key changes in its new standard stated: 'This means that the Free, Prior and Informed Consent concept will not be applicable for local communities in this version of the FSC Canada National Forest Management Standard, and will be applicable only to Indigenous Peoples' (FSC Canada 2016a, pp. 8, 9).

In 2014, FSC Canada committed to take large-scale, intact forest landscapes into account whenever it considers any change to indicators within standards, with the goal of ensuring minimal disturbance to ecosystems that have not been significantly altered by human economic activity. The Aboriginal Peoples chamber put forward the concept of ICLs as a means of implementing FPIC in this context and as an alternative forest management method led by indigenous peoples. The concept affirms the ongoing normative significance of traditional indigenous land management systems and their relevance to standard-setting:

> Indigenous Cultural Landscapes are living landscapes to which Indigenous peoples attribute social, cultural and economic value because of their enduring relationship with the land, water, fauna, flora and spirits, and their present and future importance to their cultural identity. An ICL is characterized by features that have been maintained through long-term interactions with the landscape based on land-care knowledge, and adaptive livelihood practice. They are landscapes over which Indigenous peoples exercise responsibility for stewardship. (FSC Canada 2016c, pp. 1–2).

Both of these revisions to FSC Canada standards and policies valorize indigenous legal norms, radically reconceptualizing the normative framework for FSC certificate holders. For this reason and others, the negotiation process resulted in a number of significant shifts from Draft 2 to the final draft of the national standard. These included attention to the impact of FPIC on privately owned forests, increased acknowledgement of the challenges posed if affected indigenous communities decline to participate in FPIC processes, and decisions to develop a simplified certification process for smallholders and to continue working on the ICLs concept until 2019 (FSC Canada 2018c). The focus of the national standard remains on benefit sharing and relationship-building with indigenous peoples impacted by forest management activities, and a fundamental commitment not to proceed with forest development without indigenous consent (or acquiescence, in the case of indigenous non-engagement in FPIC processes). At FSC Canada's 2018 annual general meeting, members of the leadership team referred routinely to embedding the international legal norms contained in UNDRIP and ILO C169 in the national standard. Their consensus appeared to be that FPIC and indigenous legal normativity are now so deeply interwoven throughout the standard that no revision could reverse their cumulative effect.[5] The May 2019 removal of FSC International's outstanding conditions on final approval of the Canadian National Standard has allowed FSC Canada to move beyond such calculations and turn its attention to implementation of this ambitious agenda.

This study suggests that by changing the frame of reference used to assess the human rights and ecosystem impact of forest development, FSC Canada's standard-setting process serves as an alternative route to establishing a de facto veto for indigenous peoples over forestry projects in Canada, and does so in part on the basis of indigenous legal norms. As discussed below, a requirement for ongoing consent has proven to date to be unattainable via official state channels.

Interview subjects involved in FSC Canada and FSC International explained the FSC's steadfast commitment to Principles, Criteria and indicators that operationalize FPIC and related indigenous norms by saying that they seek to implement 'the highest standards' in their work.[6] They spoke of a sense of obligation to put international human rights norms into practice. One interviewee described FSC Canada as involved in a process of clarification and anticipation of the development of international human rights standards; another spoke of it as being subject to international legal norms.[7] Interview subjects consistently felt they did this work with a high degree of legitimacy because of FSC's participatory, democratic structure.

15.4 FPIC'S ORIGIN IN INTERNATIONAL LAW

FPIC's origin in contemporary international law can be traced to the International Labour Organization's Convention (No. 107) on Indigenous and Tribal Populations of 1957 (ILO C107), Article 12.1 of which states that indigenous peoples 'shall not be removed without their free consent from their habitual territories', except where government development of those lands is the justification.[8] ILO C107's authority is, however, diminished by the fact that it was drafted by UN agencies without consulting indigenous peoples. Although ILO C107 is the first modern international agreement to address indigenous peoples' human rights, it is shaped by paternalistic assumptions regarding indigenous cultural inferiority.

The limitations of the model of informed consent established in ILO C107 were remedied in part by several subsequent international legal developments including a 1975 judgment of the International Court of Justice (ICJ) on self-determination, revisions to ILO C107's indigenous consent provisions in the 1980s, and the 1985 commencement of negotiations on the text of UNDRIP. In its 1975 *Western Sahara* opinion, the ICJ addressed the competing colonial claims of Spain, Mauritania and Morocco to the territory of the indigenous Sahrawi people.[9] The Court linked the right of FPIC with the right of self-determination and recognized consent as the necessary legal foundation for relations between states and indigenous peoples. In 1985, the ILO Committee of Experts charged with revising ILO C107 took up this theme. The Convention had come to be regarded as deeply flawed, in large part because of political pressure exerted by the transnational indigenous peoples' movement. The ILO revision process resulted in ILO C169, which superseded ILO C107 and included a stronger recognition of indigenous rights. Most notably, ILO C169 asserts the foundational role of consent that is free, prior and sought through culturally appropriate indigenous institutions where any policy or development that could impact indigenous peoples' societies or territories is at stake. ILO C169 enhanced international legal recognition of indigenous peoples' right of self-determination within the existing framework of states, but still fell short as a comprehensive statement of the FPIC principle. While ILO C169 gained substantive legitimacy from many indigenous activists and allies, its process legitimacy (Clarkson & Wood 2010, pp. 36–7) was weak due to incomplete input from indigenous peoples and the absence of indigenous representation on the drafting committee.

ILO C169 has nonetheless had an impact far beyond its 23 parties. Its influence is due in part to the UN's inauguration of a Working Group on Indigenous Populations (WGIP) to develop an international instrument on indigenous rights just as the ILO Committee of Experts was completing its work. The responsibility for drafting lay formally with the five independent members of WGIP. As the process unfolded, indigenous peoples participated actively, and after a contentious decade-long period of consultation and development, an open-ended, inter-sessional working group was created to elaborate a draft declaration of the UN General Assembly (UNGA) based on WGIP's text (Davis 2008).

The resulting UNDRIP[10] was adopted by an overwhelming majority of the UNGA in September 2007, with 144 votes in favour, 11 abstentions, and four majority settler-states opposed – Australia, Canada, New Zealand and the USA. Article 19 of the Declaration affirms: 'States shall consult and cooperate in good faith with the Indigenous Peoples concerned through their own representative institutions in order to obtain their free, prior and informed consent before adopting and implementing legislative or administrative measures that may affect them.' Indigenous peoples' right of FPIC is also invoked in articles concerning relocation and resource exploitation, among others. UNGA declarations are not traditionally considered a source of international law in the way that treaties are. However, norms articulated in UNGA declarations can contribute to the formation of rules of CIL (International Law Commission 2016, p. 2).

FPIC is now widely—although not uncontroversially—regarded as a norm of CIL, one of the five conventionally recognized sources of international law.[11] A customary international legal norm is a general practice accepted as law (*opinio juris*). The International Law Commission (ILC) has stated that it is 'primarily the practice of States that contributes to the formation, or expression, of rules of customary international law', although the practice of international organizations may also contribute 'in certain cases', and the 'conduct of other [presumably non-state] actors . . . may be relevant' when evaluating whether a general practice exists (ibid.). *Opinio juris* is evidenced by 'public statements made on behalf of States; official publications; government legal opinions; diplomatic correspondence; decisions of national courts; treaty provisions; and conduct in connection with resolutions adopted by an international organization or at an intergovernmental conference' (ibid., p. 3).

FPIC is now variously referred to as both a principle and a right in international legal and political fora, and has been affirmed as a right by the UN's Committee on the Elimination of Racial Discrimination, Committee on Economic, Social, and Cultural Rights, Human Rights Committee, Expert Mechanism on the Rights of Indigenous Peoples, and Permanent Forum on Indigenous Peoples.

The most authoritative articulation of FPIC is a set of guidelines developed in connection with the UN Collaborative Programme on Reducing Emissions from Deforestation and Forest Degradation in Developing Countries (REDD). The UN-REDD Guidelines define FPIC as 'a legal norm imposing clear affirmative duties and obligations on States' (UN-REDD Programme Secretariat 2013, p. 9). The Guidelines emphasize the disproportionate role played by indigenous and forest-dependent peoples in the stewardship of forested lands and the need to build partnerships with them. The former Special Rapporteur on the Rights of Indigenous Peoples, James Anaya, emphasized that while FPIC can be overridden like other basic norms such as free speech, this requires exceptional circumstances (Special Rapporteur on the Rights of Indigenous Peoples 2013, paras. 35–6).

15.5 THE RELATIONSHIP BETWEEN INTERNATIONAL LAW AND TRANSNATIONAL NON-STATE ACTORS

The principle of FPIC is recognized as having normative force by other non-state actors as well. It is acknowledged not only in the FSC's standard, but also in the UN Guiding Principles on Business and Human Rights (UNGPs) and a variety of principles and codes of conduct developed by private and hybrid transnational actors and international organizations (for example, World Commission on Dams 2000; World Bank 2013, para. 2; Initiative for Responsible Mining Assurance 2018; Hershey Co. n.d.).

The UNGPs were created under the sponsorship of the UN Human Rights Council while the most recent revision of the FSC Canada standard was being initiated. The UNGPs promote respect for human rights in a business context. Principle 12 requires businesses to respect foundational human rights, including, at a minimum, those set out in the International Bill of Human Rights and the ILO's Declaration on Fundamental Principles and Rights at Work. It adds:

> Depending on circumstances, business enterprises may need to consider additional standards. For instance, enterprises should respect the human rights of individuals belonging to specific groups or populations that require particular attention, where they may have adverse human rights impacts on them. *In this connection, United Nations instruments have elaborated further on the rights of indigenous peoples*; women; national or ethnic, religious and linguistic minorities; children; persons with disabilities; and migrant workers and their families. (United Nations 2011, p. 15, emphasis added)

In addition, Principles 17–20 of the UNGPs, which address human rights due diligence, discuss the requirement of consultation with those whose human rights may be affected by corporate activities.

Despite their limitations, the UNGPs and the associated voluntary principles and codes of conduct adopted by non-state actors of various stripes provide evidence of a growing recognition of the perceived authority of international human rights standards – including the right of FPIC – over non-state entities. Many, like the FSC's P&C, contain an explicit acknowledgement that the human rights norms to which they voluntarily bind themselves (including FPIC) are rooted in international human rights law, specifically, the Universal Declaration on Human Rights and ILO C169.

Notably, the motivation of non-state actors such as the FSC aligns with the defining quality of a customary international legal norm, namely that it is followed out of a sense of legal obligation (*opinio juris*) (International Law Commission 2016, p. 2). What mechanism could explain such a normative relationship between non-state actors and international legal rules?

15.6 HOW INTERNATIONAL LEGAL NORMS BIND TRANSNATIONAL PRIVATE ACTORS

The question of how a private transnational actor becomes an international law-applying agent is of more than academic interest if we seek to determine whether TBGIs can be harnessed to advance marginalized actors. In this Part, I investigate whether the FSC's claims to be bound by international legal norms can be explained in terms of formal rules of international law.

To determine whether private transnational actors can be subjects and appliers of international law, it is important to identify the mechanism(s) by which international legal norms exert compliance pull on them, if only because of the widespread positivist conviction that in 'any legal system, whether a given norm is legally valid, and hence whether it forms part of the law of that system, depends on its sources, not its merits' (Gardner 2001, p. 201). This inquiry insulates the question of whether specific international legal norms are legally binding upon private transnational actors from debate over their social justice content.

Domestic legal theory offers various means by which international norms might exert mandatory force for non-state actors with only minor theoretical alteration. One suggestive starting-point is a theory of how constitutional human rights norms exercise influence on the obligations ascribed to third parties in domestic contexts. This theory of 'structural effects' is important in constitutional courts' reasoning in Canada, Italy, Israel, Germany, Spain, Japan and South Africa (Barak 2001, pp. 22–5; Teubner 2012, p. 132).

According to former Israeli Supreme Court Justice Aharon Barak, human rights in domestic settings bear on the 'horizontal' relations between private parties in one of two ways. In countries where human rights are constitutionalized, they apply indirectly in private law through a 'cascade effect' (Barak 2001, p. 21). On this view, constitutional human rights pass into private law via public policy:

> The point of departure for indirect application is that human rights have always played a role in private law. Indeed, at the foundation of the private law system are human rights ideals such as personhood, self-realization and dignity. The specific private law rules – for example, protection of one's good name or property – reflect the rights of the private individual (as against the state and other private parties). At the same time, 'value' concepts such as 'good faith', 'reasonableness' and 'negligence' reflect, *inter alia*, an appropriate balance of opposing human rights. Moreover, the concept of public policy essentially absorbs human rights originating in the constitution. From time immemorial, confrontations between human rights – for example, freedom of contract versus freedom of occupation – have been resolved within the framework of the public policy principle, which weighs conflicting rights according to their relative status in the constitutional system. Indeed, public policy is the channel through which constitutional values flow into private law. (Ibid., pp. 21–2.)

Barak concludes that whereas '[i]n the past, common law human rights infiltrated private law by means of private law value terms . . . [n]ow constitutional human rights do the same' (ibid., p. 22). On this model, human rights apply to third parties indirectly, within the existing structures of the (domestic) private law system, but their constitutional origin lends them greater normative status than common law-derived human rights, and this structural effect allows courts to grant a wider range of remedies when constitutionalized human rights are violated.

This model also explains the weaker role of human rights in the private law of countries where constitutionalization of human rights has not occurred. In such cases, value terms serve as vehicles for conveying common law human rights into the private law even in the absence of constitutionalized human rights norms.

The International Commission of Jurists, a transnational organization of legal professionals, endorses a variant of this theory at the international level. In an article outlining the findings of its 2008 report on the subject of transnational corporate responsibility for human rights abuses (International Commission of Jurists 2008), former Canadian Supreme Court Justice Ian Binnie advocates third-party responsibility for human rights abuses (Binnie 2009). The Commission's main goal in this connection is to establish a formal legal framework of accountability for human rights violations by transnational corporations (TNCs). This approach complements and extends the UNGPs developed under the aegis of the UN Human Rights Council.

The Commission argues for civil enforcement of human rights where the violators are international corporations. In his discussion of the Commission's position, Binnie echoes Barak in suggesting that attribution of obligations to third parties should start from the existing principles of civil liability that already protect some human rights, and in advocating the development of new tools to address violations using established private law techniques (Binnie 2009, p. 50).

Binnie highlights promising elements of criminal liability such as the law of corporate complicity, as well as more traditional criminal and civil avenues for redress. His civil-law prescriptions accord with the structural effects theory of constitutionalized human rights. This approach assumes a constitutionalist reading of international law and relies on a public policy-type mechanism for transmitting human rights norms to transnational non-state actors, along the lines suggested by Barak.

A variety of constitutionalist readings of international law might support a 'structural effects' account of the indirect application of constitutional human rights norms to non-state actors (for example, Fassbender 1998). However, most or all face the challenge of the 'weak public' character of nascent global civil society (Brunkhorst 2005, pp. 159–61). More importantly, it is difficult to see how a direct analogy to the policy-making function of a national government can be readily developed in the international legal arena on a conventional constitutionalist reading due to the lack of centralized, hierarchical legislative and executive bodies.

Another theorist who seeks to extend the structural effects approach to the transnational realm may help to answer this challenge. Gunther Teubner (2012) shares Binnie's and the Commission's preoccupation with remedies for TNCs' human rights violations, and Barak's preference for an 'indirect third-party effects' approach to the application of human rights to private actors. Teubner joins the conversation about constitutionalist interpretations of international law from a functionalist, systems-theoretical perspective, while situating himself squarely in the camp of the 'structural effects' account of the uptake of constitutional human rights norms by non-state actors.

Teubner holds that human rights norms have what he calls 'horizontal effects' on transnational actors through a two-stage process of generalization and respecification akin to that described by Barak in the domestic setting (Teubner 2012, pp. 131–42). A 'social positivization' of concrete human rights norms occurs through their institutionalization in conflict resolution bodies such as the WTO Appellate Body and the arbitration tribunals of private regulatory regimes such as the Internet Corporation for Assigned Names and Numbers (ICANN) and the International Chamber of Commerce (ibid., p. 129). Teubner notes that the human rights at issue are often 'scandalized norms' that temporarily arouse the attention of global publics when a local crisis occurs, such as the Bhopal disaster of 1984 or the Rana Plaza garment factory collapse of 2013 in Bangladesh. Such norms are integrated into global law as secondary rules that are incorporated into the decisions of arbitral tribunals associated with the aforementioned diverse regulatory bodies.

Teubner also tries to account for the source of public policy-making that seems to be absent when the structural effects model is translated to the transnational arena. He adopts Andrew Hurrell's (2007, p. 53) notion of a common law constitution to describe how 'fundamental rights are positivized in transnational (public and private) regimes: an iterative decision-making process occurs between the rulings of arbitration tribunals, decisions of national courts, contracts of private actors, social standardizations, and the scandalization actions of protest movements and NGOs' (Teubner 2012, p. 130).

Teubner's account of the positivization of fundamental rights leans heavily on processes of arbitral review to explain how transnational actors become subject to international human rights norms such as FPIC. Although the FSC possesses a quasi-judicial review procedure in which the secondary rule incorporation process outlined by Teubner occurs, this does not seem to be the primary means by which international human rights norms exercise normative force within that organization. Instead, the participatory democratic structure of the FSC is regarded by activist members as having been both responsible for the strengthening of the indigenous consultation norm, and the source of the perception that the FSC is an addressee of international law. A more promising explanation of the normative processes at work in this case might be achieved by regarding transnational actors such as the FSC as formal addressees of international law, rather than only as its indirect subjects, as the existing theories outlined above allow.

15.7 FPIC AND THE CANADIAN STATE

After being actively involved in the process of drafting UNDRIP over more than a decade, Canada was one of only four countries that voted against it in 2007. The Canadian government's concerns at the time revolved primarily around Article 26, dealing with FPIC and land.

Between 2009 and 2012, all four UNDRIP-opposing countries altered their positions, deciding ultimately to endorse or support the Declaration. In its 2010 endorsement, the Canadian government reiterated the concerns it had expressed at the time of the 2007 General Assembly vote. These reservations concerned provisions of UNDRIP that addressed 'lands, territories and resources; free, prior and informed consent when used as a veto; self-government without recognition of the importance of negotiations; intellectual property; military issues; and the need to achieve an appropriate balance between the rights and obligations of Indigenous peoples, States and third parties' (Government of Canada 2010). The Canadian government indicated that despite these concerns, it was 'now confident that Canada can interpret the principles expressed in the Declaration in a manner that is consistent with our Constitution and legal framework' (ibid.). This confidence appeared to rest on the government's key assertion that it saw UNDRIP as 'a non-legally binding document that does not reflect customary international law nor change Canadian laws' (ibid.).

With the election of a new federal government in 2015, Canada changed its position on UNDRIP. In May 2016 it announced its unreserved support for the General Assembly resolution. In an address to the UN Permanent Forum on Indigenous Issues, the Canadian Minister for Indigenous and Northern Affairs, Carolyn Bennett, announced that Canada was now an unqualified supporter of UNDRIP and pledged 'nothing less than to adopt and implement the declaration in accordance with the Canadian Constitution' (Fontaine 2016a). This change of official policy seemed to herald a reversal of the previous government's rejection of the principle of FPIC and the associated idea of a veto for indigenous peoples. However, subsequent events have raised doubts about this interpretation of the government's still ambiguous position.

In a speech to the principal national indigenous organization, the then Minister of Justice, Jody Wilson-Raybould, cautioned that 'simplistic approaches, such as adopting the UNDRIP . . . [into] Canadian law are unworkable and, respectfully, a political distraction to undertaking the hard work required to actually implement it' (Wilson-Raybould 2016). After media reports portrayed these comments as a retreat from the government's commitment to implementing the Declaration, the Minister explicitly affirmed that the Canadian government supported all articles of UNDRIP 'without reservation' (Kirkup 2016).

The available evidence suggests that Canada's current interpretation of the meaning of UNDRIP provisions regarding FPIC 'in accordance with the Canadian Constitution' will result in little practical deviation from the existing requirements set out by Canada's Supreme Court, of good faith consultation with the aim of achieving consent.[12] This is supported by Minister Bennett's statement at the time of UNDRIP's formal adoption that 'Canada believes that our constitutional obligations serve to fulfil all of the principles of the Declaration, including free, prior and informed consent' (Fontaine 2016b). It remains to be seen how the Canadian government will reconcile its assertion of unqualified support for UNDRIP with economic development pressures and the constitutional division of powers that assigns authority over natural resources to the provinces.

Following the adoption of UNDRIP, the Liberal government of Prime Minister Justin Trudeau either granted approval or allowed approvals to stand in a series of resource development projects that faced significant opposition from potentially affected indigenous communities, including the Pacific Northwest liquefied natural gas (LNG) and Site C dam projects, both approved without the consent of First Nations on whose territory they are located. During this same period, Canadian courts have blocked a number of other resource development projects in response to pre-existing suits by indigenous plaintiffs asserting that the Crown had not fulfilled its duty to consult. These include the Enbridge Northern Gateway,[13] Alton natural gas[14] and Kinder Morgan Trans Mountain pipeline projects.[15]

The federal government's commitment to economic development and its 'thin' reading of FPIC are most evident in its handling of the high-profile Kinder Morgan Trans Mountain pipeline expansion plan. Its 2016 decision to approve the project was reportedly opposed by two-thirds of the indigenous communities potentially affected by the project. These include 51 indigenous nations whose territory is spanned by the existing pipeline and dozens of others that might be impacted. Various indigenous nations, environmental groups and local and provincial governments challenged the proposal in court. Seven First Nations were parties to a lawsuit that resulted in a 2018 Federal Court decision that the Crown's agents violated the duty to consult during the review process. Despite this opposition, the federal government has championed the project and announced in May 2018 that it would purchase the project from Kinder Morgan to ensure that it would be built. The decision was precipitated by Kinder Morgan's increasing signals of concern about proceeding with the expansion in light of the determined opposition, and the government's calculation that the political cost of the project's collapse would be prohibitive.

This inconsistency in FPIC's implementation – the robust version of the norm being operationalized by the FSC and the weaker form employed by the Canadian government – is characteristic of emerging principles of CIL.

15.8 CONCLUSION

This preliminary survey of the TBGIs associated with the FSC's advocacy of a strong FPIC norm suggests several conclusions. The FSC, led by FSC Canada and its indigenous network, has framed itself and its members as subjects of international law, while emphasizing the international legal grounds of an indigenous right of FPIC. This technique has helped indigenous and allied norm entrepreneurs within the organization to entrench generous interpretations of the two axes on which FPIC hinges – the definitions of 'legal and customary rights' and 'lands, territories and resources.' These robust readings have in turn supported a broad articulation of the as yet unsettled customary international legal norm of FPIC.

As a consequence, indigenous peoples in Canada who are affected by FSC certificate holders' activities exercise, in theory at least, a higher degree of control over, and participation in, the management of their lands, territories and resources than is available to them via Canadian government policy, legislation or jurisprudence. This control can extend to an effective veto if they so choose. This study therefore demonstrates that marginalized actors can enhance social justice outcomes by leveraging international legal norms through TBGIs. Further, the participatory governance structure of the FSC opens an access point for members of the global indigenous peoples' movement to exercise international legal agency. This study illustrates how non-state actors such as the FSC and the transnational indigenous peoples' movement can be understood as agents with the capacity to contribute to the development of CIL, in legal formalist terms.

This survey of selected policies and principles of FSC Canada, their root norms in international law, and the contrasting interpretations of those norms by the Canadian state also suggest some theoretical considerations that are relevant in determining how a hybrid or private transnational actor could be an addressee of international law. The chapter offers insights into the complex, iterative process of norm formation at transnational and intra-state levels. This process involves horizontal interstate norm consolidation that is often, but not always, manifested in treaties and declarations of international organizations. Treaties and other interstate normative expressions influence the FSC and, we see, are in turn affected by the FSC and other transnational actors, both in their substance and in their practical interpretation. The process of intra-state norm consolidation is influenced by these same international norms to which the FSC and the Canadian state themselves also contribute.

Such a process could be responsible in part for the shift in the Canadian federal government's policy toward UNDRIP and the customary international legal principle of FPIC. However, this course alteration is now being tested as indigenous peoples' rights to participate in decision-making about their lands, territories and resources are being pitted against the exigencies of economic development and certainty as the Trans Mountain pipeline expansion is cast as a zero-sum game, according to the classic agonistic model of colonialism.

It thus seems possible that the greatest contribution of FSC Canada's TBGIs around FPIC may come in the future. With its new national standard, FSC Canada has undertaken to demonstrate the feasibility of a robust reading of FPIC. It has committed much of its moral and political clout to deflating the myth that recognizing indigenous rights to land and resources and respecting an indigenous right of veto can occur only at the cost of economic development. If FSC Canada succeeds, this would effectively undercut states' perpetual argument that a strong interpretation of FPIC would be unworkable and economically destructive.

A happy by-product of this outcome could be the transformation of international law itself, as the FSC and like-minded, non-state actors working in concert with the transnational indigenous peoples' movement inject penumbral readings into the core meaning of FPIC. In traditional, formalist international legal theory, only states determine the core of settled meaning of an international legal norm. This study suggests that this assumption is inadequate to describe the reality of transnational legal processes today. It appears that the FPIC norm may be influenced by international organizations, the transnational indigenous peoples' movement and other hybrid and private transnational actors, including the FSC. These actors' influence on the development of the norm could, in effect, exercise an osmotic pull on the restrictive core meaning of the norm of indigenous consultation and cause an expansion of the norm to encompass what were once penumbral elements, such as the effective veto advocated by the FSC and other non-state actors. As a consequence, it can be posited that over time, states' *opinio juris* and state practice may evolve (and may have already evolved). The result could be an indirect ratcheting up of international social justice norms through the detour of CIL formation. This chapter suggests that FPIC is an incipient example of this process.

NOTES

1. Interviews with Neil Sterritt, Jr., Don Ryan (Hanamuxw), Herb George (Satsan) and Russell Collier (Summer 1996).
2. 'Aboriginal rights' is a term of art referring to rights recognized by the Canadian state as attaching to indigenous peoples in Canada. *Calder et al. v. Attorney-General of British Columbia*, [1973] SCR 313 established the continuing existence of aboriginal

title; *Delgamuukw v. British Columbia*, [1997] 3 SCR 1010 set out the test for proof of aboriginal title and confirmed the Crown's obligation to consult with indigenous peoples before infringing their aboriginal rights.

3. Constitution Act, 1982, s. 35(1) (Canada).
4. Convention (No. 169) Concerning Indigenous and Tribal Peoples in Independent Countries (adopted 27 June 1989, entered into force 5 September 1991) 1650 UNTS 383 (Indigenous and Tribal Peoples Convention, 1989).
5. Personal observation of the FSC Canada Annual General Meeting, Montréal, Canada (29 May 2018).
6. Interview with Subject No. 6 (9 February 2017).
7. Interviews with Subjects No. 6 (9 February 2017) and No. 7 (29 May 2018).
8. Convention (No. 107) Concerning the Protection and Integration of Indigenous and Other Tribal and Semi-Tribal Populations in Independent Countries (adopted 26 June 1957, entered into force 2 June 1959) 328 UNTS 247 (Indigenous and Tribal Populations Convention, 1957).
9. *Western Sahara* (Advisory Opinion) [1975] ICJ Rep 12.
10. United Nations Declaration on the Rights of Indigenous Peoples, UNGA Res 61/295 (13 September 2007) UN Doc A/RES/61/295 (UNDRIP).
11. See Oman 2019, Chapter 5 for elaboration of the evolving process by which norms acquire customary international legal status, and the role that transnational actors are now playing in it.
12. *Haida Nation v. British Columbia (Minister of Forests)*, 2004 SCC 73, [2004] 3 SCR 511.
13. *Gitxaala Nation v. Canada*, 2016 FCA 187, [2016] 4 FCR 418.
14. *Sipekne'katik v. Nova Scotia (Environment)*, 2017 NSSC 23.
15. *Tsleil-Waututh Nation v. Canada (Attorney-General)*, 2018 FCA 153.

REFERENCES

Barak, Aharon (2001), 'Constitutional human rights and private law', in Daniel Friedmann and Daphne Barak-Erez (eds), *Human Rights in Private Law*, Oxford and Portland, Hart, pp. 13–42.

Binnie, Ian (2009), 'Legal redress for corporate participation in international human rights abuses: a progress report', *The Brief (American Bar Association)*, Summer, 44–51.

Brunkhorst, Hauke (2005), *Solidarity: From Civic Friendship to a Global Legal Community*, Cambridge, MA: MIT Press.

Clarkson, Stephen and Stepan Wood (2010), *A Perilous Imbalance: The Globalization of Canadian Law and Governance*, Vancouver: UBC Press.

Davis, Megan (2008), 'Indigenous struggles in standard-setting: the United Nations Declaration on the Rights of Indigenous Peoples', *Melbourne Journal of International Law*, **9**, 439–71.

Fassbender, Bardo (1998), 'The United Nations Charter as constitution of the international community', *Columbia Journal of Transnational Law*, **36** (3), 529–619.

Fontaine, Tim (2016a), 'Canada officially adopts UN declaration on rights of Indigenous Peoples', *CBC News*, 10 May, accessed 10 April 2019 at http://www.cbc.ca/news/indigenous/canada-adopting-implementing-un-rights-declaration-1.3575272.

Fontaine, Tim (2016b), 'Canada supports UN Indigenous rights declaration: now what?' *CBC News*, 11 May, accessed 10 April 2019 at http://www.cbc.ca/news/indigenous/canada-un-indigenous-rights-questions-1.3578074.

FSC Canada (2005), *Forest Stewardship Council Regional Certification Standards for British Columbia: Main Standards*, October, Toronto: FSC Canada.

FSC Canada (2016a), *Forming Draft 2 of FSC Canada's National Forest Management Standard: A Summary of Key Changes from Draft 1 to Draft 2*, 19 December, Toronto: FSC Canada, accessed 10 April 2019 at https://ca.fsc.org/preview.forming-draft-2-of-fsc-canadas-national-forest-management-standard.a-1356.pdf.

FSC Canada (2016b), *FSC Canada Guidance on Free, Prior and Informed Consent (FPIC), Working Draft 1*, 24 November, Toronto: FSC Canada, accessed 10 April 2019 at https://ca.fsc.org/download-box.1273.htm.

FSC Canada (2016c), 'Intact forest landscapes & indigenous cultural landscapes: working together to find a functional approach', discussion paper, Toronto: FSC Canada, January, accessed 10 April 2019 at https://ca.fsc.org/preview.ifl-icl-discussion-paper.a-1105.pdf.

FSC Canada (2018a), *Annual Report 2017*, Toronto: FSC Canada, accessed 10 April 2019 at https://ca.fsc.org/download-box.2115.htm.

FSC Canada (2018b), *Forest Management Standard Update*, 26 October, accessed 10 April 2019 at https://ca.fsc.org/en-ca/newsroom/technical-updates/id/910.

FSC Canada (2018c), *Heading to the Finish Line: Public Summary of Significant Changes to Draft 2 of FSC*, Toronto: FSC Canada, accessed 10 April 2019 at https://ca.fsc.org/download-box.2048.htm.

FSC International (2002), *FSC International Standard: FSC Principles and Criteria for Forest Stewardship FSC-STD-01-001 V4-0 EN.*

FSC International (2012a), *FSC Guidelines for the Implementation of the Right to Free, Prior and Informed Consent (FPIC)*, version 1, (30 October).

FSC International (2012b), *FSC International Standard: FSC Principles and Criteria for Forest Stewardship* (10 February) FSC-STD-01-001 V5-0 EN.

FSC International (2015), *FSC Principles and Criteria for Forest Stewardship* (22 July) FSC-STD-01-001 V5-2 EN.

FSC International (2019a), *FSC Facts and Figures April 5, 2019*, Bonn: FSC International, accessed 10 April 2019 at https://ic.fsc.org/file-download.facts-figures-april-2019.a-8329.pdf.

FSC International (2019b), *FSC Forest Management Certification: Historical Figures*, February, accessed 10 April 2019 at https://ic.fsc.org/file-download.fsc-forest-management-from-start-till-2011.a-8313.pdf.

Gardner, John (2001), 'Legal positivism: 5½ myths', *American Journal of Jurisprudence*, **46**, 199–227.

Government of Canada (2010), *Canada's Statement of Support on the United Nations Declaration on the Rights of Indigenous Peoples,* 12 November, accessed 10 April 2019 at http://www.aadnc-aandc.gc.ca/eng/1309374239861/1309374546142 (Archived).

Hart, H.L.A. (1958), 'Positivism and the separation of law and morals', *Harvard Law Review*, **71** (4), 593–629.

Hershey Co. (n.d.), *Pulp and Paper Sourcing Policy*, accessed 10 April 2019 at https://www.thehersheycompany.com/content/dam/corporate-us/documents/legal/pulp-and-paper-sourcing-policy.pdf.

Hurrell, Andrew (2007), *On Global Order: Power, Values, and the Constitution of International Society,* Oxford: Oxford University Press.

Initiative for Responsible Mining Assurance (2018), *IRMA Standard for Responsible Mining, Version 1.0* (June) IRMA-STD-001, accessed 10 April

2019 at https://responsiblemining.net/wp-content/uploads/2018/07/IRMA_STANDARD_v.1.0_FINAL_2018.pdf.

International Commission of Jurists (2008), *Corporate Complicity & Legal Accountability,* Geneva: International Commission of Jurists.

International Law Commission (2016), *Identification of Customary International Law, Text of the draft conclusions provisionally adopted by the Drafting Committee*, Sixty-eighth session, Geneva, 2 May–10 June and 4 July–12 August 2016, UN Doc. A/CN.4/L.872.

Kirkup, Kristy (2016), 'Government supports Indigenous declaration without reservation: Wilson-Raybould', *CBC News*, 20 July, accessed 10 April 2019 at http://www.cbc.ca/news/indigenous/government-supports-undrip-without-reservation-1.3687315.

Oman, Natalie (2019), *The Responsibility to Protect in International Law*, London: Routledge.

Special Rapporteur on the Rights of Indigenous Peoples (2013), *Extractive Industries and Indigenous Peoples, Report of the Special Rapporteur on the Rights of Indigenous Peoples, James Anaya, to the Human Rights Council*, UN Doc. A/HRC/24/41.

Teubner, Gunther (2012), *Constitutional Fragments: Societal Constitutionalism and Globalization*, Oxford: Oxford University Press.

Tollefson, Chris, Fred Gale and David Haley (2008), *Setting the Standard: Certification, Governance and the Forest Stewardship Council*, Vancouver: UBC Press.

United Nations (2011), *Guiding Principles on Business and Human Rights: Implementing the United Nations 'Protect, Respect and Remedy' Framework*, New York and Geneva: United Nations.

UN-REDD Programme Secretariat (2013), *Guidelines on Free, Prior and Informed Consent*, Geneva: UN-REDD Programme Secretariat.

Wilson-Raybould, Jody (2016), Remarks delivered to the 37th Annual General Assembly of the Assembly of First Nations Annual General Assembly, Niagara Falls, Canada, 21 July.

World Bank (2013), *Operational Manual: BP 4.10 – Indigenous Peoples,* July 2005, revised April 2013, Washington: World Bank Group, accessed 10 April 2019 at https://policies.worldbank.org/sites/ppf3/PPFDocuments/090224b08230184e.pdf.

World Commission on Dams (2000), *Dams and Development: A New Framework for Decision-Making*, London and Sterling, VA: Earthscan.

16. Interactive strategies for advancing marginalized actors in transnational governance contests: Labour and the making of ISO 26000

Stepan Wood

16.1 INTRODUCTION

In this chapter I explore the drafting of the ISO 26000 guidance standard on social responsibility (ISO 2010b) as a case study of the circumstances in which marginalized actors can take advantage of transnational business governance interactions (TBGIs) (Eberlein et al. 2014; Wood et al. 2015) to achieve regulatory outcomes that advance their interests. I argue that organized labour exploited interactions between the International Organization for Standardization (ISO) and the International Labour Organization (ILO) to achieve results in ISO 26000 that belied its structural disadvantage. I present the case study in Part 2. In Part 3 I examine the theoretical implications of the case, proposing a triadic strategy in which an *underdog* takes advantage of interactions between a *regulator* and a *booster* to advance its interests in transnational governance and enhance regulatory standards.

16.2 LABOUR, ILO AND THE MAKING OF ISO 26000

My goal in this chapter is to investigate the circumstances in which TBGIs can be harnessed to advance the interests of marginalized actors. Organized labour's role in the development of ISO 26000 is a promising case by which to explore this question because labour is marginalized in ISO and technical standardization generally, yet it secured a remarkably favourable outcome compared to other leading social responsibility (SR) initiatives.

16.2.1 ISO, ILO and Social Responsibility

ISO, established in 1947, is the leading source of voluntary standards for global business, with 163 national member bodies, 22000 international standards and 1.6 million organizations certified to its management systems (MS) standards as of 2017 (ISO 1997, 2017, 2018). Business interests dominate ISO's leadership and standards development (Murphy and Yates 2009; Wood 2012b). The International Labour Organization (ILO) celebrated its centenary in 2019. Its mission is to advance social harmony via tripartite dialogue among workers, employers and states. A specialized agency of the United Nations, it has 187 member states. It is the authoritative source of international labour standards (ILSs), which take the form of legally binding conventions and non-binding recommendations.

ILO was active in the field of SR long before the term was coined. ISO moved into the field in 1993 with the ISO 14000 environmental management standards. Building on the success of these standards, a working group of ISO's consumer policy committee (COPOLCO) recommended in 2002 that ISO develop corporate SR standards (ISO 2002). ISO established an Ad Hoc Group on Corporate Social Responsibility (AHGCSR) to advise it whether to do so. The AHGCSR recommended that ISO develop such standards only if it recognized its lack of authority to set social expectations within the remit of representative political institutions, voluntary initiatives' lack of legitimacy compared to authoritative intergovernmental instruments, and ILO's 'unique mandate as the organization that defines, on a tripartite basis, international norms with respect to a broad range of social issues' (ISO 2004b, p. 1).

ISO received mixed feedback from its audiences about the prospect of ISO SR standards (Tamm Hallström and Boström 2010, pp. 30–35). Business actors believed SR was too diverse and contested for standardization and opposed the growth of an SR consulting and certification industry. Government representatives recognized the potential of voluntary standards to support public policy goals but lamented ISO's democratic deficit and feared that ISO standards could become trade barriers. Some intergovernmental organizations favoured voluntary standards; others saw ISO as an unwelcome interloper. Public interest NGOs ranged from ambivalent to hostile. Other standardization bodies saw ISO as a competitor but also a potential force magnifier for their standards. Labour saw ILO as the authoritative forum for labour standards and believed ISO was captured by business. ILO was ambivalent, considering ISO an unrepresentative and inappropriate forum for addressing SR but also as a possible avenue toward greater uptake of ILSs.

ISO's Technical Management Board (TMB) decided to go ahead with the development of a guidance standard and invited ISO member bodies to nominate up to six experts in six stakeholder categories: industry, government, labour, consumers, NGOs and others (ISO 2004a). The ISO Working Group on Social Responsibility (WGSR) met eight times between March 2005 and May 2010, growing from 225 experts representing 43 national standards bodies and 24 international organizations (IOs) at its first meeting to 450 experts from 99 national standards bodies and 42 IOs when it finished its work in 2010. The WGSR's records are publicly available on the Internet, opening a rare window into non-state standardization processes.[1] This archive of almost 3000 documents was the main source for my research, along with participant observation as a member of Canada's national mirror committee[2] and an observer at two WGSR meetings.

16.2.2 Labour's Disadvantage and Unlikely Success in the ISO 26000 Process

Labour was entirely absent from the COPOLCO working group that provided the initial impetus for ISO's move into SR, and vastly outnumbered on the AHGCSR. Only one of the AHGCSR's 20 members represented labour, while nine (including the chair) were from industry and one was from ILO. Labour was also outnumbered in the WGSR. It was the smallest stakeholder category throughout the drafting of ISO 26000, starting at around 7 per cent of WGSR membership and ending at around 10 per cent. Industry was the largest group throughout. The 'Others' category – later refined as Service, Support, Research and Others (SSRO) – was also among the largest. Consultants and standards body employees, whose interests align broadly with industry's, comprised a large fraction of this category. Labour was under-represented in WGSR leadership positions compared to its share of overall WGSR membership. The WGSR chair and vice-chair were from industry. Labour experts held only one of around 20 leadership positions in the WGSR for the first two and a half years. Its share of leadership positions dropped to zero in late 2007 when three drafting task groups were replaced by a single Integrated Drafting Task Force (IDTF). ILO also advocated for labour's interests in the WGSR and sat on several key subgroups including the Chair's Advisory Group (CAG), IDTF and Editing Committee.

Despite being vastly outnumbered, labour secured remarkably favourable results in ISO 26000 in comparison to SR initiatives developed in other business-oriented fora. Labour's lead representative in the WGSR called ISO 26000 'the best concise, yet comprehensive, statement on social responsibility and labour to date', and a 'welcome antidote' to CSR initiatives' tendency to dilute firms' responsibilities to workers (Justice 2011, p. 31).

Like most SR initiatives, ISO 26000 embraces ILO's four fundamental rights at work: freedom of association and the right to collective bargaining; the elimination of forced labour; the effective abolition of child labour; and the elimination of discrimination with respect to employment and occupation. But unlike many SR initiatives, ISO 26000 emphasizes that SR embraces a wide range of other labour rights, including the right to freely chosen work, the right to work in just and favourable conditions, the right to a standard of living adequate for health and well-being, and the right to unemployment, illness, disability, old age and bereavement benefits.

ISO 26000's treatment of labour issues compares favourably with other leading contemporary SR initiatives and even with ILO's own articulations of the ILSs.[3] ISO 26000 covered a far wider range of labour issues than the UN Global Compact (UNGC), Social Accountability International's SA 8000:2008 standard (Social Accountability International 2008) and the Business Social Compliance Initiative (BSCI) Code of Conduct (Foreign Trade Association 2009).[4] Its articulation of organizations' responsibilities in relation to the four fundamental rights at work was more ambitious than SA 8000's or BSCI's and far more detailed than the UNGC's. ISO 26000 compared even more favourably on issues beyond fundamental rights at work, including wages, working conditions and occupational health and safety. It even covered an array of labour standards absent from these other initiatives, including employment promotion, employment security, training, benefits, tripartite consultation, employment policy and community development.

ISO 26000 also came closer than SA8000, the BSCI and the official guide to the UNGC's labour principles (International Labour Organization 2008) to matching the scope, specificity and rigour of ILO's own articulation of ILSs. ISO 26000 even took a stronger stance than ILO itself on some issues. Whereas the ILO Tripartite Declaration of Principles Concerning Multinational Enterprises and Social Policy (ILO MNE Declaration) (International Labour Organization 2006) emphasized respect for state sovereignty, provided no guidance on resolving conflicts between national law and international norms and failed to mention collective agreements as voluntary commitments firms should honour, ISO 26000 urged organizations to respect collective agreements, treat international norms as a floor, and resolve conflicts between national law and international norms in favour of the latter to the greatest extent possible. It urged organizations facing such conflicts to review their relationships and activities, try to influence others to remedy the conflict and avoid complicity in others' violations of international norms. ISO 26000 provided that an organization 'should ensure that the conditions of work comply with national laws and regulations and are consistent with applicable international labour standards, . . . should respect higher levels established through other legally binding instruments such as collective agreements, [and] should observe at least those minimum provisions defined in international labour standards as established by ILO, especially where national legislation has not yet been adopted' (clause 6.4.4.2). Significantly, this expectation applied to all ILSs regardless of ratification status.

ISO 26000 also defined the organizational scope of SR more broadly than ILO. Whereas the ILO MNE Declaration spoke of the responsibility of various organs *within* a multinational enterprise, ISO 26000 extended an organization's responsibility to encompass 'all policies and practices relating to work performed within, by or on behalf of the organization, including subcontracted work' (clause 6.4.1.1). It also stipulated that in some circumstances an organization has a responsibility to exercise leverage over other actors within its sphere of influence: an organization 'should make reasonable efforts to encourage organizations in its sphere of influence to follow responsible labour practices, recognizing that a high level of influence is likely to correspond to a high level of responsibility to exercise that influence' (clause 6.4.3.2).[5]

Labour experts in the WGSR repeatedly applauded the draft standard's definition of SR, its consistency with the ILSs, its deference to ILO, its comprehensive yet concise account of responsible labour practices, its suitability for all organizations, its respect for authoritative intergovernmental instruments, its refusal to endorse private voluntary initiatives, its repudiation of organizations' self-definition of their responsibilities and its overall length and detail. ILO's comments were similar. It expressed strong support for the guide's treatment of labour practices and labour-related human rights, declaring these sections to be concise and fully consistent with ILSs and the ILO MNE Declaration. Only at the final vote did ILO curb its enthusiasm, opining merely that the finished product did 'not appear to conflict with international labour standards as currently understood and applied' (ISO 2010a, para 4).

16.2.3 Understanding Labour's Success

How did labour succeed in securing in ISO 26000 a 'comprehensive distillation of responsible labour practices' (International Trade Union Confederation 2010) that was unprecedented in global SR initiatives?

Effective leadership, organization, strategic concentration of limited resources and relative homogeneity of interests played a part, but other groups also enjoyed these advantages along with greater numbers and resources. The key to labour's success appears to have been its ability to take advantage of the delicate relationship between ISO and ILO at a moment when ISO needed the legitimation that ILO could offer. These ISO-ILO interactions went through three phases corresponding to three of the components of a regulatory governance process: agenda setting, including forum selection; norm formation within the selected forum; and evaluation and review (Eberlein et al. 2014, pp. 6–7).

16.2.3.1 Agenda setting and forum selection: Remaking the ISO-ILO relationship

The initial interaction between ISO and ILO in the field of SR mainly concerned putting the topic of SR on ISO's agenda. This interaction destabilized the existing ISO-ILO relationship and tentatively formalized a new one.

ISO and ILO had a longstanding relationship in which ILO participated in and occasionally initiated the development of ISO standards affecting the workplace. This collaboration was restricted to what ILO viewed as narrow technical standards. This relationship came under pressure in the mid-1990s when the British Standards Institution (BSI) lobbied to internationalize its own occupational health and safety management system (OHSMS) standards through ISO. ISO initially declined in the face of objections that ILO was a more appropriate forum. ILO began work on its own OHSMS guidelines in 1997.[6] BSI forged ahead outside ISO, spearheading the publication of OHSAS 18001 in 1999 and then proposing a new ISO technical committee to develop OHSMS standards. Facing opposition from ILO and its labour and employer constituencies, the BSI proposal failed and ILO's OHSMS Guidance was published in 2001 (International Labour Office 2001).

ISO's initial exploration of SR standardization further destabilized the ISO-ILO relationship. The 2002 COPOLCO report endorsing the feasibility of ISO SR standards gave little attention to workers and did not recognize ILO's distinctive mandate (ISO 2002). ILO and labour worried that ISO, whose standards were driven by trade liberalization and market demand rather than pursuit of social justice, might not respect ILO's authority and standards (ILO 2007). These concerns led the AHGCSR to recognize that the 'ILO is the only intergovernmental body that was created specifically to develop international labour standards', that 'ISO is not an intergovernmental organization and therefore cannot define on its own substantive expectations in the area of social responsibility', and that 'ISO must recognize and respect the legitimacy and competence of existing bodies that have been setting SR standards for many years or decades – in particular ILO and other UN bodies' (ISO 2004c, pp. 50–51). The AHGCSR recommended that ISO should develop SR standards only if it recognized ILO's unique mandate to define international standards on a broad range of issues affecting workers (ISO 2004b, p. 1).

Realizing that it needed ILO's support or acquiescence to legitimize its move into SR standardization, ISO negotiated a Memorandum of Understanding (MOU) with ILO that gave the latter unprecedented procedural and substantive rights within ISO (ISO and ILO 2005). The MOU provided that any ISO SR standard would be 'fully consistent with' and 'in no way detract from' the ILSs and their interpretation by ILO organs (ibid., Article 2.1). It made ILO instruments 'the authoritative and definitive source of reference and minimum baseline' for any ISO SR standard relating to labour (ibid., Article 6.1). This was a significant departure not just for ISO but also for ILO. Up to this point, only some core ILSs were considered a minimum floor for all ILO member states. Now ISO was promising to extend the same treatment to all ILO instruments regardless of ratification status. Never before or since has ISO provided such an *ex ante* guarantee.

The MOU also gave ILO and its tripartite constituency the right to participate fully in all ISO bodies concerned with any ISO SR standard. It gave ILO the right to review and comment on any drafts implicating ILO issues before circulation within the WGSR and to have its comments circulated with the drafts. ISO agreed to seek ILO's full and formal backing for any draft standard before circulation to ISO member bodies for ballot or comment, and if such backing was not forthcoming, to circulate ILO's comments together with the draft prior to any ISO vote.

The only quid pro quo for ISO's concessions was ILO's implicit acceptance of ISO as a forum for SR standards development, provided however that ILO participation did not imply endorsement of any ISO standard and was conditional upon ISO's performance of its MOU obligations. That ISO extracted no concessions from ILO other than this qualified acquiescence indicates its need to reach an agreement and the fragility of its authority to develop SR standards. In return, ISO gained access to ILO's legitimacy, authority and expertise. By contrast, the risks for ILO were substantial, mainly in the form of potential dilution of ILO's authority and standards. But cooperation with ISO also offered ILO potentially greater penetration of ILO standards through ISO's worldwide network of standards developers and users.

While much of the credit for these procedural and substantive protections goes to ILO itself, some goes to its labour and employer constituencies. The International Confederation of Free Trade Unions (ICFTU, which later became the International Trade Union Confederation – ITUC), the International Organization of Employers (IOE) and their respective member organizations played important roles in the AHGCSR and beyond, initially opposing ISO's development of SR standards and then lobbying for a special role for ILO and its standards. Without their efforts it is not clear that ISO would have made the concessions it did in the ISO-ILO MOU.

By the time the WGSR first met in March 2005, the framework was in place for a new ISO-ILO relationship. Instead of occasional ad hoc cooperation on a limited range of technical issues, ILO was now preparing for sustained participation in ISO standard-setting on contested matters of social policy. The MOU formalizing this new relationship gave ILO procedural and substantive guarantees not enjoyed by any other participant in ISO standard-setting before or since. Alongside this formal agreement, ISO made several decisions that helped secure ILO's cooperation, including that ISO 26000 would be a guidance standard (not for certification), would not be a management system standard, would recognize the difference between authoritative intergovernmental instruments and voluntary private initiatives, would not address issues that could only be resolved through representative political processes, and would be developed through an open and transparent process designed to ensure meaningful participation of a full range of interested parties.

Organized labour played a significant part in forging this new relationship. Although there was only one labour representative on the AHGCSR, labour's influence was magnified by ISO's legitimation deficit in the SR field and the wide recognition (including by major employer groups) of ILO as the authoritative source of ILSs. These factors also put labour in a good position to take advantage of the new ISO-ILO relationship in its favour during the drafting of ISO 26000.

16.2.3.2 Norm formation: Leveraging the new ISO-ILO relationship

With the shift from agenda setting and forum selection to norm formation, the dynamics of governance interactions changed. The earlier phase was characterized by interactions among a small number of actors. The new phase was much more open-ended and involved many more participants interacting within and outside a forum – the WGSR – that quickly took on a life of its own. During this phase, labour leveraged ISO-ILO interactions in two ways. First, it rode a wave of support for ILO and the ILSs built up by participants from all stakeholder categories and by ILO itself. Second, labour actively promoted ILO's special status to advance its own interests.

Through this combination of passive and active piggy-backing (Buhmann 2015), labour prevailed on most of the issues that mattered to it.

One might be tempted to discount organized labour's role in this case on the basis that the result would have been the same regardless of its actions. But while ILO was assertive, its labour constituency was an important source of support and exercised significant influence of its own in both the agenda setting and norm formation phases. Without the active support of its labour and employer constituencies, it is doubtful that ILO would have enjoyed the influence it did within ISO. Moreover, my argument is not that ISO 26000 would have been different but for organized labour's efforts. The point is that organized labour took advantage of governance interactions between ISO and ILO in a manner that advanced its interests. Taking advantage can entail actively steering and shaping interactions, or it can mean simply hitching one's wagon to another actor's star. Conservation of resources is a priority for all regulatory actors, and especially for actors facing severe resource constraints. The fewer resources an actor must expend to achieve a given regulatory outcome, the better. From this perspective, the most successful strategy is one in which the actor enjoys a given result without expending any resources. Finding suitable coat-tails to ride, jumping on and knowing when to jump off are important questions for regulatory actors. In such cases the actor cannot claim to have influenced the outcome, but it has still taken advantage of a particular constellation of governance interactions to advance its interests.

In the WGSR, labour rode ILO's coat-tails and benefitted from a widely shared deference to ILO and its core labour standards. Even before the WGSR first met, many ISO member bodies and experts highlighted the need to cooperate with ILO and respect its instruments. One of the WGSR's first acts was to acknowledge ILO's special status and promise to consult it continually to ensure effective and timely implementation of the ISO-ILO MOU. ILO encouraged this deference, emphasizing its history as an SR pioneer, its mandate to promulgate ILSs, and its representativeness. It characterized the ILO Declaration on Fundamental Principles and Rights at Work as an 'absolute minimum that cannot be questioned' (ISO 2005, Annex D). It insisted that ISO 26000 must be fully consistent with the ILSs, that it must distinguish clearly between authoritative intergovernmental instruments and private initiatives, and that ILO could not possibly agree to a standard that promoted or endorsed any private initiatives.

Even participants wishing to scale back worker protections treated ILO instruments as the benchmark. One delegation, for example, commented:

> We do not want the ISO to get into the business of setting labour standards. This is why we want the text to be closely related to existing ILO standards. Therefore this is not the place to promote a 'wish list' of things that we would want but haven't been able to get at ILO. (ISO 2008, p. 391)

Few participants were openly sceptical of ILO and its standards. A few industry and government participants proposed unsuccessfully to delete references to ILO instruments and eliminate the entire section on fundamental rights at work. Others argued, sometimes successfully, that ISO 26000 should reflect only widely ratified ILO instruments.

Not only did many participants invoke ILO standards as the touchstone for their positions on labour issues, they also often deferred to ILO expertise. Numerous participants urged having ILO rewrite provisions related to labour. When ILO did so, experts from various stakeholder groups invoked this fact to reject subsequent proposals to scale back worker protections.

In short, participants routinely justified their positions in terms of consistency with ILO standards and deference to ILO's authority. This meant that basic labour rights and standards were not concessions to be secured through bargaining but accepted foundations on which to build. As a result, gains for labour accumulated throughout the negotiations even in the face of sustained resistance from some industry and government participants.

Labour experts did not merely ride this wave, they actively leveraged ILO's special status by emphasizing ILO's unique mandate and urging full implementation of the ISO-ILO MOU. They lobbied successfully for references to ILO instruments, many not widely ratified. They urged successfully that organizations should observe ILSs even when they conflict with national laws. When they were happy with a draft's treatment of labour issues, they invoked its consistency with ILO standards as a reason to keep it. Commenting on one draft's labour practices clause, for example, labour experts observed:

> Importantly all of it can be related to legitimate expectations and principles in international instruments of ILO. It does not create any new expectations and therefore it does not replace ILO and its function of setting international labour standards. (ISO 2007, p. 2)

This occurred against the background of widespread recognition that labour was under-represented and disadvantaged in the negotiations. WGSR participants recognized this disadvantage early on. The ICFTU (which later became ITUC) pointed out that the WGSR's process did not ensure balanced participation of all relevant interests. It lobbied to qualify the statement in ISO 26000's draft introduction that ISO 26000 was developed through a multi-stakeholder process, opining that the WGSR's procedures 'would have to be significantly revised in order to be considered a genuine multi-stakeholder process' (ISO 2008, p, 60). The IOE agreed. Ultimately a caveat was added that 'a full and equitable balance of stakeholders was constrained by various factors' (ISO 2010b, foreword).

Despite labour's disadvantage, it was viewed by WGSR participants as second only to industry in influence, according to a 2008 survey (Schmiedeknecht 2008, p. 16). Survey respondents attributed labour's disproportionate influence to the ISO-ILO MOU (ibid., pp. 18–19). Labour experts achieved substantial success on most major issues on which they took public positions in the negotiations, and many of their efforts to expand workers' rights and protections beyond ILO's core labour standards succeeded. Industry frequently resisted this expansion but lost most battles on this front.

16.2.3.3 Evaluation and review: Reconsidering the ISO-ILO relationship

ISO and ILO began to reconsider their relationship even before the ink was dry on ISO 26000. In the late stages of the WGSR's work, ISO struck a high-level group to consider whether ISO should apply the WGSR's innovations, including representation by stakeholder groups and enhanced rights for external organizations such as ILO, to other ISO standards development. The group received highly positive feedback about these innovations from most WGSR participants but negative feedback from many ISO national member bodies, which felt that these special arrangements undermined their authority as the primary arenas for stakeholder input. The high-level group agreed, recommending that ISO not change its established procedures and that stakeholder engagement occur within ISO national member bodies (ISO 2011, p. 5).

ILO had its own concerns about the time and resources required to participate effectively, the risk that tripartite dialogue would be compromised when the WGSR switched to voting by ISO member bodies rather than experts, and the risk that ISO SR standards might be used for private third-party certification in competition with ILO instruments. Employer and worker constituents expressed concern that ISO 26000 could lead to a proliferation of private standards, such private standards could undermine ILO's exclusive competence to set ILSs, and ILO standards could be hijacked by profit-seeking standardization and certification bodies.

During the development of ISO 26000, some ISO member bodies proposed other ISO standards that would address ILO issues including

OHS and human resource management. ILO repeatedly voiced its resistance to such standards and its determination to participate only if afforded guarantees like those in the ISO-ILO MOU. ISO deferred to ILO in some cases but went ahead in others. In 2013, it accepted BSI's latest proposal to develop an ISO OHSMS standard, to be known as ISO 45001. ISO and ILO concluded a new MOU in relation to this work that was noticeably weaker than the 2005 MOU (ISO and ILO 2013). ILO was soon disappointed with the implementation of the new MOU, complaining that the draft standard was inconsistent with the ILSs and that the committee's decision-making lacked transparency.[7] ILO's concerns were repeatedly dismissed by the committee's leaders, who took the position that they could ignore the ILSs if that was the committee consensus. In the end, ILO concluded that ISO 45001 was inconsistent with the ILSs. ITUC and IOE also expressed reservations (International Trade Union Confederation 2017; International Organization of Employers 2017).

ILO also believed that ISO neglected its obligation under the MOUs to give ILO adequate advance notice of any new work implicating ILO issues, including a proposed revision of ISO 26000. When ILO suggested that any ILO participation in further ISO SR work would be governed by the 2005 MOU, ISO claimed that the 2013 MOU had superseded the 2005 MOU and gave ILO notice of termination of the 2005 agreement. ILO in turn terminated the 2013 MOU and suspended all cooperation with ISO until further notice (ILO 2017a, 2017b).

How and why the ISO-ILO relationship fell apart is a question for another day. The important point is that the leverage that this special relationship conferred on labour within ISO may have been confined to a brief time when ISO's self-perceived legitimation deficit impelled it to seek to enrol ILO and its regulatory resources to enhance its own regulatory capacities.

16.3 LESSONS FOR THEORY AND PRACTICE

What lessons can be drawn from this case for efforts to advance marginalized actors' interests in transnational governance contests? In my case study, structurally weak actors – representatives of organized labour – were able to prevail in a transnational governance contest against more powerful adversaries – including representatives of industry and governments – by taking advantage of the uneasy interaction between an organization that lacked certain regulatory resources (including legitimacy, expertise and regulatory standards) and another that could supply some of those resources. In this section I explain my case study using theories of legitimation and enrolment and propose a triadic strategy to harness TBGIs to advance marginalized actors and improve the quality of transnational regulation. In this strategy an *underdog* exploits legitimation differentials between a *regulator* and a *booster* to advance its own regulatory agenda.

16.3.1 Legitimation and Enrolment

Legitimation is the process by which an actor claims the authority to perform one or more components of a regulatory governance process and relevant audiences validate this claim. Would-be regulators act strategically to gain legitimacy. According to Suchman, *informing* strategies seek to identify audiences that are predisposed to accept a regulator's authority and alert them to the regulator's activities; *converting* strategies seek to cause undecided or opposed audience members to change their evaluations and accept the regulator's authority; and *conforming* strategies change the regulator's structures, processes or outputs to conform to audience members' expectations (Suchman 1995). Regulators 'seek to justify the exercise of power by claiming to set certain constraints upon its exercise' (Szablowski 2007, p. 18). For legitimacy to endure, audiences must believe that these constraints are generally observed (ibid., p. 19). Audiences forgive some transgressions (Black 2008, p. 145), but legitimacy does not endure long if exposed as superficial or manipulative (Gulbrandsen 2005, 2010; Fransen 2012).

Legitimation is aimed at enrolling actors into desired roles as rule makers, rule takers, monitors, enforcers, adjudicators and so on. Enrolment is the process by which an actor accepts an assigned role in a network, making its resources available for mobilization by others (Latour 1984). Such resources include organizational capacity, convening power, communication networks, personnel, money, technology, information, expertise, reputation and legitimacy (Wood and others, Chapter 1; Verbruggen and Havinga, Chapter 2).

ISO used a conforming strategy with ILO and labour. It sought to justify its development of SR standards by assuming special constraints. Procedural constraints included a formal multi-stakeholder approach, transparent records and enhanced notice-and-comment rights for ILO. Substantive constraints revolved around deference to norms set by representative political institutions in authoritative intergovernmental instruments. This principle had its strongest expression in the ISO-ILO MOU, which guaranteed that any ISO SR standard would be fully consistent with the ILSs and their interpretation by ILO organs, and would treat ILO instruments as the authoritative reference and minimum baseline for labour standards.

This conforming strategy allowed ISO to enrol numerous actors into desired roles and mobilize their symbolic and material resources in support of its goals. Chief among these was ILO, which was perceived as authoritative by most audiences from whom ISO sought legitimacy. The ISO-ILO MOU enabled ISO to enrol not only ILO but also labour, industry, NGOs, governments and other stakeholders who repeatedly cited it as a prerequisite for the WGSR's work. These actors put their time, money, expertise, connections, reputations and pre-existing norms at ISO's service.

The legitimating constraints that facilitated this enrolment were largely observed in practice, except the multi-stakeholder approach. Many participants doubted the authenticity of many experts' stakeholder designations and were critical of the imbalance among stakeholder categories. Later, when the ISO 26000 project was coming to an end and audiences' attention was turning elsewhere, ISO reconsidered the WGSR model and – in ILO's view – began to ignore the constraints of both the 2005 and the subsequent 2013 MOUs. These perceived transgressions eventually led ILO to withdraw its cooperation.

Regulators do not have conclusive control over their own legitimacy; rather, legitimacy is an endowment bestowed or withdrawn by audiences (Black 2009). Successful legitimation strategies appeal to legitimating ideas prevalent among target audiences (Szablowski 2007, p. 19). Audiences' abilities to affect a regulator's legitimacy vary, as do the bases on which they grant or withhold legitimacy. The ability of ILO to affect ISO's legitimacy in the field of SR was substantially greater than that of labour unions alone, due to the former's organizational resources and high legitimacy in the eyes of a broad audience (Tamm Hallström and Boström 2010, p. 145). Likewise, ISO's core constituencies of transnational corporations, national standards bodies and related service providers had greater influence than marginal audiences like labour. That said, the tight coherence of labour around a peak organization, ITUC, enhanced its influence over ISO's legitimacy compared to heterogeneous, less organized stakeholder groups (ibid., pp. 127–8).

ILO and labour responded to ISO's legitimation strategies initially with hostility because they believed ISO was dominated by big business and unlikely to uphold ILSs. ISO's conforming strategy brought them around to cautious acquiescence. Simply by participating, they conferred some legitimacy on ISO, but this legitimacy was outcome-contingent. In the end both ILO and ITUC were satisfied with ISO 26000. This legitimacy did not prove resilient to perceived transgressions, however. In the development of ISO 45001, ISO invoked a more traditional basis for legitimacy: technical expertise in the service of business. This may have appealed to its core audiences, but it sacrificed legitimation from ILO and labour.

These events underline the proposition that legitimacy is shifting, variable and constantly renegotiated as regulators face multiple and conflicting legitimation demands (Cotterrell 2016, p. 254). This is especially true in transnational settings, where legitimacy 'must be repeatedly created, recreated, and conquered' through 'a continuous and intensive negotiation' (Tamm Hallström and Boström 2010, p. 160). Regulators often face a dilemma: 'what they need to do to be accepted by one part of their environment, within and outside the regulatory regime, is contrary to how they need to respond to another part' (Black 2008, p. 153).

Which legitimation demands will regulators heed? Julia Black suggests that this is not a simple matter of the anticipated legitimacy gains for the regulator. Rather, a regulator will be more likely to accept an audience's legitimation demands where:

> it perceives itself to have a relatively high dependence on or interconnectedness with the legitimacy claimant; where the content of the claim and the discourse in which it is expressed is congruent with the organization; where acquiescence would not pose severe constraints on its discretion; where the claimant can directly or indirectly coerce the regulator; where the claims being advanced are widely diffused; and the consequences of acquiescing are relatively certain. (Black 2008, p. 156)

When claiming that anticipated legitimacy gains are not decisive, Black refers to legitimacy gains with the particular audience making the demand. It is true that ISO did not expect to gain a great deal of legitimacy with ILO or labour as a result of accommodating their legitimation demands. It expected them to tolerate and take part in ISO's work, little more. But it expected enrolment of ILO to garner substantial legitimacy for ISO with other audiences, and in fact it seems to have done so. I would therefore add a seventh factor to Black's hypothesis, namely the anticipated legitimacy gains for the regulator from *all* audiences as a result of acceptance of the particular audience's demands. The greater the overall gains, the more likely the regulator is to accept the demands.

Applying these factors to my case study reveals a puzzle: four of seven factors appeared neutral at best, and three clearly disfavoured ISO's acquiescence to labour's demands; yet most of labour's demands were met in the drafting of ISO 26000. First, accepting labour's legitimacy demands would place significant but not severe constraints on ISO's discretion. Labour essentially advanced the same demands as ILO:

that ISO 26000 be fully consistent with and in no way detract from the ILSs as interpreted by ILO, that ILO instruments be the authoritative reference and minimum floor, and that ISO 26000 recognize the primacy of authoritative intergovernmental instruments. These were significant constraints, but ISO reserved the discretion to determine which labour issues to include, which instruments to cite, the form of the standard (guidance or certification), its detail and precise wording. Labour's procedural demands were significant but ultimately modest departures from ISO norms. ISO's ordinary rules already required committees to seek the full and formal backing of liaison organizations for draft standards, and ITUC and ILO would surely have been accepted as liaison organizations under ISO's ordinary rules. The WGSR's transparency innovations were also modest: records were posted publicly, but meetings were closed to the public and media. These constraints, taken together, can be considered substantial but not severe. This factor therefore neither clearly favoured nor disfavoured ISO's acquiescence to labour's demands.

A second factor that appeared neutral was the diffusion of labour's legitimacy claims in ISO's institutional environment. These claims were widely diffused in ISO's external environment insofar as they reiterated ILO's claims of authority to set labour standards and asserted a general norm of balanced and effective participation by all stakeholder categories. They were not widely diffused insofar as labour claimed special status distinct from other stakeholder groups. The idea that any stakeholder was more important than others was not prevalent in the standardization community except in relation to industry, the primary user of standards.

Third, the consequences of acquiescing to labour's legitimation demands were somewhat uncertain, given the number of organizations representing labour and the absence of a written agreement setting down the terms of their engagement. That said, they overlapped substantially with ILO's demands, the consequences of which were relatively certain: acquiescence would enable ISO to proceed with developing SR standards within agreed procedural and substantive constraints. This factor was therefore either neutral or modestly favourable to labour.

A fourth factor that did not clearly disfavour labour was the anticipated overall legitimacy gains for ISO from all audiences as a result of acceptance of labour's demands. Stakeholders of all categories frequently emphasized the importance of respecting labour standards and having labour on board. But most of their attention was directed at ILO, and it is not clear that any legitimacy gains with these wider audiences could have been attributed specifically to ISO's acceptance of the demands of labour as distinct from those of ILO.

The remaining three factors clearly disfavoured ISO's acceptance of labour's legitimation demands. First, ISO saw the benefit of having labour on board but did not seem to perceive itself as particularly dependent on labour for the performance of its regulatory role; nor did it appear to feel much sense of inter-organizational or interpersonal connection with labour, in contrast to its lengthy ad hoc collaboration with ILO. Second, the congruence of labour's legitimation demands with ISO's own cognitive and normative frameworks was low. ISO sits at the apex of a system of voluntary standardization rooted in an ideology of technical expertise, voluntarism, free enterprise and trade liberalization (Wood 2003, 2005, 2012b; Murphy and Yates 2009). Labour formulated its claims in terms of social justice, workers' rights, tripartite dialogue, democratic accountability and limitation of unbridled markets. Finally, labour had very limited means to coerce ISO. Its only credible threat was to walk away. It relied on persuasion and ISO's goodwill. This became clear later, when ISO ultimately forged ahead with a process and outcome for ISO 45001 over the objections of ITUC, IOE and ILO.

Why, then, did ISO accept labour's legitimation demands? The answer seems to be that organized labour was able to ride ILO's coat-tails. Five of the seven factors favoured ISO's acquiescence to ILO's demands. First, ISO perceived itself to be dependent upon ILO for the ability to write SR standards affecting labour issues. It also seems to have seen itself as interconnected with ILO by virtue of their overlapping activities in OHS and other labour-related issues, their history of ad hoc cooperation, their shared status as influential, venerable, non-partisan IOs devoted to the betterment of society, and the overlap of their business/employer constituencies.

The congruence of ILO's legitimation demands with ISO's cognitive and normative frameworks was greater than it was for organized labour. In addition to social justice, workers' rights, tripartite dialogue and democratic accountability, ILO couched its claims in terms of its own political representativeness and authority to promulgate binding international law. This resonated with ISO's understanding of its own limitations: voluntary standards should eschew politics and should not conflict with authoritative legal norms set by representative political authorities. During the negotiation of the ISO-ILO MOU, ISO said that it was 'in ISO's own interest not to develop standards that conflict with national or international law' (Anonymous 2005, on file with author). This factor therefore modestly favoured acquiescence to ILO's demands.

Black's third factor was probably neutral: acquiescence to ILO's demands posed substantial but not severe constraints on ISO's discretion. I discussed this factor earlier in relation to labour. Fourth, like labour, ILO lacked the means to coerce ISO to accept its demands. This factor disfavoured ISO's acquiescence. Fifth, ILO's legitimacy as the authoritative source and interpreter of ILSs was very widely diffused in ISO's external environment, favouring acquiescence to its demands. Finally, the consequences of acquiescing to ILO's legitimation demands were more certain than those of labour alone. Acquiescence would enable ISO to proceed with developing SR standards within the constraints described earlier. It would secure ILO's participation in the WGSR. Finally, as I argued above, it promised to deliver substantial legitimacy gains with other audiences including government, NGOs and industry.

In short, conditions favoured ISO's acquiescence to ILO's demands but not labour's. Labour appears to have taken advantage of ILO's stronger position to secure gains it probably could not have achieved on its own. What strategic lessons can be drawn from this success?

16.3.2 Underdogs, Boosters and Regulators: Leveraging Legitimation Differentials

My case study suggests a generalizable triadic strategy for marginalized actors to prevail in transnational governance struggles by leveraging the legitimation differential between a regulator facing a legitimacy deficit and an actor with abundant legitimacy. In my case study, ISO pursued a forum-shifting strategy, proposing itself as an alternative to existing international SR standard-setters. It supported this shift with a conforming strategy aimed at accommodating the concerns of certain resistant audiences. It employed a mix of contractual and organizational modalities to achieve this accommodation: contractual in the form of an MOU with ILO; organizational in the form of enticing actors into ISO with the promise of modified standard-setting rules and procedures.

Labour entered this alternative forum reluctantly and faced a substantial disadvantage there. ISO had little reason to accept its legitimation demands. And yet it achieved a remarkably favourable outcome in the labour-related content of ISO 26000. It did so by taking advantage of the uneasy relationship between an organization – ISO – that lacked certain important regulatory resources (especially legitimacy) and another – ILO – that could supply those resources. This case shows that a weak actor can magnify its impact by exploiting the interaction between a regulator with a legitimation deficit and an actor with what might be termed loosely a legitimation surplus. The strategy I describe shares some features with but is distinct from other triadic models of regulatory governance such as orchestration (Abbott and Snidal 2009; Abbott et al. 2015a) and intermediation (Abbott et al. 2017). The first condition for the strategy is the presence of an actor that wishes to achieve regulatory goals but finds itself at a systematic disadvantage that it cannot overcome on its own. I will call this actor the *underdog*.

The second condition is that the regulator the underdog wishes to influence has a legitimation deficit with audiences, other than the underdog, from whom the regulator seeks legitimacy. Such a legitimation deficit gives the regulator an incentive to seek to enrol actors to endow it with the legitimacy it lacks. In turn it creates an opening for those actors to influence the regulator in ways that might help the underdog. Underdogs may be able to widen this opening by accentuating this legitimation deficit – something that labour did in the context of ISO's move into the SR field. Such delegitimation tactics may be insufficient on their own to achieve the underdog's goals, but can be part of the underdog's strategy. The regulator in this model is similar to that in the orchestration and RIT (regulator-intermediary-target) models in that it lacks capacities needed to achieve its regulatory goals (Abbott et al. 2015b; Abbott et al. 2017). What is distinctive about my account is that one of these capacities must be legitimacy.

The third condition is the presence in the regulator's environment of an actor that enjoys high legitimacy and is amenable to enrolment or is already enrolled by the regulator into a role in the regulatory regime. An organization that enjoys high legitimacy with a regulator's target audiences presents an attractive target for a legitimacy-poor regulator to enrol in support of its own regulatory agenda. This actor is similar to an intermediary in the orchestration/RIT models insofar is it possesses capacities that the regulator lacks or that the intermediary can provide more effectively or efficiently (ibid.). In my account, the capacities the actor can provide must include legitimacy, though they can also include other resources.

The legitimacy-rich actor does not necessarily play the role of an intermediary as defined in the orchestration/RIT models, namely acting in conjunction with a regulator to change the behaviour of regulatory targets (ibid.). In my approach the actor can be enrolled into the position of intermediary, target, beneficiary or even regulator. In my case study, ILO was enrolled as a regulator – a participant in ISO rulemaking. What makes my strategy distinctive is that the capacity-rich actor is enrolled doubly: by the regulator to boost the regulator's legitimacy, and by the underdog to boost the underdog's effectiveness. I call this actor the *booster*.

The relationship between the regulator and the booster follows the pattern of legitimation and enrolment I described earlier: the legitimacy-rich actor has capacities the regulator lacks, the regulator deploys legitimation strategies to enrol the legitimacy-rich actor into the desired role, the legitimacy-rich actor responds with its own legitimation demands, and the legitimacy-rich actor is (or is not) enrolled into the desired regulatory role and confers (or does not confer) legitimacy on the regulator.

The role of the underdog is more complicated. It takes advantage of the legitimation differential between the regulator and the booster. It relates to the regulator as a legitimacy-granting or withholding audience and in this sense is positioned similarly toward the regulator as the booster is, except that the regulator lacks incentives to respond to its legitimation demands. So the underdog accentuates the regulator's legitimation deficit and the booster's corresponding surplus. It advocates the regulator's acquiescence to the booster's legitimation demands, and if this happens it exploits the regulator's enrolment of the booster to advance its own goals. It can do so proactively, as when labour experts actively invoked ILO's special status to advance their interests, or passively, riding a wave of legitimacy conferred on the booster by other audiences. This was seen when labour rode the wave of support for ILO built up by participants from all stakeholder categories and by ILO itself.

The underdog enrols the booster and its regulatory capacities – especially its legitimacy with other audiences from whom the regulator seeks legitimation – as a force multiplier. This does not imply that the booster would not have got involved but for the underdog's efforts. It is possible that the booster would have participated for other reasons. The underdog enrols the booster not in the sense that it causes the booster to do something it would not otherwise have done, but in the sense that it takes advantage of the booster's capacities to advance its own agenda, and the booster allows this to happen.

In short, the case of organized labour, ILO and ISO 26000 shed light on the interactive dynamics of legitimation in transnational governance by suggesting a triadic strategy in which a marginalized actor advances its interests by accentuating and taking advantage of the relationship between a regulator with a self-perceived legitimation deficit and a potential booster with an abundance of legitimacy in the same regulatory space.

NOTES

1. The WGSR archive is available at http://www.iso.org/wgsr (accessed 11 April 2019).
2. 'Mirror committee' is the term for the committee that provides input to an ISO member body regarding positions its representatives should take in international negotiations.
3. A brief methodological note is in order. I derived 137 distinct elements of ILSs in 28 subject areas from ILO's official summary of ILSs (International Labour Office

2014) (excluding instruments adopted after 2010) and the version of the Tripartite Declaration of Principles Concerning Multinational Enterprises and Social Policy (ILO MNE Declaration) in force when ISO 26000 was published (International Labour Organization 2006). While these two sources do not embody all the details of the ILSs, they give an accurate picture of what ILO considers the key features of ILSs and how they apply to business firms. I assessed the scope, specificity and rigour of ISO 26000, SA8000:2008 (Social Accountability International 2008), the BSCI Code of Conduct (Foreign Trade Association 2009) and the official guide to the UN Global Compact's labour principles (International Labour Organization 2008) against these 137 elements. 'Rigour' refers only to the ambition of the standard, not its degree of obligation, since ISO 26000 as a guidance document was precluded from using obligatory language.

4. These were three of the best known and widest used cross-sectoral SR initiatives when ISO 26000 was being drafted. The UNGC was and remains the world's highest-profile SR initiative. It is a platform for making general commitments and sharing best practices. SA8000:2008 was a certification standard for corporate social accountability, focusing on labour practices. Like ISO 26000, it was produced by a purportedly multi-stakeholder process in which labour was vastly outnumbered. BSCI was a self-regulatory code of conduct produced by the leading European association of multinational businesses.
5. For a comparison of ISO 26000's treatment of the concept of sphere of influence with that of the 2011 UN Guiding Principles on Business and Human Rights, see Wood 2012a.
6. OHS is the term employed by ISO and most of its member bodies, whereas ILO uses the term OSH (occupational safety and health). For consistency, I use the term OHS in this chapter.
7. In the interest of full disclosure, I was retained by ILO in 2014–15 to advise it on effective participation in this ISO committee.

REFERENCES

Abbott, Kenneth W., Philipp Genschel, Duncan Snidal and Bernhard Zangl (eds) (2015a), *International Organizations as Orchestrators*, Cambridge, UK: Cambridge University Press.

Abbott, Kenneth W., Philipp Genschel, Duncan Snidal and Bernhard Zangl (2015b), 'Orchestration: global governance through intermediaries', in Kenneth W. Abbott, Philipp Genschel, Duncan Snidal and Bernhard Zangl (eds), *International Organizations as Orchestrators*, Cambridge, UK: Cambridge University Press, pp. 3–36.

Abbott, Kenneth W., David Levi-Faur and Duncan Snidal (2017), 'Theorizing regulatory intermediaries: The RIT model', *Annals of the American Academy of Political and Social Sciences*, **670** (1), 14–35.

Abbott, Kenneth W. and Duncan Snidal (2009), 'Strengthening international regulation through transnational new governance: overcoming the orchestration deficit', *Vanderbilt Journal of Transnational Law*, **42**, 501–78.

Anonymous (2005), *Summary Record of Meeting between ISO and ILO Concerning Guiding Principles for a Memorandum of Understanding (MoU) between ISO and ILO*.

Black, Julia (2008), 'Constructing and contesting legitimacy and accountability in polycentric regulatory regimes', *Regulation and Governance*, **2** (2), 137–64.

Black, Julia (2009), 'Legitimacy and the competition for regulatory share', LSE Law, Society and Economy Working Paper No. 14/2009, LSE Law Department.

Buhmann, Karin (2015), 'Business and human rights: understanding the UN guiding principles from the perspective of transnational business governance interactions', *Transnational Legal Theory*, **6** (2), 399–434.

Cotterrell, Roger (2016), 'Transnational legal authority: a socio-legal perspective', in Roger Cotterrell and Maksymilian Del Mar (eds), *Authority in Transnational Legal Theory: Theorising Across Disciplines*, Cheltenham, UK and Northampton, MA, USA: Edward Elgar, pp. 253–79.
Eberlein, Burkard, Kenneth W. Abbott, Julia Black, Errol Meidinger and Stepan Wood (2014), 'Transnational business governance interactions: conceptualization and framework for analysis', *Regulation and Governance*, **8** (1), 1–21.
Foreign Trade Association (2009), *BSCI Code of Conduct*, Brussels: Foreign Trade Association.
Fransen, Luc (2012), 'Multi-stakeholder governance and voluntary programme interactions: legitimation politics in the institutional design of corporate social responsibility', *Socio-Economic Review*, **10** (1), 163–92.
Gulbrandsen, Lars H. (2005), 'Sustainable forestry in Sweden: the effect of competition among private certification schemes', *Journal of Environment and Development*, **14** (3), 338–55.
Gulbrandsen, Lars H. (2010), *Transnational Environmental Governance: The Emergence and Effects of the Certification of Forests and Fisheries*, Cheltenham, UK and Northampton, MA: Edward Elgar.
International Labour Office (2001), *Guidelines on Occupational Safety and Health Management Systems, ILO-OSH 2001*, Geneva: International Labour Organization.
International Labour Office (2014), *Rules of the Game: A Brief Introduction to International Labour Standards*, 3rd revised edn, Geneva: International Labour Organization.
International Labour Organization (2006), *Tripartite Declaration of Principles Concerning Multinational Enterprises and Social Policy*, Geneva: International Labour Organization.
International Labour Organization (2007), 'Report of the Director-General, Fifth Supplementary Report: collaboration between the ILO and ISO', Governing Body, 298th Session, Geneva, March, GB.298/15/5.
International Labour Organization (2008), *The Labour Principles of the United Nations Global Compact: A Guide for Business*, Geneva: International Labour Organization.
International Labour Organization (2017a), 'Review of the implementation of ILO–ISO agreements', Governing Body, 331st Session, Geneva, 25 October, GB.331/INS/10.
International Labour Organization (2017b), 'Decision on the tenth item on the agenda: review of the implementation of ILO–ISO agreements', accessed 11 April 2019 at) http://www.ilo.org/gb/decisions/GB331-decision/WCMS_592322/lang--en/index.htm.
International Organization of Employers (2017), *Employers Concerned by ISO 45001: An Unbalanced and Impractical Standard for SMEs*, October 3, accessed 11 April 2019 at https://www.ioe-emp.org/en/news-events-documents/news/news/1506662935-employers-concerned-by-iso-45001-an-unbalanced-and-impractical-standard-for-smes/?tx_ioerelations_pi1%5BcurrentPid%5D=&tx_ioerelations_pi1%5Bnews%5D=113970.
International Organization for Standardization (ISO) (1997), *Friendship Among Equals: Recollections from ISO's First Fifty Years*, Geneva: International Organization for Standardization.
International Organization for Standardization (ISO) (2002), 'The desirability and feasibility of ISO corporate social responsibility standards', Final Report of the

Consumer Protection in the Global Market Working Group of the ISO Consumer Policy Committee (COPOLCO), International Organization for Standardization, May.
International Organization for Standardization (ISO) (2004a), *New Work Item Proposal: ISO 26000 Guidance on Social Responsibility*, 1 October, Geneva: International Organization for Standardization.
International Organization for Standardization (ISO) (2004b), 'Recommendations to the ISO Technical Management Board', Report of the Ad Hoc Group on Corporate Social Responsibility, ISO/TMB AHGCSR N32, 30 April.
International Organization for Standardization (ISO) (2004c), 'Working report on social responsibility', Report of the Ad Hoc Group on Corporate Social Responsibility, 30 April.
International Organization for Standardization (ISO) (2005), 'Draft minutes of the second meeting of ISO/TMB/WG social responsibility', Working Group on Social Responsibility, ISO/TMB/WGSR N54 rev1, 15 February.
International Organization for Standardization (ISO) (2007), 'Comments received on ISO/WD 26000.3, Clause 6', Working Group on Social Responsibility, ISO/TMB/WGSR N120 Part 2, 21 September.
International Organization for Standardization (ISO) (2008), 'Comments received on ISO/WD 26000.4.2', Working Group on Social Responsibility, ISO/TMB/WGSR N151, 15 August.
International Organization for Standardization (ISO) (2010a), 'Comments of the International Labour Office for circulation with ISO/FDIS 26000', Working Group on Social Responsibility, ISO/TMB/WGSR N194.
International Organization for Standardization (ISO) (2010b), *ISO 26000:2010, Guidance on Social Responsibility*, 1st edn, Geneva: International Organization for Standardization.
International Organization for Standardization (ISO) (2011), 'Report and recommendations to the ISO/TMB on alternative models of standards development operations and participation in ISO,' Report of Process Evaluation Group, ISO/TMB 36/2011 Annex 1, June.
International Organization for Standardization (ISO) (2017), *The ISO Survey of Management System Standard Certifications 2016: Executive Summary*, Geneva: International Organization for Standardization.
International Organization for Standardization (ISO) (2018), *Annual Report 2017: Building for a Better Future*, Geneva: International Organization for Standardization.
International Organization for Standardization and International Labour Organization (2005), 'Memorandum of understanding between the International Labour Organization and the International Organization for standardization in the field of social responsibility', ISO Doc No. ISO/TMB/WGSR N18, 4 March.
International Organization for Standardization and International Labour Organization (2013), 'Agreement between the International Labour Organization (ILO) and the International Organization for Standardization (ISO)', ILO Doc No. GB.319/INS/INF/1 Appendix, 6 August.
International Trade Union Confederation (2010), 'ITUC Comment on ISO 26000 FDIS', Brussels, ITUC, 10 September.
International Trade Union Confederation (2017), *ITUC Statement Following Approval of the ISO Standard 45001 on Occupational Health and Safety Management Systems*, 26 September, accessed 11 April 2019 at https://www.ituc-csi.org/ituc-statement-following-approval.

Justice, Dwight W. (2011), 'Labour practices', in Adrian Henriques (ed.), *Understanding ISO 26000: A Practical Approach to Social Responsibility*, London: British Standards Institution, pp. 21–31.
Latour, Bruno (1984), 'The powers of association', *Sociological Review*, **32**, 264–80.
Murphy, Craig N. and JoAnne Yates (2009), *The International Organization for Standardization (ISO): Global Governance Through Voluntary Consensus*, London and New York: Routledge.
Schmiedeknecht, Maud (2008), 'ISO 26000: reflecting the process of a multi-stakeholder dialogue-an empirical study', Kostanz Institute for Intercultural Management, Values and Communication (KIeM) Working Paper No. 29/2008.
Social Accountability International (2008), *SA8000: 2008 Social Accountability 8000*, New York: Social Accountability International.
Suchman, Mark C. (1995), 'Managing legitimacy: strategic and institutional approaches', *Academy of Management Review*, **20** (3), 571–610.
Szablowski, David (2007), *Transnational Law and Local Struggles: Mining, Communities and the World Bank*, Oxford and Portland, OR: Hart.
Tamm Hallström, Kristina and Magnus Boström (2010), *Transnational Multi-Stakeholder Standardization: Organizing Fragile Non-State Authority*, Cheltenham, UK and Northampton, MA, USA: Edward Elgar.
Wood, Stepan (2003), 'Green revolution or greenwash? Voluntary environmental standards, public law, and private authority in Canada', in Law Commission of Canada (ed.), *New Perspectives on the Public-Private Divide*, Vancouver: UBC Press, pp. 123–65.
Wood, Stepan (2005), 'Three questions about corporate codes: problematizations, authorizations and the public/private divide', in Wesley Cragg (ed.), *Corporations and the Challenge of Globalization*, Cheltenham, UK and Northampton, MA, USA: Edward Elgar, pp. 245–88.
Wood, Stepan (2012a), 'The case for leverage-based corporate human rights responsibility', *Business Ethics Quarterly*, **22** (1), 63–98.
Wood, Stepan (2012b), 'The international organization for standardization', in Darryl Reed, Peter Utting and Ananya Mukherjee-Reed (eds), *Business Regulation and Non-State Actors: Whose Standards? Whose Development?*, New York: Routledge, pp. 81–94.
Wood, Stepan, Kenneth W. Abbott, Julia Black, Burkard Eberlein and Errol Meidinger (2015), 'The interactive dynamics of transnational business governance: a challenge for transnational legal theory', *Transnational Legal Theory*, **6** (2), 333–69.

PART III

Conclusions

17. Harnessing TBGIs to advance regulatory quality and marginalized actors

Stepan Wood, Errol Meidinger, Burkard Eberlein, Rebecca Schmidt and Kenneth W. Abbott

17.1 INTRODUCTION

This book asks whether and how transnational business governance interactions (TBGIs) (Eberlein et al. 2014; Wood et al. 2015) can be harnessed to enhance the quality of regulation and to advance marginalized interests. The chapters explore numerous ways to mobilize TBGIs in pursuit of these goals, as well as constraints on doing so. In this concluding chapter, we synthesize key findings about the effects of TBGIs (Part 2) and explore their theoretical and practical implications for identifying and shaping interactions that foster regulatory quality or advance marginalized interests (Part 3), before concluding with some reflections on lessons learned and future research directions (Part 4).

17.2 FINDINGS

The chapters paint a mixed and not particularly optimistic picture of the prospects for harnessing TBGIs to improve regulatory quality and advance marginalized interests. Table 17.1 summarizes the authors' findings and projections. TBGIs appear to have advanced both regulatory quality and marginalized actors in just three chapters (Chapters 4, 15 and 16); the picture is unclear, mixed or negative in the rest.

17.2.1 Regulatory Capacities

The chapters reveal that the relationship between TBGIs and regulatory capacities is bidirectional: interactions affect regulatory capacities, and

Table 17.1 Effects of TBGIs on regulatory quality and marginalized actors

Effects on regulatory quality	Effects on marginalized actors	Chapters
Positive	Positive	4. Schmidt (sustainable mega-events) 15. Oman (FPIC in the Forest Stewardship Council) 16. Wood (ISO 26000 and organized labour)
Positive	Negative	2. Verbruggen & Havinga (GFSI)
Possibly positive	Unknown	7. Westerwinter (networks of transnational public-private governance initiatives) 12. Bach (OGCI)
Mixed	Mixed	3. Meidinger (SSCM) 8. Henriksen and Seabrooke (professional-organizational networks)
Negative	Unknown	5. Winn (SEPA) 6. Auld and Renckens (MSC audits)
Unknown	Negative	9. Casey (GLOBALGAP) 10. Carodenuto and Cashore (REDD+ and FLEGT/VPA deforestation and forest legality regimes in Cameroon) 11. Paiement (EU Renewable Energy Directive) 13. Gao and Chen (Asian derivatives trading) 14. Foley (fisheries eco-certification)

regulatory capacities shape interactions. Uneven distribution of regulatory resources influences TBGIs in at least two ways. It tilts interactions in favour of those who already have resources (see especially Foley, Chapter 14), and it drives actors who lack resources to interact with others in the hope of securing them (see especially Verbruggen and Havinga, Chapter 2). Three elements of regulatory capacity emerge as particularly significant to the cases explored in this book: material and symbolic resources, network resources and learning capacity.

First, the chapters find a strong relationship between TBGIs and the distribution of material and symbolic resources. Starting with material resources, the chapters suggest that a major factor impeding the enhancement of marginalized actors' material resources is the reluctance of powerful actors to redistribute such resources (Auld et al. 2015, p. 117). Lead firms offer suppliers inadequate material incentives to support genuine movement toward sustainability (Meidinger,

Chapter 3). Fisheries and food safety certification schemes do little to improve small-scale producers' livelihoods (Verbruggen and Havinga, Chapter 2; Foley, Chapter 14). And REDD+ and FLEGT/VPA did not help marginalized Cameroonian producers (Carodenuto and Cashore, Chapter 10).

In contrast, several chapters find that TBGIs enhanced the symbolic resources of particular actors or regulatory regimes. Interactions with state actors enhanced GFSI's legitimacy and credibility and state actors' knowledge and competence (Verbruggen and Havinga, Chapter 2). The IOC mobilized host cities' legitimacy, credibility and local knowledge (Schmidt, Chapter 4); and both ISO and labour leveraged ILO's legitimacy (Wood, Chapter 16). On the negative side, TBGIs hindered the development of symbolic resources in the case of SEPA (Winn, Chapter 5), where cognitive limitations impaired the legitimacy of EU regulation and bank self-regulation alike, while limiting the capacity of the regulatory regime. Mixed effects on symbolic resources were also seen with GLOBALGAP (Casey, Chapter 9), REDD+ and FLEGT in Cameroon (Carodenuto and Cashore, Chapter 10), fisheries eco-certification schemes (Foley, Chapter 14), and two-level professional-organizational networks (Henriksen and Seabrooke, Chapter 8).

Second, the chapters suggest that network resources can help or hinder efforts to enhance regulatory quality and advance marginalized actors. Westerwinter (Chapter 7) suggests that inter-organizational network ties can enhance regulatory quality by providing information about members' missions, goals and participants; unlocking the resources of well-connected organizations; and facilitating exchange of information and lessons learned (see also, Smith and Fischlein 2010). Other chapters point to drawbacks of networks. Auld and Renckens (Chapter 6) observe that assessor mobility may compromise audit firms' independence. Henriksen and Seabrooke (Chapter 8) note that the pursuit of issue control by professionals within networks is responsible for many of the obstacles to productive TBGIs documented in this book. And Gao and Chen (Chapter 13) suggest that networks spread the Western models that leave little room for the agency of marginalized East Asian actors.

Third, the chapters suggest that capacity for learning fosters productive interactions. Schmidt indicates that certain host cities' openness to experimentation and innovation fostered an upward spiral in social and environmental standards for Olympic Games. An iterative, global-local cycle of norm development, implementation, review and revision promoted policy learning. But the frustrating local-global interactions over the deforestation and forest legality regimes in Cameroon provide an illuminating contrast (Carodenuto and Cashore). Rather than iterated loops of norm development, experimentation and adjustment, policy momentum was unidirectional from global to local, with no feedback loops to facilitate learning.

Aside from iterative regulatory cycles, other interactions that appear to enhance learning are modelling, mentoring, professional mobility and overlapping membership. Bach observes that modelling is often bidirectional: the same organization models itself after others and presents itself as a model to be emulated. Modelling based on unreflective imitation, driven by regulators' incentives to satisfice or to appear sophisticated (Braithwaite and Drahos 2000, pp. 585–92), is unlikely to promote learning. We see evidence of such uncritical emulation in Asian derivatives governance (Gao and Chen). Meidinger's chapter suggests that personal relationships based on mentoring, cajoling and information-sharing can promote mutual learning and enhance suppliers' capacity for adaptation and innovation, though these benefits are often limited by an emphasis on productivity. Overlapping memberships (Westerwinter) can promote learning via epistemic arbitrage and diffusion of knowledge, as can mobility of professionals across organizations. Yet mobility may lead to an undersupply of competent professionals due to free-riding on other organizations' training efforts (Auld and Renckens).

17.2.2 Regulatory Outputs

We consider two main regulatory outputs in this book: the design of regulatory institutions and the content of regulatory programs. We begin with institutional design, which both shapes and is shaped by TBGIs. Some findings of the chapters relate to institutional design generally; others relate to design features particularly relevant to advancing marginalized actors, namely participation, transparency and accountability.

On institutional design generally, Verbruggen and Havinga find that mutual enrolment by states and private food safety schemes improved institutional design by lowering states' enforcement costs, facilitating risk-based prioritization of state resources and increasing the efficiency of food safety regulation. Gao and Chen observe similarly that isomorphic TBGIs generated efficiencies for Asian derivatives regulators and market participants. In contrast, interactions around SEPA triggered the creation of the self-regulatory European Payments Council, which could have enhanced regulatory efficiency and innovativeness (Winn). But an effective co-regulatory process never emerged, as EU regulators refused to grant the Council a substantial regulatory role.

Schmidt, Oman and Wood document improvements in participation, transparency and accountability as a result of TBGIs. Local-global interactions led to more open, inclusive governance of Olympic Games, at least for well-resourced actors (Schmidt). Interactions enhanced indigenous voice and participation in FSC Canada and FSC International (Oman). And TBGIs led (temporarily) to a more transparent and inclusive ISO standard-setting process (Wood).

In contrast, Paiement concludes that delegating enforcement of biofuel sustainability standards to voluntary schemes reduced participation, transparency and accountability, especially for vulnerable stakeholders. In Cameroon, international organizations' preference for technical policy tools inhibited inclusive and transparent forest governance (Carodenuto and Cashore). Interactions with states and non-governmental organizations (NGOs) produced modest improvements in participation and transparency in GLOBALGAP, but did not dislodge industry dominance (Casey). Similarly, interactions in fisheries eco-certification created some movement toward transparent and inclusive governance but did not substantially empower marginalized actors (Foley). Adopting Western regulatory models facilitated peripheral East Asian actors' participation in derivatives regulation; changes imposed by the G20 after the global financial crisis enhanced transparency but hindered East Asian participation, further concentrating trading in Western market institutions (Gao and Chen). Similarly mixed pictures can be observed in Meidinger and Bach's chapters.

Turning to the ambition and scope of regulatory standards, TBGIs facilitated tougher audit and fraud standards in GFSI member schemes (Verbruggen and Havinga), along with stronger and wider standards for FPIC in the FSC (Oman), sustainability in the IOC (Schmidt) and labour in ISO (Wood). On the other hand, it is unclear whether auditor competition and assessor mobility improves or weakens MSC audits (Auld and Renckens), whether OGCI will produce an upward regulatory ratchet or regulatory capture (Bach), and whether changing supply relationships will advance sustainability and marginalized workers (Meidinger). Foley finds some strengthening and expansion of fisheries eco-certification schemes but no prospect for genuine empowerment, while Casey finds that the price for tougher GLOBALGAP verification standards was neglect of sustainable agriculture and marginalized producers' capacities. Finally, the EU's unresponsive and inflexible interactions with banks delayed the creation of SEPA (Winn), while its incomplete oversight facilitated the proliferation of biofuels certification schemes with poor transparency, accountability and participation (Paiement).

17.2.3 Regulatory Outcomes

TBGIs enhanced the uptake of transnational business governance programs in several cases. For example, interactions amongst GFSI, its member schemes and governments increased the number of firms implementing GFSI-benchmarked food safety standards, expanded member schemes' share of the food safety certification market and improved compliance with state regulations (Verbruggen and Havinga). In contrast, uptake of stronger Olympic sustainability standards was limited by local circumstances and sunk-cost effects (Schmidt), uptake of SEPA was hindered by banks' inability to recoup costs (Winn), and uptake of REDD+ and legality standards in Cameroon was limited by a mismatch between the chosen regulatory instruments and the local political economy (Carodenuto and Cashore).

The picture is similar for regulatory synergies. The spread of SSCM codes and contracts has been accompanied by some harmonization of expectations and practices in certain sectors (Meidinger). TBGIs around the Olympics have increased harmonization of sustainability standards for the entire event-management sector (Schmidt). Oman points to potential alignment amongst the FSC, international human rights law and domestic law. Gao and Chen find that TBGIs led to harmonization of derivatives regulation around Western models. Counter-examples include the EU's delegation to non-state biofuels certification schemes, which led to divergence in institutional design and a downward trend in ambition, inclusiveness, transparency and accountability (Paiement).

17.2.4 Impacts, Tensions and Trade-offs

The chapters that consider the impacts of TBGIs on social or environmental conditions are generally less optimistic. Schmidt finds that TBGIs produced social and environmental improvement for some Olympic Games but not others. Meidinger concludes that lead firm-supplier interactions perpetuate suppliers' subordination. Foley concludes that TBGIs perpetuate the structural inequity of fisheries production. TBGIs in Cameroon deepened the marginalization of informal and non-expert forest operators and benefitted a few export-oriented multinationals (Carodenuto and Cashore). Interactions around GLOBALGAP perpetuated the marginalization of small-scale producers (Casey). On the positive side, however, Oman suggests that interactions around FPIC will vindicate indigenous peoples' right to consent to forest operations in their territories.

The chapters also reveal tensions amongst regulatory capacities, outputs, outcomes and impacts, and between regulatory quality and marginalized actors. For example, more ambitious standards, including for conformity verification, can hurt small-scale producers. There can also be trade-offs between different regulatory capacities. GLOBALGAP, for example, chose to enhance its enforcement capacity at the expense of building marginalized producers' capacities (Casey). Increasing regulatory uptake and synergy often conflict with advancing marginalized interests. Thus, food safety governance interactions disadvantaged marginal players in global agrifood markets even as they enhanced synergies and uptake (Verbruggen and Havinga). Likewise, increased uptake of biofuel certification standards benefitted powerful agribusiness interests at the expense of marginalized communities (Paiement). Interactions in derivatives regulation increased uptake and synergy but deepened the marginalization of Asian state and market actors (Gao and Chen).

17.3 PROMOTING AND HINDERING PRODUCTIVE INTERACTIONS

Building inductively on these findings, we identify several factors that enable or hinder productive TBGIs, by which we mean interactions that improve regulatory quality or advance the interests of marginalized actors. The first factor, the distribution of regulatory resources (3.1), yields the richest insights. Varying configurations of regulatory resources influence cooperation, competition, regulatory enrolment and legitimation. We break this factor down into four components: distribution of regulatory resources (3.1.1), compatibility of capacities and of goals (3.1.2), legitimation deficits and differentials (3.1.3), and organizational clusters of capabilities (3.1.4). Other factors include the presence of regulatory entrepreneurs (3.2), characteristics of regulatory environments (3.3), openness and inclusivity of regulatory governance organizations (3.4), conflicts between individual and collective interests (3.5), mismatched problem-solving logics (3.6), iterative regulatory cycles (3.7) and cross-scalar linkages (3.8). Five of these factors both hinder and promote productive interactions, four promote productive interactions, and two are only hindrances (Table 17.2). For each factor, we consider practical implications for harnessing TBGIs in productive directions.

Table 17.2 Factors that promote or hinder productive interactions

Factors that both promote and hinder productive interactions	Factors that promote productive interactions	Factors that hinder productive interactions
Uneven distribution of regulatory resources (3.1.1) Regulatory entrepreneurs (3.2) Regulatory environments (3.3) Iterative regulatory cycles (3.7) Cross-scalar linkages (3.8)	Compatible capacities and goals (3.1.2) Legitimacy deficits and differentials (3.1.3) Capacity clusters (3.1.4) Open and inclusive governance (3.4)	Conflicting interests (3.5) Mismatched logics (3.6)

17.3.1 Distribution of Regulatory Resources

17.3.1.1 Uneven distributions

We have so far treated regulatory resources as capacities that regulators mobilize to achieve their goals, but the chapters highlight that regulatory resources are also rewards regulators reap when they achieve their goals. Successful regulators enjoy a range of rewards including prestige, legitimacy, revenues, participants and regulatory market share. These in turn help constitute regulators' capacities to achieve their goals. Regulatory resources – understood as both capacities and rewards – are distributed unevenly. Some, including adherents and market share, are also finite.

The uneven distribution of regulatory resources drives TBGIs, as actors who lack the resources to achieve their goals seek to enrol other actors into desired roles, mobilizing their regulatory capacities in support of their own agendas or a shared agenda (Black 2003). For example, developed states' limited capacity to regulate production outside their borders drives them to interact with developing states and transnational governance schemes. Those schemes' lack of state-based democratic legitimacy drives them to interact with states (Verbruggen and Havinga; Paiement). Developing states' desire for material and symbolic resources drives them to interact with developed states and international organizations (Carodenuto and Cashore).

Enrolment occurs when an actor accepts an assigned role in a network (Latour and Woolgar 1986). Regulatory roles include rule-maker, rule-taker, beneficiary, intermediary, legitimator, adviser, interpreter, verifier, enforcer, adjudicator and so on. The main goal of enrolment, as

Verbruggen and Havinga note, is to mobilize the enrolled actor's material and symbolic resources in support of the enrolling actor's agenda. The enrolling actor does not control the enrolled actor, but must rely on indirect and uncertain 'action at a distance' (Grabosky 1995). The enrolled actor must be convinced that there is a net benefit (including avoided costs) to accepting the role. The principal benefit for the enrolled actor is the prospect that it can in turn mobilize the resources of other actors or the network. While the benefits of enrolment are often asymmetrical, enrolment is cooperative in the sense that the enrolled actor accepts and benefits from the arrangement.

Every successful case in this book of harnessing TBGIs to enhance regulatory quality or advance the interests of marginalized actors depended on enrolling other actors, and thus mobilizing their resources. Olympic host cities enrolled local firms, NGOs and standardization bodies, while the IOC enrolled local actors' legitimacy and innovativeness, enhancing its regulatory capacity and ratcheting up sustainability standards (Schmidt). ISO enrolled the ILO and other intergovernmental organizations to lend legitimacy, expertise and authority to ISO 26000; organized labour enrolled the ILO to boost its impact on negotiations; and the ILO enrolled ISO's credibility with business (Wood). States enrolled the monitoring and enforcement capacities of private schemes, which in turn enrolled states' legitimacy and credibility (Verbruggen and Havinga).

The chapters explore a variety of enrolment techniques, including recognition of non-state certification as compliance with state law, which can be analysed as orchestration, delegation or rule-referencing (Foley; Paiement); meta-regulatory benchmarking of governance schemes (Verbruggen and Havinga); emulation of regulatory models (Bach; Gao and Chen); creation of participatory governance fora (Foley; Wood); maintenance of direct relationships and regular interactions with suppliers (Meidinger); and piggy-backing on others' regulatory capacities (Wood).

Not all governance interaction is aimed at mutually beneficial enrolment, however. Competition for resources and influence also drives interactions. Actors compete to gain scarce regulatory resources including market share and material rewards. Transnational governance schemes compete for authority, legitimacy and regulatory turf (Verbruggen and Havinga; Foley; Wood); audit firms compete for certification business (Auld and Renckens). ISO simultaneously competed with other standard-setters for authority and adherents, and enrolled them to cooperate in its standard-setting activities (Wood). The chapters emphasize the cooperative dynamics of enrolment, but competition and other antagonistic interactions remain widespread.

The chapters show that both competition and cooperation have ambivalent impacts on regulatory quality and marginalized actors. Competition can lead to upward or downward regulatory races. Auld and Renckens, for example, find that competition amongst audit firms could enhance or reduce audit rigour. Similarly, enrolment is normatively ambivalent: it can work for or against better regulation and marginalized actors. The combination of GFSI benchmarking of non-state food safety standards and states' recognition of these standards results in upward convergence, enhanced legitimacy and market position for GFSI and its benchmarked schemes, and enhanced regulatory capacity for states. Yet mutual enrolment also carries risks, including subordination of food safety to profitability, compromise of law enforcement agencies' independence, and marginalization of small suppliers and alternative schemes (Verbruggen and Havinga).

Modelling can also be progressive or regressive, as Bach's study of OGCI illustrates. On the one hand, OGCI models itself on intergovernmental and industry initiatives that pursue practical solutions and enjoy legitimacy within broad global networks. On the other hand, this modelling is aimed at guaranteeing a future for fossil fuels and 'carbon majors' (Heede 2014), a prospect many observers reject. Another example is Gao and Chen's description of mimetic and normative isomorphism amongst derivatives regulators, which provided East Asian actors ready-made regulatory solutions but reinforced their marginalization. The same ambivalence characterizes orchestration and delegation. The EU's delegation of enforcement of biofuels sustainability criteria to private certification schemes, for example, led to a proliferation of schemes and some upward harmonization, but widespread regression toward less comprehensive and stringent standards, and less participation, transparency and accountability (Paiement).

Why does enrolment sometimes fail to produce the intended benefits? Winn points to cognitive limitations and failure to incentivize enrolled actors to pursue the enroller's goals. Paiement reveals another cause: the regulator's failure to enforce its own enrolment criteria. When a regulator delegates tasks to regulatory targets or to third parties who rely on targets' voluntary participation, the delegate's preference for undemanding, opaque and unaccountable regulation is understandable; the puzzle is why the delegator would accept such slippage from its declared requirements. One explanation is the regulator's lack of regulatory resources, combined with lack of political will, both of which often reflect countervailing economic interests. In the biofuels case, the main such interest was increasing international biofuel trade – an interest shared by the delegator (the European Commission) and the targets (agribusiness).

The perverse result of the Commission's incomplete enforcement was further empowerment of agribusiness via enhanced market access, at the expense not just of the European Parliament's accountability concerns but also of the interests of marginalized actors in global supply chains whose opportunities to contest biofuel standards were further curtailed by opaque and unaccountable standard-setting.

This example highlights a paradox of enrolment. The same resource deficit that drives a regulator to enrol others can contribute to regulatory failure, if the regulator lacks the resources or inclination to monitor the enrolled actors. Thus, a regulator's declared pursuit of enhanced sustainability, transparency and accountability in global supply chains can paradoxically facilitate the growth of unaccountable, opaque and lax governance.

At a more general level, regulatory actors confront a basic choice between strategies of alliance and autonomy – between forging links and going it alone. Cooperation facilitates exchange of knowledge and lessons learned, enables actors to learn about one other, and allows less well-connected actors to 'piggy-back' on well-connected actors' resources (Westerwinter; Wood; Buhmann 2015). But going it alone can help entrench a core constituency's decision-making power and organizational logic, insulating the regime against later challengers. Thus, GLOBALGAP's early institutionalization around a relatively homogeneous core of actors enhanced its internal cohesion, shared commitment and legitimacy with its constituency (Casey). While powerful actors have greater 'go-it-alone power' (Abbott and Snidal 2009), marginalized interests can also create regulatory regimes on their own – for example, some ethical fisheries certification schemes discussed by Foley. More often, however, their lack of resources drives them toward strategies of enrolment.

17.3.1.2 Compatibility of capacities and goals

The chapters indicate that complementary capacities facilitate productive interactions. For example, private food safety schemes enjoyed audit, inspection, information-gathering and enforcement capacity, along with expertise, financial resources and strategic position in global supply chains; states enjoyed legitimacy and credibility that could strengthen recognized schemes (Verbruggen and Havinga). These capacities were complementary in that each party could supply capacities the other lacked. Their complementarity facilitated the strengthening of standards and audit practices amongst GFSI member schemes, and allowed states to conserve limited enforcement resources. In the Olympic example (Schmidt), the IOC lacked environmental credibility and expertise and had limited capacity to innovate and implement rules; host cities lacked the prestige to attract desired resources for urban development. Each offered the other capacities it lacked, enhancing the material and symbolic resources of each, and helping to strengthen environmental and social standards for Olympic Games.

Capacities are not complementary if an actor cannot utilize them. In Cameroon, international policymakers sought to mobilize highly technical capacities through technology and financial transfers, training and technical support. But the local actors that most needed international support lacked the capacity to benefit from these transfers; non-experts and the entire artisanal forest industry were effectively excluded (Carodenuto and Cashore). In the SEPA case (Winn), the banks had technical capacity and expertise to design and implement SEPA; they lacked material incentives and the legitimacy to pressure the EU to provide them. EU regulators refused to create such incentives, partly due to limited cognitive capacity leading them to underestimate the cost of SEPA implementation and ignore the public goods characteristics of proprietary payment systems.

Compatibility of regulatory goals also facilitates productive interactions. Goals need not be identical to be compatible. One actor's pursuit of narrow self-interest can be compatible with another's pursuit of collective goals. Goal compatibility is necessary for successful orchestration (Abbott et al. 2015), but not for all regulatory intermediation (Abbott et al. 2017). Similarly, the chapters suggest that goal compatibility is conducive to but not strictly necessary for productive TBGIs.

Finally, particular combinations of goals and capacities can promote or hinder productive interactions. Even if actors' goals are aligned, incompatible or redundant capacities can foil productive interaction; and incompatible goals can foil productive interaction even where capacities are complementary. Compatibility of goals with goals, capacities with capacities, and goals with capacities facilitates harnessing TBGIs to enhance regulatory quality or advance marginalized actors, while incompatibility hinders them. Those seeking to promote productive TBGIs should cultivate and exploit such compatibilities.

17.3.1.3 Legitimation deficits and differentials

Legitimacy is a crucial regulatory capacity. Legitimation deficits and differentials emerge as important in promoting interactions that improve regulatory quality and advance marginalized actors (Wood). A regulator's legitimation deficit with certain communities offers an opening for productive interactions. MSC, for example, suffered a legitimacy deficit with small-scale producers, who exploited this deficit to carve out niches for ethical eco-certification programs and pressure MSC to change its governance and standards in their favour (Foley). Transnational food safety schemes' legitimation deficits allowed Canadian and Dutch regulators to pressure them to ratchet up food safety standards and audit practices (Verbruggen and Havinga). And the IOC's legitimation deficit allowed progressive forces in prospective host cities to enhance environmental and sustainability standards for Olympic Games (Schmidt).

Not all legitimation deficits are equal, however. A deficit provides a meaningful opening for productive interactions only if it significantly impedes the regulator's pursuit of its goals. The chapters identify several circumstances where this is not the case. First, a regulator may not benefit substantially from an audience's approval or be substantially harmed by its disapproval. This may explain the limited responsiveness, even indifference, of some transnational regulatory schemes to the disapproval of marginalized producers and communities (Verbruggen and Havinga; Casey; Paiement; Foley). It also helps to explain discrepancies in the sustainability performance of different Olympic Games: Russia was less affected by delegitimation around the Sochi Games than the UK was for the London Games (Schmidt). Second, accommodation of an audience's legitimation demands might compromise a regulator's legitimacy with a core constituency, as in GLOBALGAP's tripartite supply chain partnership (Casey). Third, even if a regulator desires an audience's approval, that audience's limited resources or attention may prevent it from monitoring the regulator's behaviour. Even the relatively well-resourced EU failed to apply its own transparency requirements when recognizing private biofuels certification schemes (Paiement).

Discrepancies between regulatory actors' legitimacy endowments can enlarge the openings offered by legitimation deficits, allowing marginalized actors to piggy-back on actors that enjoy high legitimacy. Thus, organized labour rode the coat-tails of the ILO – which enjoyed abundant legitimacy on labour standards – to exploit ISO's legitimacy deficit in the field of social responsibility. The Olympic example (Schmidt), however, hints at a downside of this strategy: powerful actors can also use it to advance their own interests. OGCI offers a cautionary tale in this respect: recognizing the oil industry's massive legitimation deficit on climate change, OGCI seeks to enrol the legitimacy and credibility of the UN by securing attendance and endorsement by UN climate change officials and the International Energy Agency (Bach).

17.3.1.4 Capacity clusters

Arenas combining complementary capacities represent a third configuration that enables productive interactions. We see this in the context of

Olympic host cities, which combine business capacity, expertise and cutting-edge technologies, and have access to deep pools of expertise and resources not readily available to a specialized regulator such as the IOC (Schmidt). The FSC's multi-stakeholder governance enables it to assemble diverse regulatory capacities in a single organization (Oman). This is less a function of size than of the range and complementarity of regulatory capacities clustered in a forum, and the forum's interconnectivity in governance networks. Learning to identify and utilize existing regulatory capacity clusters – or develop new ones – may be an important strategy for enhancing regulatory quality and advancing marginalized actors.

To conclude this discussion, the ambivalence of enrolment and related interactive strategies makes it important to understand what drives cooperative and competitive interactions. Harnessing interactions to improve the quality of regulation or advance marginalized actors is partly a matter of knowing when and with whom to cooperate, when and with whom to compete and when to carve out one's own unique regulatory niche. These choices in turn depend on the distribution of regulatory resources. Are the relevant actors' goals compatible? Are their regulatory capacities complementary? Do some actors or institutions enjoy more legitimacy than others? Are there organizational clusters of regulatory capacities? These questions point toward a strategic binary. Regulatory actors should forge cooperative links where goals are compatible, capacities are complementary, there are strong potential allies on whom to piggy-back or cluster, and there are no distinctive niches or network holes to be filled productively. Conversely, it makes sense to 'go it alone' and compete where goals are incompatible, capacities are not complementary, there are no strong potential allies to support clustering or piggy-backing, or there are distinctive niches or network holes to be filled productively.

17.3.2 Networks of Enterprising Experts

Networks of individuals with relevant expertise can be key conduits for interaction, with either positive or negative impacts on regulatory quality and marginalized actors. Networks can form around established, formally organized professions; emerging, specialized occupations; ad hoc, project-driven coalitions; state or interstate bureaucracies; activist communities; or other expert communities. Experts and activists occupy strategic positions in many transnational governance regimes. Their role in linking organizations, influencing agendas and spreading knowledge, norms and techniques is well documented (for example, Haas 1992; Keck and Sikkink 1998).

Expert networks can channel TBGIs in productive directions. Consultants and auditors helped disseminate and ratchet up food safety standards (Verbruggen and Havinga). With transnational reach and a wealth of information about audited firms, they helped diffuse standards and practices, manage their interpretation and verify their implementation. In derivatives trading, networks of financial professionals spread Western models, reducing compliance and transaction costs and providing emerging market actors with proven regulatory recipes and access to international markets (Gao and Chen). Transnationally organized indigenous norm entrepreneurs exploited political openings to strengthen FPIC in FSC standards, and possibly in law (Oman). An ad hoc coalition of local government officials, business leaders, environmental NGOs, event managers and standardization professionals catalysed a regulatory innovation – sustainable event-management systems – that quickly spread far beyond the world of sport (Schmidt).

Many of these experts are what Henriksen and Seabrooke call issue professionals – individuals recognized by peers as knowledgeable in a particular field, who eschew formal organizations in favour of informal networks. Sometimes they are insiders exploiting the 'small world' characteristics of their specialized fields to build personal networks, mobilize organizations and influence agendas; in other cases they fill structural holes in sparse network regions. Their mobility can diffuse knowledge and practices (Auld and Renckens). And they can often counter or reshape formal organizations' efforts to control issues (Henriksen and Seabrooke).

Issue professionals can offer pathways around blockages to better regulation or advancement of marginalized interests. For example, indigenous rights advocates exploited FSC's inclusive governance, the relationship between FSC International and FSC Canada, and the moral power of international human rights law to circumvent blockages in Canada to the realization of an indigenous right to consent to forestry operations (Oman). Oman's chapter offers a rare example of marginalized actors successfully employing a strategy of forum-shifting (Helfer 2004) or institutional bypass (Prado and Hoffman 2017). Powerful actors often use these strategies, but weak and marginalized actors seldom can (Braithwaite and Drahos 2000, p. 571). Oman's example demonstrates that forum-shifting can be a viable strategy for marginalized actors where they have a network of skilled, mobile experts who can advance their agenda across organizational lines.

By the same token, experts and their networks can frustrate efforts to improve regulatory quality or advance marginalized actors, as they pursue issue control, prestige, regulatory turf and revenue (Henriksen and Seabrooke). Awareness of these issues can help advocates promote productive interactions.

17.3.3 Environmental Conditions

Another lesson of the chapters is that the environments in which actors operate condition TBGIs. Three environmental factors are particularly salient in this book: isomorphic pressures, early institutionalization and local variation. These features are constituted and reproduced by interaction, but also shape and constrain it.

First, environmental conditions can create isomorphic pressures that lead organizations to resemble one another (DiMaggio and Powell 1983; Beckert 2010). One such condition is the presence of deeply and widely institutionalized norms, which constitute the discursive structures in which interaction occurs (Casey). The most influential norms discussed in this book include participation, transparency, accountability, democracy, sustainability and human rights. Implementation of institutionalized norms and mimicry of proven models can enhance regulatory credibility and efficiency, reduce compliance costs, and reduce the uncertainty that hampers institutional design (Gao and Chen). Norms can also help to advance marginalized interests, as illustrated in several chapters (Oman; Wood; Casey).

Institutionalized norms can instead pull in the opposite direction, as with the national sovereignty norm that accentuated regulatory incapacities in Cameroon (Carodenuto and Cashore), the norm of productive efficiency that inhibits SSCM (Meidinger) and the neoliberal market norms that limit the transformative potential of eco-certification (Foley). Superficial convergence around norms of transparency, accountability and openness can often mask continuing dominance by powerful economic interests (Casey; Gulbrandsen 2005; Fransen 2011). And as Gao and Chen document, isomorphic pressures can reinforce relations of domination and limit marginalized actors' room for resistance.

The isomorphic pressures generated by institutionalized norms can be limited, however, by early institutionalization around a homogeneous actor group. Such institutionalization can enhance an organization's regulatory capacity by providing internal cohesion, shared commitment and legitimacy with a core constituency. But it can also entrench a specific actor's dominance and preferred organizational logic, inhibiting productive interactions. Even though democratization norms predisposed GLOBALGAP toward external audiences' legitimation demands for transparency and participation, the early entrenchment of retailers' dominance and preferred organizational logic of control limited the potential for effective participation by marginalized actors. On the other hand, FSC's early institutionalization of a predominantly civil society membership and a dual logic of empowerment and control has been remarkably resilient (Auld et al. 2015).

Third, local variability can enable or constrain productive interactions. In the Olympic example (Schmidt), host jurisdictions' differences in state and civil society institutions, regulatory standards, rule of law and societal values had major effects on the sustainability standards and performance of particular Games, preventing the emergence of a consistent upward ratchet. The Cameroon example shows that local political economy can hinder productive global-domestic interactions (Carodenuto and Cashore). The GFSI case suggests that differences between authoritarian developing and liberal democratic developed states explain differences in food safety-related interactions (Verbruggen and Havinga). Finally, MSC's insensitivity to local circumstances spurred the emergence of locally embedded eco-certification schemes, but the global neoliberal political economy limits these schemes' ability to empower marginalized actors (Foley).

17.3.4 Open and Inclusive Governance

The chapters indicate that inclusive and open governance fosters productive interactions by enhancing legitimacy and other symbolic resources, promoting ambitious regulatory standards and advancing marginalized interests. FSC is a clear example: its inclusive multi-stakeholder design allowed indigenous advocates to secure an Aboriginal chamber in FSC Canada and a permanent indigenous committee at FSC International (Oman), and gives it a counter-hegemonic potential that MSC lacks (Foley). Open institutional structures also offered entry points to promote ambitious social and environmental standards for the Olympics and advance the agendas of some marginalized actors (Schmidt).

Yet openness and inclusivity alone are insufficient to advance marginalized interests. Marginalized actors also require sufficient organizational and material resources, and their claims must be salient to other governance actors. The salience of a claim (Kingdon 2011) is partly a function of actors' attention (Peters and Hogwood 1985; Epstein and Segal 2000). Marginalized actors and their allies can influence attention through strategic action, even if they cannot resolve issues on their own. In the FSC and Olympics, for example, high salience of marginalized actors' claims combined with open institutions to achieve beneficial effects. But in EU biofuels regulation, the low political salience of claims for transparency, participation and accountability, evidenced by the Commission's neglect of these features in its early recognition decisions, may have facilitated the rise of opaque, exclusive and unaccountable schemes (Paiement).

It is important also to note that exclusionary, industry-dominated institutions inhibit the advancement of marginalized interests, from OGCI's exclusive club structure (Bach), to industry's domination of GLOBALGAP (Casey) and lead firms' control of supply chain management (Meidinger). But the basic point remains: open and inclusive governance breeds more open and inclusive governance, provided regulatory actors are organized and sophisticated, with salient claims.

17.3.5 Conflicting Interests

As in all forms of regulation, the pursuit of self-interest can prevail over collective interests, inhibiting provision of collective goods. Most transnational regulation purports to provide collective goods: financial stability (Gao and Chen, Winn); food safety (Verbruggen and Havinga, Casey); sustainable fisheries (Auld and Renckens, Foley); sustainable forestry (Carodenuto and Cashore, Oman); sustainable supply chains (Meidinger); sustainable mega-events (Schmidt); socially responsible business (Wood); and so on. Beyond these substantive goals, regulatory regimes themselves have public goods characteristics (as Winn points out in the case of SEPA) and can be impeded by collective action problems such as free-riding, rent-seeking and capture.

Conflicts between private and collective interests impede productive governance interactions. Auditors and certifiers, for example, have a conflict of interest between maximizing their profits and furthering the public interest the regulatory scheme purports to pursue (Lytton and McAllister 2014). And private interests often prevail. Meidinger warns of this dynamic in SSCM, where pursuit of sustainability is hindered by the continuing dominance of profit maximization within lead firms and in their supply relationships. These conflicts can also combine with environmental conditions to hinder productive interactions. For example, the tendency of concentrated economic interests to prevail in regulatory contests is amplified by a global political economy dominated by Western multinationals and capital-exporting states, asymmetrical global supply chain relations, and an ideology of market-driven development. This negative interaction between political economy and economic self-interest is revealed not just in Foley's Coxian critique of the transformative potential of fisheries eco-certification but also in the governance of derivatives markets (Gao and Chen) and transnational supply chains (Carodenuto and Cashore; Casey; Verbruggen and Havinga; Paiement; Meidinger).

17.3.6 Mismatched Logics

Mismatched problem-solving logics also impede productive interactions. Auld et al. (2015) argue that different inter-subjectively defined governance problems have different problem-solving logics. Two such problems are overcoming the marginalization of peripheral actors in the global economy and ameliorating the adverse social and environmental impacts of global production. Regulatory governance institutions focused on overcoming marginalization embody a logic of empowerment, which seeks to redistribute power, control and resources via inclusion in regulatory decision-making or, more rarely, redirection of resources to facilitate self-determination (ibid., pp 111–12). Institutions focused on ameliorating social and environmental impacts employ a logic of control, prescribing rules of conduct, monitoring their implementation, accrediting certifiers to verify compliance, and tracing products as they move through global value chains (ibid., p 111).

These logics can conflict with one another, with local conditions, or with chosen policy instruments. Casey explains GLOBALGAP's limited democratization in terms of a clash between the founders' logic of control and newcomers' logic of empowerment. The poor prospects of SSCM can be understood in terms of the same conflict (Meidinger). Incompatible logics can instead create productive tension and set regulatory systems in motion. Auld et al. (ibid.) argue that private governance schemes face pressure to accommodate both logics, and typically evolve from one logic toward the other. The problem from our perspective is institutional entrenchment of logics that systematically favour vested interests.

Productive interactions are also obstructed when problem-solving logics conflict with local conditions or regulatory instruments. In Carodenuto and Cashore's chapter, for example, international actors embraced a logic of empowering marginalized actors, but their choice of highly technical policy tools was not calibrated to local circumstances and seemed likely to deepen the exclusion of marginalized actors and the opacity of forestry practices.

17.3.7 Iterative Regulatory Cycles

Capacity for learning is one of several capacities that contribute to the quality of regulation. Iterative, self-conscious cycles of regulatory innovation, implementation and review not only enhance regulatory quality through learning, they can also offer entry points for weaker actors. The IOC, for example, set down initial rules for bids; prospective host cities proposed innovative environmental and social standards to differentiate their bids; the IOC, facing critical scrutiny and lacking the credibility or expertise to develop its own sustainability rules, incorporated these innovations into its regulatory framework, for both the originator and future prospective hosts; and subsequent aspiring host cities proposed further regulatory innovations (Schmidt). Cyclical regulation was harnessed by both weaker actors and advocates of better regulatory quality. NGOs and other local actors could participate in preparing some host city applications, influencing the international standards that the IOC later adopted.

Oman's chapter shows how indigenous peoples' representatives navigated an iterative cycle of regulatory interaction between international and national FSC organs to ratchet up the FPIC norm. It also illustrates a potential limitation: a regulatory change welcomed by one marginalized actor can be seen as regressive by another. In particular, FSC International's extension of the FPIC norm to non-indigenous communities was seen by many in the developing world as a step forward, but by Canadian First Nations as an unwelcome dilution of the distinctive rights of indigenous peoples. Finally, Meidinger's analysis of SSCM suggests that actors' efforts should be directed toward institutionalizing virtuous regulatory cycles to ensure their continuity.

17.3.8 Cross-Scalar Linkages

These regulatory cycles share another characteristic: they cut across local and global scales. The chapters suggest that regulatory quality and marginalized interests can be advanced by exploiting cross-scalar regulatory dynamics. Assemblage theory (Sassen 2008; DeLanda 2016), discussed by Paiement, emphasizes the multiplicity of actors, agendas, governance levels and sources of authority that come together in polycentric governance arrangements. As Lynn Staeheli (1994, p. 388) asserts, 'To the extent that oppositional movements can move across scales – that is, to the extent that they can take advantage of the resources at one scale to overcome the constraints encountered at different scales in the way that more powerful actors can do – they may have greater potential for pressing their claims.' The chapters contain numerous examples of cross-scalar dynamics (see Table 1.2). Eight chapters describe interactions that cross micro and meso scales (Bach; Carodenuto and Cashore; Casey; Henriksen and Seabrooke; Meidinger; Oman; Schmidt; Wood). One investigates interactions at meso and macro scales (Gao and Chen), while one combines micro, meso and macro scales (Foley). Oman's study illustrates the intersection of multiple spatio-organizational scales, from subnational (FSC BC) to national (FSC Canada and the Canadian state) to global (FSC International, intergovernmental organizations, public international law and the global indigenous peoples' movement). Cross-scalar assemblages, like several of the factors we consider, can promote or hinder productive interactions. The biofuels example (Paiement) shows that they can disempower weaker actors and inhibit transparency and accountability; the Olympic and FPIC examples (Schmidt; Oman) show that they can empower the former and enhance the latter.

17.4 CONCLUDING REMARKS

Can TBGIs be harnessed to enhance regulatory quality and advance marginalized interests? It is clear that there is no single pattern or relationship, let alone strategy, linking TBGIs to these desired outcomes. We can, however, identify factors that shape the prospects for productive TBGIs, and explore some of their theoretical and practical implications. We found that five factors cut both ways, hindering or promoting productive interactions depending on the circumstances: asymmetrical distributions of regulatory resources (3.1.1); regulatory entrepreneurs (3.2); regulatory environments (3.3); iterative regulatory cycles (3.7); and cross-scalar linkages (3.8). Four factors consistently promote productive interactions: compatible capacities and goals (3.1.2); legitimacy deficits and differentials (3.1.3); capacity clusters (3.1.4); and open and inclusive governance (3.4). Finally, two factors consistently hinder productive interactions: conflicting interests (3.5) and mismatched problem-solving logics (3.6) (Table 17.2).

While the chapters suggest that the prospects for harnessing TBGIs to improve regulatory quality or advance marginalized actors are modest, the implications we draw in this chapter paint a complex and ambiguous picture in which various factors and dynamics pull in different directions, with context-specific and unpredictable outcomes. It is useful to think of this ambiguity as the co-existence of two narratives. On the one hand, there are the themes of economic self-interest, resource and power disparities, relations of domination in a global political economy, regulatory capture and issue control by professionals. Seen through this lens, the fundamental conflict between individual self-interest and collective goals in a market-driven context is a key barrier to productive interactions. The asymmetric distribution of regulatory resources and capacities is the most important arena of this conflict.

On the other hand, there are the themes of cooperative linkages, especially enrolment and mobilization, learning and experimentation, iterative regulatory cycles, networks of enterprising experts, modelling and mentoring, overlapping memberships and cross-scalar and multilevel leverage. This alternative lens directs attention to opportunities and pathways toward fostering regulatory quality or advancing marginalized interests. Success at harnessing TBGIs to these ends seems to depend on enrolling other actors and mobilizing their resources. This resonates with the idea of a polycentric world of regulation (Black 2008) where cooperative linkages across actor groups, levels and scales, and in iterative regulatory cycles are paramount. Finally, the theme of cooperative linkages connects to the four clear success factors that we distil from the chapters: complementary regulatory capacities and compatible goals (3.1.2); variable legitimacy endowments (3.1.3); capacity clusters (3.1.4); and open and inclusive regulatory governance institutions (3.4) seem to have uniquely positive effects on both regulatory quality and the advancement of marginalized interests.

Clearly, both narratives are valid. Depending on issue and context, one lens may offer more analytical or strategic traction than the other. We encourage future research to investigate the productive potential as well as the constraining effects of interactions amongst the actors and institutions involved in the transnational regulation of business conduct. Efforts to move TBGIs toward higher regulatory quality and deeper empowerment must necessarily attend to contextual conditions and be highly flexible and adaptive. The cases and analyses presented in this book can contribute to that process by providing examples to be compared, and by suggesting possible pathways for action, adjustment, analysis and learning.

REFERENCES

Abbott, Kenneth W., Philipp Genschel, Duncan Snidal and Bernhard Zangl (2015), 'Orchestration: global governance through intermediaries', in Kenneth W. Abbott, Philipp Genschel, Duncan Snidal and Bernhard Zangl (eds), *International Organizations as Orchestrators*, Cambridge, UK: Cambridge University Press, pp. 3–36.

Abbott, Kenneth W., David Levi-Faur and Duncan Snidal (2017), 'Theorizing regulatory intermediaries: the RIT model', *Annals of the American Academy of Political and Social Sciences*, **670** (1), 14–35.

Abbott, Kenneth W. and Duncan Snidal (2009), 'The governance triangle: regulatory standards institutions and the shadow of the state', in Walter Mattli and Ngaire Woods (eds), *The Politics of Global Regulation*, Princeton, NJ: Princeton University Press, pp. 44–88.

Auld, Graeme, Stefan Renckens and Benjamin Cashore (2015), 'Transnational private governance between the logics of empowerment and control', *Regulation and Governance*, **9** (2), 108–24.

Beckert, Jens (2010), 'Institutional isomorphism revisited: convergence and divergence in institutional change', *Sociological Theory*, **28** (2), 150–66.

Black, Julia (2003), 'Enrolling actors in regulatory systems: examples from UK financial services regulation', *Public Law*, 63–91.

Black, Julia (2008), 'Constructing and contesting legitimacy and accountability in polycentric regulatory regimes', *Regulation & Governance*, **2** (2), 137–64.
Braithwaite, John and Peter Drahos (2000), *Global Business Regulation*, Cambridge, UK: Cambridge University Press.
Buhmann, Karin (2015), 'Business and human rights: understanding the UN guiding principles from the perspective of transnational business governance interactions', *Transnational Legal Theory*, **6** (2), 399–434.
DeLanda, Manuel (2016), *Assemblage Theory*, Edinburgh: Edinburgh University Press.
DiMaggio, Paul J. and Walter W. Powell (1983), 'The iron cage revisited: institutional isomorphism and collective rationality in organizational fields', *American Sociological Review*, **48** (2), 147–60.
Eberlein, Burkard, Kenneth W. Abbott, Julia Black, Errol Meidinger and Stepan Wood (2014), 'Transnational business governance interactions: conceptualization and framework for analysis', *Regulation and Governance*, **8** (1), 1–21.
Epstein, Lee and Jeffrey A. Segal (2000), 'Measuring issue salience', *American Journal of Political Science*, **44** (1), 66–83.
Fransen, Luc (2011), 'Why do private governance organizations not converge? A political–institutional analysis of transnational labor standards regulation', *Governance*, **24** (2), 359–87.
Grabosky, Peter N. (1995), 'Using non-governmental resources to foster regulatory compliance', *Governance*, **8** (4), 527–50.
Gulbrandsen, Lars H. (2005), 'Sustainable forestry in Sweden: the effect of competition among private certification schemes', *Journal of Environment and Development*, **14** (3), 338–55.
Haas, Peter M. (1992), 'Introduction: epistemic communities and international policy coordination', *International Organization*, **46**, 1–36.
Heede, Richard (2014), 'Tracing anthropogenic carbon dioxide and methane emissions to fossil fuel and cement producers, 1854–2010', *Climatic Change*, **122** (1–2), 229–41.
Helfer, Laurence R. (2004), 'Regime shifting: the TRIPS agreement and the new dynamics of international intellectual property making', *Yale Journal of International Law*, **29** (1), 1–83.
Keck, Margaret E. and Kathryn Sikkink (1998), *Activists Beyond Borders: Advocacy Networks in International Politics*, Ithaca, NY: Cornell University Press.
Kingdon, John W. (2011), *Agendas, Alternatives, and Public Policies*, Revised 2nd edn, Boston, MA: Longman.
Latour, Bruno and Steve Woolgar (1986), *Laboratory Life: The Construction of Scientific Facts*, 2nd edn, Princeton, NJ: Princeton University Press.
Lytton, Timothy D. and Lesley K. McAllister (2014), 'Oversight in private food safety auditing: addressing auditor conflict of interest', *Wisconsin Law Review*, **2014** (2), 289–335.
Peters, B. Guy and Brian W. Hogwood (1985), 'In search of the issue-attention cycle', *Journal of Politics* **47** (1), 238–53.
Prado, Mariana Mota and Steven J. Hoffman (2017), 'Introduction to symposium on international institutional bypass', *AJIL Unbound*, **111**, 229–30.
Sassen, Saskia (2008), 'Neither global nor national: novel assemblages of territory, authority and rights', *Ethics & Global Politics*, **1** (1–2), 61–79.
Smith, Timothy M. and Miriam Fischlein (2010), 'Rival private governance networks: competing to define the rules of sustainability performance', *Global Environmental Change*, **20**, 511–22.

Staeheli, Lynn (1994), 'Empowering political struggle: spaces and scales of resistance', *Political Geography*, **13**, 387–91.

Wood, Stepan, Kenneth W. Abbott, Julia Black, Burkard Eberlein and Errol Meidinger (2015), 'The interactive dynamics of transnational business governance: a challenge for transnational legal theory', *Transnational Legal Theory*, **6** (2), 333–69.

Index